Murder in the Closet

Murder in the Closet

*Essays on Queer Clues in
Crime Fiction Before Stonewall*

EDITED BY CURTIS EVANS

McFarland & Company, Inc., Publishers
Jefferson, North Carolina

ALSO OF INTEREST
Mysteries Unlocked: Essays in Honor of Douglas G. Greene,
edited by Curtis Evans (McFarland, 2014)
Masters of the "Humdrum" Mystery: Cecil John Charles Street, Freeman Wills Crofts, Alfred Walter Stewart and the British Detective Novel, 1920–1961, Curtis Evans (McFarland, 2012)

Lucy Sussex's essay originally appeared in different form in *Blockbuster! Fergus Hume and the Mystery of a Hansom Cab.* Melbourne: Text, 2015.

Rick Cypert's essay originally appeared in different form in *America's Agatha Christie: Mignon Good Eberhart, Her Life and Works.* Selinsgrove, PA: Susquehanna University Press, 2005.

LIBRARY OF CONGRESS CATALOGUING-IN-PUBLICATION DATA

Names: Evans, Curtis J., 1965– editor.
Title: Murder in the closet : essays on queer clues in crime fiction before Stonewall / edited by Curtis Evans.
Description: Jefferson, North Carolina : McFarland & Company, Inc., Publishers, 2017. | Includes bibliographical references and index.
Identifiers: LCCN 2016049641 | ISBN 9780786499922 (softcover : acid free paper) ∞
Subjects: LCSH: Detective and mystery stories, English—History and criticism. | Homosexuality and literature. | Homosexuality in literature. | Gays in literature. | English fiction—20th century—History and criticism.
Classification: LCC PR830.D4 M79 2017 | DDC 823/.087209—dc23
LC record available at https://lccn.loc.gov/2016049641

BRITISH LIBRARY CATALOGUING DATA ARE AVAILABLE

ISBN (print) 978-0-7864-9992-2
ISBN (ebook) 978-1-4766-2633-8

© 2017 Curtis Evans. All rights reserved

No part of this book may be reproduced or transmitted in any form or by any means, electronic or mechanical, including photocopying or recording, or by any information storage and retrieval system, without permission in writing from the publisher.

Front cover photograph by Ivan Bastien

Printed in the United States of America

*McFarland & Company, Inc., Publishers
Box 611, Jefferson, North Carolina 28640
www.mcfarlandpub.com*

Table of Contents

Introduction
    Curtis Evans   1

Part One: Locked Doors

The Queer Story of Fergus Hume
    Lucy Sussex   18

A Redemptive Masquerade: Gender Identity in Samuel Hopkins Adams' *The Secret of Lonesome Cove*
    J. F. Norris   33

Dropping Hairpins in Golden Age Detective Fiction: Man-Haters, Green Carnations and Gunsels
    Noah Stewart   40

"Queer in some ways": Gay Characters in the Fiction of Agatha Christie
    John Curran   52

Agatha Christie: Norms and Codes
    Michael Moon   67

The Unshockable Mrs. Bradley: Sex and Sexuality in the Work of Gladys Mitchell
    Brittain Bright   78

"Less beautiful in daylight": Josephine Tey and the Anxiety of Gender
    J.C. Bernthal   93

"Mutually devoted": Female Relationships in Josephine Tey's *Miss Pym Disposes*
    Moira Redmond   106

"The man with the laughing eyes": Socialism and Same-Sex
    Desire in G. D. H. Cole's *The Death of a Millionaire*
        CURTIS EVANS   114

Humdrum Ecstasies: C. H. B. Kitchin and His Detective,
    Malcolm Warren
        MICHAEL MOON   125

"Two young men who write as one": Richard Wilson Webb,
    Hugh Callingham Wheeler, Male Couples and *The Grindle
    Nightmare*
        CURTIS EVANS   139

Queering the Investigation: Explanation and Understanding
    in Todd Downing's Detective Fiction
        CHARLES J. RZEPKA   156

"A bad, bad past": Rufus King, Clifford Orr, College Drag
    and Detective Fiction
        CURTIS EVANS   173

Foppish, Effeminate, or "a little too handsome": Coded
    Character Descriptions and Masculinity in the Mystery
    Novels of Mignon G. Eberhart
        RICK CYPERT   189

Part Two: Skeleton Keys

"The finest triumvirate of perversion, horror and murder
    written this spring": Frank Walford's *Twisted Clay*
        JAMES DOIG   200

Wayne Lonergan's Long Shadow: A Forties Murder and Its
    Literary Legacy
        DREWEY WAYNE GUNN   210

"Claude was doing all right": Homosexuality, Hard-Boiled
    Crime Fiction and the Evolution of Ross Macdonald
        TOM NOLAN   217

"Elegant stuff ... of its sort": Gore Vidal's Edgar Box
    Detective Novels
        CURTIS EVANS   225

"Adonis in person": Same-Sex Intimacy and Male Eroticism in
    the Detective Novels of Beverley Nichols
        J. F. NORRIS   241

More Than Fiction: Troublesome Themes in the Life and Writing
   of Nancy Spain
     BRUCE SHAW   249

Man to Man: The Two-Men Theme in the Novels of Patricia
   Highsmith
     NICK JONES   259

Kiss Kiss Bang Bang: Joseph Hansen's *Known Homosexual*
     JOSH LANYON   265

I Am the Most! Camping It Up in George Baxt's Pharoah
   Love Mystery Series
     J. F. NORRIS   273

About the Contributors   281

Index   285

Introduction

CURTIS EVANS

"The morality of the average mystery fan is apparently pretty straight-laced."—Marie F. Rodell, *Mystery Fiction: Theory and Technique* (1943)

In *Murder in the Closet: Essays on Queer Clues in Crime Fiction Before Stonewall*, seventeen contributors in twenty-three essays explore queer aspects of crime fiction published between the late Victorian era and the height of the Swinging Sixties, beginning with the works of the prolific author Fergus Hume, whose first detective novel, *The Mystery of a Hansom Cab*, became a worldwide bestseller upon its publication in Australia in 1886, and ending with early mysteries by American writers Joseph Hansen and George Baxt, works whose telltale titles like *Known Homosexual* (1968) and *A Queer Kind of Death* (1966) indicate that by the mid-to-late Sixties the closet door was hanging precariously on its hinges. Much of the attention in studies of queer crime fiction has focused on works published after the 1969 Stonewall riots (the street demonstrations sparked by an early morning hours police raid on the Stonewall Inn, a gay bar in Manhattan's Greenwich Village neighborhood), an event that has long been recognized as an epochal turning point in the fight for LGBTQ rights. In the years since Stonewall queer crime fiction has burgeoned, to be sure, while openly queer characters have become commonplace in all manner of mysteries, from the quaintest of cozies to the grittiest of noirs; yet there often was something queer as well about crime fiction published *before* Stonewall, and the work from this earlier period, despite the appearance of some fine genre studies on the subject, particularly those concerning queer pulps (see below), remains insufficiently explored.

In making this contention, I am not attempting to diminish advances that took place in crime fiction published after the historic stand made at Stonewall. Tellingly, Joseph Hansen's *Fadeout* (1970), the first novel in a groundbreaking, critically-acclaimed mystery series in the hard-boiled tradition that chronicles the investigations of Dave Brandstetter, an openly gay sleuth, appeared in print a year after the riots. In the preface to a 2004 edition of *Fadeout* published shortly before the author's death, Hansen noted that while he actually had completed the novel in 1967, it took a couple of years for his agent to place it with a publisher (a major one, Harper & Row). "Every place I took it to shied away," recalled Hansen of *Fadeout*. "It was a book many praised but none would publish."[1]

For many decades mystery publishers indeed had shied away from the inclusion of clearly indicated queer themes and characters in the fiction they published. Today Marie F. Rodell's Forties guidebook, *Mystery Fiction: Theory and Technique* (1943), gives bemused readers of modern crime fiction—where, to borrow from Cole Porter, anything goes—a hint of the confining strictures under which crime writers once labored. The rules-bound Rodell advised prospective mystery writers during the height of the Second World War that the depiction of sexuality in crime fiction was a metaphorical minefield, a virtual Iwo Jima of infractions:

> The morality of the average mystery fan is apparently pretty strait-laced. He will countenance murder, but not sexual transgressions ... booksellers will tell you it is true....
>
> Sexual perversions, other than sadism, are definitely taboo. And sadism must be presented in its least sexual form. Homosexuality may be hinted at, but never used as an overt and important factor in the story. An author may, in other words, get away with describing a character in such fashion that the reader may conclude the character is homosexual, but he should not so label him. All the other perversions are absolutely beyond the pale.
>
> Even references to normal sex relationships must be carefully watched. Except in the "tough" school, unmarried heroines are expected to be virgins, and sympathetic wives to be faithful to their husbands.... Abortion is considered legitimate mystery material if it is handled carefully and, of course, condemned. Apparently it is regarded by the fans as closer to murder than to sex.[2]

Rodell allowed that these taboos, which in fact encompassed a far vaster range of human sexual activity than same-sex shenanigans, limited the "field of potential material for murder fiction," but she reminded her audience of hopeful neophyte mystery authors that their chosen line of writing was escape literature and that shocks and controversies savoring of real life "are among the things the [mystery] reader is trying to escape from." Rodell advised, no doubt bloodcurdlingly to many modern crime writers, "If you have a message, if you want to write fiction with a purpose, try some other form. Mystery fiction will not serve."[3]

Yet what the well-meaning Rodell so dispiritingly detailed was "literature without bowels," as British Golden Age Crime Queen Dorothy L. Sayers back in the 1930s had bluntly complained of others who held such views, and many mystery writers of the day agreed with Sayers. In their desire that something more than a mere semblance of real life and human nature might make it into their work, these writers pressed against the artificial boundaries which people like Rodell had erected on behalf of their imagined legion of mystery-mad Mrs. Grundys. One of the points I hope *Murder in the Closet* will get across to readers is that in this pre–Stonewall period from 1886 to 1968, writers managed to include more queer material in their crime fiction than many analysts have appreciated. There are clues to this content waiting to be discovered in the pages of these writers' books, but one must, just like a keen-eyed fictional sleuth, discover and interpret them.[4]

Traditionally pre–Stonewall LGBTQ history has been seen through the powerful negative image of the closet, that dark place where all "the gay" had to be hidden away from public view, confined to its own restricted world of twilight (to use a common code word in pre–Stonewall fiction for homosexuality). In an essay in this volume, Michael Moon defines the closet as "a powerful social mechanism for regulating the open secret that same-sex desires and relationships existed, but did so largely invisibly and inaudibly." Violating what he calls the "code of the closet" could bring about "exposure, public disgrace, social ostracism, criminal prosecution." Over much of the twentieth century writers of popular fiction like crime novelists undeniably faced, whether they considered themselves queer or "normal," pressure to hoe straight rows in their writing, adhering to accepted social standards of what was deemed proper for inclusion in literature of escape. Yet historians, having come to appreciate that the pre/post Stonewall binary paints too limited a picture of pre–Stonewall queer life, have revised the confining construct of the closet, arguing that it falsely reflects, as George Chauncey has put it, "the Whiggish notion that change is always 'progressive' and that gay history in particular consists of a steady movement toward freedom."[5]

During the period between the two world wars, for example, queer people for a time became much more publicly visible in the western world, both simply as themselves, at such popular urban venues as nightclubs and drag balls, and as creative constructions in films, plays and the more daring mainstream fiction. (Chauncey has charted the course of this phenomenon in his book *Gay New York* though documentation of the Prohibition-era "pansy craze.") Similarly, during service in the Second World War "large numbers of young gay men and women came to discover their sexual identity" and not long after the conflict seemingly everyone was reading, or at least reading about, the landmark Kinsey reports on human sexuality, with their deeply intriguing scale of sexual responses indicating that homosexual activity was much more widespread than had been suspected. In these years queer subject matter began appearing more frequently in fiction, both in the form of hardbacks and what had become the ubiquitous paperback, the latter frequently decked out in provocatively sexualized covers. This movement toward greater sexual frankness in entertainment media became something of a pride parade by the mid-to-late-Sixties as legal impediments to free speech fell.[6]

Aggregately, the essays in *Murder in the Closet* lend support to the view that in crime fiction published before Stonewall more queer things made it out from behind seemingly secured closet doors onto printed pages than many have been inclined to credit. Like the clever culprits in their books, mystery writers knew a thing or two about getting past locked doors.

* * *

The essays in Part One of *Murder in the Closet*, entitled "Locked Doors," look at queer aspects to crime fiction from the late Victorian era to the celebrated Golden Age of detective fiction (traditionally defined as the period falling between the First and Second World Wars) and into the 1940s, the decade when Marie F. Rodell laid down the law to crime writers. Concerning authors who began publishing crime fiction before the advent of the Golden Age, Lucy Sussex in a piece of literary and historical detective work takes up the queer case of Arthur Conan Doyle contemporary Fergus Hume (1859–1932), the author of the worldwide blockbuster crime tale *The Mystery of a Hansom Cab* and a prolific maker of mysteries for some forty years thereafter, while J. F. Norris analyzes an intriguing problem of gender identity in *The Secret of Lonesome Cove* (1912), a deeply fascinating, if now almost entirely forgotten, detective novel by the muckraking American journalist and author Samuel Hopkins Adams (1871–1958).

The next dozen essays in *Murder in the Closet* deal with queer goings-on in the work of British and American Golden Age mystery writers, in whose hands so-called clue-puzzle detective fiction reached its apogee. Employing the between-the-wars beauty parlor metaphor of "dropped hairpins," which George Chauncey has explained was the coded language by which gay men in this era could obliquely communicate with each other in public without giving themselves away to "potentially hostile straight observers," Noah Stewart looks at the ways in which Golden Age British and American mystery writers, mindful of the admonitions of the Marie F. Rodells of the publishing world, portrayed queer characters without explicitly labeling them as such. Stewart finds certain character types that were coded as gay or lesbian: prissies/sissies and the gunsel (among men) and man-haters, vampires and, altogether more positively, the happy couple (among women). Yet he notes that not all of these characters necessarily must be read as gay or lesbian: sometimes a cigar may be just a cigar and a priss just a priss.

The next group of essays scrutinizes mystery fiction by the British Crime Queens Agatha Christie (1890–1976), Gladys Mitchell (1901–1983) and Josephine Tey (1897–1952). "Gay characters in the fiction of Agatha Christie are notable only for their scarcity," writes John Curran is his essay on the most renowned of the Queens of Crime, in which he nevertheless goes on to discuss rather a queer company of characters, most of whom, he concludes, "can confidently be identified as gay," though some to his mind offer more "ambiguous examples." In the second Christie essay, Michael Moon suggests supplementing the traditional method of discovering queer characters—what he calls "collecting and sorting types (or stereotypes)"—by scrutinizing the interplay of fluctuating conceptions of normativity and queerness in Christie's crime fiction. Moon tantalizingly urges that we "consider the hypothesis that virtually anyone in it might be queer in one way or another, or perhaps in a number of ways."

In his reference work *Gay and Lesbian Characters and Themes in Mystery Novels: A Critical Guide to over 500 Works in English* (1993), writer Anthony Slide condemns Crime Queens Ngaio Marsh and Gladys Mitchell for what he deems anti-queer crime writing. Marsh to him is the "most homophobic of the classic mystery writers," while Mitchell, he declares, "was homophobic and her books are dated and unappealing."[7] Although readers of Noah Stewart's aforementioned essay, with its discussion of Ngaio Marsh's gunsel characters Claude and Lionel in her mystery *Death in Ecstasy* (1936), may find it difficult to disagree with Slide's characterization of Marsh's writing as it relates to gay men, Brittain Bright demonstrates that such criticism of Mitchell's work is considerably wide of the mark. Bright aptly characterizes Mitchell's psychiatrist detective Mrs. Beatrice Adela Lestrange Bradley as "unshockable" and notes that by the early 1930s Mrs. Bradley "had advocated birth control, dismissed the idea that pornography was a malign influence, blithely overlooked incest and infidelity, and acknowledged homosexuality." Nor, notes Bright, is Mitchell's sleuth "defined by her sex; while she is heterosexual, she is forcefully and notably unfeminine." Bright looks not only at Mitchell's handling of gay and lesbian characters but sexuality in general and demonstrates how the author's sleuth subverted norms with cackling abandon.

It has been intimated that both Gladys Mitchell, who lived for years with the writer Winifred Blazey, and Ngaio Marsh were lesbians, a claim that similarly has been made about Scottish writer Josephine Tey, an author who, as J.C. Bernthal notes in his essay, has long been highly-regarded by critics in the UK and U.S. and is currently undergoing a tremendous resurgence in popularity, with many modern crime writers naming her as their favorite Crime Queen. In their respective essays on Tey, J.C. Bernthal and Moira Redmond address intriguing questions of gender identity and sexuality in two of Tey's most admired crime novels, respectively *To Love and Be Wise* (1950) and *Miss Pym Disposes* (1946).

From British Crime Queens we turn to a pair of trebly-initialed British male authors of detective fiction, G. D. H. Cole (1889–1959) and C. H. B Kitchin (1895–1967), in essays by me and Michael Moon. One of twentieth-century

Britain's most active and important socialist intellectuals, Cole, along with his accomplished wife, Margaret, yet found time to produce a sizeable body of detective fiction. Cole's second mystery novel, *The Death of a Millionaire* (1925), the subject of my essay, reflects both the author's politics and his own same-sex inclinations, aspects of life that were inextricably intertwined in the author's mind. Unlike Cole, Kitchin eschewed marriage, yet over his life he maintained two successive long-term partnerships with men. In his essay on Kitchin, Moon makes the case that English stockbroker Malcolm Warren, Kitchin's amateur sleuth in four well-regarded detective novels published between 1929 and 1949, "is, in several senses, as his creator was, 'gay' or 'queer.'"

From essays on Cole and Kitchin we turn to another one by me concerning a pair of British expatriate mystery writers, Richard Wilson Webb (1901–1966) and Hugh Callingham Wheeler (1912–1987), who settled in the United States between the two world wars, became American citizens and produced, under no less than three different pseudonyms (Q. Patrick, Patrick Quentin and Jonathan Stagge), some of the finest mid-twentieth-century crime fiction in their adopted country. Webb and Wheeler offer us what currently seems a rare example of a same-sex mystery writing couple, though the two men have been unacknowledged as such in traditional (i.e., heteronormative) crime genre histories. In my essay I sort through mysteries in the two men's lives and provide an analysis of the treatment of male couples in the queerest of the "Q. Patrick" crime novels, *The Grindle Nightmare* (1935).

Of much different personal origin was Todd Downing (1902–1974), a part–Choctaw Golden Age detective novelist from Oklahoma. Downing's once much-praised body of crime fiction, recently reprinted, drew heavily on his knowledge of Mexico, and modern academic interest in the author has centered on his depiction of indigenous American characters and themes. Yet it is Downing's seeming homosexuality and the queer aspects of his crime fiction, originally addressed more briefly in my book *Clues and Corpses: The Detective Fiction and Mystery Criticism of Todd Downing* (2013), which is detailed in the essay by Charles J. Rzepka.

Todd Downing's favorite crime writer in the 1930s, prized by him even above Agatha Christie, Ellery Queen and John Dickson Carr, was Rufus King, scion of an elite New York family with artistic connections on his mother's side. King, who during his time at Yale had performed a series of star turns in drag roles in college musicals, produced some of the most ingenious and transparently queer crime fiction of the Golden Age. In the next essay I look at King and his classic detective novel *Murder by Latitude* (1930), as well as the two detective novels by Clifford Orr, another gay American Golden Age mystery writer who as a student at Dartmouth was greatly involved in the world of Ivy League theatricals.

In the last essay in Part One, Rick Cypert takes on one of the most prolific and popular twentieth-century American crime writers, Mignon Eberhart (1899–1996), once known as "America's Agatha Christie." Cypert analyzes the way Eberhart, historically significant in the history of American crime fiction for marrying murder with romance, treats the subject of masculinity in her work. The frequently ingenuous young women who take center stage in Eberhart's mystery thrillers tend to learn, after much travail, that it generally would be wise for them in future to steer clear of men who are "a little too handsome."

* * *

Recently the period extending from the end of the Second World War to the mid-to-late-Sixties has been dubbed, in contravention of conventional wisdom about the epochal cultural impact of Stonewall, no less than the "golden age of gay fiction." "The Homophile Movement of the 1950s and 1960s was accompanied by an unprecedented surge of gay literature, gay novels in particular, in both Britain and America," Ian Young has noted in his essay "The Paperback Explosion: How Gay Paperbacks Changed America." Among other things fiction in the postwar years saw the rise of lesbian pulp novels and the appearance of what has been called the first book with an overtly gay detective, Rodney Garland's *The Heart in Exile* (1953), though Lou Rand's campy crime novel *The Gay Detective* (1961)—"so flaming you could roast marshmallows over it," quipped lesbian pulp fiction writer Ann Bannon—arguably has the better claim, if one means "detective" in the classical sense. Yet the Cold War era also saw the "lavender scare" in the United States and the United Kingdom and the resulting largescale, centrally-organized government persecution of homosexuals. (One of the individuals arrested and incarcerated in this period was the accomplished gay English author Rupert Croft-Cooke, who wrote detective fiction under the pseudonym Leo Bruce.) The situation was, as Michael Bronski has explained in writing of the United States at this time, complicated:

> Here was a country obsessed with ridding its government of "subversive" homosexuals, yet it idolized performers like Liberace and Little Richard.... The country enshrined motherhood and the domesticated female while at the same time buying millions and millions of lesbian pulp novels and making Marilyn Monroe and Jayne Mansfield stars. The country both savored and ignored rumors about Rock Hudson's "hidden life" while accepting him as Hollywood's leading symbol of manly heterosexual romanticism. This same country embraced the new masculinities presented by James Dean and Montgomery Clift while promoting a revival of patriotic, individualist masculinism to backbone the ongoing Cold War against Soviet and Chinese communism. It lionized Marlon Brando in black leather while it editorialized against the national outrage of youth motorcycle gangs. It was the country, finally, that promoted an apotheosis of the healthy male body in slyly homoerotic (and antiqueer) Charles Atlas ads in comics that were sold on drugstore magazine shelves only inches away from copies of *Physique Pictorial* and *Grecian Guild Quarterly*.[8]

8 Introduction

In Part Two of *Murder in the Closet*, entitled "Skeleton Keys," we move toward the more explicitly queer crime fiction of the 1950s and 1960s, following two essays dealing with subjects that anticipated the trends of these later decades. The first piece, by James Doig, concerns *Twisted Clay* (1934), a remarkably pulpish crime novel about the dark, dark doings of a psychotic lesbian (or perhaps more accurately bisexual) serial killer. Banned for many years in Australia, the native country of its author, Frank Walford (1882–1969), *Twisted Clay* was published with considerable hype in both the United Kingdom and, especially, the United States, where one reviewer, apparently quite a connoisseur of the outlandish, named the novel "the finest triumvirate of perversion, horror and murder written this spring." The lurid novel seems to anticipate the hugely popular lesbian pulp fiction of the 1950s, though it is spiked with more than a dash of the noirish nastiness which one finds in the nightmarish crime fiction of Jim Thompson.

In the second essay Drewey Wayne Gunn anatomizes a real life criminal case combining bisexuality and bloody murder. The once-infamous 1943 slaying of the beautiful young American high society heiress Patricia Lonergan was a sordid affair in which were implicated all those explicit aspects of sex that Marie F. Rodell, whose mystery writing guidebook was coincidentally published the same year, wanted kept out of "escapist" crime fiction. Patricia Lonergan's supposed murderer, her dreamily handsome husband Wayne, had been sexually involved with Patricia's artist father before he wed Patricia, just one of many details that led newspapers to go wild over the story, for the first time making extended direct discussion in their crime coverage of homosexuality. Gunn looks at mid-century American crime novels inspired by the case, named by Raymond Chandler one of the "crimes of the century."

Raymond Chandler himself has drawn the attention of those interested in queer literary history, with more than a few people on occasion having argued that Chandler's detective and even Chandler himself were latently homosexual. The next two essays study queerness in the writing of Ross Macdonald (1915–1983), Chandler's greatest successor, and the late man of letters Gore Vidal (1925–2012), a crime fiction dilettante who in the 1950s wrote a trio of mysteries under the name "Edgar Box." In his essay on Ross Macdonald, Tom Nolan points out that as the author mastered his craft and worked through his own personal emotional issues he developed a distinctively humane (and less hard-boiled) voice; and concurrently his depiction of queer characters matured beyond the cheap and easy sneers of Chandler and Dashiell Hammett, writers who "used [homosexuals] to exemplify moral decay." Macdonald also starkly contrasted in this respect, as in others, with the graphically sexual and violent yet morally primitive hard-boiled mystery fiction of Mickey Spillane, the toughest of tough guy crime writers. My essay on Gore Vidal's "Edgar Box" detective novels contrasts Spillane's writing with Vidal's

Box work, which was memorably dubbed "Spillane in mink" on account of its sexual sophistication, or what today we might be more prone to term queer sensibility. Yet Vidal's frank portrayal of same-sex desire in the first of the Box novels, *Death in the Fifth Position* (1952), is compromised not only by the constraints of the publishing business at that time, but the author's own restricted conception of masculinity.

The next two essays cross back over the pond to Great Britain, to look at the mid-century crime writing careers of Beverley Nichols (1898–1983) and Nancy Spain (1917–1964). Best known today for his popular series of books on gardening and old home renovation, Nichols also published, among many other works, five detective novels between 1954 and 1960. Though classic clue-puzzlers in the manner of between-the-wars Golden Age detective fiction, these mysteries nevertheless include evidence of a gay sensibility at work, J. F. Norris explains in his essay, including a sympathetically (though at times somewhat awkwardly presented) lesbian couple, depictions of male intimacy and a wry disguised sex scene between two men, one gay, one straight.

Over her much shorter life iconic lesbian Nancy Spain was a similarly versatile and productive author, publishing, among other things, detective fiction, children's books, biographies and personal memoirs. Spain's detective novels, which originally appeared between 1946 and 1955, are notable for bedlam humor and a markedly queer and campy sensibility. Spain herself lived openly with literary editor Joan "Jonny" Werner Laurie and their two sons, Nicholas and Thomas, though the couple never officially "came out," their lesbian relationship being more in the nature of an open secret. In his essay on Spain, Bruce Shaw scrutinizes how the author dealt with children in her fiction and in her own life with Jonny Laurie. Suggesting the confines Fifties cultural norms in the UK imposed on even the most sexually adventurous individuals, Spain and Laurie passed off both their sons as the birth children of Jonny from an earlier marriage, though in fact Spain had given birth to Tom, the product of a one-nighter with Philip Youngman-Carter, the much-philandering husband of British Crime Queen Margery Allingham.

Though Spain in her lifetime was far better known, at least in the United Kingdom, than the American Patricia Highsmith (1921–1995), another lesbian crime writer and the subject of the next essay, Highsmith's modern-day fame has far eclipsed Spain's, along with that of many another mid-century crime novelist. Roundly considered one of the most important crime writers of the twentieth century, Highsmith has been the subject of two massive biographies and her 1952 lesbian novel, *Carol* (originally published as *The Price of Salt*, under the pseudonym Claire Morgan), was recently adapted into a much-acclaimed film. In her crime fiction, however, as Nick Jones points out in his essay in this volume, Highsmith by her own admission was preoccupied with the "two-men theme": "the fluidity of identity, the nature of obsession and the tension between attraction and repulsion." The two-men theme is of central importance in Highsmith's first crime novel, the influential *Strangers on a Train* (1950), and recurs throughout her fiction of the 1950s and 1960s, most famously in the classic *The Talented Mr. Ripley* (1955).

With the last two essays in this volume, we move to examples of mid- to late-Sixties crime fiction where queerness has unashamedly emerged from the literary closet: James Colton's *Known Homosexual* (1968) and George Baxt's early Pharoah Love trilogy, consisting of the novels *A Queer Kind of Death* (1966), *Swing Low, Sweet Harriet* (1967) and *Topsy and Evil* (1968). "James Colton" was the Sixties pseudonym of Joseph Hansen (1923–2004), creator, as discussed above, of the landmark Dave Brandstetter detective novels, which originally appeared between 1970 and 1991. Under the Colton pen name Hansen between 1964 and 1971 published eight erotic gay pulp novels, including two mysteries, *Known Homosexual* (1968) and *Hang-Up* (1969). As Josh Lanyon notes in her essay on *Known Homosexual*, the novel was reprinted twice, each edition with modifications from the hand of the author himself, who two decades after its original publication admitted of "my first try at a mystery" that "I still like it."

With George Baxt's outrageously camp early Pharoah Love trilogy we are confronted with quite a queerer set of characters than those ever encountered in Hansen's crime writing (although interestingly both *Known Homosexual* and the Love trilogy have black protagonists). In an essay in *The Golden Age of Gay Fiction*, Josh Lanyon has observed that while Hansen's Dave Brandsetter "was not the first gay detective to hit mainstream crime fiction ... he was the first *normal* gay detective."[9] Certainly "normal" is not a word that could be applied to the outrageous inhabitants of Baxt's early mysteries, including the series detective himself, Pharoah Love, "a celebration," writes J. F. Norris in his essay on the Love trilogy, "of all that is hip and swinging." Somewhat recalling Marie F. Rodell's admonitions from a quarter-century earlier, Anthony Boucher, then dean of American crime fiction critics, from his august post at the *New York Times Book Review* warned of *A Queer Kind of Death*, the first novel in the trilogy, that "'staid' readers may well find it shocking"; yet Boucher himself was delighted with Baxt's book. The word "staid" says it all, I think: it was no longer the "morality of the average mystery reader" that was at issue, but the aesthetic limitations of the primly unadventurous. By the late Sixties that which was indisputably, even blatantly, queer had finally arrived, like Cinderella decked out in all her finery, at the crime and mystery fiction ball—and, queerly enough, midnight never struck.

* * *

The essays in *Murder in the Closet* open new vistas for the study of queer aspects of crime fiction published before Stonewall. My own decades-long experience with reading both vintage crime fiction and works about vintage crime fiction has convinced me that much more work remains to be done on the subject, with many Golden Age writers who could provide scholars needed illumination in their treks having gone almost entirely ignored or, if not ignored, misinterpreted. Too many crime and mystery genre studies still focus almost exclusively on a relatively small number of British "Crime Queens"— authors of so-called "cozy," classical mystery (Christie, Sayers, Tey, Allingham, Marsh)—and American "tough" writers of hard-boiled and noir crime fiction (Chandler, Hammett, Highsmith, Jim Thompson, David Goodis, James M. Cain, etc.). With the exception of Patricia Highsmith, gay and lesbian writers of vintage mystery have been mostly left out of the picture. Though some writers have urged queer readings of the lives of Josephine Tey, Ngaio Marsh and Raymond Chandler, these readings remain highly speculative. In the case of another prominent author of mid-twentieth-century crime fiction, American noirist Cornell Woolrich, the influential queer reading of his life has, it seems to me, crossed over from the realm of the highly speculative into the region of the frankly regrettable, relying heavily on the stereotype, so familiar in depictions of pre–Stonewall homosexuals, of the *self-hating gay man*:

> By all accounts, Cornell Woolrich was a real son of a bitch. A self-hating gay man who once married a naive young woman as a cruel joke, refused to sleep with her and then left her a written account of his escapades with other men, he lived most of his life with an overbearing mother who said she would die if he ever left her. When she finally did die years later, Woolrich drank himself into a decade-long stupor, developed gangrene and died weighing 89 pounds. It was a miserable end to a thoroughly rotten life [Jake Hinkson, *The Night Editor*].
>
> I say it again, the man was a creep—not because he was gay, but because of the diary, and because he left it behind for Gloria to read. Then there's the fact he lived with his mother until he was 53, when she died. By itself that would just be kind of odd; taken with everything else it tends to red-line the creep factor. (It sounds like Sebastian and Violet Venable in *Suddenly, Last Summer*.)[10] [Jim Lane, *Jim Lane's Cinemadrome*].

These withering assessments of Woolrich as a "self-hating gay man" draw upon Francis M. Nevins' Edgar-award-winning Woolrich biography, *First You Dream, Then You Die* (1988), a book which I contend in my blog essay "The Black Legend: The Private Life of Cornell Woolrich and the Perils of Popular Memory" seems to provide only a shaky basis for the author's conclusion that "the secret of understanding" Woolrich and his fiction is Woolrich's "self-hated, self-contempt" as a gay man.[11] It is far from clear to my mind that Woolrich actually was gay (see my blog essay), self-hating or not, but in any event the case for the link between Woolrich's putative mental condition and his writing is, in my estimation, never credibly made by Nevins in his biography. Here are examples of Nevins' literary analysis of the author's work and its supposed relationship to gay self-hatred:

- "I was carrying Death around in my mouth," the reporter tells us near the end [of the story "Death Sits in the Dentist's Chair," where a dentist fills cavities with cyanide], and if one is determined to find subtle traces of Woolrich's homosexuality everywhere in his work, one might as well begin here.
- While struggling with Cook over a gun, the hobo is shot in the mouth [here we go again, homosexual symbol seekers!] and killed.
- ... they arrange for a pickpocket accomplice to take a ride on the same train that is bringing Bull to the state pen, sit in the seat behind the mobster and quietly puncture Bull's rear end with a hypodermic full of germs [homosexuality symbol hunters take notice!] ...
- ... the evocation of [a male character's] death ... suggests a savage homosexual coupling....[12]

Nevins' examples seem risibly reductive to me. Since Woolrich was a "self-hating gay man," so the reasoning seems to run, inevitably any time in his tales that poison, bullets or germs enter a man's mouth or buttocks it symbolizes homosexuality. It is disappointing to see Nevins in his hunt for "homosexual symbols" focus so relentlessly on sex acts. Is it Woolrich who associated gay sex with death, or is it his biographer, writing during the height of the AIDS crisis, who has imposed this meaning on Woolrich's texts?

Concerning Woolrich and his alleged gay self-hatred, Nevins was even more emphatic on another occasion, stating in 2010 that "Woolrich was perhaps the most deeply closeted, self-hating homosexual male author that ever lived." How many others are we meant to think there were, one wonders? For his part, Nevins has extended this gay self-hatred thesis to additional twentieth-century mystery writers. In a 1977 article in the esteemed fanzine *Armchair Detective*, Nevins brought his psychological insights to bear on Golden Age detective novelist Milton M. Propper (1906–1962), while at the website *Mystery*File* he passingly pathologized Patricia Highsmith: "If you think Cornell Woolrich was something of a psychopath and a creep, you don't know the meaning of those words till you've encountered Highsmith. Both, of course, were homosexual. I gather from [Joan Schenkar's biography of Highsmith] that Highsmith ... was never terribly comfortable with being a lesbian."[13]

I believe modern mystery criticism must progress beyond such conceptually constrained analysis and develop fuller and more nuanced treatments of queer life and writing before Stonewall. To do this, however, we must read the books. Scholar Jaime Harker has recently contended that "mainstream gay texts," such as pulp fiction and popular novels, have been left "understudied and often undervalued by queer critics."[14] Vintage crime writing with strong queer elements, often written by LGBTQ authors, falls into this category as well. Following the example of authorities on mainstream queer fiction like Harker, Wayne Gunn, Michael Bronski, Susan Stryker and Ian Young, *Murder in the Closet* further opens the door to scholars of twentieth-century mystery to attitudinally unblinkered approaches that will help lead us to a better understanding both of pre–Stonewall crime fiction and cultural history generally.

Notes

1. Joseph Hansen, Preface to *Fadeout* (1970; repr., Madison: University of Wisconsin Press, 2004). An 18 August 1970 notice in *Kirkus Reviews* emphasized the new voice in Hansen's *Fadeout*, making reference to what it termed the novel's "unleashed homoeroticism" and observing dryly that the author leveled "remarks at the straight society with a Mattachine gun" (a pun on the name of the Mattachine Society, a homophile organization founded in 1950, though ironically the Society at this time was being criticized by many within the gay rights movement for being insufficiently confrontational). Obviously even after Stonewall, writers of queer mysteries still faced cultural attitudinal challenges. Suggesting the limitations that existed even in the Seventies, Hansen recalled not only that *Ellery Queen Mystery Magazine* editor Frederic Dannay (the surviving half of the team that had created the classic fictional detective Ellery Queen back in 1929) had rejected for publication in *EQMM* a Hansen short story about Dave Brandstetter on the grounds that his readers were "not ready for homosexuality," but also that a film studio in the late Seventies had wanted to option the rights to the Dave Brandstetter mysteries, though only if "Brandstetter's not gay." See Bill Mohr, "Emotions Doesn't Change Facts: Remembering Joseph Hansen," *Los Angeles Review of Books: The Magazine*, 5 December 2014. To date not a single Brandstetter novel has yet been filmed. Hansen himself noted that he only made his real sales breakthrough with the Brandstetter mysteries in the 1980s, when Harcourt, Brace's imprint Owl reprinted the novels in paperback.

2. Marie F. Rodell, *Mystery Fiction: Theory and Technique* (New York: Duell, Sloan & Pearce, 1943), 91. Rodell's conclusion that "non-sexual" sadism and abortion were tolerable subjects for mystery readers (the latter because it was more pertained to murder than sex) offers an interesting reflection on the morality of the times, as least as people such as Rodell conceived it.

3. Rodell, *Mystery Fiction*, 92, 93.

4. Some mystery writers of the period even managed to get away with explicitly labeling homosexuality as such in their books. For example, in *The Weeping Willow Murders* (1934), a character makes this homophile declaration: "The handsome and athletic Fritz ... is, my dear, a homosexualist. There are many thousands of men like him, most of whom are otherwise normal; indeed, some of 'em are quite brilliant and gifted. Few go in for murder. Fritz doesn't, I am sure." Charles Koonce, *The Weeping Willow Murders* (Kansas City: Burton, 1934), 64–65. Similarly, a character in another novel, nettled by multiple insinuations from the catty murderee-to-be, retorts: "Nancy, I'm not an anarchist, nor a nihilist, nor a Lesbian. Please, for the love of heaven, don't go round telling people so." Emma Lou Fetta, *Murder in Style* (New York: Doubleday, Doran, 1939), 15.

5. George Chauncey, *Gay New York: Gender, Urban Culture and the Making of the Gay Male World, 1890–1940* (New York: Basic Books, 1994), 9.

14   Introduction

6. John D'Emilio and Estelle B. Freedman, Foreword to Allan Berube, *Coming Out Under Fire: The History of Gay Men and Women in World War II* (1990; repr., Chapel Hill: University of North Carolina Press, 2010), x. On the "pansy craze," see Chauncey, *Gay New York*, part III, chapter eleven, especially pages 311-13 and 324-25, where Chauncey discusses the craze's influence in contemporary stage plays, films and books. Of the latter he notes that the early 1930s saw "publishers race to satisfy the public's growing interest in the gay scene, for a flurry of gay-themed novels appeared between 1931 and 1934." See also Laura Horak, *Girls Will Be Boys: Cross-Dressed Women, Lesbians, and American Cinema, 1908-1934* (New Brunswick: Rutgers University Press, 2016). On queer pulp fiction see, for example, Susan Stryker, *Queer Pulp: Perverted Passions from the Golden Age of the Paperback* (San Francisco: Chronicle Books, 2001); Michael Bronski, ed., *Pulp Friction: Uncovering the Golden Age of Gay Male Pulps* (New York: St. Martin's Griffin, 2003); Drewey Wayne Gunn, ed., *The Golden Age of Gay Fiction* (Albion, NY: MLR Press, 2009); and Drewey Wayne Gunn, *The Gay Male Sleuth in Print and Film: A History and Annotated Bibliography* (2005; new ed., Lanham, MD: Scarecrow, 2013). In the United States a series of court decisions greatly limited the legal definition of obscenity, giving vastly freer rein to authors of queer fiction. See Roger H. Tuller, "'A Subject of Absorbing Interest to Mankind': U. S. Supreme Court Obscenity Rulings, 1934-1977," in Gunn, *Gay Fiction*, 135-41.

7. Anthony Slide, *Gay and Lesbian Characters and Themes in Mystery Novels: A Critical Guide to over 500 Works in English* (Jefferson, NC: McFarland, 1993), 113, 126.

8. Ian Young, "The Paperback Explosion: How Gay Paperbacks Changed America," Gunn, *Gay Fiction*, 3; Bronski, *Pulp Friction*, 14-15. On Rodney Garland's *The Heart in Exile*, see Ian Young, "The Two Rodney Garlands: A Literary Mystery," Gunn, *Gay Fiction*, 63-74, and Drewey Wayne Gunn's "Down These Queer Streets a Man Must Go," Gunn, *Gay Fiction*, 197-98. On Lou Rand's *The Gay Detective*, see Gunn, "Queer Streets," in Gunn, *Gay Fiction*, 198-99 and Susan Stryker and Martin Meeker, Introduction to Lou Rand, *The Gay Detective* (1961, repr., San Francisco: Cleis, 2003). For an overview of the career of Marijane Meaker (b. 1927), one of the most important lesbian and crime pulp fiction authors of the postwar period, see Jon L. Breen's essay "Vin Packer," in Jon L. Breen and Martin H. Greenberg, eds., *Murder off the Rack* (Lanham, MD: Scarecrow Press, 1989). Vin Packer was Meaker's crime fiction pseudonym. On Cold War persecution of LGBTG people see John D'Emilio, "The Homosexual Menace: The Politics of Sexuality in Cold War America" [1989], in John D'Emilio, *Making Trouble: Essays on Gay History, Politics, and the University* (London: Routledge, 1992), 57-73; Alkarim Jivani, *It's Not Unusual: A History of Lesbian and Gay Britain in the Twentieth Century* (London: Michael O'Mara, 1997); Nicolas C. Edsall, *Toward Stonewall: Homosexuality and Society in the Modern World* (Charlottesville: University of Virginia Press, 2003); David K. Johnson, *The Lavender Scare: The Cold War Persecution of Gays and Lesbians in the Federal Government* (Chicago: University of Chicago Press, 2004). For a specific example see the case of Newton Arvin, Smith College professor, National Book Award winner and onetime lover of Truman Capote, who was arrested in 1960 on account of his possession of male physique magazines. See Barry Werth, *The Scarlet Professor: Newton Arvin: A Literary Life Shattered by Scandal* (New York: Nan A. Talese, 2001).

9. Josh Lanyon, "The Play of Shadows and Light: Hansen Before Dave," in Gunn, *Gay Fiction*, 153.

10. Quotations are drawn from Jake Hinkson, Review of *Fear in the Night* (1947), 24 February 2010, *The Night Editor*, at http://thenighteditor.blogspot.com/2010/02/fear-in-night-1947.html; Jim Lane, Review of *Night Has a Thousand Eyes*, 6 May 2011,

Jim Lane's Cinemadrome, at http://jimlanescinedrome.blogspot.com/2011/05/lost-found-night-has-thousand-eyes.html.

11. Curtis Evans, "The Black Legend: The Private Life of Cornell Woolrich and the Perils of Popular Memory," 12 May 2014, *The Passing Tramp*, at http://thepassingtramp.blogspot.com/2014/05/the-black-legend-private-life-of.html; "Underappreciated Literature: Cornell Woolrich" (Nevins interview with Leonard Lopate), 14 July 2006, *The Leonard Lopate Show*, at http://www.wnyc.org/story/52432-underappreciated-literature-cornell-woolrich/.

12. Quotations are drawn from Francis M. Nevins, *First You Dream, Then You Die* (New York: Mysterious Press, 1988), 129, 141, 157, 299.

13. Francis M. Nevins, "The World of Milton Propper," *Armchair Detective* 19 (July 1977): 197–203 and "First You Read, Then You Write," 22 June 2010, *Mystery*File*, at http://mysteryfile.com/blog/?p=2142; For other views of Propper see my 23 November 2012 review of Propper's *One Murdered, Two Dead* (1936) at my blog *The Passing Tramp*, http://thepassingtramp.blogspot.com/2012/11/a-proper-crofts-he-is-one-murdered-two.html, and a comment from J. F. Norris on my blog essay "The Black Legend."

14. Jaime Harker, *Middlebrow Queer: Christopher Isherwood in America* (Minneapolis: University of Minnesota Press, 2013), 179.

Part One
Locked Doors

The Queer Story of Fergus Hume

Lucy Sussex

> Adam Lind, aged 25, handsome, gay, and to a certain degree clever, was a clerk in the Hibernian Bank, Melbourne, a situation of no great responsibility.—Fergus Hume, "The Queer Story of Adam Lind"

Fergus Hume (1859–1932) is best known for *The Mystery of a Hansom Cab*, a book first semi-self-published as a "shilling shocker" (paperback) in Australia in 1886. When reprinted in London the following year, it became the biggest and fastest-selling mystery novel of the nineteenth century: 300,000–500,000 copies sold. The novel's success helped consolidate the emergent detective genre into a distinct and lucrative publishing category. It preceded into print the first Sherlock Holmes story, "A Study in Scarlet," and without it, Holmes might never have become a series hero. Conan Doyle had intended his narrative to be a one-off; as did Hume, who fatally did not believe the *Hansom Cab* would succeed outside Australasia. Hume sold his copyright for £50, then a large sum ("A Study in Scarlet" earned Conan Doyle half that amount), but could have made thousands of pounds from the book. He never repeated the success, despite a long career, producing some 140 novels, predominantly mystery, of which some are very fine.

Hume in his literary context follows on from the Sensation (crime) novels of Wilkie Collins and Mary Braddon of the 1860s, to both of whom he paid tribute. His model was the crime procedurals of French writer Emile Gaboriau, as translated and reprinted to huge sales by the publisher Vizetelly, and exported to the British colonies. Hume also left an important early statement of the detective-writers' craft vs. the critical reaction in *When I Lived in Bohemia*:

But if you write a detective novel, you state a hard and fast criminal case, and in order to carry it out to a logical conclusion you are as bound by that case as though it actually happened. Then you must have all police-court business at your fingers' ends, be well up in legal matters, know something about the medical profession, and be careful about every statement you make. You must conceal the real criminal, lay the blame on all the other characters in the book; yet, when the end comes, you have to prove that it is quite natural the real criminal should have committed the crime.

Look at all the work, observation, logic, analysis, and memory involved in the writing of such a book, and yet when it is done and presents a perfect picture of a difficult criminal case, then critics dismiss it with the contemptuous remark "that it is a shilling shocker!"

Not much is known about Hume's private life, and that is no doubt how he preferred it. He was born in England of Scottish parents, the family emigrating to New Zealand during his early childhood. He would declare in an 1892 preface to the *Hansom Cab* that he "belonged to New Zealand," although when he left the Southern Hemisphere for England in 1888, he never returned. His parents, James and Mary Hume, ran the insane asylum in Dunedin, New Zealand, and Fergus was the youngest of their five children. He became a lawyer, although preferring writing as a career. Crime fiction was not his intended destination, that being a successful dramatist, something he never achieved. Although he had some minor success in New Zealand, when he emigrated to Melbourne in 1885, then the richest city in the Southern hemisphere, he could not place his plays. He only wrote the *Hansom Cab* to draw Melbourne theatre managers' attention to his writing, after having enquired of a bookseller what was selling—and being told Gaboriau. The book's success turned him into a crime writer, and typecast him with the public.

Hume never married, and left no known diaries, nor do many letters survive. Yet in the process of researching *Blockbuster*, my book about the *Hansom Cab*, a possibility emerged, not proven, but still tantalizing. When the words queer and gay appeared in Hume's 1889 story "Adam Lind," it meant little to the casual reader and the story itself was conventional, heterosexual. The semantic and social changes since have given us gay marriage, queer theory, developments unimaginable in Hume's era. They have also made it possible to read Hume's life and work for clues to his personal preferences, the hidden life of a very private man. If actively gay, he would have lived, from 1885 and the passing of the Labouchère amendment, which criminalised "gross indecency" between men, in secrecy and fear. Such necessitated discretion—but still a case can be made for Fergus Hume having his own, secret, queer story.

In understanding Hume, it is necessary to place him in context, growing up in the Australasian colonies in the nineteenth century, which made him a writer, and a man. The ideal of the era was heterosexual virtue, the royal model of Queen Victoria and Prince Albert, surrounded by offspring. Photograph albums and family trees tell a different story: the large families had many spinster aunts, many bachelor uncles. Economics might have kept some single, others might have been unlucky in love. Or did they prefer not to marry, seeking alternatives for which, given discretion, an innocent explanation existed? How many people lived at odds with the prevailing heterosexual culture is unknown, but some fascinating traces survive: in letters, photographs, archives, and even the works of Fergus Hume.

Victorian morality separated the sexes, resulting in homosociality outside the domestic circle: in schools, the workplace, the clergy and armed services. In the Australian colonies it was a feature of the convict system, and also goldmining, from where the term "mate" derives: initially a partnership, then the term for male friendship, but just how far did it go? With the premium on female virtue, and the lack of reliable contraception, relations between the sexes could be fraught. Same-sex affection was far less problematic, even permitted to be romantic: males posed arm in arm, schoolgirls were allowed their crushes. Agnes Murphy, a journalist and co-worker with Hume on the Melbourne magazine *Table Talk*, wrote in her autobiographical novel *One Woman's Wisdom* (1895):

> "I can never understand people who are not enthusiastic about girls. Now, to my thinking," and [Mary's] eyes danced roguishly, "it must always be more delightful to kiss the fresh soft lips of a girl than the mustached mouth of a man. If I were a poet I should write all my verses to girls, just to show how one of their own sex appreciates them."[1]

This passage passed unremarked, for lesbian expression was essentially unregulated by law. For males sodomy incurred severe penalty, although it was relatively rarely prosecuted. Unless caught in the act, it was hard to prove. Nor did sexual practice define the homosexual identity. For most of the century there was no real conception of such: same-sex acts were what people did, rather than something that distinguished them from the heterosexual norm. However, criminology was beginning to identify a "type," and activities that would, with the Labouchère amendment, be penalized. Its first prominent victim came ten years later, with the 1895 imprisonment of Oscar Wilde.

Although Fergus Hume grew up in Dunedin, a Scots Presbyterian settlement, beneath the public rectitude can be read a different narrative. From his childhood onwards it would have been possible to encounter individuals with same-sex attractions. An 1879 New Zealand government report on mental asylums cited inmates' "abominable vices," the euphemism for homosexual practices.[2] The Humes' connection with their patients was intimate; they lived on the asylum premises and some patients even lodged with the family. For his schooling, Hume went to Otago Boys' High, a public school on the English model. Typically the Greek classics featured in their curricula, where could be found depiction of intense male, even homosexual relationships—

something paralleled in the schools themselves. *Tom Brown's Schooldays* might have presented one school story; a quite different view appeared in the first homosexual autobiography, by John Addington Symonds (1840–1893), who attended Harrow: "Every boy of good looks had a female name, and was recognized either as a public prostitute or as some bigger fellow's 'bitch.' Bitch was the word in common usage to indicate a boy who yielded his person to a lover." Symonds lived a double life, as a classicist, husband, father, and lover of men. He also defended his private practices, in layered texts, outwardly on the classics, but inwardly seeking precedents for his covert erotics, which he termed "the ways of evasion," a means of communication. Hume studied Classics to university level, both knew and cited Symonds' work—which he arguably read on its two levels.[3]

The first descriptions of Fergus Hume are as a bright child, and a dandy dresser. Among the sober-minded Scots of his hometown, he stood out as a Masher: a male youth sub-culture noted for their smart, flashy clothes. The well-dressed Masher sported a bowler hat, moustache curled with wax, high stiff collar above a starched shirt, diamond studs (paste, for the poorer), well-tailored jacket and waistcoat, buttoned gloves, tight trousers, and patent leather boots. Essentially being a Masher was not much more than a young man's fashion statement, but Hume, with his arts criticism and aspirations to be a dramatist, shaded into the Aesthete of Oscar Wilde—a cultural figure whose influence extended to New Zealand. Young Hume had heard of him. As a Masher Hume would have been the object of jokes, and a certain unease—the reactionary journalist Eliza Lynn Linton decreed the masher "effeminate" and "of the fringe between the sexes."[4]

A tale told with variations about the young Hume is that this young peacock used the street as a public place of display, not only in dress but for discussions or arguments. Once the topic was really arcane, metempsychosis, the transmigration of the soul. Hume would have encountered the—hardly Presbyterian—concept from the classics, Plato, at the least, but it also figured in Theosophy, with its blend of Oriental and Occidental beliefs. Reincarnation would prove a persistent notion throughout his writing, with references to characters having met and loved repeatedly in different lives. In an article on Gilbert and Sullivan's operas, which he adored, he wrote: "No one now-a-days—at least, not openly—is a convert to the doctrine." But covertly? Did he himself feel like an old soul, or else someone born into the wrong body?[5]

There seems more here than the usual adolescent sense of being a misfit. Like Classical precedent, Theosophy could provide a means for the expression of same-sex desire. For those who felt ill-fitted for their times, it could be used as explanation, a coded statement similar to the "ways of evasion," as when the Australian novelist Rosa Praed in her *Nyria* (1904) gave her relationship with the medium Nancy Harward classical precedent: they had originally met in previous, Imperial Roman lives. In Hume's mystical fiction, the body and the transmigrating soul are not necessarily of the same gender. In *The Gentleman Who Vanished*, which features astral travelling and the taking over of bodies, Seer Dr. Rothersmire declares: "What attracted me most about the young lady [...] was not her beauty of face and form, although in both of those she was pre-eminent, but the strong masculine spirit which inhabited her feminine body." The apparently heterosexual attraction is spiritually homosexual. It is odd stuff, even for the Victorian advanced/arcane novel, though not going so far as to describe the logical reverse: the female spirit in the man's body. That was, as described by some contemporary sexologists, the "invert," the effeminate homosexual male.[6]

Sexual ambiguity could also be found in Hume's great love: the stage. Here was a site where the Victorian rigid rules of class, race and gender could be suspended, onstage; a centre for sexual display, not always heterosexual. In his novel *Across the Footlights*, Hume describes two theatrically-minded siblings: "Nature had made a mistake by giving the masculine nature to the girl and the feminine nature to the boy."[7] It was a motif that reappeared in his works—men who have pronounced aspects of the female, and women who are manlier than the Victorian norm generally permitted.

As an aspiring playwright, Hume sought performance for his plays, and he courted—at least professionally—touring theatrical troupes. His most noted theatrical association was with the young, handsome and celebrated English actor Philip Beck. He rescued a seriously ill Hume from debt prior to the *Hansom Cab*'s publication and in return demanded a Faustian bargain: collaboration, which involved a legal agreement. The pair co-wrote a published poem, and the stage adaptation of Hume's novel *Madame Midas*, the sequel to the *Hansom Cab*, which was a star vehicle for Beck. They were close: Beck lodged with Hume and his siblings in Melbourne, and after the success of the novel internationally, they travelled to England by ship together in 1888, writing theatre skits and performing them for the passengers. The relationship, however, would be doomed. The pair fell out, it costing Hume a "stiffish sum" to break the agreement with Beck.[8] The actor shot himself in 1889.

The stage, then and now, is a locus for those eschewing conventional gender roles. One such was Robert Gant, an actor who in Dunedin appeared in performances of Gilbert and Sullivan, credibly performing the female contralto parts. Hume almost certainly attended the shows. Gant is a perfect example of a gay man who successfully hid by being in plain sight, like Poe's purloined letter. While living in Masterton, New Zealand, he created photographic albums with his friends, now collected by Chris Brickell, which are marked by their homoeroticism. Men kissed; and dressed in drag—but because of Gant's amateur and professional theatrics, it was unexceptionable, especially since he was the town chemist, who knew everyone's medical secrets. Nonetheless, when a young man named Gordon Lawrence was arrested in Melbourne for transvestism, at least one New Zealand paper linked him to the Gant circle in Masterton.[9]

This report was in error, but another New Zealand paper *did* link Lawrence with Fergus Hume. Unlike Gant, Lawrence took his transvestism out of the theatre, and into the streets. This 21-year-old Sydneysider, a servant/actor, made a conspicuous spectacle at the Melbourne Centennial Exhibition, October 1888, parading in drag, complete with cosmetics and a flaxen wig. The use of make-up offstage signified the prostitute: respectable women kept their faces naked. Lawrence was, if not actively soliciting, certainly performing it: he winked at passing males, and gained a train of followers.

A watching police detective arrested him, and dislodged the wig—to reveal a man's cropped hair. Lawrence's court appearance confounded spectators: "In every look, in every motion, in every line of his figure he was a woman." Lawrence was found guilty of "insulting behaviour and vagrancy," after evidence was presented of "a long career of nameless immorality." He received six months, at which sentence he screamed and fainted. Even this act was performative, it being reported that after being carried out of the courtroom he winked at the constables. Without his finery "he stood revealed as a sallow faced and unpleasant looking young man of rather vulgar type."[10]

The press stated that Lawrence was "a member of a large gang of men who practice loathsome and unnatural offences." They took female names, often from actresses. In a Sydney case of 1887, several associates of Lawrence faced the court: "It appeared that numerous complaints had been made against them, and they were watched by police. It was found that they were in the habit of walking the streets at night, impersonating females, and having powder and pearl cream upon their faces. They were in the habit of jostling men in the street and making use of disgusting expressions."[11]

These cases indicate a colonial cross-dressing subculture, shading into the rent boy. An English precedent existed from the 1870s: Ernest Boulton and Frederick Park, who as Lady Stella Clinton and Fanny Park, strolled west-end London winking, like Lawrence, at likely men. In their letters appear among the first uses of the expressions "camp" and "drag." Though charged with conspiracy to commit sodomy, they were found not guilty, something in which class figured: the pair were well-connected, with expensive lawyers. In contrast Lawrence and his friends associated with the criminal underclass, vice squad fare.

One intriguing aspect of the Lawrence case was that Fergus Hume gave him money. A theatrical columnist reported that Lawrence "was able to obtain £20 from Fergus Hume in Sydney."[12] It was not for legal fees, since Hume had left Australia with Beck for London months before the Lawrence arrest.

Twenty pounds, with modern inflation, does not seem a significant sum, but at the time—when the *Hansom Cab* paperback cost a shilling (approximately $Aust5.00)—it was considerable. That amount could buy a ticket to somewhere distant: £20 in 1888 was the price of an economy steamship fare to England. It was considerably more than colonial courtesan rates.

The question of blackmail arises. Both Lord Alfred Douglas and Oscar Wilde got blackmailed prior to Wilde's court case, paying between £15–100 to regain compromising letters. Another nastier means of extortion existed, the badger game, in which men *in flagrante delicto* would be rudely interrupted by an accomplice, demanding money with menaces. The rent boys of Sydney would have known all about this trick. "It was fatally easy to set someone up," notes Phryne Fisher series author and lawyer Kerry Greenwood. "For poor Fergus to pay out such an outrageous sum to a young man of such a profession argues infatuation or blackmail." She adds:

> If the putain went back to his profession, then either explanation would still work and they are both tragic: Fergus was desperately in love with him and tried to bribe him out of the life and the Molly took the money and went on with it anyway, possibly spending it on drink or drugs or gambling, or the Molly boy had letters or photographs (tricky at the time, so valuable now) or proof of some sort he could use to extort the 20 quid. Possibly saying that he would sail away. Then not sailing. Either way poor Fergus is cheated and shamed and possibly has his heart broken, as well.
> What a sad story.[13]

A second source for the Lawrence tale appeared in 1902, after an article in the English magazine *M. A. P.* belatedly detailed Hume's association with Philip Beck. When it reached Australia, "Valentine Day" wrote to the *Critic*:

> Well, Beck has gone, and, therefore, cannot contradict the statement that he traded on a sick man's necessities, but I know his version of the story—corroborated by the testimony of others. This was its purport: That while he and Fergus Hume were living at the Sydney Criterion Theatre, the latter got into a very tight corner. He was being blackmailed by a certain coloured Shakespearean actor and his accomplice when Beck extricated him [...] it appears to me that that he would better have shown his gratitude and discretion by preserving a discreet silence concerning his obligations to the dead man.[14]

The only time the Criterion Theatre housed Beck was when he was appearing in the play *Sophia*, a version of *Tom Jones* in which he played the villain Blifil—for a six week period from March-April 1888. Shortly afterwards Hume and Beck left for England. One of the implications of this anecdote is that the £20 came from Beck, who naturally would have been concerned to protect his investment in Hume. Another is that Lawrence would have been the "accomplice." But who was the "coloured Shakespearean actor"?

The term does not refer to an Indigenous Australian. A small population of Africans, some American freedmen and women, and others did live in colonial Australia. Occasionally they intersected with the theatre, appearing in plays such as *Uncle Tom's Cabin*, instead of white actors in blackface. The most likely candidate was not a Shakespearean actor, but certainly noted as a tragedian. In March 1888, while Beck was appearing at the Criterion, Thomas Morton's 1816 musical drama *The Slave*, set in the West Indies, was performed in Sydney's Gaiety Theatre. The title role was performed by a young actor from Barbados, Antoine Bollars, and drew "good houses." Reportedly his only previous work on the stage had been as dresser to the celebrated English actor Wilson Barrett.[15]

Bollars, like Lawrence, came to Melbourne later that year, and to the attention of the police. In early July he was arrested after an incident that one newspaper described as "an extraordinary story." It was recounted in court that Bollars had been walking about the fashionable streets of the city, dressed to the nines. From what happened one evening it was clear he was, to use the modern term, "cruising." He met/"picked up" a young man called John H. Hampden, and took him back to his lodgings. Once in Bollars' room, the actor locked the door and "behaved in a strange manner towards his visitor." Hampden claimed he was only allowed to leave after signing an I. O. U. for Bollars for £7. He went to the police.[16]

Hampden was a man of some property, sporting a diamond tie-pin. From the newspaper account, which reads as if coded, it seems the police were at some pains to protect him from any public suspicion of sexual misconduct. Of three charges laid, only one was named: "attempting to commit a criminal offence." Bollars' prison record, which notes his being in the "Theatrical line," tells a different story: "Indecent assault on a male person." He was sentenced to three years imprisonment and ten strokes from the cat o' nine tails.[17] Bollars' committal to Pentridge prison occurred shortly before Lawrence donned drag for the Melbourne Exhibition. His act may thus not only be performative, but also romantic: did Lawrence seek to join Bollars?

Fergus Hume never described Bollars and Lawrence directly in his writing—the risk and contemporary prudery would have been too great. In any case he largely kept his life out of his work. But of all the characters in the *Hansom Cab*, closest to Hume as he was then, an aspiring young man of letters in the rich colonial city of Melbourne, is journalist Felix Rolleston. Hume was recalled as witty good company, like Felix. Both were Mashers: "His well-brushed top-coat glittered, his varnished boots glittered, and his diamond rings and scarf pin glittered; in fact, so resplendent was his appearance that he looked like an animated diamond coming along in the blazing sunshine." Hume gives Felix some of the best lines in the book: "some fellows are like trifle at a party—froth on top but something better underneath." Felix speaks affectedly, as mashers did, Hume even being recalled in Melbourne as lisping.[18]

In *Madame Midas*, Felix comments that the charismatic villain Gaston Vandeloup (played by Beck in the stage version) is a "deuced good-looking chappie," several sentences later telling him: "'it's a case of we never speak as we pass by, and all that sort of thing—come and look me up,' hospitably, 'South Yarra.'" If spoken by the right actor, as with Nathan Lovejoy in the 2012 ABC (Australia) telemovie of the *Hansom Cab*, this line would be most suggestive. Glen Dolman, its script writer, deliberately drew Felix as gay: "charmingly effete, fingers encrusted with rings." Dolman comments: "Early on in researching the background of the book too, I came across an article that suggested that Hume might have been gay himself, and lived with a partner in the UK. Whether or not that was the case, I felt he was suggesting that in Felix and wanted to include that character and dynamic in the tapestry of the world I was representing." He adds:

> Re: the character of Felix Rolleston, I just drew what I picked up from the book. I felt like Hume was not only writing about a comical socialite with social ambitions beyond his financial status (hence his opportunistic marriage to Miss Featherweight), but was most likely a gay man playing by society's rules of the time. The images Hume paints of him "shimmering in diamonds," looking like a peacock, and his flamboyant turn of phrase all seemed to fit.[19]

Philip Bentley, who is writing a graphic novel version of the *Hansom Cab*, disagrees:

> What did I think of the TV depiction of Felix R? Well I think they did the most logical thing and made him a bit less of a buffoon and not as gay—I know he ends up marrying, but a modern day reading of the character as written certainly could give you that impression. I'm sure Hume wasn't intending it so, I think he wants him to be read as a fop, but these days that sort of character tends to have melded into a gay stereotype ... perhaps we can blame Kenneth Williams [an English actor and comedian].[20]

Felix is an ambiguous character. But ambiguity was one way to write homosexual desire in the 1800s. Various terms were used: Arcadian, Greek, Calamus, deriving from Walt Whitman's *Leaves of Grass*, and Uranian, coded with hidden meanings. In 1892 Fergus Hume, then a successful author in England, but trying to break out of the crime genre gave an interview to a journalist, Raymond Blathwayt. He was promoting his new utopian novel, *The Island of Fantasy*. Its aim was "to reconstruct the old Greek civilisation and adapt it to the present day." Hume's research included: "All the old classics, I super-added the Greek poets of [John] Addington Symonds; I recalled all I knew of the Tragedies; the great pathos and fatefulness of Greek life and history. I studied the whole matter almost as a science, and as a result, I feel I have got somehow into the heart of the old Grecian life."[21]

Hume also showed Blathwayt a verse from his forthcoming book of poetry, which he printed with the interview. The book of verse seems never to have been released, or else was self-published, anonymously in small circulation. It cannot at present be traced. The poem did appear in *The Island of Fantasy*.

> Venus Urania
> To rose-red sky, from rose-red sea,
> At rose-red dawn she came,
> A fiery rose of earth to be,
> And light the dawn with flame;
> Then earth and sky triumphantly
> Rang loud with man's acclaim.
> A rose art thou, O goddess fair,
> To bloom as men aspire,
> Red rose to those whose passions move,
> White rose to chaste desire;
> Yet red rose wanes with pale despair,
> And white rose burns as fire.

Venus Urania figures in classical mythology, spiritual love, as distinct from Venus Pandemos, earthly love or lust. The name indicates the origin myth: Venus Urania is of no woman born, arising from the severed genitals of the god Uranus. In Plato's *Symposium*, Uranian love is divine, but also associated with man-love, and definitely superior to that of women. Symonds uses it with precisely this sense. Wilde wrote in an 1898 letter: "To have altered my life would have been to have admitted that Uranian love is ignoble. I hold it to be noble—more noble than other forms." Significantly, the word Uranian describes a group of classically minded and pederastic poets, mostly clandestine, operating from the 1850s–1930s. Poet Chris Wallace-Crabbe, seeing the word Urania in the title of Hume's poem, immediately asked me if Hume was gay.[22]

To mention Symonds, a reconstruction of Ancient Greek civilization, and Urania in the same interview, suggests that Hume is aware of "the ways of evasion," and is using them to communicate. Arguably interviewer Blathwayt is knowingly part of this process. Since much of the interview is a plea from Hume for acceptance as a serious writer, is it also a plea for something else, concealed for the cognoscenti?

What does Hume mean by saying his intent is: "to show how a life such as that led by the ancient Greeks, and that nurtures the genius under every possible advantage, ought to be encouraged and not discouraged"? Hellenism might then be intellectually fashionable, but at the time it was also a codeword for homosexuality. "Encouraged and not discouraged" hints at much.

The Island of Fantasy is a utopia, in which an eccentric millionaire recreates ancient Greek civilisation on an Aegean island. It is also astoundingly homoerotic. Consider Count Caliphronas:

> I can tell you that his figure was as perfect as the Apollo Belvedere, and say that his face was as flawless in its virile beauty as the Antinous of the Vatican [a beautiful boy, lover of

the Emperor Hadrian], but this will give you no idea of his physical perfection. His body seemed to be instinct with the lawless fierceness of wind and wave; he moved with the stately grace of a nude savage unaccustomed to the restraint of clothing.[23]

Symonds had done much the same in his *Studies of the Greek Poets* (which contains in its later pages paeans to male athletic beauty), and also in his journalism:

> I asked a young friend of mine—a stag-like youth from Graubunden, tall and sinewy, like the young Achilles on a fresco at Pompeii—how all the gymnasts in this country came to be so brotherly. "Oh," he replied, "that is because we come into physical contact with one another. You only learn to live with men whose bodies you have touched and handled."

Joseph Bristow terms the above a "barely coded allusion."[24] Watching males in physical activity is the business of sport, unexceptionable. But the auctorial gaze in both these passages has an interest beyond the purely sporting, for beyond the frank appreciation is longing, even desire. Here classical allusions, with their authority, conceal the erotic as if with a figleaf. In comparing the bodies of young men to canonical art, the compliment becomes a matter of pure aesthetics, nothing blushworthy at all—unless the reader happens to know about the sex lives of Antinous or Achilles.

Later in *The Island of Fantasy* Caliphronas poses naked for sculptor Maurice, as Endymion (another classical figure who has become a gay icon). Maurice almost despairs "of being able to mould the soft clay into a perfect representation of this virile perfection." The tactile act reads like sublimation, or a transferred caress. Elsewhere a sequence of nude bathing features Caliphronas, about to dive: "As he stood there with his arms raised above his head, the first yellow ray of the sun flashed on his white body and enveloped in him in glory, as though he were indeed a stray Olympian." The scene culminates in Caliphronas galloping on a horse, and Maurice "thought of the frieze of the Parthenon, where nude youths ride fiery steeds in a long serene procession of marble figures."[25]

The Island of Fantasy being written in the 1890s and having a commercial publisher, precludes an erotic consummation. Instead the characters travel to the millionaire's island, a recreation of Ancient Greek culture that is distinctly sanitized. Maurice and the Count conventionally fall in love with the same, colorless maiden. It reads like an instance of the love triangle concealing the attraction between men, as identified by Eve Kosofsky Sedgwick. Pirates attack—and the island's volcano erupts and destroys this earthy paradise. The novel predated Freud, yet the symbolism of the volcano indicates extreme repression—finding vent in melodrama. But what it suggests about Hume is significant. He never wrote about men with such open desire again, a factor being the Wilde trial in 1895.

Fergus Hume was a lifelong bachelor. Women liked and helped him professionally, but the newspapers never linked him with them romantically. His female friends comprised older women, such as his sisters, and actresses, including the famous Ellen Terry. Otherwise his closest associations are with men, including the charismatic, doomed Beck. Little in his oeuvre suggests heterosexuality. His young lovers seem curiously passionless, his gaze upon attractive women brotherly rather than lustful—and nothing like the depiction of Caliphronas.

In England, Hume initially lived in London, with trips to the countryside and the continent. It is likely that he encountered Oscar Wilde, Hume on his arrival in 1888 being feted as a literary lion from the Antipodes. Indeed it would have been difficult for them *not* to meet: both men were creatures of literature and the theatre, who socialized among London's bohemians. The extensive scrutinies of Wilde's life do not mention Hume, but that does not prove they never coincided.

Hume worked hard to establish himself as a dramatist in the wake of the *Hansom Cab*'s success, wrote in other genres such as the futuristic and occult—but found that the public preferred him as a crime writer. In 1902 the *M. A. P.* feature depicted Philip Beck as a blackguard, in Hume's own testimony. Those who recalled the charming and charismatic actor fondly, such as "Valentine Day," were incensed. Furthermore, the article was termed "The Romance of Fergus Hume"—double meaning intended? As an apparent consequence of this unwelcome publicity Hume left London, for the village of Thundersley in Essex, where he spent the rest of his life. The local Rector, Thomas Noon Talfourd Major, was a friend, and had a cottage for rent. Curiously, Thundersley also housed another writer, "Nigel Tourneur," who wrote *Hidden Witchery* (1898) in the decadent/symbolist mode.[26] How much of a literary or other community existed in the vicinity is unclear.

In the 1911 UK census Hume is shown living quietly with a housekeeper, Ada Louise Peck, a widow of 69. After Major's death in 1915, Hume was obliged to vacate the cottage. He moved in with John Joseph Melville, a colourful character. Melville, though a metallurgical chemist, practiced alchemy: on at least four occasions he persuaded rich capitalists that he could extract gold from base metals. An article by Jeremy Parrott, with information from Marie Dalton, a distant Hume relation, described Melville as Hume's "companion."[27] This article informed Glenn Dolman's reading of Felix Rolleston. Yet Melville had a wife, Florence Amelia, and lived with her at Thundersley. When Melville died in 1929, he left his property to Florence and Hume moved out, to lodgings. He died three years later, in genteel poverty, but respected by his local community.

In "Venus Urania" Hume talks of chaste desire, a burning white rose. It suggests a safe option: celibate love, allowing companionship, manly affection, if not sex. Thus Hume could have lived unproblematically and chastely with the Melvilles. He and John Melville had similar interests, in the Classics and languages, alchemy, Theosophy. Hume, though he would novelise the occult, never expressed anything openly autobiographical. In contrast Rosa Praed wrote *Nyria*, in which she revealed she and Nancy Harward had been Imperial noblewoman and slave girl in ancient Rome. But then, as lesbians, the two had the legal freedom to be more openly expressive in print.

From Marie Dalton comes the information that John Melville believed that he was the reincarnation of philosopher Roger Bacon, a famous alchemist. Hume, in turn, was the reincarnation of a French nobleman, guillotined in the Revolution, something he "remembered" vividly. It represents a curious link to Robert Gant, who had something of a fetish for images of mock-beheading: "I wonder what it would feel like?" is the caption in one of Gant's albums, below a photograph of a young man gazing at the axe and block.[28] Fergus Hume could have answered that question. Though Freud's superego and id had yet to gain currency, a coded meaning seems likely here, to lose your head, and with it (societal) control of the body. With the head and heart separated, carnal desires could be expressed, in death, and beyond.

Of Hume's gay contemporaries, Wilde paid the price for public exposure. Gordon Lawrence served his time afterwards disappeared. Antoine Bollars would reappear under various aliases in the Australian prison system, for minor offences.[29] Others more discreet lived quietly and happily. Robert Gant would retire with a male partner decades his junior, quiet suburban bachelors. He created for himself an antipodean idyll, where homosociality shaded into passion undreamt of by the wider, censorious world. Praed and Harward lived together unto death. Similarly Agnes Murphy and her partner Aimee Moore worked in theatrical and musical circles, but also became militant suffragettes. Was Hume another who by living unobtrusively similarly escaped censure?

It is possible to speculate about Hume's private life. Blackmail seems near certain with Lawrence and Bollars. Beck committed suicide from the loss of Hume, an association that was as much professional as personal. Certainly Hume used forms of communication and expressions associated with same-sex love. *The Island of Fantasy* is either consciously or unconsciously homoerotic. "Venus Urania" suggests he took the option of chastity, prudent in the era of Labouchère, which allowed companionship with Melville without danger. Ultimately, though, Hume tantalizes but never reveals his personal mystery.

Note: An earlier version of this material was published in *Blockbuster! Fergus Hume and The Mystery of a Hansom Cab* (Text, 2015).

Notes

1. Agnes Murphy, *One Woman's Wisdom* (London: Routledge, 1895), 207–8.
2. New Zealand Lunatic Asylum 1879, [41].

3. John Addington Symonds, *The Memoirs of John Addington Symonds*, ed. Phyllis Grosskurth (London: Hutchinson, 1984), 94.
4. "The Masher," *Otago Witness*, 13 June 1889, 32.
5. Fergus Hume, "Satirical Opera," *Table Talk* (26 June 1885): 2.
6. Fergus Hume, *The Gentleman Who Vanished: A Psychological Phantasy* (London: White, 1890), 21; Joseph Bristow, *Effeminate England: Homoerotic Writing After 1885* (Buckingham: Open University Press, 1995), 5.
7. Fergus Hume, *Across the Footlights* (London: White, 1912), 6.
8. (Christchurch) *Star*, 14 March 1890, 2.
9. *Daily Telegraph*, 12 Oct. 1888, 3.
10. *South Australian Register*, 3 Oct. 1888, 6; *Clarence and Richmond Examiner*, 13 Oct 1788, 6. The best account of Gordon Lawrence is in Suzanne Davies, "Sexuality, Performance, and Spectatorship in Law: The Case of Gordon Lawrence, 1888," *Journal of the History of Sexuality* (Jan. 1997): 389–408.
11. *Sydney Morning Herald*, 17 July 1887, 12.
12. *Otago Witness*, 26 Oct. 1888, 28.
13. Kerry Greenwood, Email to Lucy Sussex.
14. *The Critic*, 18 Oct. 1902, 12.
15. *Otago Witness*, 20 April 1888, 28.
16. *Age*, 5 July 1888, 6.
17. *Ibid.*; VPRS 515/P0001/1401, p. 338, at Ancestry.com.
18. Fergus Hume, *The Mystery of a Hansom Cab* (1886; repr., Melbourne: Text, 1999), 110, 48; *Bulletin*, 15 Nov. 1902, 13.
19. Fergus Hume, *Madame Midas* (1888; repr., London: Hogarth, 1985), 217; Glen Dolman, Script, *The Mystery of a Hansom Cab* (telemovie); Glen Dolman, Email to Lucy Sussex.
20. Philip Bentley, Email to Lucy Sussex.
21. Reprinted in *Maitland Mercury*, 19 Jan. 1893, 6.
22. Wilde, Letter to Robert Ross, *Complete Letters of Oscar Wilde*, ed. Merlin Holland and Rupert Hart-Davis (New York: Holt, 2000), 1019.
23. Fergus Hume, *The Island of Fantasy* (London: Griffith Farran, 1892), 44–5.
24. Quoted in Bristow, *Effeminate England*, 130.
25. Hume, *Fantasy*, 85, 92.
26. Reprinted in *Evening Post* (New Zealand), 24 Sept. 1902, 9; Information from Douglas A. Anderson.
27. Jeremy Parrott, "Fergus Hume: Mystery Man," *Book and Magazine Collector* 232 (July 2003):46.
28. Chris Brickell, *Manly Affections: The Photographs of Robert Gant, 1885–1915* (Dunedin: Genre, 2012), 137.
29. VPRS 515/P0001/1401, p. 338, at Ancestry.com.

WORKS CITED

Brickell, Chris. *Manly Affections: The Photographs of Robert Gant, 1885–1915*. Dunedin: Genre, 2012.
Bristow, Joseph. *Effeminate England: Homoerotic Writing After 1885*. Buckingham: Open University Press, 1995.
Davies, Suzanne. "Sexuality, Performance, and Spectatorship in Law: The Case of Gordon Lawrence, 1888." *Journal of the History of Sexuality* (Jan. 1997): 389–408.
Dolman, Glen. Script for *The Mystery of a Hansom Cab*, 2011.
Hume, Fergus. *Across the Footlights*. London: White, 1912.

——. *The Gentleman Who Vanished: A Psychological Phantasy.* London: White, 1890.
——. *The Island of Fantasy.* London: Griffith Farran, 1892.
——. *Madame Midas.* 1888. London: Hogarth, 1985.
——. *The Mystery of a Hansom Cab.* 1886. Melbourne: Text, 1999.
——. "The Queer Story of Adam Lind." *Manchester Times* Supplement (5 Oct. 1889): 5.
——. "Satirical Opera." *Table Talk* (26 June 1885): 2.
——. *When I Lived in Bohemia.* Bristol: Arrowsmith, 1892.
Murphy, Agnes. *One Woman's Wisdom.* London: Routledge, 1895.
Parrott, Jeremy. "Fergus Hume: Mystery Man." *Book and Magazine Collector* 232 (July 2003): 39–50.
Reports on Lunatic Asylums in New Zealand. Appendix to the Journals of the House of Representatives. AtoJS Online.
Symonds, John Addington. *The Memoirs of John Addington Symonds.* Edited by Phyllis Grosskurth. London: Hutchinson, 1984.
Wilde, Oscar. *Complete Letters of Oscar Wilde.* Edited by Merlin Holland and Rupert Hart-Davis. New York: Holt, 2000.

A Redemptive Masquerade
Gender Identity in Samuel Hopkins Adams'
The Secret of Lonesome Cove

J. F. NORRIS

Long before Robert Bloch is credited with having turned the world of horror and crime fiction upside down with his creation in the novel *Psycho* (1959) of Norman Bates, now a cliché character amalgamation of arrested development and Oedipal nightmares, crime fiction writers were dabbling with a variety of plot tricks involving cross dressing, gender identity issues and dissociative personality disorders. As early as 1933 a troubled murderer with a schizoid identity crisis appears in a novel by the inventive detective fiction writer Harriette Ashbrook, while in 1946 Helen Eustis in *The Horizontal Man* shocked readers with a twist which anticipated Norman Bates by thirteen years. Gladys Mitchell, Dorothy L. Sayers, and Agatha Christie all played with cross-dressing as a gimmick in their mysteries: women disguise themselves as men and men turn out to be women in a number of their works. Richard Marsh, a Victorian sensation writer who wrote both crime and supernatural fiction, even tinkered with androgyny in *The Beetle* (1897) and *The Joss: A Reversion* (1901). Both novels feature as antagonists a shapeshifting creature that at its whim changes not only its form but its sex. Yet perhaps the most astonishing instance of these early experiments in using a gender identity crisis for a surprising effect is found in a little known detective novel published a dozen years after the turn of the twentieth century: *The Secret of Lonesome Cove* (1912) by Samuel Hopkins Adams.

Primarily known for his crusading investigative journalism, through which he exposed everything from patent medicine frauds to scandals in the Harding administration, Samuel Hopkins Adams also dabbled in genre fiction after leaving his job as a reporter with the *New York Sun*. Two of his detective novels incorporate elements of weird fiction: *The Mystery* (1907), co-written with adventure novelist Stewart Edward White, and *The Flying Death* (1901), an impossible crime mystery with a denouement as startling and rule breaking as John Dickson Carr's *The Burning Court*. His *Average Jones* (1911) made Ellery Queen's *Queen's Quorum*, the quintessential honor roll of notable detective fiction books that exemplify the best work done in the short story form. In his third and final detective novel, *The Secret of Lonesome Cove*, Adams unfolds the startling tale of a dead woman who carried a disturbing secret to her grave and how her true identity was kept hidden by town officials and relatives in order to prevent scandal.

Adam's detective protagonist, Professor Chester Kent, is typical of his era—unmarried, preternaturally intelligent with a horde of arcane knowledge, eccentric in manner and dress, but above all insightful and compassionate in his dealings with all those he encounters. Kent awes the small New England seaside village that is the setting for his novel with his knowledge of entomology, climatology, ornithology, and postmortem biology; and he even gives a demonstration of jiu-jitsu. He is the epitome of what Julian Hawthorne and later Carolyn Wells liked to call the Transcendent Detective, with an array of astute observations and superhuman talents.

Within minutes of observing the unknown woman's corpse—lashed to a wooden grating, her left wrist encased in one half of an ancient manacle while the other half hangs free with a smashed lock—Kent knows she has not drowned, as most of the crowd has assumed. Though damp, her expensive silk dress is not soaked through with water; her horrible head wound is still bloody, not washed away as would happen if she were submerged in the ocean; and, most telling of all, a dry cocoon of a grain moth with a living insect inside proves that the grating has not been in the water for several days. Therefore, Professor Kent deduces, either the dead woman fell or was struck with a blunt weapon and then tied to the grating. Why she was tied and manacled are questions too puzzling for Kent to immediately comment upon, but his explanation of those enigmas will come in time.

The solution of the mystery of the woman's identity is further delayed as the medical examiner and sheriff are about to have the townspeople file in for a viewing of the corpse, in order to see whether anyone recognizes her. Suddenly the doctor notices something horrifying, shuts the coffin and abruptly removes the body from viewing. Hours later, after having given the excuse that the body needed to be made more presentable in order to avoid the possibility of upsetting any viewers, the local officials finally commence the identity parade. Elder Dennett, who had briefly seen the body on the shoreline, remarks that it now has a cut on the right cheek, though earlier in the day there had been no cut. Professor Kent marches forward, puts on his magnifying monocle for closer scrutiny of the wound and also takes time to examine the woman's right wrist. He begins to formulate his solution then and there. He makes the first of his many cryptic remarks in the novel, hinting that while the woman certainly died violently, he doubts that she was murdered.

Investigation of the death is complicated by eyewitness accounts of the woman having been seen in the company of a man. Others claim they heard the scream of a man coming from Hawkill Cliffs, just above where the body was discovered. Gansett Jim, a semiliterate Amagansett Indian, accuses young Francis Sedgwick, a portrait painter, of being the woman's killer, declaring that he saw Sedgwick with the woman on a few occasions, including the very day she died. As the last man seen with her, Sedgwick becomes the prime suspect in her death; and the young artist joins forces with Professor Kent to clear his name.

Having never been formally identified, the woman is quickly buried as a Jane Doe. Professor Kent learns that the burial was rushed at the insistence of millionaire businessman Alexander Blair, who seems to have personal reason for quieting talk about her violent death. Blair has a son named Wilfrid, a former playboy whose hedonistic lifestyle and spendthrift ways have squandered much of the Blair fortune, though all that has changed now that Blair has succumbed to tuberculosis and been shut up in a summer house, where he is cared for in his final days. Rumor has it that Wilfrid has no disease at all and that Blair has removed his profligate son to a place where he can be watched more closely and do no harm to the family name and holdings. Professor Kent finds this all highly intriguing, especially when Wilfrid Blair's wife, who left him after a few months of marriage, enters the story, telling a woeful tale of stolen jewels. Among them is an antique topaz necklace that Francis Sedgwick saw the mystery woman wearing the day she died. Is this mystery woman yet another of Wilfrid's many lovers? And is it merely coincidence that Wilfrid dies of his illness mere days after the mystery woman expired?

Intricately plotted and filled with a rich variety of unusual characters, from the gossipy Elder Dennett to the fraudulent spiritualist Preston Jax, *The Secret of Lonesome Cove* is an admirable model of early twentieth century detective fiction. But the novel is not merely good entertainment. Interspersed in the tale are brief mentions of the sort of progressive causes Adams espoused in his newspaper and magazine journalism. Alexander Blair's wealth is touched by scandal and corruption: "Haven't you heard of him and the Fabric Trust?" Dennet asks of Kent. When Professor Kent introduces himself to Preston Jax, the conman astrologer gasps and exclaims, "The Kent that broke up the Coordinated Spiritism Circle?" Evidently Samuel Hopkins Adams' days as a muckraking journalist never left him.

Beneath the intricate plot and Professor Kent's brilliant deductions is found a subversive tone rare in works of this era. When the secret in the book's title is revealed, the reader finds an early form of gender dysphoria mixed with a wispy occult influence. The Jane Doe who lies buried in a potter's field and the late playboy Wilfrid Blair are, in fact, one and the same person.

How came Wilfrid Blair to undergo such a personality transformation, a modern reader might ask? The story is couched in a sort of mysticism rounded out with pat explanations of a psychologically troubled soul. By making the young man a student of the occult, Adams seems to have an "excuse" for this transformation. Wilfrid came to believe that he was the reincarnation of his great grandmother, Camilla Grosvenor, whom he greatly resembles. Slowly but surely her personality overtook him until he became Camilla Grosvenor reborn. His mission in this newfound female identity was to prove his devotion to a true love, to fulfill for that love "a reward greater than [one] can dream."

Calling himself "Astraea," Wilfrid began a correspondence with the con artist Preston Jax. Astraea's letters to Jax were inspired by Jax's own words, Astraea having seen in Jax no less than Hermann von Miltz, her reincarnated lover of forty years ago. In her letters Astraea speaks of Fate and how all is ordained by the stars, as Jax himself had told her. Her language is filled with romantic metaphors of ships sailing in the night, "stars, swinging in mighty circles, rushing on to a joint climax." She wishes to "open the doors to the past and sway the world as we sought to do in bygone days." Guided by the stars and her heart, Astraea planned to make right Camilla's act of desperation that went wrong so many decades ago.

Unbeknownst to Jax, who failed to see through these thickets of purple prose, Astraea hatched a plot to reunite lovers in the same fashion as the suicide pact made by Camilla and Hermann after they were denied marriage by Camilla's xenophobic father. With Hermann's body never having been recovered all those many years ago, Astraea glimpsed an opportunity to join their souls forever in eternal love. It is a bittersweet echo of the past. Bigotry led to tragedy in the previous century, just as prejudice of a different sort in the modern day has led to the cover-up of what Wilfrid did and who he became.

Marjorie, Wilfrid's ex-wife, summarizes the real theme of the novel: "He left me nothing to love, but to find disgrace and shame even to the end of his life!" This bleak sentiment she utters when she realizes that Wilfrid stole the necklace and other jewels and recognizes his handwriting in a letter Astraea wrote to Preston Jax. Shame is the ugly shadow that casts a dark light on everyone connected to Wilfrid and is the motivating factor in the unthinkable acts that follow the discovery of Astraea's corpse.

To Alexander Blair family honor is all. He rushes to get Astraea buried and later stages a phony funeral for his son. Although he claims he is also protecting Marjorie from public humiliation, it is clear that Blair's action in kidnapping and imprisoning Wilfrid was more to spare himself the humiliation of "the scandal of [Wilfrid's] life" than to save the young man or protect his former daughter-in-law. He also believes Francis Sedgwick killed Wilfrid and his last ditch efforts to literally bury the past are also carried out to avoid the potential disgrace of a murder trial and testimony on the witness stand.

When he hears the truth revealed from Professor Kent, Wilfrid's father at last shows some remorse. He laments his failure in protecting his son ("We thought it was melancholia."), but rationalizes it as well. As Astraea his son had become secretive and "very silent," making it all the more difficult to "cure" his affliction. Holed up in her room, Astraea spent most of her silent hours furtively writing letters to Preston Jax and managing to mail them without anyone's knowledge. There was no way that Blair, nor anyone else, could have suspected what she was plotting.

Marjorie is appalled when she discovers that the coffin in the Blair private graveyard which she believed contained the body of Wilfrid holds nothing but a large sandbag. In a moment of unexpected poignancy she utters a bold statement exposing Alexander Blair's selfishness: "Whatever Wilfrid may have been, he was my husband. I bear his name. And to leave him in a nameless grave is to dishonor not him alone, but myself."

Despite the presence of a cross-dressing character in *The Secret of Lonesome Cove*, the only traces of gay sensibility in the story come in the chapter when Preston Jax is first introduced. In keeping with genre fiction of this era, it is Jax who one would expect to be cast as the effeminate male. Sax Rohmer's closetful of occult mystics and evil warlocks have always been noted for looking womanly, having effeminate features and generally making the übermacho protagonist sick to his stomach each time he views the villain. From Antony Ferrar in *Brood of the Witch Queen* (1918) to the title character in *Fire-Tongue* (1921), men who turn to the dark side and dabble in witchcraft and the occult in order to become more powerful are portrayed as deviant and are made to appear even less male by feminizing them. Jax is also cast in this role, but Adams chooses to make him boyish and a bit dangerous: "They beheld a man of undistinguished size and form, eked out by a splendid pomposity of manner.... It was a remarkable face, small, calm, and compacted of muscles.... There lurked in the countenance a suggestion of ingenuousness. The man looked like a bland and formidable baby. He looked even more like a puma."

Ironically it is Jax who makes the only specific gay reference in the entire book, even if it is only expressed in his thoughts to the reader. Upon their first meeting he is suspicious of Chester Kent, thinking he might be an undercover policeman on another spiritualist sting operation, but when he takes in Kent's "swellness" in attire and manner he becomes envious. He wonders whether he can "persuade the visitor to disclose his tailor to the stars," since Jax himself is something of a clothes horse. Yet when he notices the monocle in Kent's left eye he comes to this conclusion: "The visitor was obviously 'light.'"

When discussing Wilfrid's alter ago as Astraea, the characters make no mention of sexual inversion. The entire personality shift is described as the manifestation of a "diseased mind" and yet the entire story is predicated on the ruse that we believe the dead body found on the shore is a woman, just as Wilfrid believed he was a woman. The skill with which Adams delineates the two halves of one person into two wholly believable separate characters is something at which to marvel. That the unknown woman is suspected of having been Wilfrid's mistress, whom he has paid off with the Grosvenor jewels, is only one of the clever bits of misdirection that cements the errant notion in the reader's mind.

While one may argue that Adams in *The Secret of Lonesome Cover* employed cross-dressing merely as a gimmick in order to surprise the reader, the skill with which Adams presents Astraea as a fully developed woman is remarkable. Although all the clues are present—the telltale cut on the cheek indicating the corpse's face was shaved, the man's scream from Hawkill Cliffs, the portrait of Camilla Grosvenor bearing a great likeness to Wilfrid, the destruction of all images of Camilla and Astraea—the solution still comes as an eyebrow raising shock. An astute reader of detective fiction may catch on early in the novel, yet so intricate is the story in its complications and twists, so compelling is Chester Kent as the omniscient detective, so puzzling the different mysteries layered onto the primary mystery of Astraea's secret identity, that he might just as easily doubt his formulation of yet another Norman Bates gimmick. With a finale so satisfying and unexpectedly moving, the reader may not even realize that he has completed a murder mystery in which there was no murder!

Whether or not he was aware of having done so, Samuel Hopkins Adams in *The Secret of Lonesome Cover* fashioned one of detective fiction's first transgendered characters. Whether the manifestation is called a fixation, an obsession or "a strange and complete assumption of personality," it cannot be denied that Wilfrid Blair truly believed himself a woman. His is a transformation not only of gender but of the soul; he undergoes a kind of redemptive masquerade.[1]

Astraea looks ever heavenward, focusing on her spiritual destiny. She seems to be making amends for Wilfrid's earthbound dissolute playboy life. Astraea literally throws away jewelry and gives away one hundred dollar bills, contrasting with Wilfrid's selfish spendthrift habits. She sees love in its purest, most spiritual form, never as lust or desire. Some of her last words are only whispers of awe: "The stars! The stars! See ours, how they light our pathway across the sea!" Her final moments of earthly life are tinged with a divine madness, a savage reverence for infinity, as all the while she remains oblivious of what the reader knows will be her inescapable Fate. The concluding scenes of her misguided attempt to bring about happiness for two lost souls at the edge of Hawkill Cliffs are all the more heart wrenching when we watch her once again end her life alone.

NOTE

1. At the time of the publication of *The Secret of Lonesome Cove*, notes to historian George Chauncey, people who addressed the subject often spoke of homosexual behavior as resulting from "sexual inversion," i.e., people having inverted their gender (hence the term "inverts"). Males who sexually desired other males "were regarded as virtual women, or, more precisely, as members of a 'third sex' that combined elements of the male and female." Gay rights pioneer Karl Heinrich Ulrichs in the 1860s had characterized male sexual inversion as representing the existence of a "woman's spirit in a man's body." George Chauncey, *Gay New York: Gender, Culture and the Making of the Gay Male World, 1890–1940* (New York: Basic Books, 1994), 48–49. In the 1920s Samuel Hopkins Adams under the pseudonym Warner Fabian published two racy bestselling novels, *Flaming Youth* (1923) and *Unforbidden Fruit* (1928), which frankly dealt with the sexual mores of the flapper. The latter title, written to capitalize on the notoriety generated by the lesbian-themed play *The Captive* (1926), included several references to female sexual inversion. See Laura Horak, *Girls Will Be Boys: Cross-Dressed Women, Lesbians, and American Cinema, 1908–1934* (New Brunswick: Rutgers University Press, 2016), 151, 161–62. Intriguingly, Adams in his cryptic dedication to *The Secret of Lonesome Cove* indicated that he had to some extent based the novel on a real life tragedy:

TO ONE UNKNOWN
The only living being who possesses the secret of the strangely clad and manacled body found beneath the cliffs of Cornwall on April 19, 1909, this story, changed in the setting as he will understand, is blindly inscribed.

WORKS CITED

Adams, Samuel Hopkins. *The Secret of Lonesome Cove*. New York: Bobbs-Merrill, 1912.
Chauncey, George. *Gay New York: Gender, Culture and the Making of the Gay Male World, 1890–1940*. New York: Basic Books, 1994.
Horak, Laura. *Girls Will Be Boys: Cross-Dressed Women, Lesbians, and American Cinema, 1908–1934*. New Brunswick: Rutgers University Press, 2016.

Dropping Hairpins in Golden Age Detective Fiction
Man-Haters, Green Carnations and Gunsels

Noah Stewart

Introduction

About a hundred years ago, at the outset of the Golden Age of detective fiction (roughly 1920–1940, here abbreviated GAD), homosexual activity was punished as a crime in the Western world. Bars and nightclubs catering to homosexuals were rarely advertised, and men and women in large cities created a kind of underground network where information about homosexuality and homosexuals was encoded and reserved to people whom others could be sure were clearly not associated with law enforcement. Lives, families, and careers frequently depended on the ability of homosexuals to pass as heterosexual in social situations.

All this renders the task of the social historian more difficult when it comes to discussing the twentieth-century precursors of today's LGBTQ population. Nothing was obvious; there were no easy ways to identify any individual's non-heterosexual preferences unless that individual was more than usually candid. Heterosexual society in the 1920s and 30s reduced homosexual characters to a limited set of readily discernible stereotypes. Homosexual males were "known" to be effeminate, lisping, and prissy; homosexual females were heavy-set, masculine-looking, and physically aggressive. If someone fit that limited set of stereotypes, they were labeled as being homosexual. Most homosexual people "passed" by concealing their true lives and relationships behind sham marriages and extreme secrecy.

And so the process of discerning homosexual characters in Golden Age detective fiction is weirdly similar to the process of discerning homosexuals themselves at that time. You will never be told that someone is a homosexual in so many words, although you may hear a character spoken of pejoratively as a "Miss Nancy" or a "man-hater" by another. Instead, the way to understand what you are being told about a character is to make small but telling observations about their dress, habits, speech patterns and lifestyle in general.

Among male homosexuals of the time, the process of providing tiny clues to an acquaintance that may alert that person to a shared sexual preference was known as "dropping hairpins." When Monday morning water cooler chatter turned to how one man had spent the weekend with his fiancée or wife, another might mention casually that he had been to a specific nightclub—known only to the cognoscenti as a hangout for "queers." If the listener was aware of the meaning of the "dropped hairpin," a small bond of understanding was forged; if not, no harm was done to the speaker's heterosexual reputation.

So as we sift through GAD looking for homosexual characters, be warned in advance: nothing is obvious. The clues are usually tiny and susceptible to multiple meanings, because that is the nature of dropping hairpins. Nothing is said in certain terms. Nevertheless if one goes looking there are small threads that can be teased out of the larger tapestry, which divide easily into male and female references. Both have a few major stereotypes into which most of the examples fall and these are outlined below in the body of this essay. Readers of GAD fiction should keep these hairpins mentally at hand as they encounter fictional characters that authors may (or may not) have meant us to see as homosexuals.

Male Homosexuals in GAD

"Prissies" and "Sissies"

It is not likely that mystery readers in the 1920s and 1930s generally were familiar with the habits and practices of homosexuals in everyday life. Mystery writers may have felt that readers were capable of identifying the effeminate male, mostly because "prissies" and "sissies" remained stock characters in films of the Twenties and Thirties. The professions of these roles were widely varied but were frequently found in hairdressing, clothing design, tailoring, art, theatre and dance; and they were often depicted by actors like Franklin Pangborn and Edward Everett Horton.

Identifying the way in which the stereotype is likely to manifest itself in Golden Age detective stories, though, is a far cry from finding frequent occurrences of it. One of the most obvious male homosexual characters in literature of the period—although this author's first novel was published in 1941, just barely outside the classic time boundaries of the Golden Age—is Mr. Cecil, a character in two mystery novels by Christianna Brand. In his first appearance in 1941's *Death in High Heels*, where he is a dress designer at a shop where someone is murdered, he is described as follows:

> Cecil ... was a slim, fair man, with huge, brown, long-lashed eyes, a well-modelled nose and over-feminine mouth; at first sight one took him for a youth, but soft living had given him, too early, pouches beneath the eyes and a suspicion of a paunch. His trousers were draped over girlish hips and his suit and shirt were a miracle of lavender grey; over his forehead a lock of yellow hair was trained to fall, and be pushed back with a graceful hand.

Mr. Cecil is apparently not intended to be seriously considered as a suspect when compared to three or four career women in the shop who have both motive and strength of will; he has no apparent motive and actively weeps when asked to assume an ordinary responsibility. And his profession, male dress designer, is one to which the public apparently felt confident ascribing homosexuality, at least so far as Christianna Brand was concerned.

Mr. Cecil is more clearly identified as homosexual than many other GAD characters, mostly because much later, in 1955's *Tour de Force*, he is said to be actually "in hot pursuit of [the tour guide] Fernando...." (In *Death in High Heels*, he also has a male friend referred to as "the boyfriend" by his female coworkers.) Mr. Cecil can stand for a number of other such characters, young or young-ish, effeminate, employed in design, the theatre, the arts, etc. However there is a large category of characters in GAD who are not easily identifiable as homosexual; their professions, if any, are not so clear-cut as dance instructors or hairdressers, and their mannerisms are not so easily identified as effeminate. There are many characters in GAD mysteries like Anthony Berkeley's Ambrose Chitterwick, solver of murder mysteries in two 1929 detective novels, *The Poisoned Chocolates Case* and *The Piccadilly Murder*. He is a milquetoast who resides with and is tyrannized by an ancient aunt. Such men are older, small-framed, prissy, precise and "confirmed bachelors." But are they meant to be read as homosexuals? Hard to say.

My best example of the "sissy," Philo Vance, is an important one, for he constitutes the single case known to me where it is arguably suggested that the detective and protagonist of a GAD novel is himself a homosexual male. Philo Vance, a well-read dilettante with a passion for art and a talent for amateur detection, was a huge presence in the GAD tapestry; S. S. Van Dine's *The Benson Murder Case* (1926), the first Vance detective novel, and several which followed it were bestsellers in the United States. In Chapter Two of *Benson*, District Attorney Markham visits Vance's home to invite him to consult on the murder, but Vance is not yet dressed for the street. After Markham suggests that Vance should "get a move on, you orchid," the following exchange takes place:

> [Vance] rang for [his valet] and ordered his clothes brought to him. "I'm attending a levee which Mr. Markham is holding over a corpse and I want something rather spiffy. Is it warm enough for a silk suit? ... And a lavender tie, by all means."

> "I trust you won't also wear your green carnation," grumbled Markham.
> "Tut! Tut!" Vance chided him. "You've been reading Mr. Hichens. Such heresy in a district attorney! Anyway, you know full well I never wear boutonnieres. The decoration has fallen into disrepute. The only remaining devotees of the practice are roués and saxophone players.... But tell me about the departed Benson."

To the reader of 2016, this passage is possibly incomprehensible; Philo Vance sounds strange and affected, and is prepared to wear a lavender tie in public. To the well-informed reader of 1926, though, something was being said very clearly. Lavender was not then a generally understood symbol of homosexuality, but the reference to "Mr. Hichens" and the wearing of a green carnation refers to an 1894 novel by Robert Hichens called *The Green Carnation*—where the lead characters are closely based on Oscar Wilde and Lord Alfred Douglas. The book was a scandalous success, and the wearing of a green carnation in one's buttonhole became a hint that the wearer was "unnatural."

Was Van Dine saying that Philo Vance was a homosexual? Without any certain knowledge of what Van Dine had in mind, we cannot say for sure. My view is that the staid Markham was merely teasing his well-dressed friend about his devotion to sartorial perfection. Note that Vance turns down the suggestion that he should wear such a boutonniere, though he claims this is consideration of fashion; he seems to be saying that boutonnieres are associated with disreputable and socially unacceptable people, rather than reinforcing his heterosexuality to his friend by refusing to wear one.

But that one brief and enigmatic exchange seems to stand for a number of references in Golden Age detective fiction. It identifies homosexuality as being associated with extravagance in clothing, using a reference from literature; Vance is highly affected in speech and manner, and a devotee of "advanced" artistic movements. Generally speaking, when you come across a character effeminate in manner, mincing in step, affected in speech and superbly well dressed and color coordinated, this is when you find the "sissy"—a possibly homosexual character.

The Gunsel

A second common stereotype that I have noted in a broad look at the breadth of GAD detective novels is that of the "evil minion" or "gunsel." This is a character whose homosexuality is unspoken, but for whom it forms just one aspect of a constellation of anti-social traits that are largely criminal: drug use/drug dealing, blackmail, pernicious gossip, low-level criminal activity. Often—not always, but often—these characters are associated with and serve a more powerful evil character in a joint enterprise (because, it seems, their lack of masculinity vitiates their ability to run a criminal enterprise on their own).

I have here called this stereotype the "gunsel" because of a well-known story about how this word came to have its present meaning, that of a henchman carrying a gun. The word actually comes from a Yiddish term for "gosling," a young goose, which was once American English underworld slang for a "young male kept as a sexual companion, especially by an older criminal." During the 1929–30 serialization of Dashiell Hammett's hard-boiled detective novel *The Maltese Falcon* in the pulp magazine *Black Mask*, Hammett—at war with Captain Joseph Shaw, the editor of *Black Mask*, about the amount of profanity in story— managed to sneak in the word gunsel because Shaw apparently believed it was criminal slang for a gunman. The word only survived Captain Shaw's desire to improve the moral tone of his magazine because he did not know that it bore any relation to homosexuality.

I have two contrasting examples to offer that depict this stereotype in action. The first is a type that repeats throughout the oeuvre of GAD Crime Queen Ngaio Marsh. In her *Death in Ecstasy* (1936), evil cult leader Father Garnette has two repellent acolytes, Claude and Lionel, who "lisp" and "mince":

> "And now, these two"—[Alleyn] looked a little doubtfully at Claude and Lionel—"these two young men."
> Claude and Lionel answered together in a rapturous gush.
> "What?" asked Alleyn.
> "Do be quiet, Lionel," said Claude. "We share a flat in Ebury Street: 'Ebury Mews.' Well, it isn't actually a flat, is it, Lionel? Oh dear, I always forget the number—it's too stupid of me."
> "You are hopeless, Claude," said Lionel. "It's 17, Ebury Mews, Ebury Street, Inspector Alleyn, only we aren't very often there, because I'm in the show at the Palladium and Claude is at Madame Karen's in Sloane Street and—"
> "I do not yet know your names."
> "Lionel, you are perfectly maddening," said Claude. "I'm Claude Wheatley, Inspector Alleyn, and this is Lionel Smith."
> Alleyn wrote these names down with the address, and added in brackets: "Gemini, possibly heavenly."

Claude has opportunity but no motive for the novel's murder, and is said twice by Alleyn not to have the "guts" to do murder. Alleyn also writes in his notes, "Horrible youth.... Perhaps the Greeks had a word for him." Claude is employed by the cult leader to transport things like drugs and pornographic books to and from his followers.

My second example of the "homosexual evil minion" is a creation of Anthony Boucher in *Nine Times Nine* (1940); Robin Cooper is an accessory of the evil cult leader Ahasver and is constantly referred to throughout the book as a "cherub" because of his youth (approximately 21) and his beaming smile. He does not really become clear as a character until he is being investigated by the detectives for a possible role in some deception that surrounds the murder, and then his full stereotype comes into play. Here is a brief snippet that shows his conversational style: "Now let me see, did I leave the Temple Monday? Oh, yes, of course, I had to go see the printer. He'd sent us a frightfully messy proof of the weekly Letter of Light, and I simply had to explain all the corrections myself."

Boucher had a slightly more enlightened attitude for 1940. After making fun of his speech patterns ("And don't stamp your foot at me, you gweat big dweadful man!" says the police lieutenant to Robin mockingly), the detective says something more insightful:

> "...I am fascinated by our sweet little Robin."
> "Why, Lieutenant!" Matt imitated the cherub's birdlike cadences.
> "It's a good act. It's a honey of an act. But it is an act, and he slipped at the end. He's no ecstatic hanger-on of the Ancients. He knows what he's about; and unless my guess is way off, he's probably about as influential as any member of the Temple."
> "You think so? Him?"
> "The stupid tendency of the normal male is to discount everything said or done by one who seems effeminate. You think, 'Nuts, he's a swish—the hell with him.' It's about as clever a front as you can pick. Smart lad, our Robin."

Admittedly this is still offensive—"the normal male"—but Boucher sees more under the surface than most.

Female Homosexuals in GAD

The stereotypical lesbian is less obvious in GAD stories, possibly because there were fewer stereotypical manifestations that authors would feel would be known to the reading public. The best-known film stereotype of the period was Marlene Dietrich as a barroom entertainer who wears a tuxedo and kisses a girl in the 1930 film *Morocco*. It is reasonable to assume that the reader of 1930 would have understood a female character in a country-house mystery who came down to dinner in a tuxedo to be a lesbian but, alas for posterity, no writer, I presume, ever tried that specific gambit.

I have identified three major "types" of lesbian character in Golden Age detective fiction: "man-haters," "vampires," and the "happy couple."

The Man-Hater

The characteristics of the "man-hater" stereotype are difficult to unravel from their association with early feminism. The Twenties in England and to a lesser extent in the United States were a time of political upheaval with respect to the rights of women, and some women were said to avoid the company of men as a kind of political statement. It is hard to say at this great remove whether the reader of this time would understand the avoidance of men as a kind of encoded lesbianism, or merely a political statement indicating that the possessor of such attitudes was outside the social and/or political norm.

In Dorothy L. Sayers' *Strong Poison* (1930), we meet a supporter of accused murderess Harriet Vane—one Eiluned Price, "a short, stout girl with a pugnacious nose and a twinkle." Chapter Eight tells us "she scorns anything in trousers, but she's a good friend at a pinch," and she's later described as being "anti-man." Lord Peter Wimsey interviews her in connection with his murder investigation:

> Wimsey was introduced, and Eiluned Price immediately inquired, rather truculently: "Can he drink coffee, Marjorie? Or does he require masculine refreshment? ... [B]ecause some of your male belongings need stimulating, and we haven't got the wherewithal, and the pub's just closing." She stumped over to a cupboard, and Sylvia said, "Don't mind Eiluned; she likes to treat 'em rough."

Later on in the same chapter, Eiluned says:

> "No, thanks"—as Wimsey advanced to carry the kettle—"I'm quite capable of carrying six pints of water."
> "Crushed again!" said Wimsey.
> "Eiluned disapproves of conventional courtesies between the sexes," said Marjorie.

I would be sympathetic to the view of a student of social history, or even just a fan of Sayers' writing, who suggested that to read Eiluned Price as a lesbian would be going beyond the text. Frankly, it is a toss-up, and there is evidence on both sides. The issues surrounding Sayers herself and her own political and sexual views are better left to her biographers, but there are aspects of the writer's life that could legitimately bear upon this question. Sayers had a university degree and a full-time job in an advertising agency at a time when those things were considered unusual and rather "mannish"; and she must have dealt with people who felt her to be unfeminine merely because of these factors in her own life.

The Vampire

Much more clearly a lesbian in Sayers' work, however, is the character of Mary Whittaker in 1927's *Unnatural Death*, who exemplifies my second stereotype: the "vampire," or "predatory Lesbian." Mary Whittaker is to my knowledge the most clearly delineated homosexual character in Golden Age detective fiction, despite the word "lesbian" never being used, and she's depicted as enticing a young girl into a life of homosexuality.

Spoiler Alert: It is impossible to talk about this character sensibly without revealing the identity of the murderer in this book and, should you not have read this particular volume, I encourage you to do so before undertaking the remainder of this section; skip to "The Happy Couple," below.

Mary Whittaker is the principal heir of a murder victim in *Unnatural Death* and Lord Peter Wimsey, suspecting her immediately, sends his associate, the elderly Miss Climpson, to investigate her in her home surroundings. From Chapter Five:

> The first impression which Miss Climpson got of Mary Whittaker was that she was totally out of place among the teatables of St. Onesimus. With her handsome, strongly-marked features and quiet air of authority ... she had a pleasant and self-possessed manner, and was beautifully tailored—not mannishly, and yet with a severe fineness of outline that negatived the appeal of a beautiful figure....

Mary Whittaker, in fact, is a trained nurse who has been taking care of her elderly aunt Miss Agatha Dawson, whose death is the mystery underlying this novel. In Chapter Eight, Miss Climpson in a letter to Lord Peter retails the local gossip upon two major topics. One is that Miss Whittaker "means to set up farming" with a local girl, Miss Findlater, whom Miss Climpson describes as a "very gushing and really *silly* young woman."

> However, Miss Findlater has evidently quite a "pash" (as we used to call it at school) for Miss Whittaker, and I am afraid none of us are above being *flattered* by such outspoken admiration. I must say, I think it rather unhealthy—you may remember Miss Clemence Dane's *very clever book* on the subject?—I have seen so much of that kind of thing in my rather WOMAN-RIDDEN existence! It has such a bad effect, as a rule, upon the *weaker character* of the two....

The "very clever book" by Clemence Dane, who like Sayers became a founding member of the Detection Club three years after the publication of *Unnatural Death*, is *Regiment of Women*, a 1915 novel about girls' school lesbianism. Anyone familiar with Dane's much-discussed novel would have understood what Sayers, through the verbosity of Miss Climpson, was intimating.[1]

Miss Climpson then goes on to note that the elderly Miss Agatha Dawson had lived in Warwickshire with her cousin, Miss Clara Whittaker.

> This Miss Clara was evidently rather a "character," as my dear father used to call it. In her day she was considered very "advanced" and *not quite nice* (!) because she refused several good offers, cut her hair SHORT (!!) and set up in business for herself as a HORSE-BREEDER!!! Of course, *nowadays*, nobody would think anything of it, but *then* the old lady—or *young* lady as she was when she embarked on this *revolutionary* proceeding—was quite a PIONEER.... Agatha did not care about marriage any more than Clara, and the two ladies lived together in a big house, with immense stables.... Agatha Dawson never had anything to do with the *horsey* part of the business. She was the "domestic" partner, and looked after the house and the servants.

In other words, once you plough through Miss Climpson's eccentric italicization and capitalization, Clara (butch) and Agatha (femme) are a lesbian couple of long standing; I cannot think Sayers could have expressed it any more clearly in the 1920s. After Miss Clara died, Mary Whittaker moved in to take care of Miss Agatha in her declining years. Perhaps we are meant to think that this lesbian household led to the formation of Mary Whittaker's particular sexual preferences, or merely allowed her natural desires to flourish; hard to say.

Miss Climpson disapproves, in Chapter Sixteen, of the relationship between the young Miss Findlater and what we are coming to learn is not only a predatory lesbian but also a cold-blooded murderer, Mary Whittaker, who killed Miss Agatha to inherit her money. Miss Climpson "felt sure that Vera Findlater was being 'preyed upon,' as she expressed it to herself, by the handsome Mary Whittaker." They intend to set up as joint proprietors of a chicken farm, now that Miss Whittaker has come into her inheritance. "It is natural for a schoolgirl to be *schwärmerisch*—in a young woman of twenty-two it is thoroughly undesirable." Miss Climpson, perhaps rather heteronormatively (Sayers says specifically that Miss Climpson is heterosexual), sees Miss Findlater as being somehow led astray by Miss Whittaker and pictures young Vera as more suitable for marriage to a "rabbit" (a meek male). "At any rate," thinks Miss Climpson, "I am certain that Mary Whittaker is doing Vera Findlater no good." When Miss Findlater comes to tea, in the same chapter, they have a long conversation in which Miss Climpson finally attempts to steer Vera Findlater back to heterosexuality but fails.

So Miss Findlater is about to embark on quasi-matrimony with Mary Whittaker, the two running a chicken farm together. But first Mary Whittaker must escape the attentions of the detectives who are closing in on her. As an escape route in case of danger, she has rigged up a false personality of one Mrs. Forrest. "The idea was, I suppose, to build up a double identity, so that, if Mary Whittaker was ever suspected of anything, she could quietly disappear and become the frail but otherwise innocent Mrs. Forrest." A tiny clue has led to the Mrs. Forrest persona becoming involved in the periphery of the case, and Mrs. Forrest—not yet known to the reader as being Mary Whittaker in disguise—is attempting to seduce Lord Peter. Lord Peter suspects that what is going on is soon to become blackmail, with some male confederate bursting in, and so is on high alert in Chapter Fifteen: "Swathed to the eyebrows in gold tissue, with only two flat crescents of yellow hair plastered over her cheekbones, she looked, in an exotic smoking-suit of embroidered tissue, like a young prince out of the Arabian Nights."

In other words, she is made up like a male. Something is indeed "off" for Lord Peter:

> Suddenly he became aware that she was trying—clumsily, stupidly, as though in spite of herself—to get him to make love to her.... Mrs. Forrest was handsome enough, but she had not a particle of attraction for him. For all her make-up and her somewhat outspoken costume, she struck him as spinsterish—even epicene.... Wimsey had felt her as something essentially sexless, even then. And he felt it even more strongly now. Never had he met a woman in whom "the great It," eloquently hymned by Mrs. Elinor Glyn, was so completely lacking.

"The great It" refers to "sex-appeal":

> "Well, damn it all, I'll risk it," thought Wimsey. "I must and will know what it's all about."
> ... He pulled her suddenly and violently to him, and kissed her mouth with a practised exaggeration of passion. He knew then. No one who has ever encountered it can ever again mistake that awful shrinking, that uncontrollable revulsion of the flesh against a caress that is nauseous. He thought for a moment that she was going to be actually sick.

I will submit that this is the closest that a writer in 1927 would be able to come to saying that the character was a lesbian and that kissing a man made her want to vomit. Admittedly this is somewhat encoded. My thirteen-year-old self, upon reading this book for the first time, had no idea why she found Lord Peter so repulsive except that she was faking wanting to kiss him, and it took me years to come to the realization of what was not being said in this passage. But I think it makes sufficiently clear to any reasonably well-informed adult what is going on.

Unnatural Death is not a traditional whodunit; Lord Peter's investigation focuses upon Mary Whittaker from a very early stage. I will suggest that this is the reason why Sayers could create such a thoroughly evil character and get as close as possible to talking about her as a Lesbian. We are told she is probably guilty from a very early stage in the book, so there is no question of over-emphasizing her personality and her putative capacity to do the evil of murder, because she is already seen as being guilty of the evil of murder. If she is already a murderer, she would not scruple at introducing a young girl to Lesbianism; crime begets crime, so to speak.

The Happy Couple

This stereotype is based on the idea that two women of any sexual preference, who are deprived of the opportunity for marriage and children for one of a wide variety of reasons, can form a domestic partnership and live in a rural community together. Sometimes this is a sexual relationship, sometimes not. In GAD it recurs in the form of two characters who are sisters or cousins or unrelated widows or spinsters who run a small business together— a farm, a guest house, a village shop, or a tea house. These situations are generally found in the work of GAD writers who specialize in the "village mystery."

As we have just seen, however, in the plans of Mary Whittaker and Vera Findlater, it can also be a way of setting up a lesbian relationship in a way that was apparently acceptable to society at the time. (And remember, within the world of GAD, it is not necessarily what the social history of the real world would tell us, but what authors felt that readers would accept as true, that was more commonly the topic of mysteries.) Dorothy L. Sayers twice in *Unnatural Death* indicates that a long-term lesbian couple can operate, respectively, a horse breeding establishment and a chicken farm. And we have the much more mainstream point of view expressed by Agatha Christie in 1950's *A Murder Is Announced*: the example of Miss Hinchcliffe and Miss Murgatroyd.

Spoiler Alert: Although I do not discuss the identity of the murderer, you may find out more about this excellent mystery than you care to know in advance of reading it. Please avoid the remainder of this section if you should.

Hinchcliffe and Murgatroyd run a farm together in the small village of Chipping Cleghorn. "Hinch" is decidedly butch—she has a "formidable grip," is "as tall as a man," and one character describes her as taking up "a manly stance in front of the fireplace"—and the "rather fluttery" Miss Murgatroyd is more feminine, with her "round, good-natured face." They are present at what they think is going to be a game of "Murder" at a fellow villager's home, but instead a real murder takes place. Amy Murgatroyd, unbeknownst to everyone including herself, is in possession of a vital clue. When the murderer realizes that this is the case, Murgatroyd is murdered. When Hinch and Miss Marple discover the body, Hinch "in a low quiet voice" avows: "'I'll kill whoever did this … if I once get my hands on [that person]….'" And later: "Nobody offered Miss Hinchcliffe sympathy or mentioned Miss Murgatroyd's death. The ravaged face of the tall vigorous woman told its own tale, and would have made any expression of sympathy an impertinence." Finally, when the identity of the murderer is revealed, it takes the full strength of a policeman to hold Hinch off from physically attacking the killer. It is clear, at least to this reader, that this is more than a strong friendship.

Let us be clear, though: there is nothing in the text of this novel to which I can point and say, "This means they are a lesbian couple." If a specific reader chooses to be willfully blind to the possibility that Hinchcliffe and Murgatroyd are a romantic couple, that option is slender but available. It ignores the fact that Golden Age writers spent a lot of time and effort to make you think you knew things about specific characters that you actually did not. To conceal the homosexuality of a couple behind a thin veil of refusal to make a direct statement is well within the abilities of Agatha Christie, who routinely convinced us that certain characters could not possibly be guilty when indeed they were. I think that the reader will agree with me that the examples in Sayers and Christie are references to homosexuality.

Conclusion

Finding LGBTQ characters, or their early counterparts, in Golden Age detective fiction of the 1920s and 1930s is a difficult and tenuous process, since few authors were sufficiently daring (or even sufficiently knowledgeable) to include characters considered anti-social at the time. Since the level of knowledge of LGBTQ people had not gone beyond then-current stereotype, it is worth examining the appearance of stereotyped characters across the wide expanse of GAD fiction to see whether they offer any clues as to the social history of LGBTQ people. I do not suggest that all unmarried middle-aged men who have fussy personal habits and are fastidious in their sartorial choices should be read as homosexuals. What I do suggest is that it is a valuable exercise to avoid falling into the trap of heteronormativity by automatically consigning all such characters to heterosexuality. The reader may find it valuable, either when examining new works or revisiting old favorites, to proceed as if the sexual preferences of the characters were capable of being wider in scope than everyday heterosexuality, and that is all that the social historian can expect.

NOTE

1. On the predatory lesbian "vampire" in literature from this period, see Lillian Faderman, *Surpassing the Love of Men: Romantic Friendship and Love between Women from the Renaissance to the Present* (New York: William Morrow, 1981), 341–55. Faderman notes that Sayers was familiar with *Regiment of Women*, which Faderman terms the "most noxious of the lesbian vampire novels," and asserts that Mary Whittaker "was certainly modeled" after the lesbian vampire in Dane's novel (p. 346).

BIBLIOGRAPHY

Berkeley, Anthony. *The Piccadilly Murder*. London: Collins, 1929.
_____. *The Poisoned Chocolates Case*. London: Collins, 1929.
Boucher, Anthony [as H. H. Holmes]. *Nine Times Nine*. New York: Duell, Sloan and Pearce, 1940.
Brand, Christianna. *Death in High Heels*. London: John Lane, 1941.
_____. *Tour de Force*. London: Michael Joseph, 1955.
Christie, Agatha. *A Murder Is Announced*. London: Collins, 1950.
Dane, Clemence. *Regiment of Women*. New York: Macmillan, 1917.
Faderman, Lillian. *Surpassing the Love of Men: Romantic Friendship and Love between Women from the Renaissance to the Present*. New York: William Morrow, 1981.
Hammett, Dashiell. *The Maltese Falcon*. New York: Knopf, 1930.
Hichens, Robert. *The Green Carnation*. London: Heinemann, 1894.
Marsh, Ngaio. *Death in Ecstasy*. London: Geoffrey Bles, 1936.
Sayers, Dorothy L. *Strong Poison*. London: Gollancz, 1930.
_____.*Unnatural Death*. London: Ernest Benn, 1927.
Van Dine, S. S. *The Benson Murder Case*. New York: Scribner's, 1927.

"Queer in some ways"
Gay Characters in the Fiction of Agatha Christie

JOHN CURRAN

Introduction

Gay characters in the fiction of Agatha Christie are notable only for their scarcity. Fewer than a dozen characters in the Queen of Crime's entire body of work can confidently be identified as gay. In an output of over 60 novels, 150 short stories and 15 plays, and, consequently, many hundreds of characters, this might seem anomalous. But Agatha Christie was born in 1890, during the famously repressed reign of Queen Victoria, an era when discussion of sex and sexuality was unthinkable in polite society. Furthermore, while, somewhat illogically, female sexuality was never illegal, male homosexual activity, even in private, was a criminal offence in the UK before 1967. This situation goes some way to explaining why Christie was more comfortable—and, arguably, more convincing—portraying lesbian characters, and sometimes couples, in her work. The sexual revolution of the 1960s coincided with the declining years of her literary activity and ingenuity and her not entirely successful attempt to come to terms with "Swinging London" of the 1960s can be judged in *Third Girl* (1966).

A more likely explanation for Christie's reticence may lie in the following passage from the first chapter of *A Caribbean Mystery* (1964):

> In the course of her duties in a country parish, Jane Marple had acquired a comprehensive knowledge of the facts of rural life. She had no urge to *talk* about them—much less to *write* about them—but she knew them. Plenty of sex, natural and unnatural. Rape, incest, perversion of all kinds. (Some kinds, indeed, that even the clever young men from Oxford who wrote books didn't seem to have heard about.)

Substitute "Agatha Christie" for "Jane Marple" and this, surely, is Christie's own rationalisation of what could be seen as, at best, odd.

A brief exchange from that same novel shows that Christie was aware—

and had been for over thirty years (see below)—of the homosexual connotations of the word "queer." Raymond West, her nephew, arranges a house-sitter for his aunt as she embarks on a Caribbean holiday and explains: "'He'll look after the house all right. He's very house-proud. He's a queer. I mean—' He broke off, slightly embarrassed...." Yet he should not have been embarrassed, because both Jane Marple and Agatha Christie were perfectly aware of the world around them, as Christie demonstrated, sometimes overtly or, more frequently, covertly throughout her career.

A 1923 short story, "The Double Clue," is the first example of a coded, and therefore somewhat uncertain, reference indicating possible homosexuality, and it is not until twenty years later that unambiguous examples can confidently be identified:

- Mr. Pye from *The Moving Finger* (1943)
- Hinchliffe and Murgatroyd from *A Murder Is Announced* (1950)
- Christopher Wren and Miss Casewell from *The Mousetrap* (1952)
- Alec from *The Rats* (1962)
- Clotilde Bradbury-Scott from *Nemesis* (1971)
- minor characters from "Greenshaw's Folly" (1960), *The Mirror Crack'd from Side to Side* (1962) *and Hallowe'en Party* (1969)

More ambiguous examples of major characters include:

- Lord Edgware from *Lord Edgware Dies* (1933)
- Mr. Shaitana from *Cards on the Table* (1936)
- Mr. Ellsworthy from *Murder Is Easy* (1939)

While there is little doubt about the orientation of the first half-dozen listed above, that fact is of little or no importance either to Christie or her detectives. Taste in sexual partners is of relevance in only two cases, although in both cases it is the reason that they kill. Fewer than twenty Christie characters can be perceived, or at least interpreted, as gay, and the evidence for some is far from overwhelming. It has fallen—not, it would seem, unwillingly—to adapters of Christie to interpret characters and reassign sexual orientation where, clearly, none was originally intended. The most egregious examples will be considered later.

Unambiguous Examples

The Moving Finger (1943)
"He fairly skipped down the street."

Miss Marple makes her shortest ever appearance in a mere dozen pages of *The Moving Finger*. The setting, a country village devastated by poison-pen letters and, later, murder, is typical Christie, and the plot and solution show the detective novelist at the height of her powers. Among the inhabitants of Lymstock we meet:

> Mr. Pye ... an extremely ladylike plump little man, devoted to his *petit-point* chairs, his Dresden Shepherdesses and his collection of bric-a-brac.... His small plump hands quivered with sensibility as he described his treasures, and his voice rose to a falsetto squeak as he narrated the exciting circumstances under which he had brought his Italian bedstead home from Verona.

The reader is left in no doubt about Mr. Pye's sexuality, although the hints are far from subtle: "ladylike," "*petit-point* chairs," "falsetto squeak" and, the final nail in the coffin of Mr. Pye's heterosexuality, an Italian bedstead. Tellingly, as with Horace Bindler (see below), when he parts company with the narrator, "[Mr. Pye] fairly skipped down the street." During the investigation the narrator and his sister, Jerry and Joanna Burton, discuss possible suspects but, unlike the description above, their estimate of Mr. Pye is compassionate and somewhat poignant:

> "Not—not an ordinary man—but a certain kind of man. I was thinking, really of Mr. Pye.... He's the sort of person who might be lonely—and unhappy—and spiteful. Everyone, you see, rather laughs at him. Can't you see him secretly hating all the normal happy people, and taking a queer perverse pleasure in what he was doing?"
> "[Inspector] Graves said a middle-aged spinster."
> "Mr. Pye," said Joanna, "*is* a middle-aged spinster."
> "A misfit," I said slowly.

Even the local policemen discuss Mr. Pye in non-derogatory terms: "I don't think a man wrote the letters—in fact I'm sure of it—and so is [Inspector] Graves—always excepting our Mr. Pye, that is to say, who's got an abnormally female streak in his character."

Throughout the book there is much talk about "repression" and "frustration" as a motivation for writing anonymous letters and even the Burtons' unmarried housekeeper, Partridge, is considered. The use here of the word "queer" carries no homosexual overtone: "queer in some ways—a grim spinster—the sort of person who might have religious mania." So Mr. Pye's homosexuality can be viewed as an integral part of the plot, introduced in order to distribute suspicion among other unmarried—and, therefore, automatically "frustrated"—characters: Emily Barton, Aimee Griffith and her brother Owen, Miss Ginch, Elsie Holland, Megan Hunter, and even Joanna and Jerry Burton. With this level of reader-misdirection at play, we should not be surprised when Christie eventually unmasks one of the (relatively few) married characters as the killer.

A Murder Is Announced (1950)

"I'll kill whoever did this...."

Christie began work on *A Murder Is Announced* in 1948, in a Britain emerging from the Second World War and dealing with unemployment, food-rationing, housing shortages, identity cards and army deserters, all of which are included in the plot of Miss Marple's greatest case. And at the centre of this unrecognisably altered social landscape is a lesbian couple, Hinchcliffe (we never learn her first name) and Amy Murgatroyd. This pair of middle-aged women is not just the clearest example of a gay couple in the Christie oeuvre, it is also the most understated. In fact, their most remarkable feature is that they are completely unremarkable. They are treated in a totally matter-of-fact manner by Christie, by Miss Marple, by the police and, most significantly of all, by the inhabitants of Chipping Cleghorn. So unremarkable are they that finding a relevant quotation to indicate their relationship is impossible. They are merely two women sharing their lives together.

It is not until the murder of Amy, late in the novel, that Hinchcliffe's true feelings emerge. Up to that point the couple's conversation was an easy mix of amiable banter and good-humoured criticism. In the wake of the death of Hinch's partner, however, deeper passions become evident, in the woman's vow to "kill whoever did this."

Perhaps because of the devastating social effects of the recent war, Christie felt more comfortable than previously in introducing such unequivocally "different" main characters; and, of course, female homosexuality activity was not a criminal offence. Possibly bolstered by this unremarked-upon experiment, Christie, when she began plotting *Mrs McGinty's Dead* (1953) a few years later, included in her Notebook, among a list of possible characters, "two young men who live together." Regrettably, this was not pursued by the author.

Three Blind Mice/The Mousetrap (1952)
"He's very attractive, isn't he?"

The world's longest running play, *The Mousetrap*, has a complicated genesis. It began life as a radio play, *Three Blind Mice*, written at the request of the BBC as part of an evening's programming to celebrate the 80th birthday of Queen Mary and was first broadcast on 30 May 1947. Christie subsequently rewrote it as a long short story, also called "Three Blind Mice," first published in 1950. Only then was it adapted as a stage play which opened in London's West End on 25 November 1952; and the rest is history.

The play is notable for the inclusion of not just one, but two, gay characters. Equally notable is the fact that one of these, Miss Casewell, does not appear in either the radio version or the novella but was added for the stage version. While the balance of male/female was, arguably, distinctly uneven in its radio and print incarnations—five males and two females, one of whom is murdered midway through the story—the addition of an extra female character made artistic, and "whodunit," sense. But with an unequivocally gay character already present in every version why make the new female character, in the relatively small *dramatis personae*, also homosexual? Post-*A Murder Is Announced* "bravery"?

One of the snowed-in guests at Monkswell Manor guest-house is student architect Christopher Wren, described, on his stage entrance, as "a rather wild-looking, neurotic young man" with "a woven artistic tie" who desires a bedroom with "a four-poster with little chintz roses." The equivalent passage in the novella describes him as "a young man" with "a high-pitched querulous voice," while the radio script baldly states that he has "a shrill rather pansy voice."

On Christopher's arrival the disapproval of Giles, the guest-house owner, is palpable when he calls him a "twerp," adding, "I've no use for that kind (Significantly)"—although he does so when Christopher is off-stage. In the novella version Christopher casually observes that "[the Navy] is much less tolerant than the army or air force," after which "Mr. Wren skipped out into the hall."

It is interesting to compare the various versions of Christopher in the radio script, the novella and the stage play. Onstage he voices his opinion of Sergeant Trotter: "My dears, how melodramatic. He's very attractive, isn't he?" This is amended slightly from the novella version—"He's very handsome, don't you think so? I always think that policemen are very attractive."—while in the original radio script he merely says, though in "a shrill pansy voice": "Too terribly hearty and all over snow."

In the radio script he explains his nervous breakdown thus: "I suppose really that I went a bit queer," although the word "queer" is manually deleted, while the equivalent scene in the novella omits the word completely. But in all versions Christopher uses the full quota of clichéd "gay" forms of address:

- "But, darling, they're so frightfully against me."
- "My dear," he said. "*Such* ructions."
- "But it's too thrilling, you must agree, my dears. It's absolutely too thrilling."
- "You mustn't give way to nerves, darlings."

The second gay character appears only in the stage version where, on her entrance, she is described as "a young woman of manly type" with "a deep manly voice" who "straddles in front of [the fire] in manly fashion." Three uses of the word "manly" in the space of ten lines leaves little doubt that Miss Casewell is to be perceived as a lesbian. She laughs "stridently" and shakes hands "vigorously"; and it is difficult to believe that her first name, Leslie, was not chosen on account of its sexual ambiguity.

When alibis are checked she explains that she was writing a letter and produces it. Sergeant Trotter begins to read from it, "Dearest Jessie,"—"h'm—a friend of yours, or a relation?" to which she replies, "None of your damned business."

As with Miss Casewell, the name of the letter's recipient is androgynous.

The Rats (1962)
"Mad—of course he's mad."

One of Christie's least-known theatrical offerings is the triple bill of one-act plays, *Rule of Three* (1962), consisting of *The Rats, Afternoon at the Seaside* and *The Patient*. Totally contrasting in tone and technique, each displays a different aspect of the Queen of Crime. *The Rats* is a claustrophobic tale of an adulterous couple, Sandra and David, caught in a murderous trap from which escape is impossible, during the course of which we meet Alec, who is described as: "a young man of twenty-eight or nine, the pansy type, very elegant, amusing inclined to be spiteful. He has a very artificial manner and is dressed in the height of fashion…."

Although his conversation is littered with "My dears" and "darlings," his "elegant … height of fashion" clothing is designed, in all likelihood, to camouflage the fact that he wears gloves throughout his stage appearance, a detail that will later prove significant. While there is no denying that Alec is a thoroughly nasty character and a murderer, it is important to note that he is the first of only two homosexual killers in Christie's crime fiction whose crimes are directly attributable to their sexual orientation. As realisation of his and Sandra's predicament dawns, David observes: "You said [Alec] was devoted to your first husband. You've only got to take one look at Alec to know what kind of devotion that was."

In the recently published *Curtain Up: Agatha Christie: A Life in Theatre* by Julius Green we learn that this line went through a few less cryptic drafts before arriving at this relatively anodyne version. It began as "Alex—obviously a homo—it was that kind of devotion I should guess." And, when disallowed by the Lord Chamberlain (effectively the UK stage censor at that time), it became "Alex—obviously a queer…" and, later again, "Alex—obviously a bit feminine.…" And although David adds that Alec is "Mad—of course he's mad." this observation should not be seen as a logical deduction from Alec's homosexuality; rather, it is David's verdict on the (undeniably ingenious) extremes to which Alec was willing to go to exact revenge on those responsible for the death of the man he loved. The remark actually tells us as much about David as it does about Alec.

Nemesis (1971)
"One of the most frightening words there is in the world."

Without the word ever being mentioned it is clear that elderly Clotilde Bradbury-Scott harbored homosexual feelings for young and beautiful Verity Hunt and this doomed one-sided relationship is the source of the entire plot of *Nemesis*, the last Miss Marple novel that Christie wrote. In a telling conversation mid-way through the book, Elizabeth Temple, who is soon to be the killer's next victim, explains her interpretation of Verity's death:

> "Love!" she said.
> Miss Marple queried the word sharply. "Love?"
> "One of the most frightening words there is in the world," said Elizabeth Temple.

In conversation with Miss Marple, Clotilde and her sisters, Lavinia and Anthea, skirt delicately round the situation:

> "Verity," she said, "was a girl we cared for very much. She lived here for a while. I was very fond of her."
> "And she was very fond of you." said Lavinia.
> "Of course, you couldn't know that our sister Clotilde, was particularly fond of [Verity]."

And in a final confrontation with Miss Marple, Clotilde acknowledges her hopeless and eventually fatal love:

> "Because you loved her," said Miss Marple.
> "Of course I loved her. I was devoted to her. And she loved me."

Although she is the second example of a gay murderer in Christie's crime fiction, Clotilde evokes far more reader sympathy than does Alec. Interestingly, both characters appear during Christie's final decade as a writer.

Some minor characters unquestionably fall into the clichéd gay category:

"Greenshaw's Folly" (1960)
"But, my dear, how wonderful."

Horace Bindler, a collector of architectural "monstrosities," appears as a minor character in the opening passage of the Marple novella "Greenshaw's Folly." His brief conversation is replete with "My dears" and his first sight of the eponymous Folly is greeted with: "'But, my dear, how wonderful.' His voice rose in a high screech of aesthetic delight...."

A sadly stereotypical gay character (especially this late in Christie's career), he explores, in the company of Raymond West, the Greenshaw house and grounds and, when Raymond led the way "Horace skipped after him..." (230); as did Mr. Pye, twenty years earlier.

The Mirror Crack'd from Side to Side (1962)
"...a willowy young man..."

Equally stereotypical is film producer Jason Rudd's private secretary, Hailey Preston, described as "a willowy young man with wavy hair" and again, at a later stage, as "that willow wand of a young man." Miss Marple alarms him with a cryptic "village parallel":

> "You remind me very much," she said, "of someone I knew called Gerald French [who] ... had an unfortunate past."

"You don't say," said Hailey Preston, slightly ill at ease. "What kind of a past?"
"I won't repeat it," said Miss Marple. "He didn't like it talked about."

The novel also features a character "almost as willowy as Hailey Preston," the photographer's assistant, Johnny Jethroe. He is "a young man with exuberant hair and a pink and white face" wearing "a kind of lilac smock." True to clichéd form, he soon says "My dear" and "How perfectly rapturous!"

Hallowe'en Party (1969)
"She was a bit queer they say."

Minor characters in *Hallowe'en Party*, mentioned in connection with an earlier unsolved murder, are Janet White and Nora Ambrose, described by a teacher colleague as: "Over-sexed ... but in different ways." When Janet was strangled "[Nora] left the school and took another post in the North of England—she was, naturally, very upset. They were—great friends."

Worldly-wise students Nicholas and Desmond—*Hallowe'en Party* is notable for the number of children whose actions and conversation are implausibly adult—give Poirot the benefit of their wisdom:

> "You remember, one of the teachers got strangled a year or two ago. She was a bit queer they say."
> "Lesbian?" asked Nicholas, in a man of the world voice.
> "I shouldn't wonder. Do you remember Nora Ambrose, the girl she lived with? ... She had a boyfriend or two, so they said, and the girl she lived with got mad with her about it."

This relationship moves center-stage in the 2010 television adaptation in the *Agatha Christie's Marple* series.

A final clear, and also regrettably stereotyped, example comes from Dame Agatha's non-crime output as Mary Westmacott, the name under which she published, between 1930 and 1956, six bittersweet romantic novels. *A Daughter's a Daughter* (1952) is the novelization of a rarely-performed play, written, in all likelihood, in the 1930s. First presented in 1956, when it ran for just a week, it was revived in London's West End in 2004, and received very positive reviews. As its title suggests, it concerns a corrosive mother/daughter relationship and briefly features a Basil Mowbray, "an artistic young man of twenty-eight." The novel describes his entrance thus: "Mr Mowbray darted in. There was no other term for it. It was the skimming motion of some gay insect.... He was young and affected in manner."

His dialogue—slightly different in each version—is replete with "My dears" and "How absolutely adorable!" He is described as "having a thing about Victorian jewellery" and in the script one line reads: "(Utters squeal) 'Oh dear, I've just seen the time.... Ta, ta, everybody.'" The eponymous daughter, Ann, is unequivocal in her opinion of her mother's friend:

"It's no good, mother, I don't like your pansy friend."
"Oh, but darling, he's very amusing, so marvellously spiteful about people."

The inclusion of such a clichéd and stereotypical character is difficult to justify; he plays no significant part in the story and, unlike *The Mousetrap's* Christopher Wren, a close counterpart from Christie's crime output, he is not even amusing.

Ambiguous Examples

More contentious are major characters from three classic Christie novels and a very early short story, who pose unanswered—and unanswerable—questions.

"The Double Clue" (1923)
"…young man with his white effeminate face and affected lisping speech…"

The earliest example of a (possibly) gay character occurs in a Poirot short story, "The Double Clue," in which the detective undertakes to locate some missing jewelry on behalf of a Mr. Marcus Hardman, an ardent collector of "old lace, old fans, and antique jewelry." He is described, much as Mr. Pye would be twenty years later in *The Moving Finger*, as "a small man, delicately plump with exquisitely manicured hands and a plaintive tenor voice."

The first suspect to be interviewed by Poirot and his sidekick Captain Arthur Hastings is "young man about town," Mr. Bernard Parker. "We found him reclining on some cushions, clad in an amazing dressing-gown of purple and orange," comments a palpably disgusted Hastings. "I have seldom taken a greater dislike to anyone as I did to this particular young man with his white effeminate face and affected lisping speech."

It is clear from Hastings' patently heteronormative reaction to Parker that it is the latter man's effeminacy, and not his potential criminality, that angers the good Captain. When Poirot asks Hardman about his connection to Parker, the question appeared to embarrass Mr. Hardman considerably: "He is—er—he is a young fellow. Well, in fact, a young fellow I know."

Although there is a criminal connection between the two men, it is possible, though by no means certain, that they share a sexual relationship too.

Lord Edgware Dies (1933)
"…he's a queer man—he's not like other people…"

One of the most enigmatic relationships—if such it is—in the Christie output is that of Lord Edgware and his butler in *Lord Edgware Dies*. When

Poirot is asked by Edgware's estranged wife, the actress Jane Wilkinson, to intervene on her behalf in the matter of a divorce, she explains: "he's a queer man—he's not like other people.... He should never have married— anyone. I know what I'm talking about. I just can't describe him, but he's queer."

This use of the word "queer" is open to interpretation, as is the punctuation dash before the word "anyone." Is it a significant pause? Is Jane telling Poirot that her former husband is homosexual or that he is merely peculiar (though in a nasty way)—or, possibly, both? We know from *Three Act Tragedy*, published two years later, that the use of the word "queer" to indicate homosexuality was familiar to Christie: "'I like men to have affairs,' said Egg. 'It shows they're not queer or anything.'" In the case of Lord Edgware, however, the evidence for sadomasochism is, arguably, stronger than that for homosexuality. Consider Poirot's observation as he and Hastings leave Edgware's house: "I should imagine [Edgware] practices many curious vices and that beneath his frigid exterior he hides a deep-rooted instinct of cruelty."

Taken in conjunction with the presence on Edgware's bookshelf of tomes on mediaeval torture and the Comte de Sade, Edgware's own admission— that he "enjoy[s] the *macabre*. I always have. My taste is peculiar."—would tend to confirm his interest in the infliction of pain (although this does not, of course, rule out a parallel interest in handsome young men). Is it mere coincidence that on arrival at his home Poirot and Hastings are ushered in to Edgware's presence by, Hastings explains, "one of the handsomest young men I have ever seen. Tall, fair, he might have posed to a sculptor for Hermes or Apollo. Despite his good looks there was something vaguely effeminate that I disliked about the softness of his voice." After this paragon of male beauty disappears during the course of the novel, Inspector Japp reports: "Seems he's mixed up with a couple of rather disreputable nightclubs. Not the usual thing. Something a great deal more recherché and nasty." It is doubtful that a senior policeman—even in the 1930s—would consider homosexuality "recherché," whatever he might think about its being "nasty." But clubs devoted to the practice of sadomasochism would almost certainly merit that description.

Cards on the Table (1936)
"...and he smelt of scent."

The question of whether Mr. Shaitana, the murder victim in *Cards on the Table*, is gay is a problem that might vex even Poirot. Shaitana is described as giving "wonderful parties—large parties, small parties, *macabre* parties, respectable parties and definitely 'queer' parties," yet it is by no means certain that these parties are anything other than merely peculiar. Certainly Shaitana's final affair, around which the novel revolves, with its guest list of four undetected murderers and four potential investigators, could be considered such, especially when the peculiarity extends to the murder of the host. At the party this exchange occurs:

> "What a queer man he is!"
> "Dr. Roberts?"
> "No, Mr. Shaitana."

This, however, may be just an overall impression, one that is in keeping with the authorial observation that: "'Every healthy Englishman who saw [Mr. Shaitana] longed earnestly and fervently to kick him!" Major Despard, one of the suspects in Shaitana's slaying, during the course of his questioning explains his reasons for disliking Shaitana: "He was too well dressed—he wore his hair too long—and he smelt of scent." Despite these comments Shaitana's sexual tastes remain enigmatic.

It was left to television—famous, as every crime reader knows, for its fidelity to source material—to settle the question in the 2006 adaptation of this novel for the program *Agatha Christie's Poirot*. This episode, one of the poorest of the entire series, leaves the viewer in no doubt about Shaitana's sexual predilections: he is accompanied by a pretty young boy in the opening scenes. But just in case this liberty was not sufficiently tasteless, Dr. Roberts, clearly heterosexual in the original novel, is depicted as having an affair with a patient's husband; in fact, the doctor's closet homosexuality is now the motive for his crime. And lest any viewers remained unconvinced of the producers' *bona-fides* as purveyors of modern, edgy drama, there are final revelations of gay orgies involving the police investigator—thankfully, not Inspector Japp of the novel— and strong hints that one of the suspects, Anne Meredith, and her housemate, Rhoda Dawes, are more than "just good friends."

Murder Is Easy (1939)

"…the gentleman at the curio shop is a queer one…"

Like Lord Edgware and Mr. Shaitana, the sexual orientation of Mr. Ellsworthy from *Murder Is Easy* is also open to question. His description on his first appearance certainly conforms to the clichéd perception of gay males: "a very exquisite young man dressed in a colour scheme of russet brown. He had a long pale face with a womanish mouth, long black artistic hair with a mincing walk." He is a knowledgeable collector (and seller) of antiques, like *The Moving Finger*'s Mr. Pye, as well as an enthusiastic gossip: "'Now who told you that?' cried Mr. Ellsworthy, clasping his hands together…. 'Gossip and malice and scandal—all so delicious if one takes them in the right spirit.'"

Yet the word "queer," used frequently in connection with Ellsworthy and, later, his friends, in this case relates, I contend, not to homosexuality but its original meaning of "odd" or "peculiar":

- "Oh, no—I think [Ellsworthy]'s dreadful." She drew a little nearer.
- "There's a lot of talk about him. I was told that he had some queer ceremony in the Witches' Meadow—a lot of his friends came down from London—frightfully queer-looking people."
- "The gentleman hasn't got at all a good reputation here, sir. All sorts of goings on. And friends down from town and many queer happenings."
- "I wouldn't like to say anything definite"—Mrs. Church passed a hungry tongue over her thin lips—"but the gentleman at the curio shop is a queer one."

"Odd" and/or "peculiar" is certainly an accurate description of these "friends from town," but the likelihood of all of these visitors participating in potential "gay" goings-on is, at best, debatable:

"Three extraordinary people have arrived at the Bells and Motley. Item one, a man with shorts, spectacles and a lovely plum-colored silk shirt! Item two, a female with no eyebrows, dressed in a peplum, a pound of assorted sham Egyptian beads, and sandals. Item three, a fat man in a lavender suit and co-respondent shoes. I suspect them of being friends of our Mr. Ellsworthy. Says the gossip writer: 'Someone has whispered that there will be gay doings in the Witches' Meadow tonight.'"

Yet, despite that jocular description, it seems that the "extraordinary people" are gathering not for a gay orgy but something more sinister (even by 1930s standards):

"As I see it, this murderer must be crazy. And that, you see, brought me straight to Ellsworthy. Of all the people down here, he's the only one who is definitely queer. He is queer, you can't get away from it!"
Luke said doubtfully, "There are a good many of his sort—dilettantes, poseurs—usually quite harmless."
[...]
"Well, it seems that he has a kind of little coterie—a band of nasty friends. They come down here from time to time and celebrate."
"Do you mean what are called nameless orgies?"
"I don't know about nameless but certainly orgies. Actually, it all sounds very silly and childish."
"I suppose they worship the devil and do obscene dances."
"Something of the kind. Apparently they get a kick out of it."

And, indeed, such it proves to be, when Ellsworthy and some of these friends are seen with blood on their hands as a result of slaughtering a cockerel during the "queer happenings" in the local woods. At the close of the novel it is clear that such "nameless orgies" will be brought to an abrupt end: "I think something unpleasant is going to happen to our Mr. Ellsworthy. [Superintendent] Battle is planning a little surprise."

So, despite the repeated use of the words "queer" and "gay" in connection with these three characters, it is arguable that Edgware is a sadist, Shaitana a particularly nasty blackmailer and Ellsworthy a devil-worshipper (although that does not, of course, rule out the possibility that they are also gay). It is important to remember that throughout her career it was Agatha Christie's purpose to misdirect the reader's attention and to make the guilty seem innocent and the innocent guilty. Ambiguity of any sort, even sexual, was part of the ludic strategy she adopted towards this end.

Brief mention was made above of the possible relationship between Anne Meredith and Rhoda Dawes in *Cards on the Table*. Similarly, question marks can be appended to Miss Marple's *Nemesis* guardians, Miss Barrow and Miss Cooke, and to Barbara Allen and Jane Plenderleith in "Murder in the Mews." Although evidence is lacking in all of these cases, the actions of the last-named are not far removed from those of Alec in *The Rats*.

Adaptations

Some modern adaptations of Christie insert gay sensibilities—plots, themes and even (hitherto "straight") murderers—in defiance of fidelity, logic and taste. Mention has already been made of the sweeping changes made to *Cards on the Table*. While these were completely unjustifiable they stopped short at changing the identity of the murderer. Not so the 2004 TV adaptation of *The Body in the Library* from the *Agatha Christie's Marple* series. Instead of the murderous heterosexual couple of the novel the scriptwriter, for no discernible reason, amended this to a lesbian couple. The changes to *Nemesis*, from the same series, are so laughably preposterous that any resemblance to the original novel seems accidental. The lesbianism of the novel is, needless to remark, retained, although the sisters are now nuns.

A more acceptable, and somewhat justifiable, change was made to the 2003 adaptation of *Five Little Pigs* in *Agatha Christie's Poirot*, where Philip Blake admits to Poirot that he was in love, not with Caroline, but with her husband Amyas, "the friend I loved better than anyone in the world." Less convincingly, Tim Allerton, in the 2004 adaptation of *Death on the Nile*, cryptically admits his homosexuality to Rosalie Otterbourne when she tries to kiss him. This modification, which adds nothing to the plot, was presumably "inspired" by Tim's claustrophobic relationship with his mother. A further minor example can be found in the dramatization of *Taken at the Flood* from the same TV series.

Likewise, the BBC Radio adaptation of the little-known story "Swan Song" changes the perfectly acceptable heterosexual pairing which provides the killer's motive to a lesbian one. There seems no valid reason for this other, as with *The Body in the Library* (above) than a misguided determination to make Christie, in that ubiquitous catch-all of producer-speak, "relevant."

Conclusion

Christie's treatment of gay characters is distinctly even-handed, with depiction of lesbian characters more matter-of-fact and less clichéd—with the exception of Miss Casewell—than that of males. The clearly recognisable examples range from the sadly stereotypical (Mr. Pye and Miss Casewell) to the matter-of-fact (Hinchcliffe and Murgatroyd); from the figure of fun (Christopher Wren) to the utterly nasty (Alec); and to the sympathetic (Clotilde Bradbury-Scott). Gay characters can be nasty (Edgware, Ellsworthy) or nice (Murgatroyd, Mr. Pye); sinister (Shaitana, Alec) or sad (Clotilde).

Of those discussed, only two—Alec (*The Rats*) and Clotilde Bradbury-Scott (*Nemesis*)—are revealed as killers motivated by their sexuality. And gay characters as victims slightly outweigh this number: Amy Murgatroyd (*A Murder Is Announced*), Lord Edgware (*Lord Edgware Dies*) and Mr Shaitana (*Cards on the Table*). Victims, unlike killers, are murdered for reasons other than their sexual tastes. As far as Christie was concerned they were all characters; and, more importantly, suspects.

Note: This essay does not purport to include a complete list of gay, and/or possibly gay, characters in the work of Agatha Christie.

Works Cited

All novels and short stories are from the HarperCollins Facsimile reprint series 2006–2010. Original UK publication dates and alternate U.S. titles are included.

Works by Agatha Christie
- Detective Novels and Short Story Collections
  The Adventure of the Christmas Pudding 1960
  The Body in the Library 1942
  Cards on the Table 1936
  A Caribbean Mystery 1964
  Death on the Nile 1937
  Five Little Pigs 1943
  Hallowe'en Party 1969
  The Listerdale Mystery 1934
  Lord Edgware Dies (*Thirteen at Dinner*) 1933
  The Mirror Crack'd from Side to Side (*The Mirror Crack'd*) 1962
  The Moving Finger 1943
  A Murder Is Announced 1950
  Murder in the Mews 1937
  Murder Is Easy (*Easy to Kill*) 1939
  Nemesis 1971
  Poirot's Early Cases 1974
- As Mary Westmacott
  A Daughter's a Daughter (1952)

Part One: Locked Doors

- PLAYS
    The Mousetrap 1952
    The Rats 1962
- SHORT STORIES
    "The Double Clue" (December 1923) in *Poirot's Early Cases* (1974)
    "Greenshaw's Folly" (December 1956) in *The Adventure of the Christmas Pudding* (1960)
    "Murder in the Mews" (September 1936) in *Murder in the Mews* (1937)
    "Swan Song" (September 1926) in *The Listerdale Mystery* (1934)

Works by Other Authors

Green, Julius. *Curtain Up: Agatha Christie A Life in Theatre*. London: HarperCollins, 2015.

Agatha Christie
Norms and Codes

MICHAEL MOON

Codes

Bletchley, a town fifty miles northwest of London, has become a household word in recent years—famous now for having been World-War-II-era Britain's best-kept secret. Throughout the war, fifty-eight acres of an estate there known as Bletchley Park served as the headquarters of the UK's foremost "secret weapon," a brilliant team of cryptographers who succeeded in cracking a number of the enemies' supposedly unbreakable codes, thereby giving Allied forces increasing access to Axis military plans and secrets. Some historians have argued both that the codebreakers' successes were a unique factor in ultimately enabling the Allies to win the war, and that their efforts may have shortened the length of the war by as much as two years.

It does not appear to have become widely known until quite recently that Agatha Christie's name had, at one time during the war, become linked to the remarkable (and remarkably secret) cryptographic projects going on at Bletchley Park. In February 2013, a story began appearing in newspapers about how Christie had at least briefly become a person of interest to the top command of Britain's Secret Service—one of whose highest priorities was preserving the heavy veil of secrecy around the codebreaking project. Michael Smith, author of several books about Bletchley Park, appears to have broken the story; he tells a succinct version of it:

> Security remained so tight that when Agatha Christie's spy novel *N or M*, published in November 1941, included a character called Major Bletchley, there was an investigation. [Dilwyn, widely known as "Dilly"] Knox [one of Bletchley Park's top decoders], who knew Christie well, invited her to tea and asked her about the name's origins. She explained that she was once stuck at Bletchley [train] station and found the place so boring that she thought it the ideal name for the tiresome old major.[1]

Christie's apparently coincidental naming of her character notwithstanding, a very high standard of top-secrecy was maintained around Bletchley Park throughout the war. This is especially impressive given the size of the operation there, for at its peak in January 1945, around 9,000 personnel were working at the facility. The relatively small teams of mathematicians, economists, and linguists who did the bulk of the codebreaking were assisted by large staffs of workers called "computers," humans who carried out by hand the computing of enormous amounts of raw data that were retrieved from enemy code transmissions.[2] Fifty years after the end of the war, some former workers still considered themselves to be bound by their oath of silence. But in recent decades a noisy world has broadcast the achievements of the codebreakers and their staffs far and wide; Bletchley has even spawned its own television detective series, *The Bletchley Circle*, about the postwar adventures of a group of women who had worked together at the Park.

Some aspects of the wartime history of the project have become especially interesting to students of feminist and LGBTQ matters. In all, of the 12,000 people who worked at Bletchley Park sometime during the war, nearly 10,000 were women, many of whom worked as "computers." Alan Turing, routinely hailed in recent decades as "The Father of Modern Computer Science," was a major contributor to some of the most decisive breakthroughs in the wartime work at Bletchley, providing much of the math necessary to crack sophisticated codes as well as participating in the design of some of the first proto-computing devices used to streamline the tasks that the large teams of "human computers" had been carrying out. Working closely with Christie's friend Dilly Knox, Turing is generally credited with, among many other contributions that he made to the Allied war effort, having broken the Nazi's Enigma codes.

Besides being an eminent mathematician and a pioneering and uniquely important figure in the development of modern computing, Turing was also a sexually active gay man who appears in retrospect to have been "out" to an unusual degree in the UK of the 1940s. Some years after the war, Turing broke—this time in the sense of violated—another "code," this one not a "code" in the sense of transmitting information in encrypted form, but a "code" in the sense of a largely implicit but widely shared understanding among members of a particular social class of how its privilege depends on at least the outward, social performance of certain forms of "discretion" and self-control. The twentieth-century institution of "the closet" has come to be understood as a powerful social mechanism for regulating the open secret that same-sex desires and relationships existed, but did so largely invisibly and inaudibly—at least until someone allegedly violated the code of the closet, thereby bringing about a supposedly inevitable train of likely catastrophes on themselves: exposure, public disgrace, social ostracism, criminal prosecution.

Turing, however, appears to have been less heavily invested or involved in the code of the closet than many other members of his generation who engaged in same-sex relations of one kind or another. He seems to have more or less inadvertently breeched this code when he told police who were investigating a burglary at his home in early 1952 that another man whose name he had mentioned to them as part of a narrative of events leading up to the burglary had been a sex-partner of his. Convicted of "gross indecency" for admitting to having had sexual relations with another man, Turing was tried, convicted, and given a choice of being sentenced to prison or accepting a form of probation that stipulated that he be regularly injected with a synthetic estrogen designed to suppress his sexual functioning (this treatment was an early form of what came to be known as "chemical castration"). Turing chose probation, and he was subjected to the estrogen injections for a year.[3]

A couple of years later, Turing died of cyanide poisoning, aged forty-one. An inquest ruled his death a suicide, but there is a persistent minority opinion (held by, among others, philosopher Jack Copeland), that Turing accidentally inhaled cyanide fumes while electroplating spoons in his tiny spare room at home. Near the end of 2013, Queen Elizabeth II issued Turing a posthumous pardon; a public outcry then arose about why 50,000 other UK "sex offenders" convicted under the same laws had not been retroactively "pardoned" at the same time.[4]

Poisons, inquests, police investigations, secrets revealed: it is no wonder that a recent reviewer of Hugh Whitemore's popular 1986 play about Turing, *Breaking the Code*, said that the bare outlines of Turing's story sound "like Agatha Christie, but gay and geeky."[5] But, as some queer readers of Christie have been aware for a long time, her mysteries themselves can be pretty "gay and geeky." If one happens to be attuned to some of the major types (some would say stereotypes) that have figured in the twentieth century's limited public image-repertoire of queers, Christie's stories may be seen as presenting more than a sufficiency of them: single older gentlemen fascinated with the minutiae of social prestige (*The Mysterious Mr. Quin*) or the display of fine furnishings (*The Moving Finger*); village-dwelling middle-aged female couples barely visible as such against the immediate background of the larger community of women left permanently single by World War I (*A Murder Is Announced*); unusually beautiful young men who often have a disturbing effect on the communities through which they pass (*Halloween Party*); distinguished headmistresses who form intense attachments to certain of the older girls (*Nemesis*); a "bad-tempered and bitter" aristocratic male with a "queer, secretive" look and a fondness for reading the Marquis de Sade, and his butler, who puts a visitor in mind of a classical nude sculpture of Apollo and yet has "something vaguely effeminate" about him that the visitor "dislike[s]" (*Lord Edgware Dies*).

The examples gestured toward here are hardly the only such characters to be found in Christie's fiction. Indeed, as readers have pointed out before, Christie's two main series detectives—Hercule Poirot and Jane Marple—are themselves hardly exemplars of twentieth-century models of heterosexuality for their respective genders. Without claiming flatly that Poirot "is gay," one may observe that some of his most distinctive qualities, such as his "foreignness," his fastidiousness of dress and manner, and the oblique view he often takes of the goings-on around him, mark him as queer-ish if not downright queer. One wonders, moreover, if Christie didn't marry off Poirot's flatmate Captain Arthur Hastings, sending him to live with his bride in Argentina, about the time that it occurred to her that readers might wonder about—i.e., suspect—two unmarried men permanently sharing a fashionably modern London flat. Yet despite or perhaps at least partly because of the exorbitance of his many mild but conspicuous violations of the norms of "English manliness," Poirot is the object of widespread affection and high professional respect in the many novels and stories in which he figures. Similarly, without needing to claim that Marple "is lesbian," one may note that her immersion in the feminine networks of the village combined with her character-defining disregard for masculine illusions of superiority and her drive and ability to penetrate layers of deceit and misdirection mark her as someone who might be seen as "deviant" in her society in a number of ways—at the same time that she might also be seen (as she is by many of her fellow villagers) as an in many ways thoroughly conventional gentlewoman of her time and place.

Several thoughtful students of Christie's work have already provided models of ways of decoding the queer or queer-ish characters and modes of behavior that recur in her fiction. Pioneering Australian gay activist and social theorist Dennis Altman and his friend the late poet Dorothy Porter discovered ways of "Queering Agatha" that Altman has written about, acknowledging that "it's not difficult to find coded homosexual references in Christie." For Altman, the "queerness" of Christie's work "lies in the way in which she suggests another and less ordered world lying beneath the conventional middle class English prejudices and class structures."[6]

More recently, UK scholar Owen Emmerson has compared the "codings" of lesbian and gay characters and characteristics that Christie carries out in her fiction with the sometimes quite different kinds of "recodings" and "decodings" of them that various adapters have introduced into the two recent Miss Marple television series—the BBC series first screened in 1984–92 (starring Joan Hickson) and the ITV series first screened in 2004–13 (starring first Geraldine McEwen and then Julia McKenzie).[7] After some reviewers and on-line fans expressed dismay over the introduction of "openly" lesbian characters and situations into these twenty-first-century adaptations, BBC saw fit to promote a reissue of their Thatcher-era Marple series as being for "fans of a good murder mystery without extra lesbianism" (both Altman and Emmerson cite this egregious ad-line).

For all his concern with the translational labor of codings, recodings, and decodings that he sees going on in Christie and her adapters, Emmerson attempts to move beyond the "spot-the-stereotype" way of piling up Christie's references—often undeveloped and very much in passing—to gossiping spinsters, spiteful old bachelors, lovelorn headmistresses, and oddly "statuesque" young butlers. He does so by introducing the concept of heteronormativity as a kind of big picture in relation to which Christie's many, largely fragmentary, references to queerish characters and characteristics can be assembled into supposedly larger patterns and analyzed, like so many chips of mosaic glass. The "big" concept serves Emmerson reasonably well in identifying and critiquing the different kinds of homophobia that are dominant in the various television adaptations of Marple—in the early AIDS (as well as the Thatcher) era of the 1980s, as well as in the ostensibly more open and understanding early 2000s. And yet the introduction of the idea of a hetero norm or norms into the conceptual mix actually gives him little more to say about the place or status of queers and queerness in Christie's own stories than the familiar method of collecting and sorting types (or stereotypes) had already done.

Norms

In a recent article, Robyn Wiegman and Elizabeth A. Wilson have taken a long and searching look at such concepts as normativity and antinormativity, heteronormativity and its supposed converse, arguing that queer theory has suffered from its over-commitment to a reductive and inflexible (mis)understanding of the meaning and function of norms and normativity that posits all norms as allegedly oppressive and all antinormative impulses, acts, and projects as socially and politically progressive. Wiegman and Wilson say that they return to the idea of a norm "in order to revivify what is galvanizing (indeed what is queer), about its operations." Rather than being unfailingly restrictive, constricting, and exclusionary, they go on, a norm "may be a more capacious event than one might suspect." What the study of norms discovers over and over again is not necessarily that there are sets of rules to which all must bend but that "we are all comparable" in an unpredictably numerous and various range of ways, and that "normativity," rather than being by definition an airless space of regimentation and tyranny, "is a structure of proliferation"—or, as queer legal theorist Janet Halley has written, "The idea of the average depends on deviation; normalcy can be articulated as such only if it has outliers." Wiegman and Wilson venture yet another way of characterizing a norm: as "a wide-ranging, ever-moving appraisal of the structure of a set," asserting that a routinized practice or understanding of "antinormativity misses what is most engaging about a norm: that in collating the world, it gathers up everything ... it values everything; it plays." They quote French philosopher of biology George Canguilhem, "Wherever there is *life* there are norms."[8]

Historians of the mystery novel, of twentieth-century popular fiction and fiction in general, have been hard put to it to say exactly what it is that has made Agatha Christie by far the bestselling and most widely translated author of her time and since—or what it is that continues to make her fiction, all of it written between forty and nearly a hundred years ago, still one of the hottest and most profitable "franchises" in the realm of global media. Her exceptional ingenuity as a plotter and the reliable delivery of suspense and surprise in her narratives, combined with her straightforward ability as a storyteller and a scene-setter (whether in a country village or in various "exotic" locales) and a writing style simple enough in syntax and vocabulary to be readily accessible to bright children and some first-time readers of English: these are the reasons most often put forward for the remarkably enduring popularity of her work. But Wiegman and Wilson's revivification of the concept of norms suggests to me another possible reason, a far from negligible one, for the notably long-lived and widespread enjoyment that many readers have taken and continue to take in her work. This factor may be best understood not by the casual reader of one or two of her novels—even of the most highly acclaimed ones, such as *The Murder of Roger Ackroyd*, *Death on the Nile*, *Murder on the Orient Express*, or *And Then There Were None*—but by those of us "fans" who have read—often at quite different times of our lives—all or most of her mysteries.

One way to try to articulate my own pleasure in reading Christie as I have found myself, having some time ago exhausted the long list of reputedly "good ones," in recent years finally reading all the alleged "dogs" of her oeuvre, her 1970s novels that fellow fans had long steered me away from—*Elephants Can Remember*, *Passenger to Frankfurt*, even *Postern of Fate*—might be to say that Christie really had a way with a norm, a norm as Wiegman and Wilson have invited us to rethink its workings and ranges, as playful, unpredictable, highly mobile, curious, omnivorous, generous in according value and attention—in several of the broader senses of the term, queer. Deprecators of Christie's work have long dismissed it as a set of meretriciously clever crossword or jigsaw puzzles disguised as prose fictions of a certain length and, most of all, of an exorbitant marketability to the broadest (and by implication lowest) common denominator. The young Gertrude Stein, despairing of ever finding an audience among the artists and intellectuals that she knew, says in *The Making of Americans* that she wrote for herself and strangers. Christie somehow succeeded in finding a way of writing that permitted her to speak with an intimate and welcome familiarity to an incoherently, perhaps unprecedentedly, wide range of readerships. As critic Gillian Gill eloquently puts it in her own assessment of the basis of the uncanny appeal of Christie's work to masses of readers of several generations, "Agatha Christie makes no claim to know her readers, merely to respect and enjoy us. She loves us enough to leave us alone, and we love her for it."[9]

The basis for her innumerable readers' pleasure in her work is, I believe, of a piece with the wildly stochastic (i.e., formally unpredictable) quality that Christie achieved through her lifelong engagement with the play of norms in her fiction. It is in this quality that we may discover something (some things) lastingly and ponderably queer about her work. It is perhaps in her casts of characters, and the play of recurrence-with-variation from story to story and from decade to decade that this quality most clearly and reliably manifests itself. We may recall at this point that Christie was not only an enormously successful author of mystery novels and stories, she was also one of the handful of extremely popular and successful playwrights in the English-speaking world of the twentieth century. (*The Mousetrap* is only the best known of a host of theatrical works of Christie's.)[10] When I consider one of her novels after another, and in relation to each other, I am struck by her eminently practical theatrical sense of what constitutes a significantly compelling mise en scene, and, most of all, of how to put together a cast of characters that will in some ways be familiar enough to be readily legible to a wide—potentially very wide—audience, while, at the same time, somehow also being weird, anomalous, uncanny enough to keep many viewers engaged, even fascinated, by the proceedings.

Christie and the Play of Norms: The Example of N or M?

Rather than thinking of queer characters or characteristics or meanings as being "encoded" in her work and needing "decoding," I am more interested in thinking about how a wide variety of such phenomena—characters "queer" in many senses of the term—seem to fluctuate and mutate around what one might take to be the norm in many of her works. Take for example her mystery novel *N or M?*, the work of Christie's published in the dark early days of World War II that had briefly raised questions "in the highest circles" about whether she might be treasonously signaling the existence of top-secret Bletchley Park to her readers. Jonathan Goldberg pointed out to me early in my research for this essay that the title *N or M?*, its letters moved together, can be read as a single word put into question: *norm?* Christie has been routinely acclaimed for the ingenuity of her plotting since the appearance of *The*

Mysterious Affair at Styles in 1920, but in addition to the originality with which she refashioned standard plots in sometimes uncannily striking new forms, her work also deserves recognition for the ways in which she keeps cobbling together casts of characters of a notably diverse sort, across social classes, genders, occupational categories, and so on, that still, taken together, make some sort of sense as a striking kind of collective singularity. Here we find the kind of collection gathered and collated by the roving and playful norm as it amasses and places in often random juxtapositions to each other qualities, values, and behaviors, in what may strike us as unexpected, incongruous, grotesque, discomfiting, and/or comic relations.

Take for example the highly miscellaneous assortment of persons whom amateur detectives Tuppence and Tommy Beresford encounter on their arrival at the somewhat seedy seaside rooming house in Leahampton where most of the action takes place in *N or M?* Although each of the residents of the boardinghouse seems a very representative type of a familiar if not over-familiar kind, the Beresfords already know before actually encountering any of them in person that at least one may quite likely be one of the pair of master spies at the head of a major enemy plan to invade the UK, whom it is Tuppence and Tommy's job to suss out and foil. In his first conversation with his new wartime boss, Mr. Grant, about the high-level counterespionage mission he and Tuppence are in the process of taking on, Tommy and Grant face the kind of challenge that Christie's readers often encounter, how to become aware of the singularity or particularity of someone who, "on the face of it," seems just like a dozen (or a thousand) people one has encountered before—whether in life or in British detective fiction. The fate of Europe and at least of England is said to hang in the balance as the Beresfords work to unmask an immensely threatening pair of individuals whose best disguise may be their appearance of utter ordinariness—"normativity." Tommy asks Grant what kind of town Leahampton is, what kind of people live there:

> "And Leahampton itself?"
> "Just like any other of these places. There are rows of them. Old ladies, old Colonels, unimpeachable spinsters, dubious customers, fishy customers, a foreigner or two. In fact, a mixed bag."
> "And N or M amongst them?"
> "Not necessarily. Somebody, perhaps, who's in touch with N or M. But it's quite likely to be N or M themselves. It's an inconspicuous sort of place, a boardinghouse at a seaside resort."[11]

When Tommy confers with Mr. Grant again later in the novel, once more about the inhabitants of the boardinghouse and the possibility or likelihood that one or both of the members of the enemy super-spy team have infiltrated the country and are living in some kind of disguise there, Tommy reports that so far only the landlady, Mrs. Perenna, strikes him as possibly "suspicious." Otherwise, he says, the boardinghouse is occupied by "a young mother, a fussy spinster, the hypochondriac's brainless wife, and a rather fearsome-looking old Irishwoman. All seem harmless enough on the face of it." Tommy and Grant have a little earlier reviewed the male population of the boardinghouse, which includes the aforementioned Major Bletchley, whose name (as we have seen) had briefly roused suspicion about Christie's own possible intention of blowing Bletchley Park's deep wartime cover. Here the character so named is said to "seem[ ] the ordinary type of retired officer. If anything, a shade too typical." A Mr. Cayley, also resident in the house, is checked off as "seem[ing] a genuine hypochondriacal invalid." And a young German man called Carl von Deinim is brushed aside as a possible enemy spy—his being German would make him too obvious.[12]

Taken together, the denizens of the boardinghouse are evoked with quite a stew of descriptors: "suspicious," "young," "fussy," "brainless," "fearsome-looking," "Irish," "harmless enough," "ordinary," "a shade too typical," "genuine," "hypochondriacal," "German." Some of these terms may express Mr. Grant's misogyny ("fussy," "brainless," "fearsome-looking" women) and/or his ethnic prejudices ("fearsome-looking Irish"), but a significant number of them (roughly half) betoken the effort to discern which of this motley assortment of apparently marginal- and insignificant-seeming persons is one of Hitler's "two ... most highly trusted agents" and a major threat to the Allied war effort. The vocabulary of "suspicious," "seem[ing]," "[-]looking" (i.e., "appearing") "genuine" shades into the complementary group of evaluative descriptors, "harmless enough," "ordinary," "typical," "too typical," and even (the sometimes crucial nuances of "typical" requiring it) "a shade too typical." After Tuppence and Tommy's first evening with this crew, they acknowledge to each other the difficulty they are having in taking their extremely serious mission seriously, "Can you honestly say you think any of these people ... could be a dangerous enemy agent," Tommy asks, and Tuppence admits, "It does seem a little incredible."[13] And yet one of these apparently stereotypically all-too-ordinary characters will climactically be exposed as the super-agent the Allies are seeking.

Besides focusing on identifying and analyzing the encoding of historically recognizable queer "types" in Christie's fiction, I believe it may be useful for understanding the richness and enjoyability of the work to consider the hypothesis that virtually anyone in it might be queer in one way or another, or perhaps in a number of ways. It has often been observed that a significant part of the interest that many readers take in her work is a response to the powerful sense that her narratives produce that virtually anyone might commit a murder. My discussion of *N or M?* provides only one example among dozens that Christie's mysteries provide us, of the kind of scrupulous attention and imagination that may be required in order for one to understand the possible gulf between who someone appears to be (or who we may take them to be) and the kind or kinds of actions and deeds of which they are capable, for better and/or worse, or have actually already performed and may well perform again. A Christie mystery novel published a couple of years before *N or M?* was entitled (in its UK edition) *Murder Is Easy*. The book was retitled *Easy to Kill* by Christie's U.S. publishers. Perhaps the U.S. publishers (Dodd, Mead) thought that her original title for the book, *Murder Is Easy*, sounded cynical, was potentially too shocking, or posed a possible threat to American morals: murder is *easy*? Is that such a scandalous revelation? Only a step away from that very sad but demonstrably not untrue observation about humans and human wretchedness, "Murder Is Normal."

Notes

1. Michael Smith, *Bletchley Park: The Code-Breakers of Station X* (Oxford: Shire, 2013), 32. Thanks to the participants in my short-course on Agatha Christie's work, held at the Fox Center for Humanistic Enquiry at Emory University in Fall 2014—especially to Carole Hahn, Ashley Shelden, Elizabeth Wilson, and Weny Worrall. I wish to thank the staff at the Fox Center, Amy Erbil and Colette Barlow, for their support of the course, and Millie Seubert, Jonathan Goldberg, and Marcie Frank for their interest in this essay. Finally, thanks to Curtis Evans for providing a venue for the essay and for his very stimulating ongoing research on the history of detective fiction.

2. Facts and figures about the size of the groups working together at Bletchley Park come from Smith, *Bletchley Park*.

3. For information about Alan Turing's life I have depended on Andrew Hodge's remarkably fine biography, *Alan Turing: The Enigma* (New York: Simon & Schuster, 1983).

4. See, for example, Hayley Dixon, "Alan Turing pardon should apply to all homosexuals, say campaigners," *The* [London] *Telegraph*, 24 Dec 2013.

5. Marke B., "'Breaking the Code' depicts the enigma of Alan Turing," posted on 48 Hills website 20 Aug 2015, at http://www.48hills.org/2015/08/15/breaking-code-alan-turing/.

6. Dennis Altman, "Reading Agatha Christie," posted on Inside Story website 5 Jan 2009, at http://insidestory.org.au/reading-agatha-christie/.

7. Owen Emmerson, "Queering Agatha Christie," posted on Headmaster Rituals website 13 June 2014, at https://headmasterrituals.wordpress.com/2014/06/13/queering-agatha-christie-2/

8. Robyn Wiegman and Elizabeth A. Wilson, "Introduction: Antinormativity's Queer Conventions," *differences: A Journal of Feminist Cultural Studies* 26:1 (2015), 13–17.

9. Gillian Gill, "Afterword: The Secret of Success," *Agatha Christie: The Woman and Her Mysteries* (New York: Free Press, 1990), p. 208.

10. For the fullest consideration to date of Christie's long and successful career as a playwright, see Julius Green, *Curtain Up: Agatha Christie, A Life in the Theatre* (New York: Harper, 2015).

11. Agatha Christie, *N or M?* (1941; repr., New York: William Morrow, 2012), 12.

12. Christie, *N or M?* 48–49.

13. *Ibid.*, 11, 22–23.

BIBLIOGRAPHY

Altman, Dennis. "Reading Agatha Christie." *Inside Story* (5 Jan 2009). At http://insidestory.org.au/reading-agatha-christie/.
Christie, Agatha. *N or M?* New York: G.P. Putnam's, 1941.
Emmerson, Owen. "Queering Agatha Christie." *Headmaster Rituals* (13 June 2014). At https://headmasterrituals.wordpress.com/2014/06/13/queering-agatha-christie-2/.
Gill, Gillian. "Afterword: The Secret of Success." In *Agatha Christie: The Woman and Her Mysteries*. New York: Free Press, 1990.
Green, Julius. *Curtain Up: Agatha Christie, A Life in the Theatre*. New York: Harper, 2015.
Hodge, Andrew. *Alan Turing: The Enigma*. New York: Simon & Schuster, 1983.
Smith, Michael. *Bletchley Park: The Code-Breakers of Station X*. Oxford: Shire, 2013.
Wiegman, Robyn and Elizabeth A. Wilson. "Introduction: Antinormativity's Queer Conventions." *differences: A Journal of Feminist Cultural Studies* 26:1 (2015): 1–25.

The Unshockable Mrs. Bradley
Sex and Sexuality in the Work of Gladys Mitchell

BRITTAIN BRIGHT

The author Gladys Mitchell is primarily known for her creation of a psychologist detective, the Freudian Mrs. Bradley, in a mystery series that spanned much of the twentieth century. Mitchell's novels are fascinatingly, and often disconcertingly, varied with respect to style, theme and structure; and unlike the stereotypical "whodunit?" these works reject the idea of closure. Mitchell's interest is in the process of inquiry, the endless work of detection. Her engagement with psychoanalysis and the ongoing nature of therapy focuses her narratives on conversation and interchange between characters, and it is thus that she develops these characters and explores the nature of their relationships.

Because of her interest in Freud, it is hardly surprising that Mitchell incorporates sexuality in her novels more obviously and far more frequently than many of her peers. In her varied and experimental work, Mitchell includes some patently Freudian imagery and diagnoses, but she also espouses a liberality that frequently verges on the radical. By the early 1930s, her heroine had advocated birth control, dismissed the idea that pornography was a malign influence, blithely overlooked incest and infidelity, and acknowledged homosexuality. Naturally, Mrs. Bradley is remarkably unshockable. The detective is also, crucially, not defined by her sex; while she is heterosexual, she is forcefully and notably unfeminine. As Patricia Craig and Mary Cadogan observe, "her qualities might be transferred to a male detective without loss of credibility. Allowing for the edge of fantasy [...] she exemplifies a type of professionalism which transcends sexual distinctions."[1] Indeed, by professionalising psychoanalysis as a mode of detection, and in the person of a woman, Mitchell uses the detective form to reconsider established ideas about gender, sexuality, and relationships.

As Samantha Walton points out in her study of insanity in detective fiction, Mitchell's work "helps uncover the golden age detective novel as a site in which politics and social conflict are approached both implicitly and explicitly."[2] Mitchell, and Mrs. Bradley, often point to sexuality as a potential motive, and in these novels it is a far more likely one than in those of Christie, for instance, where the threat of strong sexuality of any kind remains largely in the background. Mitchell's first novel, *Speedy Death* (1929), turns upon the sensational revelation that the murder victim, a famous explorer and adventurer who is engaged to the daughter of the house, is physically female. In this case, as in numerous others, Mitchell turns a novelistic trope on its head, and uses the preconceptions of the characters and of the reader to upset notions of a stable and socially functional sexuality.

The adventurer was a well-established secondary stock character in detective fiction; building upon H. Rider Haggard's "white hunter" Allan Quatermain, Arthur Conan Doyle created the vengeful Dr. Sterndale in "The Devil's Foot" (1910), and Christie included the explorer Major Blunt in the wide suspect pool in *The Murder of Roger Ackroyd*. Although Mitchell's reader is never introduced to Everard Mountjoy, it is natural to assume, like the newly arrived Dorothy Clark, that the explorer is "a large, hairy, loud-voiced, primitive sort of creature, with a red tie and a black beard." She is quickly disillusioned:

> "Oh, rot!" laughed Bertie. "He is a little, slim, clean-shaven, shy sort of fellow, with hardly a word to say."
> "Oh, I'd pictured him so differently. And isn't he even a sheik?"
> "Sheik be hanged! The chap seems terrified out of his life is anybody comes up and speaks to him.... He may get on well with lions and elephants, but I'm hanged if he's any catch as a fellow-guest."[3]

The explorer's profession implies an assertive masculinity that, while absent from the character's physical appearance (for obvious reasons), cannot be entirely separated from the reader's understanding. Given Mitchell's Freudian proclivities, it is almost necessary to read a dual meaning into Mountjoy's very name, drawing a connection between the pleasure of conquering the natural world (mountaineering), and the pleasure of sex with women (the Mount of Venus). This name asserts, for the physically female man, a definitive hyper-masculinity. That this masculine definition fails in the end is not, in the end, the fault of Mountjoy; instead, her engagement, exposure, and death are the result of her fiancée's repressed sexual impulses. *Speedy Death* is Mitchell's boldest experiment with gender, but it introduces themes that were to become central to her work; even as later novels dealt with controversial themes more subtly, she continued to explore sexuality as a motive, in crime and in life.

Mitchell's novels, taken as a whole, set up three distinct types of active sexuality (because not every character may be primarily distinguished by sexuality, even in the work of a self-professed disciple of Freud): repressed sexuality; Edenic, or developing, sexuality; and desirable, or confident, sexuality. Characters who fall into the first category are most often criminals, while those in the latter two are often assistants to the detective. The last category, confident sexuality, also allows Mitchell to explore the development of romantic relationships, and to speculate about the needs of the individual within a partnership.

Feminine Neuroses: Repressed and Dangerous Women

Mitchell's novels contain numerous unconventional sexual relationships, ranging from incestuous to homosexual to simply extramarital. However, the greatest threats arise from extreme interpretations of normative heterosexual behavior. As mentioned above, *Speedy Death* introduces the idea of the sexually repressed character as a likely criminal. Though most conventional discourses on criminality and sexuality after Lombroso assert that criminal women are over-sexed, Mitchell implies that there is far more danger in a lack of sexual expression.[4]

The most pronounced instance of this criminal tendency may be the obsessive paranoia exhibited by the vicar's wife Mrs. Coutts in *The Saltmarsh Murders* (1932): she is a married woman, but her own aversion to sex, coupled with her suspicions of her husband's sexual disloyalty, spurs her to commit murder. Mrs. Bradley observes her symptoms (and those of her household) before the fact: "The devil a monk would be! Took some pains to stir up Mrs. Coutts in order to test her reactions. She is absolutely unhinged on the subject of sexual relationships, and the vicar is horribly ill at ease." The jealous and stifled wife, in this case, becomes a crusader against sex itself, and as Mrs. Bradley asserts: "She probably considered that she was doing the will of God in ridding the earth of what she considered to be two dreadfully depraved and wicked people.... Of course, as the mania took root, there is no doubt that she would have considered herself a crusader against all sexual intercourse."[5]

The solution to this novel is not immediately obvious because the Wodehousian/Watsonian narrator Noel Wells "reproduces popular conservative discourses of doubt about, and good humoured resistance to, psychoanalysis."[6] Sexual motivation is evident, but easily misinterpreted: various other solutions are proposed during the course of the novel, including murder by a jealous lover. In the end, according to Mitchell, sexual inhibition is far more dangerous than sexual license.

While jealousy provides a powerful motive in Mitchell, it is rarely a straightforward one; murders are not committed by enraged lovers or by immediate rivals. For instance, the multiply unfaithful Mrs. Saxant in *Printer's Error* (1939) may be "the Delilah of the neighbourhood," but she is dismissed from that investigation as having insufficient motive to kill her lover's wife. Instead, sexual jealousy is characterized as a force that, if unacknowledged, unhinges the mind. In *Laurels Are Poison* (1942), the rivalry that leads to murder is many years in the past; rather than being concluded by the murder, though, it devolves into a bizarre game of cat-and-mouse that indicates, according to Mrs. Bradley, "a type familiar to all students of the morbid psychology of sex."[7]

In *The Devil's Elbow* (1951), there is actually no rivalry: a lonely and delusional woman murders an equally (though willfully) delusional one because she fancies the same man. "I heard Miss Pratt telling everybody she was going to meet Mr. Jeffries at the bottom of the garden," Miss Durdle confesses. "But he was mine, not hers, and so I told her." Mrs. Bradley observes, in the face of Inspector Gavin's protests about her respectability, "Respectability stands very little chance of holding the balance against the curious fancies of middle-aged spinsters, child. The cruel Mr. Gilbert knew that. I have never really liked his librettos." However, she insinuates, in a way, that it is that very desire for respectability that is a problem. Like Mrs. Coutts, Miss Durdle imposes her own conception of reality onto the world around her, with disastrous results. Her repression is evident in the language of her diary:

> My darling handsome George Jeffries hath shown his handmaid a mark of special favour. Pleaded I poverty to my lord, thinking to remain in the hotel and wash out my stockings and vest when others would sally forth with him.... But no, I was not allowed to remain behind. My lord would have me go with him. And oh, the wild lochs and high mountains! Oh, my wild heart and high hopes!
> "Lor'!" said Gavin. "Indelicate old party! She must be about twice young Jeffries' age!"
> [...]
> "There have been less obvious motives for murder," Mrs Bradley replied.[8]

Throughout the novel, suspects remark that Miss Pratt "asked for trouble" with her man-trap behavior, and she is killed because of it; however, Miss Durdle's absurd combination of courtly language and mundane detail, which in itself reveals a sexual fixation, demonstrates how far she is from a realistic and healthy attitude toward sexuality.[9] Ultimately, their actions are revealed as two different performances of the same sexual neuroses. The act that brings them together, the murder, takes place on a bank covered with hare-bells; a Freudian reading suggests that the flowers symbolize the sexual fixations of the two women, and the profusion thereof indicates an atmosphere saturated with sexual tension and deception. It is not always healthy to act upon one's sexual desires, as Miss Pratt demonstrates, but it is far more dangerous, suggests Mrs. Bradley, to deny its existence.

Mrs. Bradley herself, married at least twice (she has two names but in some books references three marriages), understands healthy desire psychologically and personally; she is sympathetic toward those who cannot, for various reasons, establish a functional sexual relationship. Lonely spinsters and children feature frequently in this capacity; the former, of course, are usually tragic figures, while the latter are typically characterized as heroes. Adolescent boys, who frequently figure in Mitchell's novels, are particularly representative of individual potential, ambition, and desire.

Mitchell's Boys: Developing Sexuality

Mitchell is, overall, more concerned with the motivations and dynamics of female sexuality, but her interest in developing sexuality is centered on adolescent boys. Perhaps because of her Freudian inclinations, Mitchell took repeated interest in this state of transition. Despite her assertion, "I have only academic knowledge of romance and sex," she also claimed a personal engagement with these characters, particularly with respect to *The Rising of the Moon* (1945), in which, she said, "I am Simon ... and my adorable brother Reginald is Keith."[10] Many of these boys find themselves simultaneously fascinated with a criminal investigation and with a woman, suggesting the potential dangers of the latter as well as the seductive appeal of the former. Women, like crimes, are puzzles to be solved.

The boys' adolescent sexuality may accurately be termed "Edenic," because boys are often characterized as ideal creatures in Mitchell's universe. As Mrs. Bradley and other character regularly assert, "Creation should have begun and ended with boys." These "inimitable and preternaturally favoured beings" exhibit, in many ways, an exemplary masculinity, as well as a trust in their own impulses.[11] Boys' ideas about, and performances of, heroism are genuine even if they are yet immature; the teenage Aubrey in *The Mystery of the Butcher's Shop* (1929) tempers an act of valor (attempting to protect his cousin by concealing evidence) with one of mischief (burying a fish in a hole resembling a grave), but he is more straightforward in both his motivations and his confessions than his adult relatives. Aubrey is the first iteration of the adolescent boy in Mitchell's work, and many of his characteristics define similar characters in later works: he is restless and inquisitive; his actions are bold and decisive, though rarely foolhardy; he is sensitive to atmosphere and environment, but maintains a distinct sense of self despite its influence;

and he attempts to behave with greater maturity for the benefit of an older girl.

More prominent are the boys in *Come Away, Death* (1937), who are in many respects the most reasonable and realistic characters in the novel; however, they too prefigure Mitchell's most notable boy character, Simon Innes, who is the narrator of *The Rising of the Moon*. This novel, one of Mitchell's rare but evocative forays into first-person narration, eloquently portrays the thoughts and desires of a thirteen-year-old boy, who is equally enthralled by the murder investigation and by his family's beautiful lodger Christina. Boys are also, potentially, a more obvious vehicle for the presentation of developing sexuality. Psychologist Deborah L. Tolman asserts that in adolescence girls succumb to male notions of sexuality, and thus become distanced from their own sense of self, becoming "ambivalent about desire" or learning to "disappear desire."[12] It is no coincidence that most of the intelligent and rational adults in Mitchell's universe are women, but that all of her intelligent and rational adolescents are boys: there is something about that developmental stage that seemed to her less authentic—or at least less legible (scriptable?)—about girls. She returns to girls as they become young women; the next section will address young female characters, chiefly Laura Menzies, who are close enough to adulthood to have gained a level of personal and sexual confidence.

Simon's growing awareness of his sexuality in *The Rising of the Moon* is one of Mitchell's most personal, and provocative, achievements. The conflict between Simon's understanding of himself as a child and as an adult is most developed through his interaction with Christina: he is sexually attracted to her, but emphasizes his youth to achieve an intimacy with her that would not be possible if he were even an older teenager. His tentative approaches to the sexual nature of his feelings for her are gentle and clumsy in equal measure.

> "Here, Christina!" I said. "Come in a minute and talk to us. We haven't seen you all day!"
>
> "That's not my fault," she said, laughing and coming in and shutting the door. "I can't see in the dark. Where are you?"
>
> "Here," I said; and pulled her down on to my bed, and put my arms round her. She smelt good, and her hands were small and soft, not big and always half-covered with cuts and scratches and callouses, like mine. She always seemed clean and fresh, and made me think of the cool bunches of bluebells that we used to gather in the woods beyond Dead Man's Island and bring home on the backs of our bicycles for her to put in jars. I tried to pull her down to lie beside me, but she would not let me do that. She had never known us as little boys, and it made a difference, I think.[13]

Simon expresses Christina's beauty through natural spaces and objects, through physical experiences of place and time that he associates with her. Her complete female physicality is still largely beyond him, so he expresses his attraction to her through an alternate, remembered physicality of nature. The flowers, as mentioned above, are also one of the many Freudian symbols in the text, nearly as evocative as the sabre and pistol that Simon and Keith carry. These symbols make explicit reference to the Freudian understanding of dreams; as such, their presence is part of the dreamlike state conveyed by much of the text. That state of transition in which Simon finds himself is akin to the border between dreaming and waking, and the way that aspects of one consciousness find their way into another.

The bluebells are also a courtly offering, an opportunity for Simon to act as her knight, a role that he attempts to take more seriously later in the novel, when Christina determines she must leave the Innes house: "'I'll get you some lodgings,' said I. 'You're not going to stay at the *Pigeons*, that I do know. June's a mean vixen, and I always thought Seabrook was an ass.'"[14] Simon alternates between characterizing himself as a child in order to be physically closer to her, and attempting to act "like a man" in order to take the role he really desires, that of her lover. When Christina dresses up to go to a dance, Simon cannot restrain his impulses:

> She put her arms round me, and I hugged her harder than I meant to, so that she lost her balance and came into my arms. I kissed her hard on the mouth, in the way that I had seen a man do before she smacked his face. That had been after a dance. She did not attempt to smack mine. She said, pushing me off and laughing:
> "Oh! Oh, darling, you'll be all over lipstick!" [...] I was blushing, but I was far more pleased than put out of countenance by the incident.[15]

This attempt at "manly" behavior (which, as Simon himself realizes, does not emulate the best example) conflicts with his typical performance of a childish role in Christina's presence. Though the boys' Aunt June does basic maternal duties by ensuring that they are fed, that they go to school, etc., it is Christina who makes small, loving gestures including tucking them in at night and buying them sweets:

> "What do you pretend, Christina, when we get on the bed with you like this?" asked Keith, as he wriggled because she was tickling his neck.
> "That I'm your mother," she answered seriously. I knew she meant it. She hated that we had not a mother. She wanted to be mother and sister and everything else in the world except what I wanted her to be. I knew I was in love with her, although it was a secret—the only one—that I ever kept from Keith.[16]

Christina tries to fulfill the boys' need for a mother figure, but in doing so she creates the conditions for Simon's desire to grow. Although he is fully aware that his feelings for her are not filial, he allows her to contextualize their relationship thus because it allows him to fulfill (or at least kindle) some aspect of his own desire.

Simon's conflation of the maternal and sexual relationship certainly implies an Oedipal aspect, but it may also allude to the construction of the lesbian relationship.[17] The fact that the novel lends itself easily to a Freudian reading means that it may not only be read for its delicate evocation of sexual desire, but for its implication of an unconscious state of sexuality. It is not difficult to draw a parallel between the developing sexual desire of the child and the process of becoming aware of same-sex desire. If Mitchell truly based the character of Simon on herself, it is certainly possible that her delicate evocations of his burgeoning desire also reflect her own experience. In any case, these boys rarely fulfill their amorous ambitions. Instead, the expression of a confident, adult sexuality is left to young women.

Laura Menzies: A Figure of Confidence

The "sidekick" character in the Mrs. Bradley novels transforms in the 1940s, from a boy into a young woman. This shift is primarily due to the introduction of Laura Menzies, who becomes an Archie Goodwin-esque secretary/assistant to the detective; while she does not narrate the stories, Laura's role as Watson makes her Mitchell's second most powerful statement of feminism (the first, of course, being the intimidating, wealthy, hyper-intellectual Mrs. Bradley herself). Largely replacing other, temporary, usually male Watsons, including Simon Innes and Noel Wells, Laura is denied their narrative control, but is a powerful character nonetheless. Like Simon, Laura represents an alternative, irreverent approach to detection that highlights Mrs. Bradley's eccentricity and her identification with youth; she is first introduced when she is Mrs. Bradley's student at Carteret College. However, Laura represents a very different approach to the subject of sexuality. Regularly described as "Amazonian," she is a figure of desire as well as aspiration.

When she strips off her clothes to dive into a freezing river in search of evidence in *Laurels are Poison* (1942), she exhibits masculine confidence, independence, and skill: "tall and big-limbed in her scanty bathing suit," she resists stereotypes of feminine physicality by proving physical strength and taking physical risks. A similar activity in a later novel has a rather different implication: masquerading as the naiad in *Death and the Maiden* (1947), she exhibits a decidedly feminine sexuality:

> "The water-nymph!"
> Mrs. Bradley glanced, stared, looked at the surrounding reeds and willow trees, and then again at the water. A splendid, naked figure, firm, buxom and rosy, had just dived over a great clump of flowering rushes and, entering the water like a spear-thrust, had left nothing but widening ripples and the half-echo of a splash to convince the watchers that they had not been mistaken.
> [...]
> [Mrs. Bradley] leaned on the rail and had the felicity to find, in the six-foot pool below the bridge, her handsome and graceless secretary.
> "Rather an outsize in grayling or trout," said Mrs. Bradley.
> "Hullo," said Laura. "Lucky it was you, and not the bishop or someone!"[18]

Though "handsome and graceless" rather than ultra-feminine, Laura is convincing in her brief appearance as a sexually appealing mythological being. Her motivations for a nude bathe are not entirely clear; she hints that she is working on the case by acting as a decoy naiad, but it is evident that she is also simply enjoying her swim. In this outing as in several others, Laura's powerful physicality is contrasted with those of her friends, the voluptuous Kitty and the small, wiry Alice, who are often "hypnotized ... by the spectacle of Laura in action."[19] The other "Musketeers," as Laura calls this group, act as a counterpoint to Laura's bold, almost masculine confidence: Kitty is ultra-feminine in both appearance and behavior, and Alice is nondescript, modest, and diffident, at least until action is needed. Laura naturally dominates the actions of the group, not by manipulation but through an apparently irresistible energy.

Linguistically, Laura plays the role of the fool, but her oblique exchanges with Mrs. Bradley demonstrate a similarly robust intelligence. *Twelve Horses and the Hangman's Noose* (1956), a novel in which Laura takes a prominent investigative role, offers insight into her most intimate relationships, those with her employer and her husband:

> "I did get prizes at school, including one of deportment," said Dame Beatrice with a triumphant leer. "I feel that you cannot match that."
> "I got a prize in my kindergarten for my cheerfulness," said Laura proudly. "It has stood me in good stead all my life. If you notice, I *am* cheerful. I feel I owe it as a duty, since I accepted the prize."
> "And what was the prize, child?"
> "A cruet set. A bit of a blow to one who had designs upon an infant's tricycle. But that's Fate. And Fate, as the Master of English Prose has indicated, is apt to lie in wait with a wet sandbag. Mind you, one becomes accustomed to these things. That's philosophy, that is."[20]

Such conversations depict a comfortable relationship in which two intelligent women indulge rather playful spirits. Laura colorfully paraphrases where Mrs. Bradley would quote, but there is no question that, despite her casual speech, she has an equally wide frame of reference and worldly knowledge. As B. A. Pike observes, her expression is "picturesque yet pertinent, with a vigorous crackle of metaphor, it moves in a headlong rush of slang, quotation, imprecation and flight of fancy."[21] In language, as in action, Mitchell emphasizes that Laura, like her employer, is not limited by her sex, but is physically and intellectually self-defined.

Laura's disappointment at receiving a prize related to housekeeping rather than sport, echoes the terms in which her marriage is described earlier in the novel:

> Nothing would have induced Laura to perform any ordinary household task—a point which she had explained to Detective Chief-Inspector Gavin before she married him.... She would ... take a bicycle to pieces, knock a handy nail or two into a piece of wood,

remove or put in screws correctly and competently—all, in her view, activities not prejudicial to human dignity; but the usual domestic work of women she held to be beneath contempt....[22]

From her first introduction, Laura exhibits a self-confidence that distinguishes her from a typically "feminine" character, and the way that she organizes her life. Though tomboyish, and closely bonded with other young women, Laura is definitely heterosexual. However, even after she is married to Inspector Gavin, her first loyalty is to her employer; she even lives primarily with Mrs. Bradley at the Stone House, while her husband has a flat in London. He even phones to ask permission to join her while she is at work, and she answers, "Yes, chump, of course you can come down. Quite pleased to see you on the whole.... I said On The Whole."[23] Teasing her husband with the idea of her ambivalence is typical. Their relationship, which is of course always developed in the context of an investigation, is friendly as well as passionate; this balance is crucial to the depiction of Laura's independence, but also to Mitchell's idea of a healthy relationship.

Mitchell does depict other marriages with far more traditional domestic arrangements, but, since Mrs. Bradley's own marriages are in the past, it is the Gavins' relationship that forms the dominant depiction of matrimony in the series. The Gavins' marriage is functional, Mitchell argues, because it lacks the obsessive characteristics that often lead to trouble in her works. Love, it seems, can stand the kind of distance that sexual obsession cannot. The mature relationship is that of two parties who maintain independence.

The Devil's Elbow: *Between Women*

A relationship of mutual independence, however, does not have to be between a man and a woman. In *The Devil's Elbow*, Mitchell creates a similarly adventurous and mischievous character, Miss Carter, who happens to have a female partner. Miss Carter, who is a crime novelist, joins in the investigation at points, and demonstrates a mischievous sense of humor and a practicality that certainly remind the reader of Laura, who is absent from this novel.

The Devil's Elbow is, among other things, a consideration of female relationships. The coach tour group includes two pairs of sisters, an elderly lady and her browbeaten companion, two irritatingly bright (if not so young) friends, and two lesbian couples. The temporary but intimate conditions of the coach tour bring forth similarities as well as disparities between individual characters (as mentioned above in the discussion of the apparently dissimilar Miss Durdle and Miss Pratt); also, the casual immediacy of interactions in this environment offers a very different way to look at relationships than, for instance, the community in which Dorothy L. Sayers sets *Unnatural Death*

(1927). In creating this spectrum of female relationships, Mitchell is, in the words of Teresa de Lauretis, considering (and frequently rejecting), "a popular feminist fantasy *which projects onto female sexuality certain features of an idealized feminist sociality*—sisterly or woman-identified mutual support, anti-hierarchical and egalitarian relationships, an ethic of compassion and connection, an ease with intra-gender affectionate behavior and emotional sharing, and a propensity for mutual identification."[24]

Few of the relationships between these pairs enact these values. Although the sisters are dependable and companionable (to each other and others), Miss Pew is offensively dominant, while Miss Nordle and Miss Pratt (the murder victim) are immature and competitive. The second lesbian couple, Miss Bernard and Miss Moxon, are not developed as characters until the latter part of the novel, when Mrs. Bradley and Gavin visit them at their dog kennels. They are both more stereotypically "lesbian" and more dependent on each other. They use the pet names "Bernie" and "Moxie," and Miss Bernard in particular does not relate well to others, confessing that she "only like[s] dogs and old Moxie."[25]

Miss Carter and Miss Baird do demonstrate some aspects of positive feminine sociality, but, as mentioned above, their relationship is easily equated with a healthy heterosexual one. They are the first passengers with whom Jeffries, the tour guide whose letters begin the novel, forms a bond, as well as an impression of the two that proves reliable. Jeffries' (and the author's) preference for this couple is far more dependent on their extroverted social behavior than on their relationship with one another. As he describes them on the first day of the trip:

> One is good-looking, the other not. Both middle-aged, and both seem sensible. Know their way about, too. I think this trip is chickenfeed to both. Same address on the backs of their luggage labels, I noticed, so I suppose they're what Maurice Richardson calls "jovial collar-and-tie spinsters." Easy to get on with, too, which is more than I am going to be able to say in favour of some of this menagerie.[26]

Lesbians, in this case, are unremarkable as such. Carter and Baird are characterized as widely social; they are not overly attached to or dependent on one another, and take a friendly interest in the other members of their party. They are so un-suspect as suspects that Mrs. Bradley and Gavin promptly enlist them as assistants in a reenactment of the crime; later, Miss Carter joins Jeffries and fifteen-year-old Robert for a cross-country chase after a suspicious caravan, and he singles her out for praise: "I ought to have guessed Miss Carter's intentions, but the male is a bit inclined, I suspect, to doubt the female's ability to do a bit of quick thinking. However, I take off my hat to the sex in the person of Miss Carter."[27] In this case, and in a very Laura Menzies–type way, Carter is an ideal woman, i.e., a woman whose thinking is not defined by her sex.

Carter's most "feminine" sociality appears not in relation to her partner, but in their ruse to embarrass Miss Pew and give her companion, Mrs. Adderley, a break. Even in this instance, she performs what would be Laura's role in another novel, the "masculine" one of driving Miss Pew in the car and decoying her to a grouse moor. Carter and Baird, in this instance as well as others, display a "mutual independence" akin to that displayed in Laura's relationship with her husband.

Toward the conclusion of the novel, when Mrs. Bradley and Detective Inspector Gavin visit the suspects in their homes, the lesbian couples, particularly Baird and Carter, are evidently both respectable and stable:

> Miss Baird and Miss Carter shared a large, untidy house looking on to a gorse-quickened common. They had lived in it for twelve not completely unruffled but definitely quite contented years, and had bought the house with the intention of remaining there together.
> They welcomed Gavin ... and hospitably strewed the belongings (with which most of the chairs were littered) on to a well-carpeted floor. They produced gin, bitters and sherry, and invited him to sit down and help himself.

This brief sketch indicates the kind of comfortable domesticity that might easily be ascribed to a married couple of a similar age, class, and professional status. Their profession as writers is not only unisex, but, crucially, creative: Freud argued that women's sexual repression inhibited thought and creativity of other kinds, so it follows, by implication, that the creative woman cannot be repressed.[28]

Sayers wrote of the Golden Age that "the detective-story has, in fact, sprung into a popularity and a respectability almost alarming to its friends. It is pleasant, of course, to feel oneself respectable and respected, but all privilege carries with it its own responsibilities"; the same might be said of such respectability as Baird and Carter have achieved in their life together.[29] Even the rather radical Mitchell terms the transgendered Mountjoy an "invert" (the proper medical term at the time) in 1929; however, in the 1950s, she seems to argue that it is no longer necessary to assign a label to "respectable" lesbians. This lack of a label may be contrasted to the questions that arise about the sexual motivations of Miss Cann, who is single, lies about her profession, and is altogether a more questionable character.

The stability of both lesbian couples in their homes and careers is also clearly opposed to the casual, indeterminate, and immature nature of Miss Pratt and Miss Nordle's relationship. After Pratt's death, Nordle asserts first that "we were very close friends," then declares, "actually, I didn't know Lilias at all well. I mean, up to this holiday, I suppose we hadn't, well, more than hardly met, except at the tennis club." These two might colloquially be called "frenemies": they compete to outdo one another in loud vivacity and aggressive flirtation. Jeffries writes, "The vicious Pratt and her satellite Nordle apparently had a *screamingly* funny time in Edinburgh ciné-photographing the natives. 'But a *screamingly* funny time, my dear!' Pratt shrieked this out all through dinner." As Miss Nordle relates the scene to Mrs. Bradley, "she yelled and screamed all during dinner, so of course I yelled and screamed too. I wasn't going to play second to Lilias Pratt."[30] The quiet maturity of the lesbian relationship—particularly that of the independent and socially-adept couple—is very obviously characterized as more respectable and congenial than the showiness of the younger women's friendship.

Pratt and Nordle are too competitive with each other, but also too dependent on each other. Successful friendship, Mitchell implies, requires the sort of complementarity that characterizes the "three Musketeers." Romances, meanwhile, require not only complementarity but distance and balance. If her depiction of Carter and Baird's relationship recalls that of Laura and Gavin, it reaffirms not only the freedom of women to be equal partners in a relationship (and to choose a partner of the sex they desire), but the freedom to exist as individuals beside that partnership.

Conclusion

Mitchell's defining statement about gender and sexuality, then, may be an assertion of equality. Walton situates her as a pioneering feminist interpreter of Freud,[31] and certainly her heroines embody a sense of competence identifiable with any definition of feminism. Whether she develops a character like Laura over the course of numerous novels, or, like Simon, through just one probing examination, Mitchell is continually engaged with individual desires and motivations, to which, essentially, she does not assign a gender. While her characters often reflect an apparently heterosexual normativity, their behavior often challenges the "normalcy" of any individual or, conversely, traditional definitions of psychological disorder.

While it is not, perhaps, useful to speculate on how these themes relate to Mitchell's personal life, her conception of "ideal" relationships suggests that her understanding of desire involved keeping a safe distance. Her emphasis on balance, and on honesty with oneself, leads to a speculation that her description of Simon as a version of herself could be revealing; though perhaps erroneous, it is tempting to read a growing recognition of same-sex desire into the boy's development of adult desires. The status of "normality" that she accords to Miss Carter and Miss Baird may be, after all, the highest compliment from a psychoanalytic standpoint.

The various characters discussed here are only a few of Mitchell's unconventional creations, but virtually any selection of her work will reject, or at least query, standard social conventions. Her focus on the individual leads to comic, perverse, or peculiar permutations of behavior, but not to proscriptions thereof. *Brazen Tongue* (1940) concludes with a telling exchange between Mrs. Bradley and her barrister son:

> "But, Mother, you can't behave like God and decide that Burt shall be arrested and Pat get off scot-free."
> "How do you know how God behaves?" asked his mother.[32]

Mrs. Bradley makes personal judgments and believes in their value, but she grants others their right to do the same. Mitchell writes her as a seeker of truth, but one who will never conclude that her truth is the only one. This opening of the detective formula is one of Mitchell's many provocations, and one which allows her to embrace the unconventional, the unnatural, and the transformative.

NOTES

1. Patricia Craig and Mary Cadogan, *The Lady Investigates: Woman Detectives and Spies in Fiction* (New York: St. Martin's Press, 1981), 181.
2. Samantha Walton, *Guilty but Insane: Mind and Law in Golden Age Detective Fiction* (Oxford: Oxford University Press, 2015), 16.
3. Gladys Mitchell, *Speedy Death* (London: Gollancz, 1929), 9. Allan Quatermain is the hero of Haggard's *King Solomon's Mines* (1885) and numerous other novels and stories published 1885–1927.
4. Cesare Lombroso and Guglielmo Ferrero, *Criminal Woman, the Prostitute, and the Normal Woman*, trans. Nicole Hahn Rafter and Mary Gibson (1893; repr., Durham: Duke University Press, 2004).
5. Gladys Mitchell, *The Saltmarsh Murders* (1932; repr., London: Vintage, 2009), 282, 277.
6. Walton, *Guilty*, 122.
7. Gladys Mitchell, *Printer's Error* (1939; repr., London: Minnow, 2008), 106; Gladys Mitchell, *Laurels Are Poison* (1942; repr., London: Hogarth, 1986), 233–34.
8. Gladys Mitchell, *The Devil's Elbow* (1951; repr., London: Sphere, 1988), 115–16, 219–20, 221.
9. Ibid., 130.
10. Gladys Mitchell, interviewed by B. A. Pike, "In Praise of Gladys Mitchell," *Armchair Detective* 9 (October 1976), repr., *The Stone House: A Gladys Mitchell Tribute Site*, at http://www.gladysmitchell.com/.
11. Mitchell, *Elbow*, 71.
12. Deborah L. Tolman, *Dilemmas of Desire: Teenage Girls Talk About Sexuality* (Cambridge: Harvard University Press, 2005), 48.
13. Gladys Mitchell, *The Rising of the Moon* (London: Michael Joseph, 1945), 39.
14. Ibid., 142.
15. Ibid., 58.
16. Ibid., 80–81.
17. As discussed in Teresa de Lauretis, *The Practice of Love: Lesbian Sexuality and Perverse Desire* (Bloomington: Indiana University Press, 1994), 186–88.
18. Mitchell, *Laurels*, 116; Gladys Mitchell, *Death and the Maiden* (London: Michael Joseph, 1947), 122.
19. Gladys Mitchell, *The Worsted Viper* (1943; repr., London: Minnow, 2009), 43.

20. Gladys Mitchell, *Twelve Horses and the Hangman's Noose* (1956; repr., London: Penguin, 1961), 61.
21. Pike, "Praise."
22. Mitchell, *Horses*, 49.
23. Ibid., 96.
24. de Lauretis, *Love*, 185–6.
25. Mitchell, *Elbow*, 202.
26. Ibid.,19.
27. Ibid., 149.
28. Ibid., 190; Sigmund Freud, *"Civilized" Sexual Morality and Modern Nervous Illness* (1908; repr., London: Read, 2014), 27–28.
29. Dorothy L. Sayers, Introduction to second series of *Great Short Stories of Detection, Mystery, and Horror* (London: Gollancz, 1931), 11.
30. Mitchell, *Elbow*, 24, 65, 69, 105.
31. Walton, *Guilty*, 65, 91–92.
32. Gladys Mitchell, *Brazen Tongue* (London: Michael Joseph, 1940), 318.

BIBLIOGRAPHY

Mitchell, Gladys. *Brazen Tongue*. London: Michael Joseph, 1940.
_____. *Death and the Maiden*. London: Michael Joseph, 1947.
_____. *The Devil's Elbow*. 1951. Reprint, London: Sphere, 1988.
_____. *Laurels Are Poison*. 1942. Reprint, London: Hogarth, 1986.
_____. *Printer's Error*. 1939. Reprint, London: Minnow, 2008.
_____. *The Rising of the Moon*. London: Michael Joseph, 1945.
_____. *The Saltmarsh Murders*. 1932. Reprint, London: Vintage, 2009.
_____. *Speedy Death*. London: Gollancz, 1929.
_____. *Twelve Horses and the Hangman's Noose*. 1956. Reprint, London: Penguin, 1961.
Craig, Patricia, and Mary Cadogan. *The Lady Investigates: Woman Detectives and Spies in Fiction*. New York: St. Martin's Press, 1981.
de Lauretis, Teresa. *The Practice of Love: Lesbian Sexuality and Perverse Desire*. Bloomington: Indiana University Press, 1994.
Freud, Sigmund. *"Civilized" Sexual Morality and Modern Nervous Illness*. 1908. Reprint, London: Read, 2014.
Lombroso, Cesare, and Guglielmo Ferrero. *Criminal Woman, the Prostitute, and the Normal Woman*. 1893. Translated by Nicole Hahn Rafter and Mary Gibson. Reprint, Durham: Duke University Press, 2004.
Pike, B. A. "In Praise of Gladys Mitchell." *Armchair Detective* 9 (October 1976).
Sayers, Dorothy L. Introduction. *Great Short Stories of Detection, Mystery, and Horror*. London: Gollancz, 1931.
Tolman, Deborah L. *Dilemmas of Desire: Teenage Girls Talk About Sexuality*. Cambridge: Harvard University Press, 2005.
Walton, Samantha. *Guilty but Insane: Mind and Law in Golden Age Detective Fiction*. Oxford: Oxford University Press, 2015.

"Less beautiful in daylight"
Josephine Tey and the Anxiety of Gender

J.C. Bernthal

"Humans are queer, aren't they, sir?"—Sergeant Williams in
A Shilling for Candles[1]

Introduction

Golden Age detective novelist Josephine Tey is enjoying a huge resurgence of interest of late. Her books have been reissued, an extensive biography has appeared, crime writers are clamoring to claim her as an influence and she has even featured as a sleuth in a popular series of novels. This essay considers one aspect of Josephine Tey's increasing relevance in these changing times: her approach to the question of gender identity.

Josephine Tey was a notoriously private person, a fact which has ironically led to a great deal of scrutiny of her private life in recent years. Many commentators find "the idea of a deep dark secret" that Tey was hiding to be "irresistible." The crime writer Val McDermid, one of Tey's most vocal admirers, laments that, "sadly," any such secret is "destined to remain hidden."[2] McDermid is hinting that Tey may have been a lesbian; similar theories, with varying degrees of corroboration, have surrounded Gladys Mitchell, Ngaio Marsh and even the married Margery Allingham. Meanwhile, Jennifer Morag Henderson devotes frantic paragraphs in her 2015 biography of Tey to insisting that the crime writer was completely heterosexual, all the while drawing on as little evidence as those whose opinion she disputes.

It may be inspiring to find and label historical figures who might today identify along LGBTQ lines. For some people, on the other hand, anything but the presumption of heterosexuality will always be disrespectful. However, dead people are not here to have a say in how the world perceives who they are. Moreover, sexuality has not always been measured consistently, and labels like "gay" and "straight" meant different things in different decades. Surely it is arrogant, even dangerous, to suggest that in our current unequal world we have finally unlocked the full catalog of human identity, and that we can backdate our own inadequate vocabulary. To thrust these labels upon historical figures may seem anything from naive to dishonest.

Elizabeth Mackintosh, to use Tey's real name, never publicly discussed her private life but she did find pleasure in being "held to be slightly queer."[3] This remark was a reference not to her sexuality but to the fact that she disliked having a social life. Her preference for solitude was held to be odd, especially moving as she did in theatrical circles: she was a well-known playwright who numbered West End stars among close friends. I would like now to read some of Tey's detective novels through a "slightly queer" lens. What this means is that I will not seek to identify homosexual, bisexual or transgender characters but to look at themes that may run counter to received ideas about what people should do or be. As stated, my focus here is on gender as a defining element of personal identity.

Alternative Masculinities

Critical perspectives on Tey's work have been rare—even Martin Edwards' magisterial *The Golden Age of Murder* only mentions her twice, once in a footnote. (This is partly because Tey, who was almost pathologically shy, did not join the Detection Club, a high-profile body of mostly British crime writers that has existed since 1930. While Agatha Christie cultivated an aura of mysterious secrecy around her private life, Tey simply avoided the limelight). What Tey criticism exists is generally enthusiastic. Christina R. Martin has praised Tey's "[s]triking ... presentation of women characters, through whom she expressed ideas much in advance of the time in which she was writing." According to Martin, Tey presents heroines who should be "admired for [their] lack of conventional femininity," while also rejecting the idea that they have any definitive essence, feminine or otherwise. There is a sense, for Martin, "of her characters having two identities."[4] Dual identities and the question of femininity are key themes that this investigation will pursue. While I am not keen to make grand claims about the author at the expense of what the texts have to say, it is worth noting that she used two very different pseudonyms to write, and sometimes books written under one name were reissued under the other.

Several novels have been published, at one time or another, under the name Josephine Tey. Some of these were written as Gordon Daviot, Mackintosh's favored pseudonym, and later republished. Of interest here are the detective stories that feature her series character, Inspector Alan Grant. There are, in total, six: *The Man in the Queue* (1929), *A Shilling for Candles* (1936), *The Franchise Affair* (1948), *To Love and Be Wise* (1950), *The Daughter of Time* (1951) and *The Singing Sands* (1952). For reasons that will become obvious, *To Love and Be Wise* is particularly relevant.

Grant is a policeman, although he also falls into the amateur sleuth camp, because he has enough independent wealth to retire whenever he loses interest in the job. He is a remarkable detective because of his subtle characterization, far removed from the eccentricities of Hercule Poirot, Peter Wimsey and Adela Lestrange Bradley. He is also unmarried and—for the most part—not particularly interested in women, with a sensitive side that sees him mocked and revered in equal measures by other characters in the books. Like P. D. James' later detective, Adam Dalgliesh, Grant has an interest in poetry that becomes important in more than one plot.

The first appearance of the police force in a Grant novel involves a reference to "a manicured finger" belonging to a superintendent. The superintendent makes his taller, more imposing subordinates hide their stature so that they appear shorter, and he envies Inspector Grant's "dapper," "chic" "flair for the sartorial." Grant's own chief subordinate, Sergeant Williams, is "his opposite and his complement": a bulky, burly man with "terrier qualities" who could never be taken for anything but a policeman. Readers are often told that Williams has "hero-worshipped Grant for years."[5] He respects Grant for not looking the part while being able to provide brute strength and intuition when the job demands it.

In *To Love and Be Wise*, Grant and his officers drag a river looking for a corpse. Grant quotes a poem about the suspected victim's beauty. He instructs his colleague, Rodgers, on the formal techniques and social significance of poetry. Suddenly, he laughs. "I was just thinking," he explains, "how shocked the writers of slick detective stories would be if they could witness two police inspectors sitting on a willow tree swapping poems."[6] Here, Tey-the-author is further humanizing her character while also pointing out how unlike his contemporaries he is. However, Grant is not alone in this scene, reflecting on his tragic inadequacy as a "slick" hero. He is sharing his predilection for poetry with the stocky Inspector Rodgers. Rodgers has a telling response at this point: he recalls a colleague who reads police procedurals for "howlers"—mistakes about police work.

The entire police force, and not just Grant, appears in Josephine Tey's fiction as falling short of mythical masculine standards. From the manicured superintendent who makes his subordinates pretend to be shorter than they are, to the walking stereotypes in lower ranks who nonetheless envy and idolize Inspector Grant's dapper sensitivity, the force appears more emotionally complex than it does in much contemporary fiction. The police in Tey's literary world are more benevolent than readers might expect. They are also, like the criminals and suspects they investigate, frustrated by gendered expectations that surround them. At the center of this, of course, is Alan Grant.

Alternative Desires

In the final Tey novel, Grant battles strong psychological demons, falling victim to post-traumatic stress and claustrophobia, and he worries that Sergeant Williams will become aware of his sensitivity; that "admiration" will give way to "pity." The final line in this passage is an innocuous piece of dialogue, but perhaps its first two words are significant: "'Push over the marmalade,' Tommy said."[7]

The husband of Grant's cousin, Tommy shared with Grant a dormitory at school. "There was no intimacy so close," he thinks, watching Tommy with "silence and affection" and marveling that "in all essentials" the "ingenuous" boy who needed help getting dressed is still the same.[8] We need not read this sexually to appreciate the homoerotic coding, and indeed there is something deeper here. Grant, with his sense of divided self, sees in Tommy all the innocence of same-sex intimacy, which cannot happen in manhood without consequences.

Although the text makes some references to Grant forsaking family life on account of his job, this may be too easy an explanation for his unconventional relationships with women. Remarkably for a detective in fiction—even today—Grant has several close friends who are young women, without a trace of romance between them. In particular, he has a good friend in the actress Marta Hallard, a recurring character who provides a splendid insight into Tey's theatrical friendships. It is all too uncommon to find strong women characters who exist as something other than love or sex objects for the male characters and/or readers. Marta Hallard is that rare thing: a fully-realized, fully dimensional, fully engaging character who exists in her own right and who is a woman. Val McDermid calls Grant and Hallard's relationship "unconventional enough to be a striking choice."[9]

Wondering why other men—or, as he puts it, "men"—do not "go for" Hallard, Grant speculates that they may "f[ind] her intimidating" because of her lack of conventional femininity: "No questions, no hints, no little feminine probings. In her acceptance of a situation she was extraordinarily masculine." Yet this is why he likes her: "How admirable, he thought ... how truly admirable." The unfortunate word here is "masculine" in the place of "stoic" or "unemotional." Surely, Grant cannot mean he likes Hallard for being manly? After all, his chief claim to manhood—his job—depends on his asking questions and refusing to accept a given situation that he has not vetted. In their first case together, *The Man in the Queue*, it is Grant who speculates on whether a Hollywood starlet was a virgin while Hallard tears around the country in a motor car, disconcerting men who would otherwise be flirting, with her "queer taste" in clothes.[10] Perhaps the two get on well because neither is too heavily confined by social prescriptions for what men and women should be. Perhaps this is how they can share an intense and loving friendship in the face of generic precedent suggesting that they should marry.

Grant's most intense relationship is with himself. Often he is confused or angry by how invested he is in the life or death of some young man. It is Grant's curious attraction to dead men that gets him started on several cases—although in *A Shilling for Candles*, which opens with a woman's death, he is drawn to the rakish prime suspect. Things become extreme in the final novel, *The Singing Sands*. Grant is now having full arguments with internal demons, related in speech with inverted commas. After seeing a good-looking man die on a train, Grant has been drawn to the dead man's handwriting, finding it "somehow attractive," and has pursued an unofficial investigation into the incident. When he tells his demons that he is just pursuing justice in the case of a suspicious death, an internal voice responds, "You lying dishonest bastard," and asks a rhetorical question: "If the [dead man] had been a fat commercial traveler with a moustache like a badly kept hedge and a face like a boiled pudding, would you still have been interested?" Elsewhere in the novel, Grant watches his happily married cousins and contemplates marriage himself—something McDermid reads as necessary camouflage for strong "homosexual" "coding." However, even as he does so, Grant's inner voice tells him to "get away from" "the fairy-tale" and back to the man he is investigating.[11] It is just about possible to read this as intense investment in his work that gets in the way of family life—but we have seen that questions surrounding masculinity, emotion and relationships simmer beneath such tensions.

The question of homosexual desire is only raised around Grant once. Like many twentieth century crime writers, Tey tapped into queer stereotypes when creating her colorful array of characters—but making any series character, let alone a detective, homosexual was unthinkable. So unthinkable, in fact, that Tey's characters are loudly silent on the topic.

To briefly set the scene: a mysteriously beautiful young man has appeared in a quiet, conservative village where Grant happens to be visiting with Hallard. Grant himself is intoxicated when he sees Searle at a party: the man appears "divorced ... from his surroundings" and Grant is terrified at the idea that Searle is not famous, "that those cheekbones were being wasted in a stockbroker's office." But, he rationalizes, perhaps it is all a trick of the evening light, "and the young man [will] be less beautiful in daylight."[12]

Everybody is slightly afraid of the enigmatic Leslie Searle. One day, he vanishes almost without a trace. Williams asks Grant what Searle was like:

> "A very good-looking young man indeed."
> "Oh," Williams said, in a thoughtful way.
> "No," said Grant.
> "No?"
> "American," Grant said irrelevantly.... [H]e added: "He seemed to be interested in Liz Garrowby, now that I remember."[13]

In fact, Liz Garrowby was interested in him; Leslie Searle pursues friendships with men and women and inspires their mystified attraction, but he never seems romantically or sexually inclined towards anybody. For context, the above passage occurs directly after a lengthy discussion of Williams' "mild hero-worship" for Grant.[14] The idea of Searle's homosexuality is, here, unthinkable because it would mean Grant's being acquainted with the codes and implications—and would lend a new significance to the sensitive masculinity that Williams so admires. Grant quickly explains away Searle's otherness ("American"! That explains it!) and invents a heterosexual romance.

Alternative Genders

To Love and Be Wise, then, makes the fear and silences around Grant's gender nonconformity more prominent than the other books. The solution to its animating puzzle is important: it turns out that the mysterious Leslie and a barely-mentioned female cousin, Lee Searle, are one and the same. Nobody killed or abducted Leslie Searle; he simply ceased to be. According to Nicola Humble, a scholar of the twentieth-century "middlebrow," it is telling that "transvestism and hints of lesbianism ... are considerably less worrying to the text than Searle as a male homosexual."[15] This is a valid reading, but I would like to dig a little deeper. The fear of male homosexuality is part of a wider illustration of social panic concerning the prescribed rigidity of gender identities. As I hope I have indicated above, Grant himself is central to that panic.

Today, cross-dressing as a literary device may seem anything from cheap to cheesy. As early as 1992, the gender theorist Marjorie Garber proclaimed it "a classic strategy of disappearance in detective fiction.... The lady vanishes by turning into a man—or the man by turning into a woman."[16] However, there is surprisingly little of it, in puzzle-based detective fiction particularly, in the first three-quarters of the twentieth century. Agatha Christie used the device more than once and a rather egregious late Ellery Queen novel features an offensive portrait of a transgender woman as its criminal. We should not, though, assume that Tey's readers in 1950 will have been prepared for the novel's denouement. For one thing, it is not a simple case of cross-dressing;

Lee Searle has fully become Leslie Searle for a long period of time. For another, Tey has clearly not picked the "trick" out of a hat and clued it with a few references to the man's unconventionality: *To Love and Be Wise* stands as a social commentary, illustrating a variety of social pretenses and discomforts woven around the theme of an exotic man whom people are drawn to but for whom they are totally unprepared.

The word most used of Searle is "beautiful." Only Grant calls him "good-looking" and that is in a conscious understatement, as discussed; elsewhere, he too thinks of Searle as a "beautiful young man," and is "disconcerted" by the thought. Other people also find him "disconcerting": Liz, the admirer mentioned above, feels an inexplicable urge "to cross herself, or utter charms against him." She has no idea why: she has known lots of attractive men, but this is something different. There is something sinister about a man being that beautiful: "uncanny," says one character, "there is no other word." She goes on to describe having "the same 'kick' out of being in a room with him that I would get out of being in a room with a famous criminal. Only nicer, of course." The local vicar only half-jokingly describes Searle as a demon and he is twice compared to Lucifer: "A fallen glory. A beauty turned evil."[17]

Beyond the world of the novel, male beauty is too problematic to think about. As Agatha Christie put it in her 1969 crime novel, *Hallowe'en Party*, "You said of a young man that he was sexy or madly attractive.... You didn't say a young man was beautiful." Tey's reviewers, if not her readers, agreed. Writing in the *Australian Women's Weekly*, Ainslie Baker did her best to paint Tey the author as ultra-feminine: one of the "charming" leading "ladies" of detective fiction, distinguished by an "airy touch." Baker does not use the word "beautiful" when describing the plot, instead introducing Searle as a "handsome" youth—a much less challenging word when talking about a man. Baker concludes with an attempt to smooth over her palpable discombobulation: "In the last chapter Miss Tey propounds a solution whose silliness can only be partly redeemed by the preceding 236 pages of most agreeable reading."[18] In other words: let us not think about such things; let us change or ignore the details we do not like, and dismiss all this social commentary under the banner "agreeable reading."

Searle's uncanny beauty, then, has a lasting bite that reaches beyond the written word. As a presence in the novel, he brings out inconvenient truths in the other characters. Well-spoken individuals, we are told, tend to "revert ... to the vernacular" when speaking of him. Liz sees the man she eventually marries alongside Searle and realizes for the first time that he—the pretentious other man—is "human, and imperfect," with a lined face and receding hair, "not something of inhuman beauty that had walked out of some morning of the world beyond our remembering." More amusingly, a self-made millionaire who prides himself on his working class roots lets slip his privileged background, a lawyer whose practice carries several grand names admits that none of these people exist and a flamboyant foreigner whose personality is "built on [tales of] Russia" is revealed to have no grasp of the Russian language. Once gender norms are complicated, expectations must be changed and any number of social rituals may eventually be rethought. As Grant states in his most famous case, *The Daughter of Time,* "how small and queer the world looks right way up."[19]

Alternative Lives

The reader discovers that Leslie is Lee (or, rather, that Lee had been Leslie), through an intellectual discussion of "transvestism." At this stage, the successfully duped reader believes Grant is meeting Lee Searle for the first time, and that she is an artist who had little to do with her photographer cousin, Leslie. Before anything, Grant forms an impression of Lee: "She was a tall woman, and spare; very good-looking in her bony fashion and still quite young.... [S]he had the long legs that helped to give Marta her elegance."[20] Notice how completely different this description is to that of Leslie. Although we are about to learn—and the most alert readers will have worked out—that they are the same person, the descriptions here have opposing inflections. It is an inventory of features with a kind of laconic disapproval about it; there are none of the allusions to classical Greece that surrounded Leslie, no speculations on where those features are being worshipped or wasted, and certainly no sense of uncanny curiosity or soul-searching.

Instead, the subject is faintly condemned. She is "spare" rather than slim or petite, she is only good-looking "in her bony fashion," and rather than exhibiting the intoxicating vitality of youth, she is "still quite young" (she is twenty-one). Her "long legs" are not even hers, they are the exact same legs, apparently, that Marta has, and they "help" Marta but—well, the effect on Lee is not mentioned. As a woman, then, Lee Searle cannot just have an effect on Grant. Rather, all her physical qualities must be itemized for effectiveness and put into a register that contains the details of the other women he knows. Grant is more open-minded and sensitive than most policemen of fiction, but he is still a man.

This, then, is the context in which Grant unveils his discovery. Glancing around Searle's flat, he notes her peculiar books. Searle seems unphased:

> "I think all artists are attracted by the odd, whatever the medium, don't you?"
> "You don't seem to have anything on transvestism.... Is it something that doesn't interest you?"
> "The literature of the subject is very unsatisfactory, I understand. Nothing between learned pamphlets and the *News of the World.*"[21]

The topic has been gently introduced. It has been contextualized as artistic, decadent, eccentric, "odd." However, as the penny begins to drop with even the slowest reader—Grant's next line is "You ought to write a treatise on the subject"—it becomes clear that cross-dressing has social implications. In 1950, the space between scholarship and tabloids was vast. Some "learned pamphlets," indeed, were still being written in Latin, precisely to avoid being read by the uneducated, while the *News of the World*, Britain's premier Sunday tabloid which folded in 2011, has always been notorious for relying on gossip and titillation.

Some context is needed here. Today, no self-respecting middle-class person would admit to watching *The X Factor*, but to claim to have no idea of what that program is would be disingenuous at best. The same was true of the more lurid Sunday newspapers in 1950, and in the decade following World War II, they were dominated by one type of headline. Alison Oram puts it best in her study of the phenomenon: *Her Husband Was a Woman!*[22] Oram looks at two newspapers—*People* and the *News of the World*—which ran hundreds of stories between them in the 1940s and 1950s concerning "mannish" women or women who passed as men. Often, they would dress as men in order to marry same-sex partners, or for longer periods of time to join the armed forces. Oram shows that earlier stories praised these women for patriotically wishing to fight and work alongside men. As the specter of war grew very slowly fainter, the tone became more condemning as cross-dressing was linked with lesbianism, and readers were encouraged to consider conventional couples they knew as potentially unholy same-sex unions. Ultimately, the successful cross-dresser was described in exotic terms, representing a different world, unfettered by conventional morality codes, at which readers could wondrously gawp.

It is reasonable to expect that Tey's British readers will have understood some of the discussions surrounding gender-switching when *To Love and Be Wise* was published. However, these were incredibly limited versions of events, with no apparent concession to the complexity of gender identity itself. Sex reassignment surgery has been taking place since 1931, although it did not become common knowledge in Britain until the high-profile career of transsexual model April Ashley in the 1960s. Underlying each newspaper story—and, unfortunately, most scholarship—was the core principle that the person who "became a man" for sexual or career purposes was "really a woman." Moving in transatlantic, artistic, and sometimes avant-garde circles, Tey would doubtless have been aware of trans people, and of the reality that some people were not assigned the correct gender at birth. However, she claims to be writing about "transvestism."

Notably, Lee or Leslie Searle does not have a military background and is not trying to marry a woman. As far as Tey's readers were concerned, this was not a typical cross-dresser—although, in real life, gender was and remains more fluid in the artistic sphere than in any other. "Transvestism," well-known through select narratives only, is part of a brutally limited understanding of gender norms in society that Tey's novels reflect.

When Grant suggests that Leslie was Lee in disguise all along, she does not disagree. He asks her why she did it, prefixing his remark with some rather leading opinions: "Some, of course, are genuinely happier in men's things; but a great many do it from love of adventure, and a few from economic necessity. And some because it is the only way in which they can work out their schemes."[23]

Presented with a handy list of options, Searle explains the "necessity" of her "disguise"—but we can decide whether this is really a satisfactory solution. Searle spends several pages describing an English friend she occasionally saw, Marguerite, who was engaged to a local in the village and who committed suicide after it fell through. Marguerite, we hear, had "a shining quality" that entranced the young Searle. She explains that she turned up in the village to avenge the death, but found out that Marguerite had not been a very nice person after all, and, unable to do murder, she disappeared.

So far, so good, but why the disguise? Nobody in the village knew the American Searles. Following the sensational build-up, and 1,000 words on Marguerite, we get 300 words on why Lee became Leslie. The thing is mostly dealt with in one paragraph: the reasons were professional. "A girl alone is always having trouble [and] has a more difficult time getting an 'in' .... So I tried it out for a little. And it worked."[24]

To escape from the village where he has not really done much but wind people up and disconcert them with his beauty, Leslie Searle had to cease to be. Of course. (It is difficult to know which pronoun to use here. I shall now use "she" as Searle relates this story while identifying as a woman.) To achieve this, we discover, Searle threw away her Leslie things and escaped as a woman. For this, she had to get hold of "convincing" garments like "gloves" and "lipstick" that would dispel "any doubt ... as to my sex." It is interesting that more dressing up is required to be read along the lines of her "true" sex. Indeed, she describes her "real" identity tellingly: as "[a] personality all ready for [Leslie] Searle to dissolve into."[25]

Perhaps that unhappy reviewer had the right idea describing this solution as silly. Taken at face value, it does not add up. A beautiful, intoxicating man, whose very existence makes those around him explore their deepest, truest selves, turns out to be a woman in disguise who has created the persona for unrelated professional reasons and suddenly abandoned it over a casual friendship with a bizarre intensity. Anyway, it satisfies Grant, who does not press charges. "You're cured," he tells Searle, confident that she will grow out of everything. But perhaps there is another solution that Tey could not write or even contemplate.

Conclusion

Searle was clearly in love with Marguerite. Whether this was an adolescent crush or something deeper does not matter. If Searle lived for years as a man for professional reasons, that makes sense, but why turn up in the village like this? Searle makes it clear that she mostly lives as a woman, except when engaged in work, so the whole story seems fishy—unless Searle is escaping to England to explore living with a new gender identity. The disappearance comes after disillusion over Marguerite: the rejection of an easy correlation between gender and sexuality. Now that the one version of love has been dashed, if Searle has built a gender identity around romantic preferences alone, his whole new identity has fallen apart. Searle, then, has to disappear, to occupy to sexless liminality of a New York artistic studio.

Searle continues to have an uncanny impact once the text has accepted her as a woman. The novel closes with Grant entertaining a wild fantasy about taking Lee Searle to a forthcoming masquerade. Now that she is a woman, it is all right for him to desire her on his arm. But, of course, he dismisses the thought. Leslie Searle is still a disturbing presence, who has challenged received notions of gender, attraction and identity.

The detective fiction of Josephine Tey opened a range of possibilities for subsequent crime writers to explore concerning gender identity with all its internal conflicts and their consequences. As discussed, Val McDermid has claimed Tey as a key influence. McDermid's first mainstream detective novel, *The Mermaids Singing* (1995), also features a shock solution based on transgender themes. In McDermid's novel, the killer is a woman whom nobody has investigated, partly on the grounds that a man's physical strength and the psychological profile of a gay man are on the suspect profile. The twist is, of course, that she is a transgender woman. Ostensibly, McDermid writes in more enlightened times, but perhaps the restrictions on Tey's subjects and vocabulary produced a less problematic text. While McDermid perpetuates some extraordinarily damaging stereotypes about transwomen being effectively gay men who are "biologically male" and dangerously violent, Tey writes of a world that is introspectively disconcerted by new takes on the gender binary. She is self-conscious in not expressing what she is writing about. Gender identity is a strong, open theme in the Alan Grant novels, and a knotty problem with no obvious answers.

NOTES

1. Josephine Tey, *A Shilling for Candles* (1937; repr., London: Pan, 1960), 81.
2. Val McDermid, "Behind the Twitching Curtain: The Brilliant Unconventional Crime Novels of Josephine Tey," *Daily Telegraph: Arts and Books*, 15 Nov. 2014, 20.
3. Quoted in Nicola Upson, "Josephine Tey: Fact and Fiction," *Nicola Upson*, [n.d.], at http://www.nicolaupson.com/fact_and_fiction/index.html.

4. Christina R. Martin, "Josephine Tey: Scottish Detective Novelist," *Studies in Scottish Literature* 29 (Jan. 1996): 193, 197, 199.

5. Josephine Tey [originally as Gordon Daviot], *The Man in the Queue* (1929; repr., London: Arrow, 2011), 8; Josephine Tey, *To Love and Be Wise* (1950; repr., Harmondsworth: Penguin, 1978), 73-74; Josephine Tey, *The Singing Sands* (1952; repr., London: Arrow, 1988), 20.

6. Tey, *Wise*, 151.

7. Tey, *Sands*, 21.

8. *Ibid.*, 18-19.

9. McDermid, "Curtain," 21.

10. Tey, *Wise*, 161; Tey, *Queue*, 43, 97.

11. Tey, *Sands*, 18, 60, 118; McDermid, "Curtain," 20; Tey.

12. Tey, *Wise*, 9.

13. *Ibid.*, 75.

14. *Ibid.*, 74.

15. Nicola Humble, "The Queer Pleasures of Reading: Camp and the Middlebrow," in Erica Brown and Mary Grover, eds., *Middlebrow Literary Cultures: The Battle of the Brows, 1920-1960* (Basingstoke: Palgrave Macmillan, 2012), 226.

16. Marjorie Garber, *Vested Interests: Cross-Dressing and Cultural Anxiety* (New York: Routledge, 1992), 186.

17. Tey, *Wise*, 12, 15, 19, 23, 51, 60, 113.

18. Agatha Christie, *Hallowe'en Party* (1969; repr., London: HarperCollins, 2001), 140; Upson, "Josephine Tey."

19. Tey, *Wise*, 22-23, 108, 114, 130, 203; Josephine Tey, *The Daughter of Time* (1951; repr., New York: Scribner, 1995), 165.

20. Tey, *Wise*, 191.

21. *Ibid.*, 192.

22. Alison Oram, *Her Husband Was a Woman! Women's Gender-Crossing in Modern British Popular Culture* (New York: Routledge, 2008).

23. Tey, *Wise*, 193.

24. *Ibid.*, 198.

25. *Ibid.*, 198-9.

BIBLIOGRAPHY

Christie, Agatha. *Hallowe'en Party*. 1969. Reprint, London: HarperCollins, 2001.

Edwards, Martin. *The Golden Age of Murder: The Mystery of the Writers Who Invented the Modern Detective Story*. London: HarperCollins, 2015.

Garber, Marjorie. *Vested Interests: Cross-Dressing and Cultural Anxiety*. New York: Routledge, 1992.

Henderson, Jennifer Morag. *Josephine Tey: A Life*. Dingwall: Sandstone, 2015.

Humble, Nicola. "The Queer Pleasures of Reading: Camp and the Middlebrow." In *Middlebrow Literary Cultures: The Battle of the Brows, 1920-1960*. Edited by Erica Brown and Mary Grover. Basingstoke: Palgrave Macmillan, 2012. pp. 218-230.

Martin, Christina M. "Josephine Tey: Scottish Detective Novelist." *Studies in Scottish Literature* 29 (Jan. 1996): 191-204.

McDermid, Val. "Behind the Twitching Curtain: The Brilliant Unconventional Crime Novels of Josephine Tey." *Daily Telegraph: Arts and Books*, 15 Nov. 2014, 20-21.

_____. *The Mermaids Singing*. 1995. Reprint, London: Harper, 2011.

Oram, Alison. *Her Husband Was a Woman! Women's Gender-Crossing in Modern British Popular Culture*. New York: Routledge, 2008.

Tey, Josephine. *The Daughter of Time*. 1951. Reprint, New York: Scribner, 1995.
_____. *A Shilling for Candles*. 1937. Reprint, London: Pan, 1960.
_____. *The Singing Sands*. 1952. London: Penguin, 1988.
_____. *To Love and Be Wise*. 1950. Harmondsworth: Penguin, 1978.
_____ [originally as Gordon Daviot]. *The Man in the Queue*. 1929. Reprint, London: Arrow, 2011.
Upson, Nicola. "Josephine Tey: Fact and Fiction." *Nicola Upson*, [n.d.]. At http://www.nicolaupson.com/fact_and_fiction/index.html.

"Mutually devoted"
Female Relationships in Josephine Tey's Miss Pym Disposes

MOIRA REDMOND

Introduction

The all-female educational establishment is a gift to fiction writers in a quite different way from boys' schools and colleges. There is an emphasis on stress and strong feelings: in Hilary Mantel's novel *An Experiment in Love*, the narrator says of the female student dorm "What did people do for a metaphor, before the pressure-cooker was invented?"—a pertinent question.

And of course we all know what the pressure is going to lead to: lesbianism. In a similar male circle there is a feeling that homosexuality is to be expected, but probably a phase—"expelled for the usual thing" is an expression you'll find in British books (fiction and non-fiction) about boys' schools of the period. "'Expelled not for the usual thing" means caught having sex with a woman.

The girls of the mid-twentieth century will not be expelled for those reasons—but still there are dangers: there is a fear that they will "catch" lesbianism, be infected somehow, trapped into their inversion. In Mary McCarthy's *The Group*, published 1963 but set in the 1930s, the revelation of Lakey's gayness at the end is the key to, and explanation of, so much about the group of women who attended college (based on Vassar) together.

So where does Leys, the Physical Training College in Josephine Tey's *Miss Pym Disposes* (1946), fit in? One internet commentator on crime fiction, Michael Grost, says the book has a "full agenda" on lesbianism: "It depicts homosexuality as an evil force, one that harms people and destroys lives. *Miss Pym Disposes* is an example of the ugly anti-gay hatred that sometimes appears in older mystery novels."[1]

I disagree strongly with this: the book is subtle and careful, and I would say bears no such implication—I would challenge Grost to produce one word of "anti-gay hatred" in *Miss Pym Disposes*. But there is still plenty to look at in the gender politics of the book, and that is what I propose to do—I think it is fruitful to compare it with other Golden Age mysteries set in similar establishments, and interesting to look at what the characters in the book say themselves about the atmosphere in the college and the relations among the women. The book has one of the strangest outcomes imaginable for a mystery novel of the time, and the view taken concerning punishment, revenge, and important decisions sets it apart from comparable works of fiction.

First, a short summary of the plot. *Miss Pym Disposes* takes place in a training college in England: an establishment where young women learn to be PE teachers—that is Physical Education, meaning games teachers or gym teachers to modern and American readers. (There is quite a tradition in the UK of linking games teachers with lesbianism, but this does not arise in the book.)

Lucy Pym, a distinguished author and psychologist, visits Leys (short words with a Y in them abound—Pym, Tey, Leys, and there is also Lux with an x) at the request of the principal, Henrietta Hodge, whom she knew in her own schooldays. She stays for a while, becoming very friendly with many of the girls who are about to graduate and go out into the world: she observes their plans, their fears, their good and bad points, and notices the stress that builds up during their Finals period. She sees a charmingly strong friendship between two of the most attractive students.[2]

Very late on in the book, someone dies. There is a huge question mark over what has happened and why: Miss Pym realizes the truth, and then has to decide what to do. In a remarkable moment from those death penalty days, she sees that if she tells what she knows, X would die [i.e., be executed] before the first students came back to Leys in the autumn.

She dithers, and makes a decision—but then in the closing pages of the book finds out that she did not know as much as she thought she did. In a heartless closing passage she admits to herself that she failed to understand the psychology of the main characters. And then she goes on her way, without attempting to put anything right.

The reader is left stunned and shocked.

Further Education and the Murder Story

At Leys College, life is very much turned in on itself. It is a contained world, full of feeling and pressure—the ideal setting for a murder story. But the more you look at the emotional isolation of the residents, the odder it is.

None of the students has a fiancé, a boyfriend at home. Other books of the period have suitable young men presenting themselves on a Sunday for some innocent diversion, or the classic situation (in books as in life) of a young woman meeting her friend's brother, or her brother's friend. This happened to one of the teaching staff many years before, but none of the students apparently has any brothers, let alone more interesting male connections. The only exception is Teresa Desterro, the Brazilian incomer, who intends to marry, and has a handsome young admirer—but then *she* is seen as very odd by everyone else at the college. One girl has a crush on a handsome older male actor, but the other students dismiss this totally and cannot understand it.

Another Golden Age crime writer, Gladys Mitchell, frequently features post-18 education in her books, but there could hardly be a greater contrast with Tey where sexual matters are concerned. To take an example, the 1958 book *Spotted Hemlock* features two single-sex agricultural institutes where college boundaries are constantly challenged by heterosexual fancies. The boys play silly pranks (plainly displacement-activity), everyone is bursting to get out and cross the gap, and the effect is of some gigantic fertility rite/dance (the agricultural college setting, then, is about right). The women are certainly up for all this, and joint social events are much anticipated. Both sides dodge past the authority figures to search, to offer, to tease and to pretend to retreat. Compared with this "het fever" and endless high spirits, Miss Pym's Leys is very flat indeed.

At Dorothy L. Sayers' Shrewsbury College—the all-female Oxford University establishment featured in the 1935 *Gaudy Night*—the life of the mind is respected, but the call of heterosexual sex is recognized. One girl has a boyfriend whom she fears is being "vamped" by another female student, and says "Geoffrey's sound—yes, darlings, definitely sound—but I'm taking no chances." Some of the women have possibly embarrassing crushes, but they are on men—there are no girl-on-girl pashes here. Of course Harriet D. Vane (alumna of, and consultant to, Shrewsbury) has that all-time dream man, Lord Peter Wimsey, at her beck and call. Everyone puts on their gladrags—a posh new frock or a best black gown– when he comes to dinner at the college. Men intrude all the time: all the dangerous affections are male-female.

In Catherine Aird's much later *The Religious Body* (1966), the young chaps of the agricultural institute are also busy playing pranks, though in this case they are invading a convent—where they are delightfully described as "limbs of Satan" by one of the nuns.

In all these books it is seen as quite normal for men to be invading. Yet in *Miss Pym*, there is no male invasion or intrusion, and even the avowedly handsome and famous actor cannot get any attention whatsoever when he visits.

How the Female Relationships Work

Affection underpins the story—there is a range of different female bonds at Leys:

1. Miss Pym had a crush on Henrietta Hodge—the principal of Leys—when they were at school together. Lucy was a lowly fourth former, Henrietta the head girl who rescued her from bullies. It is perfectly understandable that she felt so strongly—passionate gratitude is a very proper response to being saved from bullying. She also worked in a girls' school as a teacher, so feels she "understands" girls.

2. The group of students known as "The Four Disciples" stick together, and are going to go forward into life together, in a way that seems strange, and unlikely to last. But no-one is very interested in them, nor distinguishes much among them.

3. Pamela "Beau" Nash has a queen-like position at the college. In this respect the book resembles a traditional boarding school story, with a head girl and her prefects and a lower school—reflecting Pym's early experience with Henrietta.

4. And the key bond: Beau Nash and Mary Innes, senior students, have a shining relationship of equals. It is seen as quite different, and more important, more radiant, than anyone else's friendship at Leys.

Then there is the staff, the grown-ups: young Miss Wragg has a pash for Madame Lefevre. The Swedish teacher Froken Gustavsen has a fiancé—so she is not part of the maelstrom. She retires to her room with her mother, symbolically withdrawing from the hurly burly of the internal politics and the big fights. And there is the memorable cameo of the spinster teacher who turns out to be the object of desire for a very eligible man, but who concentrates her own affection on an adored and beautiful younger sister.

Innes and Nash both have parents with convincingly happy marriages (and where does that get them?), while Rouse, the ghastly victim, has no proper family. But friendships are shown as positive, everyone is supportive of one another. Teresa Desterro—the South American truth-teller amid the plain British girls—says this about the college: "It is not a normal life they lead. You cannot expect them to be normal." She also says of the students in general: "They are like little boys of nine.... Or little girls of eleven." They have raves, they "swoon" over teachers.

But it is clear this is *pre-sexual*, not gay—they have not discovered what she considers to be the superior pleasures of men. And she notices that the adored teacher "likes better the ones who do not bring her offerings." No one else sees any of these relationships as wrong, or worrying, or abnormal.

Driving the Plot

Everyone in the book likes someone. Barbara Rouse seems to be the unloved woman, and in the end unavenged: she is unpopular, untrustworthy, even repellent. But she gets on with the Principal, and is loved in return. Henrietta seems to identify with Rouse—although she herself is charismatic and full of integrity, and obviously always was. This is the one psychological feature of the book that does not quite make sense. Would she really identify with Rouse so much? This view comes without comment: "College was Henrietta's world. She lived and moved and had her being in the affairs of Leys; it was her father, mother, lover, and child." But Henrietta's blind spot is essential to set the plot in motion—she does not see why others dislike Rouse, who is not worthy of the job she is offered.

It is one of Tey's greatest achievements that she gets us to accept, unquestioningly, that nothing could be more important than who gets a junior job in a girls' boarding school, and that this golden prize justifies sabotage and murder. Even though, actually, how could it matter who goes to take a post at whatever Roedean or Benenden is in mind? Because in truth, *in real life, at that time*, it would be assumed that most of the young women would get married and give up their jobs. That it all would be completely wiped out within a couple of years. That Mary Innes is so evidently talented she would get another job anyway. But still Tey manages to make it seem earth-shattering, an end-of-the-world issue.

This forefronting of female relationships and power dynamics is unexpectedly feminist. Tey has removed the male world of the time, and the girls are able to embed themselves in female friendship (or more), female careers, and even crimes of passion, without distraction. Only a female institution of the kind she describes would allow this to be explored at the time.

Up until the murder occurs, the "college crime" is girls stealing food—because they are always hungry. The only other worrying incident the assembled staff can remember concerns a "dreadful creature who was man-crazy and used to spend Saturday evenings hanging round the barrack gate in Larborough." This is a "crime" because the staff has chosen to describe it that way—she would have been treated more gently in a Gladys Mitchell book I suspect. It is unimaginable that the list of "crimes" in a boys' academy of similar era would resemble this in the slightest. Tey has done well in creating a world that does not live by male standards.

Miss Pym

Miss Pym is given a vague male friend in the background, Alan, but one who sounds feeble and lackluster. (Interestingly he is given the name of Tey's undoubted hero and—you would conclude from her other crime books—perfect man, Alan Grant.) Surveying the relationships at Leys, she sees that she has not experienced real passion. She is like Mr. Lockwood in Emily Bronte's *Wuthering Heights*—the complacent outsider who is going to be shocked by something much deeper than expected. Tey seems to be distinguishing between immature, childish loves which are safe—the students who adore the teachers—and real love and relationships, which come later, and are better and more satisfying. But those can be dangerous, with dramatic fall-out, and that is where Innes and Nash lie, despite their love being "merely" a college friendship.

There is a lot of emphasis on Miss Pym's femininity—her satin slipper, her expensive frock, her careful make-up—reminiscent of Mary McCarthy's *The Group* with its sharp division between very feminine and very butch women. (*The Group* makes it explicit—the butch baroness is the husband, super-feminine Lakey is the wife.) Miss Pym is different from all the women at the college, and is attractive to the students for that reason—it is not too fanciful to see her as an object of innocent adoration. And there is a rather startling scene where the student Dakers peers at Miss Pym in the bath, climbing up a partition to have a look. It is a sexless event and no one apparently minds. Miss Pym is relaxed about it.

We are lulled into thinking that Miss Pym is full of "common sense" and proper views. But few protagonists in any books turn out to be quite as wrong about people as she does—at the end she says "What did she know about psychology anyhow?" because she was utterly wrong in her conclusions and decisions. She is revealed as a deeply flawed character and, despite endless apparent sensitivities, one who is crass and heartless.

The Fall-Out

So—is this a gay story, a queer story, a hidden parable of inversion? Life here bears no resemblance to the world outside. There are no men, and this is the classic Leys joke: "There was actually a rumour once that half the girls at Leys were pregnant, but it turned out that it was only the odd silhouette that everyone made with Gray [a large textbook] stuffed up the front of their Sunday bests." Could it *be* more symbolic and significant?

A misplaced friendship causes the crime, but even so, the friendship is not blamed. The personality of one of the people involved *is*, but she is never at any point seen as transgressive—her interests or loves are not blamed.

Spoiler Alert: Plot revelations to follow.

In retrospect Mary Innes was always the obvious suspect—she was the one who had lost out through Rouse being given the job, and who might have gained through her being injured. Miss Pym has evidence that she is to blame, but decides to withhold it from the authorities: instead she speaks to Innes, and gets this assurance from her: "For the rest of my life I shall atone for the thing I can't undo. I pay forfeit gladly. My life for hers."

But then, in the final pages of the book, Miss Pym realizes that Innes is not guilty, that she is covering up, martyring herself, for her friend who committed the crime. Innes *feels* guilt because it was her own rage and disappointment that was at the root of the murder—and she perhaps blames her relationship with Nash. Conversely, the actual culprit seems to feel no shame or guilt at all, and is obviously rather annoyed with Innes and her refusal to benefit from the death of Rouse—"after I went to all the trouble of killing her" you feel is implicit in her attitude.

And at this point—to the horror, surely, of generations of readers—Miss Pym finishes packing her case, sighs that she got it so wrong, and heads off back to her comfortable life in London, feeling none of the guilt that readers surely assign to her. Nothing will be put right. Tey does not even bother to explain how or why the key clues were wrong—she gives her readers credit that they can work out for themselves that the shoes were borrowed. She never truly explains what either of the girls is or was thinking.

Innes takes all the punishment in the end. But she is *not* being punished for a sinful love. Yes, the extreme friendship between Innes and Nash led to the crime, but it would be wrong to see that as the root of the problem. It is more that Innes chose someone with different moral values—something that can happen in any kind of relationship.

Innes and Nash are "mutually devoted." The key question for some modern readers is: was there a sexual relationship? There is a case to be made that older crime novels, as they cannot make certain things explicit, have the benefit of euphemism and mystery. The author can hint at and imply various things, so the reader's own assumptions and outlook take centre stage. There must be people who would read *Miss Pym Disposes* without thinking about lesbianism at all, and others who would put it at the heart of their interpretation.

Like the Biblical David and Jonathan that Innes and Nash are compared with, there is no certainty of what is going on—the relationship is left open and readers must decide for themselves. The nearest hint we get is Mary Innes telling Miss Pym that she was awake all night "facing a lot of things," not all of them having to do with the death of Rouse.

A modern version would surely give the pair a more sexual relationship, would be more explicit. But Tey is better than that: she does not dream of telling you—the true mystery at the heart of the book is that you cannot work out whether Innes and Nash are more sexual or less sexual than you expect. A present-day writer would find it challenging to achieve that admirable ambiguity. **End Spoiler.**

Notes

1. See *Mike Grost*, at http://mikegrost.com/coles.htm#Tey.
2. In the novel Tey refers to the young women students (who would seem to be around 20–21) as "girl" throughout, as would be normal at the time of writing, so I have felt free to do the same.

Bibliography

Aird, Catherine. *The Religious Body*. London: Macdonald, 1966.
Brontë, Emily. *Wuthering Heights*. London: Thomas Cautley Newby, 1847.
Mantel, Hilary. *An Experiment in Love*. London: Viking, 1995.
McCarthy, Mary. *The Group*. New York: Harcourt, Brace, 1963.
Mitchell, Gladys. *Spotted Hemlock*. London: Michael Joseph 1958.
Sayers, Dorothy L. *Gaudy Night*. London: Gollancz, 1935.
Tey, Josephine. *Miss Pym Disposes*. London: Peter Davies 1946.

"The man with the laughing eyes"
Socialism and Same-Sex Desire in G. D. H. Cole's The Death of a Millionaire

CURTIS EVANS

Intellectuals Douglas and Margaret Cole, in their lifetimes committed, active and articulate socialists, today receive their due in political histories of the British Left; yet the mystery literature the Oxford professor and his wife individually composed (twenty-eight novels, five novellas and thirty-five short stories), though well-regarded in the between-the-wars period, is treated as a footnote, both in books about the Coles (including Margaret's 1949 memoir, *Growing up into Revolution*, and her 1971 biography of Douglas, *The Life of G. D. H. Cole*) and, with a few very recent exceptions, surveys of the mystery genre. Usually mention is duly made that the Coles were that oddity of the Golden Age, leftist detective novelists, accompanied by an addendum that their political views were not reflected in their fiction. In truth, however, much of the Coles' world view *is* reflected in their fiction, often in the form of satire directed at Britain's conservative, capitalist establishment. Moreover, material in Douglas Cole's detective novels, particularly the intense though one-sided gay romance in *The Death of a Millionaire* (1925), the most remarkably transgressive of Douglas' mystery texts, reflects the author's own complex sexuality, which intriguingly intertwined with his socialism.[1]

Prompted by the popularity of the early "Humdrum" detective novels of the Anglo-Irish crime writer Freeman Wills Crofts, Douglas Cole wrote his first mystery, a virtual Crofts pastiche, while convalescing from a mild case of pneumonia.² Published by Collins in 1923 under the title *The Brooklyn Murders*, this tale was followed two years later by another, far more notable, Douglas Cole mystery, *The Death of a Millionaire*. Like all of Douglas and Margaret's mystery fiction from 1925 onward, *The Death of a Millionaire* was credited to both spouses, though they composed their fiction separately. Detective novels by the Coles appeared annually for nearly two decades, until during the midst of the Second World War, when the highly politically-engaged couple, preoccupied with momentous events at home and abroad, simply lost interest in writing them.

The Death of a Millionaire concerns the investigation by the Coles' primary series detective, Superintendent Henry Wilson, into the mysterious demise at Sugden's Hotel in London of millionaire Hugh Radlett ("the richest man in America—and that means, in the world"). Traveling under the pseudonym Restington, Radlett had a suite reserved for him at Sugden's by the great Earl of Ealing. In the opening pages of the novel, Sugden's, a bastion of Britain's conservative ruling elite, is preparing to welcome the Earl, who is due to meet there with Radlett/Restington, and the employees are "all just a little flustered" by the imminent arrival of this august representative of British capitalism. "Though you may never have heard of Sugden's, it can hardly be that you have never heard of Lord Ealing," pronounces Douglas Cole, in the archly ironic Trollopian narrative voice that he sometimes adopted in his detective fiction:

> He is the richest man in England, and president, for the third successive year, of the Federation of British Enterprises. He has been member of several Cabinets—the urbanest of Home secretaries, the most popularly militant of War Ministers.... He owns several newspapers, and knows how to wield the power of the Press. And he is the chairman of the fairest jewel in the crown of British commercial enterprise—the Anglo-Asiatic Commercial Corporation.... Hearts needs must beat faster at such a paladin's approach.³

Lord Ealing over the course of the novel proves to be anything but a "paladin," repeatedly lying to the police and fraudulently manipulating stock prices to add to his already bursting coffers. For Douglas Cole, Lord Ealing and his Anglo-Asiatic Commercial Corporation [AACC] stand for all that is debased in British political and economic life. Though "a patrician of unblemished descent" (one must glide over the matter of the great-great-grandfather and the flower-girl), Ealing has cynically allied himself with corrupt, grasping parvenus like the obsequious Mr. Benjamin, son of a Whitechapel tailor originally "from somewhere in Central Europe," and the piggish, vulgar Sir James Vanzetti; and he uses his name and his place in government at every opportunity to benefit the AACC.⁴

When Lord Ealing discovers at Sugden's that Radlett/Restington appears to have been murdered in his room by his secretary Rosenbaum, his body carried off in a trunk, the magnate aristocrat's first thought is to find and destroy any incriminating documents concerning his shady financial dealings. (Ealing, who was authorized by the AACC to back Radlett/Restington's gold mine concession from the Soviet Union, had promised Radlett/Restington to use his influence with the British government to obtain advantages in AACC's dealings with the Soviets; and the pair also had planned to manipulate AACC stock prices to their personal advantage.) Sugden's manager and Inspector Blakie are overawed by the Earl (the manager is mainly concerned—and desperately at that—that Lord Ealing get some breakfast), but Superintendent Wilson, "easily the most celebrated detective in England," proves a tougher proposition altogether.[5]

Wilson, we learn, knows "a thing or two about that nobleman which Lord Ealing fondly believed to be quite unsuspected in official quarters. The Superintendent had few illusions left."[6] Eventually Wilson discovers the truth about both Radlett/Restington's murder and Lord Ealing's malfeasance. Unfortunately, Wilson, now a man who knows too much, must pay for his excessive knowledge of the sordid truth about people in high places in capitalist countries. After the current government falls, Wilson, realizing that Lord Ealing will return to the Cabinet and take the position of Home Secretary so that he can suppress any evidence in the Radlett/Restington affair unfavorable to him, resigns from the force and becomes a private detective.

Cole has additional objects of odium in his novel besides the rotten-to-the-core Lord Ealing and his contemptible cronies in capitalist crime. The fact that the secretary Rosenbaum, a Russian Jew, is suspected of Radlett/Restington's murder gives the author his opportunity to critique as well the conservative persecutors of Bolsheviks and Jews during recent "Red Scares" in Britain and the United States. Intriguingly, the real life British wartime Director of Intelligence (and future detective novelist), Sir Basil Thomson, comes in for direct excoriation by name during a discussion between the gullible Blakie and his wise superior:

> "Of course, sir, he had accomplices. One of these Bolshevik dens—the enemy in our midst, sir. We must call in the Special Branch."
> "My dear Blakie, don't talk like an article in the *Daily Express*. I'm not much of a believer in Bolshevik dens. Most of these fellows are a harmless lot of fanatics."
> "But Sir Basil always used to say—"
> "Oh, yes, I know all about that." Wilson's little differences with Sir Basil had been notorious, and the quoting of Sir Basil as an authority caused him to react at once.... "I remember they used to discover at least a couple of great revolutionary plots a week, before Sir Basil went."[7]

Wilson's "dear Blakie" is easily led, but the Superintendent soon finds a more obstinate, if ultimately farcical, antagonist in Brigadier-General Sir

Evan Bunker, Basil Thomson's (fictional) replacement as head of Intelligence. Of the same defensive and paranoid mentality as his predecessor (as the General's surname suggests), Bunker upon hearing the words "Soviet Union" and "Rosenbaum" immediately commences rounding up as many of the kingdom's Bolsheviks and Jews as his men can lay their hands on, under Wilson's scornful eye. Bunker, Cole informs us, "was not an intelligent man—it was said that defect of his had cost several thousand men their lives during the war—but he was immensely energetic ... the chasing of Rosenbaum afforded a magnificent opportunity for the display of the General's qualities." Bunker's men hit the streets in search of Bolshies, with less than stellar results:

> Every known haunt of advanced opinion in or near the metropolis was raided and searched from top to bottom. A full-dress raid on the King Street headquarters of the Communist Party resulted only in the seizure of a quantity of "seditious" literature. The Liberty Club in Clerkenwell, haunt of a leading Anarchist group, was raided twice, despite the fact—unknown to the Special Branch—that its members looked on Bolsheviks as a shade worse than kings or capitalists. The East End of London was combed fine for suspicious characters, and quite an army of Rosenbaums was interrogated, and several detained for a few hours until they could prove their identity. None of them was the man. Even the Nineteen Seventeen Club was politely visited, while Mr. Ramsay MacDonald was delivering a lecture on the horrors of Bolshevism.[8]

At one point, General Bunker believes he has found his man, but all is for naught:

> Bunker's crypto-Jew turned out to be a Scotsman of irreproachable antecedents, his Bolshevik desperado a respectable merchant of sound conservative principles and active in the South Streatham Lodge of the Primrose League. His name was not Rosenbaum, but, as he had said, Ivor Rose, and his partners, Lewis and Smith, were not Levi and Schmid, but the one a Welshman and the other a pure Cockney. Rose had a perfect alibi for the night of the crime, which he had spent attending a Wesleyan Conference in Birmingham ... the mysterious trunk which he had brought home ... and "secreted" in an outhouse, proved to contain, not a dead or living body, but trade samples—of Poggin's Ideal Pickles for the Home—which the worthy merchant was conveying to the United States when Bunker's zealous emissaries arrested him at Liverpool.... Not for the first time in its career, the Special Branch found itself badly bunkered.[9]

In the face of such a fiasco Wilson cannot resist tweaking the blustering, impetuous and incompetent Special Branch head over the mess he has made:

> "If we don't want him for the case, you can always deport him as an undesirable alien. That's one advantage with these Russians. There's no one to look after their interests. No fuss about *habeas corpus*, eh, General?"
> "It would be a jolly good thing for the country if habeas corpus were repealed altogether," said the General savagely.
> "Oh, I don't know," replied Wilson. "It would come very expensive if we let you imprison everybody."[10]

Cole does not rest content with ridiculing "Great Men" like Sir Basil Thomson and Brigadier-General Sir Evan Bunker for unreasoning fear of foreigners and leftists; lesser folk are lampooned as well. "A Russian," darkly declares Sugden's manager of Rosenbaum, "in the tone of one who imputes a crime." "Very foreign-looking gentleman, sir" adds a hotel porter. "Queer-looking, as you might say. Not English, I mean." On the other hand, another character in the novel, one Cole clearly means for us to admire, Hugh Radlett/Restington, is reported to have observed that "Russians were the most intelligent people on earth except the Jews—and [Rosenbaum] had the advantage of being both."[11]

The reader gradually discovers that Hugh Radlett/Restington is one of three foci of moral conscience in *The Death of a Millionaire* (besides, of course, Wilson), the other two being Lord Ealing's nephew and secretary, Arthur Wharton, and Radlett/Restington's business partner, James Pasquett. A document written by Radlett/Restington reveals that the American millionaire was actually born in England and grew up in a coal mining slum town, where he learned the horror of grinding, amoral capitalism. Here Cole draws on his familiarity with Labour issues, from the sympathetic perspective of a committed Labour man. Much of the document reads like it was drawn from a study of working conditions in late-nineteenth-century industrial Britain:

> My father, John Radlett, was a collier, but we were very poor. Father had been too active in Union affairs, and the overseer always saw to it that he got the worst working place in the pit. There was no minimum wage then. The Unions weren't so strong as I suppose they've grown since. And father couldn't chuck up his job: no one else in the district would have employed him. He was a marked man...
>
> ... My brother Edward was killed in a colliery accident when I was ten. I remember it well. The cage had fallen to the bottom of the shaft. My mother took me to the pithead, where there was a crowd of men and women waiting for the news. I was frightened, and ran away and hid in a shed. My mother found me and told me my brother was dead. After that, there were only four of us to feed.
>
> [...]
>
> I went to work at thirteen. I had some schooling at first, of course, at a rotten hole of a school pretty nearly as bad as our house. It was draughty and leaky and horribly cold in the winter...
>
> ... And, in a few months' time, came a strike.
>
> ... Father was made chairman of the Strike Committee. When the men went back—starved out—there was no job for him.... He was turned fifty by then, but he made up his mind to leave England and go to the States.[12]

James Radlett finds work with an old friend, Merritt, who made a fortune in American mines, though ultimately Radlett loses his life in a violent strike. To his surprise young Hugh inherits Merritt's money at the latter man's death and finds himself a wealthy man. After marrying a woman who proves a scheming gold-digger, Hugh arranges for his own disappearance and departs to engage in new ventures overseas. In Russia he is caught up in the Revolution and imprisoned, but eventually makes his way out, with a valuable gold mine concession, in partnership with his friend John Pasquett.

Pasquett is the pivot on which much of the novel's puzzle plot turns, the anti-Ealing of the novel, and Cole lavishes much sympathetic attention on him. "He was," Cole tells us, "a big, fair man, clean shaven, and of fine physique. But he was much more than that. He had one of those faces which are always half-smiling, as if he was perpetually amused. There was a humorous twinkle in his eye, too, and he was used to making friends at sight."[13]

One of the most devoted friends whom Pasquett makes at first sight is Arthur Wharton, Lord Ealing's nephew and private secretary. Under Pasquett's influence, Wharton too becomes a true moral agent in the novel. Wharton is the son of Lord Ealing's sister, who married a novelist from whom she was quickly estranged. The novelist went off to live in Capri, providing his son, Arthur, with a small allowance but never seeing him. Like Douglas Cole, Arthur Wharton attended Balliol College, Oxford; later he was elected to a Fellowship at All Souls, which he relinquished to go to work for his uncle, feeling "conscience of a desire to do things."[14] Wharton soon realizes, when plunged amidst the events described in *The Death of a Millionaire*, that his uncle is corrupt to his very core; and that realization leads him to repudiate Lord Ealing and the business world and return to Oxford, where decency reigns.

Arthur Wharton's relationship with James Pasquett is interesting for nonpolitical reasons as well, for it is quite obvious that the relationship is, on Wharton's part, latently homosexual. Indeed, in a novel singularly (and likely deliberately) bereft of significant female characters, Wharton functions as the "female" half of the novel's love interest, caught in the classic conflict of loyalty to a parental figure (in this case an uncle, Lord Ealing) versus love for a winning young man (Pasquett).

Before Wharton even knows the identity of Pasquett, he is powerfully struck by the man's very presence: "Arthur was glad the man with the laughing eyes was to be his fellow passenger. He observed him closely as he stood talking to the mechanic, noting his great strength and physical vigour." After departing from Pasquett's company, Wharton's only "regret is that he had failed to exchange names and addresses" with this remarkable laughing-eyed man: "The man remained in his thoughts: Arthur wanted to meet him again." Later, after the two have become fast friends, Arthur finds himself thinking about Pasquett constantly: "Arthur missed him when he was gone. Lord Ealing ... laughed at him for mooning about like a girl who has lost her lover. Arthur first blushed, and then said that really he did feel a bit like that."[15]

When Wharton comes to fear that Pasquett may be involved, like Lord Ealing, in shady business transactions and even perhaps in murder, he agonizes in the manner of a lover: "His uneasy mind suggested to him all manner of dark suspicions. He put them from him, but they thronged back to haunt him. And yet, the worse his thoughts of Pasquett, somehow the greater his affection grew.... Arthur groaned in spirit, perplexed between fear and love." Believing that Wharton will reveal what he knows of his Uncle's crooked business dealings, Lord Ealing attempts to manipulate Wharton's doubts about Pasquett to his own advantage, in the highly melodramatic fashion of a wicked uncle in Victorian sensation fiction: "Have I not seen your affection for him? ... Would you send him to prison to mark your love for him? ... I ask you, Arthur, would you send your friend to imprisonment—perhaps—who knows?—to death?"[16] A mortified Wharton decides he must keep quiet about what he knows, in case his beloved is implicated, though he tells his uncle that he holds him in contempt and will leave his employ.

Fortunately for the anguishing Wharton, Pasquett is revealed to be virtuous at the tale's end. However, Wharton ultimately must satisfy himself, after Pasquett marries a young woman, with Pasquett's firstborn son being named "Arthur." In the novel's final colloquy between the two men, Pasquett provides Cole's moral, one highly subversive of putative Golden Age verities:

> The trouble about you, Arthur, is that you've been badly brought up. You think you're a bit of an iconoclast; but away down in your mind you've a profound veneration for property, and law and order, and middle-class morality, and all the other things you criticize in those funny little books of yours. I had all that knocked out of me quite early. You see, I was brought up to be a business man—in America too. I know that law and order and the rights of property, and all the rest of the stuff your uncle puts in his speeches, are just bunkum. You only know it theoretically; when it comes to acting you're a good old Whig like the rest.... I judge for myself: I make my own laws....[17]

An obviously deliberate irony here is that Cole is having Pasquett, when making his stirring call to revolutionary action, effectively lecture Wharton about Cole's own "faults." Like Wharton, Cole was an Oxford academic writing about advanced societal reformation in "funny little books." There is another important similarity between Cole and Wharton as well, in the matter of sexuality: like Wharton, Cole clearly had homosexual inclinations. "Physically, he was always under-sexed—low-powered," reflected Margaret Cole of her husband in her biography of him. Until Douglas' marriage with her, she conceded, "his physical affections, his desire to caress, had been generally directed towards his own sex; he had fallen in love with various young men, one or two whom I afterwards met, and had written poems to them." Yet she insisted that Coles' same-sex affairs of the heart were "all very mild, and needed no sort of legal sanction; his sympathy with homosexuals, though he was naturally against their suppression, was intellectual chiefly."[18]

Margaret allowed that, with the one notable exception of herself, her husband "never seemed to have any sexual use at all" for women, regarding them "by and large ... as rather a low type of being." She argued that Douglas' antipathy for the female sex was rooted not in misogyny per se but rather in his political ideology: "[H]e thought that the mass of women were not good Socialist material.... He believed as strongly as any anti–Socialist that no woman (except Jane Austen) had ever achieved first-class honours in art or literature; and he felt that the main purpose in life of a majority of them was to distract man from his proper work...."[19]

It is apparent that in her debut detective novel, *The Murder at Crome House* (1927), Margaret Cole modeled the character of her priggish protagonist, James Flint, after her husband:

> James Flint was a tallish, slight young man of a year or two over thirty, who looked older by reason of his hairless temples and the steady gravity of his expression.... He was a lecturer and tutor in history and economics.... [He] had a positive horror, based mainly on ... practical inexperience ... of the modern young female of his own class.... [T]he Young Woman of the Period he regarded as a monster who would certainly try either to marry him or become his mistress.[20]

After Douglas was diagnosed as diabetic in 1931, Margaret noted, his "asexuality was greatly increased ... he was warned by the specialist that he must expect far less enjoyment of sex, to which according to his own account he replied, 'Thank goodness.'" Margaret admitted that her sex-life with her husband, by whom the determined woman had managed to bear three children in the 1920s, "diminished gradually to zero for the last twenty years of his life [1939–1959]," adding that concurrently Douglas "developed by degrees a positive dislike of, and disgust with, any aspect of sex almost equal to that of the early Christian fathers.... He came to feel that it was all revolting.... 'Womaniser,' I was once told by one of his secretaries, 'was his last word in condemnation of any man.'" In his penultimate detective novel, *Murder at the Munition Works* (1940), Douglas makes the book's most decidedly unappealing character, a nasty cog in the capitalist machine named Sullivan, guilty of "sexual aberrations" (to use the author's term), by which is meant that the man has engaged in copious coitus with females. "Lord bless you, dozens of them," the Sullivans' cook emphatically responds when Superintendent Wilson delicately queries whether Sullivan has had affairs with "young ladies."[21]

The late Labour party leader Michael Foot supplemented Margaret Cole's blunt appraisal of her husband's sexuality, recalling that as a professor at Oxford Douglas had succumbed to "innocent little homosexual crushes on some of his students," including a future Labour party leader, Hugh Gaitskell, seventeen years Douglas' junior. Upon Hugh's ceasing to be Douglas' pupil in the summer of 1927, two years after the publication of *The Death of a Millionaire*, the still-enraptured Douglas took the young man on country walking-tours and wrote a series of heartfelt romantic letters to him, continuing this impassioned correspondence until Hugh, as Margaret confided in her *Life of G. D. H. Cole*, politely made clear to his former teacher that "the *emotion* was not reciprocated." This attitude described by Margaret Cole and Michael Foot—that relationships between men are on some altogether higher mystical plane than those between men and women—can be glimpsed in other Douglas Cole tales besides *The Death of a Millionaire*. For example, in

The Man from the River (published in 1928, around the time Douglas was trekking in the country with Hugh Gaitskill), Douglas euphorically depicts the rural vacation idyll, unfortunately interrupted by murder, of Superintendent Wilson and his bosom pal Dr. Michael Prendergast; while in *End of an Ancient Mariner* (1933), the sympathetically presented protagonist, Philip Blakeway, rather remarkably thinks to himself, we are told, that "although he liked his wife well enough, he would unhesitatingly have burned her at the stake if Sam Fowler's interests had demanded the sacrifice." Sam Fowler is Blakeway's business partner and best friend.[22]

Margaret Cole, boasting her own circle of devoted male admirers (the English diplomat Rowland Kenney evocatively recalled her as "a provocative elfin tigress," smoking a large cigar), appears to have been disinclined to sacrifice her own sexuality on the ever-heightening pyre of her husband's puritanism. By 1937, when Margaret wrote an intriguing analysis of the marital triangle in the notorious Adelaide Bartlett murder case—witheringly likening the attitude of Edwin Bartlett toward his wife, Adelaide, to that of a master toward a favored pet dog and speculating that Edwin may have deemed the arrival of Reverend George Dyson, the third member of the triangle in the Bartlett case, "as a godsend to enable his pet dog to be kept happy and amused"—she and Dick Mitchison—a "large, self-effacing, gentle and humorous" barrister married to the novelist Naomi Mitchison who later, with the Coles' support, was elected a Labour MP—had developed a close friendship that most people in their social circles assumed was a sexual affair carried on with the equable acquiescence of their respective spouses. (In a February 1936 letter, for example, noted intellectual Isaiah Berlin matter-of-factly referred to Dick Mitchison as Margaret's "lover.") Having happily escaped the inconvenient wife's fate of burning at the stake, to which Douglas had alluded in his novel *End of an Ancient Mariner*, Margaret Cole outlived her husband by over two decades, passing away peacefully on 7 May 1980, one day after her eighty-seventh birthday, which she spent reminiscing over a long life in the company of her only son, Humphrey Cole, and Naomi Mitchison, the widow of her reputed longtime lover.[23]

NOTES

1. Julian Symons' influential but sometimes errant *Bloody Murder* (1972; 3d. ed., New York: Mysterious Press, 1992) cursorily discusses the Coles' detective fiction, decidedly downplaying its political significance and ignoring the matter of Douglas Cole's sexuality, while Martin Edwards, in *The Golden Age of Murder: The Mystery of the Writers Who Invented the Modern Detective Story* (London: HarperCollins, 2015), his recent revisionist study of the Detection Club, a social group of distinguished British detective novelists of which Douglas and Margret Cole were founding members, discusses Douglas' sexuality at length but fails to link it to his detective fiction, declaring that the author "was reluctant to fictionalize his private sexual predilections" (p. 77). This reluctance that Edwards discerns is not evident in Douglas' detective

novel *The Death of a Millionaire*, as has been noted recently by me in *The Spectrum of English Murder: The Detective Fiction of Henry Lancelot Aubrey-Fletcher and G. D. H. and Margaret Cole* (Greenville, OH: Coachwhip, 2015) and by Michael Bloch in *Closet Queens: Some Twentieth Century British Politicians* (London: Little, Brown, 2015), wherein Bloch observes passingly that in *The Death of a Millionaire* a homosexual character is portrayed in a "surprisingly positive light" for the time. In the 21 November 2014 review of *The Death of a Millionaire* found on his crime fiction blog "Do You Write Under Your Own Name?" Martin Edwards discusses the novel's scathing socialist critique of English society without making any mention of the one-sided gay romance that Douglas included in the novel. See "Do You Write Under Your Own Name?" at http://doyouwriteunderyourownname.blogspot.com/2014/11/forgotten-book-death-of-millionaire.htmlat. The best detailed sources on the lives of Douglas and Margaret Cole remain Margaret's *The Life of G. D. H. Cole* and *Growing up into Revolution*.

   2. On Crofts and other "Humdrum" detective novelists, see my *Masters of the "Humdrum" Mystery: Cecil John Charles Street, Freeman Wills Crofts, Alfred Walter Stewart and the British Detective Novel, 1920-1961* (Jefferson, NC: McFarland, 2012).

   3. G. D. H. and Margaret Cole, *The Death of a Millionaire* (1925; repr., London: Penguin, 1950), 9-10. Sugden's resembles the stately, old Bertam's Hotel of Agatha Christie's *At Bertram's Hotel* (1965), published forty years after *The Death of a Millionaire*. Presumably the authors based their respective fictional hotels on the famous Brown's Hotel.

   4. Coles, *Millionaire*, 39, 68. Cole's use of the surname Vanzetti, shared with the soon-to-be-executed Italian-American anarchist Bartolomeo Vanzetti, likely is deliberately ironic.

   5. *Ibid.* 10
   6. *Ibid.*
   7. *Ibid.*, 60-61.
   8. *Ibid.*, 101-102.
   9. *Ibid.*, 140.
   10. *Ibid.*, 214.
   11. *Ibid.*, 17, 18, 53. It should be noted that the real-life object of Douglas Cole's ire, Basil Thomson, himself briefly enjoyed a writing career as a detective novelist, between 1933 and 1937 publishing eight Crofts-like detective novels about a Scotland Yard policeman named Richardson, who with remarkable fleetness advances over the course of the series from Police Constable to Chief Constable.
   12. *Ibid.*, 86-96.
   13. *Ibid.*, 75.
   14. *Ibid.*, 114.
   15. *Ibid.*, 97.
   16. *Ibid.*, 101, 145, 170, 219.
   17. *Ibid.*, 286-287.
   18. Margaret Cole, *The Life of G. D. H. Cole* (London: Macmillan, 1971), 91-92.
   19. *Ibid.*, 92.
   20. G. D. H and Margaret Cole, *The Murder at Crome House* (New York: Macmillan, 1927), 3, 4, 27.
   21. Cole, *Life*, 93-94; G. D. H. and Margaret Cole, *The Murder at the Munition Works* (New York: Macmillan, 1940), 35, 174.
   22. Michael Foot, introduction to Betty D. Vernon, *Margaret Cole, 1893-1980: A Political Biography* (Dover, NH: Croom Helm, 1986), 21; Cole, *Life*, 169-170; G. D.

H. and Margaret Cole, *End of an Ancient Mariner* (London: Collins, 1933), 10. Superintendent Wilson appears with his great friend Michael Prendergast in two more Douglas Cole "vacation" novels, *The Missing Aunt* (1937) and *Toper's End* (1942), as well as in eleven short stories that were written, I believe, by Douglas; no vacations, romantic or otherwise, of Wilson with his wife are recorded. Of Hugh Gaitskell, the late Twenties object of Douglas Cole's affection, Martin Edwards avows that he was "resolutely heterosexual," speculating that he "was probably more attracted to Margaret." (If he really was "resolutely heterosexual," one would assume so.) However, in *Closet Queens* Michael Bloch asserts that at Oxford Gaitskell had been "a flamboyant aesthete" who had "enjoyed homosexual experiences," including a dalliance with the poet John Betjeman; and that into his later life Gaitskell "carried a strong whiff of bisexuality," despite his carrying on a long affair with Ann Fleming, wife of Ian Fleming, creator of the famous fictional spy James Bond. In any event, Margaret Cole in her *Life* notes that the friendship of Douglas and Hugh "continued for several years of collaboration after the emotion had started gently to die away" (p. 170).

23. Peddling and Politics," *Sydney Morning Herald*, 6 January 1940; Margaret Cole, "The Case of Adelaide Bartlett," in *The Anatomy of Murder* (1937; repr., New York: Macmillan, 1937), 89–90, 100–101, 113; Vernon, *Margaret Cole*, 69, 203–204; Isaiah Berlin, *Letters 1928–1946*, ed. Henry Hardy (Cambridge: Cambridge University Press, 2004), 155.

Bibliography

Berlin, Isaiah. *Letters 1928–1946*. Edited by Henry Hardy. Cambridge: Cambridge University Press, 2004.
Bloch, Michael. *Closet Queens: Some Twentieth Century British Politicians*. London: Little, Brown, 2015.
Cole, G. D. H., and Margaret Cole. *The Death of a Millionaire*. 1925. Reprint, London: Penguin, 1950.
———. *End of an Ancient Mariner*. London: Collins, 1933.
———. *The Man from the River*. New York: Macmillan, 1928.
———. *The Murder at Crome House*. New York, Macmillan, 1927.
———. *The Murder at the Munition Works*. New York: Macmillan, 1940.
Cole, Margaret. "The Case of Adelaide Bartlett." In *The Anatomy of Murder*. 1936. Reprint, New York: Macmillan, 1937.
———. *Growing up into Revolution*. London: Longmans, 1949.
———. *The Life of G. D. H. Cole*. London: Macmillan, 1971.
Edwards, Martin. *The Golden Age of Murder: The Mystery of the Writers Who Invented the Modern Detective Story*. London: HarperCollins, 2015.
———. Review of *The Death of a Millionaire* (21 November 2014). "Do You Write Under Your Own Name?" At http://doyouwriteunderyourownname.blogspot.com/2014/11/forgotten-book-death-of-millionaire.htmlat.
Evans, Curtis. *The Spectrum of English Murder: The Detective Fiction of Henry Lancelot Aubrey-Fletcher and G. D. H. and Margaret Cole*. Greenville, OH: Coachwhip, 2015.
"Peddling and Politics." *Sydney Morning Herald*, 6 January 1940, 10.
Symons, Julian. *Bloody Murder*. 1972. 3d ed. New York: Mysterious Press, 1992.
Vernon, Betty D. *Margaret Cole, 1893–1980: A Political Biography*. Dover, NH: Croom Helm, 1986.

Humdrum Ecstasies
C. H. B. Kitchin and His Detective, Malcolm Warren

MICHAEL MOON

"Had it not been for my inability to mash potatoes on Thursday, June 10, I think it quite possible that I might never have embarked on this third case of mine."[1] The opening sentence of a 1939 detective novel. Sam Spade? Philip Marlowe? Obviously not. There is nothing even remotely hard-boiled about a detective who begins by admitting that it was his failure to transform some chunks of boiled potato into creamy white peaks that opened his way into the murder case he recalls cracking in *Death of His Uncle*.

And yet, there is something about the way that the exact date and day of the week are supplied in the middle of that opening sentence that keeps it from seeming entirely fey. Coming on the heels of the mashed-potato meltdown, the precise naming of the date and the day of the week shifts the sentence into a different register from where it started—a strong if momentary whiff of police procedural?—before revealing that the present book is being told by a veteran albeit amateur detective reporting on his third successful murder investigation.

The author, C. H. B. Kitchin, had scored a major success in the burgeoning field of the detective novel when his first mystery, *Death of My Aunt*, had appeared a decade earlier, in 1929. Published under Leonard and Virginia Woolf's own imprint, the sales of *Death of My Aunt* helped subsidize some of the less profitable titles on Hogarth Press' list at the time. Malcolm Warren, the young stockbroker turned amateur detective who solved the case of his rich aunt's murder in Kitchin's first mystery, returned five years later (in 1934) to report another case in *Crime at Christmas*. Five more years passed before Kitchin brought Warren back in *Death of His Uncle*, and another full decade passed before Warren's fourth and final appearance as detective in *The Cornish Fox*.

Such was pretty much Kitchin's entire crime novel output, four Malcolm Warren mysteries stretched over two decades.[2] Kitchin had published two novels (non-criminous ones) in the mid–1920s before *Death of My Aunt* made him somewhat famous, and published six more such novels between 1931 and a posthumously published last novel in 1971 (born in 1895, Kitchin had died in 1967).

Unlike many male writers of the twentieth century, Clifford Kitchin did more than write and drink. He worked as a stockbroker when he was young, the occupation that he gave his detective Malcolm Warren. He is said to have inherited a substantial fortune and to have increased its size through investment. Later, while continuing to produce novels with fair frequency for forty years, he also farmed for a while and taught in a school for boys (I have so far been unable to discover what subject he taught; he appears to have been qualified to teach several, including Latin, Greek, and maths). He was a talented pianist and a skilled bridge player who enjoyed solving problems in algebra textbooks the way many of his contemporaries did crosswords. For a time he bred and raced greyhounds with characteristic enthusiasm—and success. He haunted the salesrooms and collected Meissen porcelain and other *objets de luxe*, interested in them as much as investments (he sold as well as bought) as in holding them as prized personal possessions.

When Kitchin was young, he was taken up by powerful political as well as literary people: he weekended and was for a time close friends with members of Prime Minister H.H. Asquith's family, whose political power had begun to fade at the time but whose social and cultural clout was still at its peak. Kitchin's early fiction was praised by Lytton Strachey, and there are snapshots of him in the National Portrait Gallery taken by Lady Ottoline Morrell, as he poses with his lifelong friend Kenneth Ritchie, later Chairman of the London Stock Exchange and member of the Queen's Privy Council. Virginia Woolf refers to Kitchin in an offhand manner in a personal letter written around the time that Hogarth Press was publishing his second Malcolm Warren mystery, *Crime at Christmas,* as "a very rich young man who used to work [as an attorney], until he took to the Stock Exchange and discovered a gift for detective stories."[3]

Despite the fact that he appeared to many of his contemporaries to excel and succeed at everything to which he turned his hand, Kitchin himself often professed to feeling an inveterate outsider, someone who felt at home in none of the various worlds in which he apparently shone at different times in his life. While it would be foolhardy to accept everything his fictional alter ego Malcolm Warren says about himself as being true of Kitchin as well, Warren does sound as though he may be speaking for his creator when he laments, "It is my fate, in Bloomsbury, to be thought a Philistine, while in other circles I am regarded as a dilettante with too keen an aesthetic sense to be a responsible person."[4] Besides feeling less than entirely welcome in either highbrow

Bohemian Bloomsbury or on the Stock Exchange, Kitchin expressed similar feelings of alienation and exclusion from the literary world of his time, having discovered after the early popular success of *Death of My Aunt* that his numerous subsequent novels did not entirely succeed in the marketplace of publishing and critical opinion as either middlebrow entertainment or art-fiction.

Kitchin appears to have been sexually active with other men throughout his life and was relatively open about the fact, despite the vulnerability of such men in the mid-twentieth century UK to blackmail, criminal prosecution, and social ostracization. Kitchin himself contributed the story to the public record that he and Kenneth Ritchie and bibliophile Richard Jennings shared a flat in Great Ormond Street in the early 1930s to which all three men were regularly bringing "trade" (young working-class men who were sexually available for money), and that for a while T. S. Eliot moved in with them, after the break-up of his first marriage. Again according to Kitchin, during the time he stayed in the flat, Eliot used to go out for the evening wearing "a bit of slap" (theatrical makeup—"paint and powder") and stay out until the three flatmates had all gone to bed.[5] Kitchin's references to cosmetics and late hours seem to suggest that Eliot was frequenting the kinds of early gay bars that figure in Radclyffe Hall's novel *The Well of Loneliness*. This early portrait of the emerging lesbian / gay scene in London had been prosecuted for alleged obscenity in late 1928, drawing considerable public attention to the existence and behavior—and rather abject glamour—of "inverts" as a new metropolitan "type" only a short time before the appearance of Kitchin's first Malcolm Warren mystery.

In 1930, when he was in early middle age, and at a time when he later claimed to still be bringing available young men back to the Great Ormond Street flat, Kitchin became involved with an accountant named Clive Preen who was about nine years his senior. Kitchin and Preen appear to have lived very happily together until 1944, when Preen unexpectedly died in a Liverpool hotel. Since Kitchin and Preen had been traveling together as "associates" of some vague kind rather than as lovers and life-partners—in keeping with the required pretense of the time—it was necessary for Kitchin, in the first hours after Preen's demise, to conceal his intense grief and pretend "for form's sake" that Preen's death meant little to him—at least until he could get home where he could express his true feelings in the company of a few trusted friends.

The Cornish Fox was published five years after Preen's sudden and devastating death. Kitchin dedicated this book, the last of the Malcolm Warren series, to Preen, writing understatedly, "To the Memory of CLIVE PREEN, who would have helped me with this story." Kitchin later wrote to a friend, "my real life began in 1930 and ended in 1944," as though to say that, as Kitchin experienced it, Preen himself, or Kitchin's relationship with Preen, had in a sense *been* Kitchin's real life.[6] Readers interested in the affective valences of Kitchin's Malcolm Warren series may want to note that the period of Kitchin's relationship with Preen (1930–44) roughly correspond to Kitchin's years as a mystery writer (1929–49).

In this essay I hypothesize that Kitchin's serial-detective, the four-times-appearing Malcolm Warren, is, in several senses, as his creator was, "gay" or "queer." The male protagonist's apparent attraction to female characters, often a motivating feature of the plot in other detective series of the time, plays no part in the Warren series. Nor does the development of a romance of some sort between the young male detective and some spunky young female character. Forms of hetero attraction and the formation and rupture of hetero emotional and sexual relations between other significant characters (i.e., others besides Warren) often play determinate parts in the plots of Kitchin's mysteries, however.[7]

Although (as I shall discuss later) there are moments in the Malcolm Warren series in which attraction and desire between men flicker into at least momentary legibility, there are many non-erotic aspects of the lives of homosexuals in the homophobic society of the interwar period and after that feature prominently in the series. One of the "gayer" things about Malcolm Warren, given the threatening atmosphere in which homosexuals of all classes lived in the UK between the wars, is his way of more or less stumbling innocently into the position of potential chief suspect in several of the murder cases narrated in the series. In this way the Malcolm Warren mysteries may be providing several different versions of a scenario in which Kitchin and many other men like him feared and dreaded finding themselves. In it, a clever young man about town goes to the country or to one of the posher suburbs of London to visit a rich relative, business client, or college friend and unexpectedly finds himself in the thick of a murder and a police investigation in which he to varying degrees appears for much of the story to be implicated. Not many of Kitchin's fellow gays are likely to have committed murder, but most if not all of them must have known how oppressive it felt to live one's otherwise ordinary-enough life "under suspicion" because of one's sexual and/or social inclinations. Three-fourths of the way through *Death of My Aunt*, Warren asks worriedly, "Inspector, can I take it that I am no longer under suspicion," but rather than responding directly, Inspector Amos Glaize spends a long paragraph explaining why Warren's query is inappropriate before grudgingly admitting to him that he is in fact "pretty well outside the picture" as far as the police are concerned at this point late in their investigation. Two-thirds of the way through the mystery novel that follows, Warren begins to panic as he lies sleepless at 4:00 a.m., at "that dismal hour when all the horrors of life and death crowd to the bedside," agonizedly wondering if, as the police continue to put their findings together, "Shall I not be the chief suspect?"[8]

Warren is not at all happy or pleased about being recurrently "suspected" by various people in his environment, including the police. Instead, he professes himself by turns to be irritated, annoyed, frightened, angry, and filled with disdain for his "suspectors." Part of the formal unity that a reader may notice in reading Kitchin's fiction, including his detective fiction, manifests itself in the Malcolm Warren novels in their frequent explorations of the powerful role that negative affect and antisocial impulses play in determining Warren's behaviors and attitudes. "I have already shown myself to be possessed of many odious qualities," Warren forthrightly tells the reader in the opening words of a chapter (13) a little past half-way through *Death of My Aunt*. He goes on: "I cannot, without distorting the facts of this story, conceal my greed, my indifference to the other people's feelings and my interest in my own, my timidity, idleness, and vacillation." All this he says by way of introducing an account of what he claims has been a rare display of courage on his part. But Warren is for many readers a thoroughly sympathetic character, partly because he is open about admitting his alleged personal shortcomings. "I am neither hero nor villain of this story," he tells the reader on page 105 of the same novel.[9] Kitchin remained a devoted reader of classical Greek and Latin poetry long after he first encountered it in school, and one of the signs of this in the Malcolm Warren series may be the classically "balanced" personality and the self-critical but also self-understanding and self-forgiving attitudes that its protagonist displays.

We may find another sign of a classical aesthetic in what critics of an earlier day valued as the "unities of time and place" that are to be discovered not only in early-modern neoclassical narratives but in the Malcolm Warren mysteries as well. Usually set in a restricted locale—the country village or country house in which many interwar mysteries are set—the Warren mysteries are even more compressed in time than many of the other mystery novels of the period. They characteristically take place entirely within the four or five days of a long weekend, with the dates and often the times of day provided as chapter headings throughout the book. Murders tend to take place on Thursday night or Friday morning and the cases to be wrapped up by Monday or Tuesday afternoon. But despite the fact that a fairly complex plot unfolds in such a compressed period of time, the narratives can hardly be described as action-packed. The moods they depict and convey tend to be highly unified, often concerning themselves with Warren's feelings and emotional responses to developments around him, and the narratives tend to examine them in expansive and even leisurely ways. The considerable discomforts and dissatisfactions of ordinary life in the middle-to-upper-class milieu in which he lives are a frequent topic of the narrations. As he walks about the grounds of his murdered rich aunt's estate toward the end of *Death of My Aunt*, he recalls to himself how he had always detested the place, and now (he says) makes "the most of [his] hatred" of his childhood and his social class before eventually reminding himself that it was his aunt's wealth that had paid for many of the comforts of his childhood and youth and that she has been murdered only a few days before as he stood at her bedside.[10]

Warren often describes himself as behaving in a selfish or cowardly way, but it seems clear enough in the series that he is a character designed to be admired overall for his frank appraisals of his motivations. There are several other types of male characters which recur from novel to novel—some of them literally. Three of the chief types of these are all described by Warren in his first-person narrations as being exceptionally good-looking men and clearly-enough attractive to him. The first of these is the bully. Clarence Ropford, a young man described as "dashing" and, like Warren (and like the young Kitchin) himself a stockbroker, appears in *The Cornish Fox* and will serve as a fair representative of the type, said by Warren to be "an oppressive bullying personality which cramps one's style, and won't live and let live." Similar characters appear in the other Warren mysteries. A second type is the comely young man who may be involved in shady dealings such as the black market or drug dealing but who turns out to be an ally of Warren's, when both find themselves in a tight corner, usually around the dramatic climax of the narrative. Jimmy Hankersley, another character in *The Cornish Fox*, will serve as a representative of this type. Envoyed to the train station to welcome and provide transportation for Warren when he first arrives in Cornwall early in the novel, Hankersley (his name may resonate with Warren's "hankering" for him) appears for his second interaction with Warren with his body on display. Walking along the local beach, Warren takes a good look at the "one genuine sun-bather sprawled at full-length on the sand," who turns out to be Hankersley. Warren goes on, "Seeing him stripped I was surprised not only by his muscles but by a general appearance of 'toughness' about his whole body, which one did not suspect when one saw him in his clothes."[11]

Warren would not attempt to flirt even mildly with the "dashing" Ropford, whom he seems to dislike and distrust almost before even meeting him, but he allows his interest in the indifferent but affable Hankersley a little freer rein. But it is really only with the third type that Warren in any sense lets himself go (so to speak), and that is with male characters such as Chief Inspector Parris, who allows his openly sociable and enjoying response to Warren to show almost without reserve. Consider his first spectacular appearance in *Crime at Christmas*, in which he comes striding into Warren's bedroom late in the evening of Boxing Day: "Inspector Parris was a tall and very good-looking man of about forty. Had he been a little thinner, he might have been a male film star. He had thick, rather greasy, light brown hair, large blue eyes, a strong though slightly snub nose, and a large but not unpleasant mouth and jaw. He came straight to my bed and held out his hand."[12]

Having first appeared in *Crime at Christmas*, Parris cycles back through *Death of His Uncle*. He is typical of a kind of male character who can appreciate Warren's good qualities and even show him affection without idealizing or ignoring his failings. Even as he is congratulating Warren on having figured out most of the complexities of the case in *Death of His Uncle* before the police were able to, he also teases Warren about his tendency as an amateur detective to "post-date" his own discoveries and suspicions in the written reports of his investigations that he makes to the police, in order to dispel any suspicions that the police in turn might have that Warren was actually withholding evidence and obstructing their investigation until it suited him to share his findings with them.[13]

At the very end of *Death of His Uncle*, Parris offers Warren his second ticket for the Sibelius concert (the fourth and seventh symphonies) that Parris is planning to attend "at the Queen's Hall on Wednesday of next week." Is there a romance budding between the amateur and the professional detective at the very end of *Death of His Uncle*? What happens *after* Parris and Warren experience together the intensities of these particular symphonies of Sibelius? Here at the end of Parris' second and final appearance in the Warren series, is Kitchin, who appears to have had sex with and/or formed sustaining emotional relationships with other men throughout his adult life, perhaps sending Parris and Warren off on a date of sorts that will take place just beyond some (but not necessarily all) of his readers' ken? Whatever love life or sex life Malcolm Warren may have, he must do so between installments of the series; whatever erotic and/or romantic experiences he may have appear to leave little in the way of traces in the novels, although (as I am suggesting) traces there are, intermittently. Eros seems to be approaching once again near the end (the climax?) *of The Cornish Fox*, where, on the next-to-last page of the novel, Warren tells the reader of his excitement about finally escaping rural Cornwall and heading back to his life in London: "How delightful it would be to exchange those restricted, geographical friendships such as one is forced to make in the country, for the spontaneous friendships which one can make in a big town without regard for local susceptibilities."[14]

Whatever may or may not be "gay" about Kitchin's Warren stories, perhaps the "queerest" thing about them is the way they suspend themselves, narratively and affectively, between the chapters and episodes of Warren's life that do not get told. Kitchin keeps giving readers accounts of Warren's life when he (usually only briefly) finds himself in the country, with a suspenseful crime-puzzle to investigate but with the prospect of no "friendships" except "those restricted, geographical" ones "such as one is forced to make in the country." Even the warm friendship that develops between Warren and Inspector Parris in *Crime at Christmas*, appears to grow even warmer in *Death of His Uncle*, and which may actually be getting hot at the very end of the latter book, looks to both men's being back in London ("at the Queen's Hall on Wednesday of next week") for its possible fulfillment.

Yet not even the aura of excitement and intense pleasure that seems to characterize the kind of metropolitan "spontaneous friendships" that Warren is at the very end of the entire series looking excitedly forward to resuming represent the most appealing and highly valued experiences and feelings that Kitchin evokes in the Warren mysteries. That is why Warren, for all his expressed preference for life in the city most of the time, also appears to have especially intense experiences of pleasure at least occasionally while living his "restricted" life in the country; it is this latter kind of episodes—Warren's various enforced rustications—that Kitchin's mystery series is all about. Probably most readers of Kitchin's fiction—whether the eight "regular" novels that he published or the four Warren detective novels—remember his work as thoroughly ironical comedy-of-manners-style writing. But there keeps recurring in his fiction—certainly in his detective novels—passages (ones that I would argue have tended to be overlooked) that evoke an almost mystical awareness of the rapturous pleasure(s) that one may take in the most ordinary, even outwardly drab, environs and experiences, and that the environs of these raptures are at least as likely, if not likelier, to be located in the country and the suburbs:

> I have always had a fondness for the shabby, slow suburban trains which run in the late evening. To me there is something romantic about their tired homeward glide between rows of little houses with their lighted windows. On such journeys I find released in me a serenely contemplative quality—a hint of the Divine essence in man—which weaves innumerable fantasies round those drawn translucent curtains and the human beings shadowed against them by the lights within, or appearing for a second in the square of an uncurtained window, for few people are shy about being seen by a passing train. I have even wondered if the guards and engine drivers, who, no doubt, know the names of every little house, ever form contacts with their momentary neighbors, here wave a handkerchief or blow a kiss, or shudder here at some tragedy which they know is being enacted within those half seen walls, and in the houses there are surely some who have made the train a real and personal thing—my realities are all personal—watch its coming with joy and its going with regret, like astronomers thrilled by the radiance of a predicted star.[15]

Here is an experience of pleasure and a fantasy of pleasure that may exceed—in the "contacts with … momentary neighbors" that Warren imagines the train men having with the "people" who are not "shy about being seen by a passing train"—even the "spontaneous friendships" that can be found only in the city. Here is a kind of "mystery" in the Warren stories that may be greater than the explicit mystery of "whodunit?" How does a reverie on and about a "shabby" train on its suburban rounds generate such intense feelings of "romance," not here between two men in particular but between the train men, on the one hand, and the people (gender unspecified) whose open windows they are passing "in the late evening"? Kitchin appears to have preferred men from social worlds much less privileged and moneyed than his own, both as casual sex-partners and as long-term domestic partners (he had another male lover for years after he lost Preen)—hence, perhaps the "shabby" but nevertheless fairly paradisiacal atmosphere of the suburban train running its "slow," "tired homeward glide between rows of little houses." It is easy to imagine Kitchin falling into a "serenely contemplative" mood, perceiving "a hint of the Divine essence in man" as he imagines the train workers ("guards and engine drivers") blowing kisses at the "human beings," men as well as women, "shadowed against" the curtains.

Kitchin's close friend and fellow novelist L.P. Hartley contributed a foreword to Kitchin's posthumously published last novel, *A Short Walk in Williams Park*, in which Hartley writes:

> What appears in most of Mr. Kitchin's novels, and not least in this one, is the sense of ecstasy. Let the subject be what it will, the Stock Exchange, the Helford River, the Fandango Restaurant, or the 444 motor bus, which carries Francis so conveniently to Williams Park, there is always round the corner not only romance and excitement but sheer ecstasy, transforming these commonplace scenes and experiences with a sudden halo of light.[16]

The term "ecstasy" for the quality that appears in most of Kitchin's novels is one that Hartley may have taken directly from Kitchin's *Death of His Uncle*. The outward occasion for what is there called "ecstasy" comes late in Warren's investigation in this third novel of his series, as he (not one to make a scene of his "whole body," as Jimmy Tankersley would do in *The Cornish Fox*), strips for a solitary moonlight swim in a country pond:

> I deposited my clothes in a little heap by a stone ... darted three yards down the grassy slope and plunged in. As I did so, a big drop of rain struck me on the forehead.... Except for the cry of a startled night-bird, there was no sound, and I enjoyed a moment of timeless ecstasy, feeling as if I were wearing the whole pond with its grasses and willows and even the mud beneath, as my garment.... It was an experience of pantheistic satisfaction—of a beneficent if sombre earth-magic—to which I should never have thought I could respond.[17]

Spoiler Alert: Taken out of context as it has been here, this moonlight swim may sound excessively and wistfully pastoral, but the reader of this passage learns soon afterwards that "most of the body" of the missing uncle for which Warren has been searching lies mutilated and decaying in this very pond. The full force of Warren's experience of "a moment of timeless ecstasy" as he submerges his body in the pond and imagines gathering its "grasses and willows and even the mud beneath" around and onto his body as his "garment" can register only once he and the reader have learned that the missing corpse, or most of it, is sharing the pond with Warren's momentarily "ecstatic" body: Warren later realizes that he had scraped his bare foot as he swam on the rock that turns out to be all that is keeping the corpse from floating to the surface. **End Spoiler.**

As we have seen, part of the "serenely contemplative quality" that Malcolm Warren said he finds on some "shabby" suburban trains earlier in *Death of His Uncle* proceeds not only from his fantasy of glances and kisses passing between the train men and some of the people in lighted windows that they pass, but also of a "shudder" that the train men feel at "the tragedy which they know is being enacted within those half-seen walls" that the train passes. Here Kitchin gives us readers a glimpse into the powerful affective charge with which he imbues his Malcolm Warren novels, in which erotic attraction both hetero- and homosexual and casual and unexpected contact with death, dead bodies, and "tragedy" are pulled together into an uncanny kind of "garment" which the reader as well as the protagonist of these stories can at times "ecstatically" don, if only for scattered and unpredictable moments. There are not only "love-scenes" (and/or sexual encounters) going on behind those illuminated curtains that can be seen from the "shabby" train, there are also domestic tragedies, including the misery that some of the same-sex couples in these houses experience as objects of suspicion and persecution. But there is also sometimes the bliss ("ecstasy") of erotic and emotional fulfillment and/or mutual devotion and sustenance that they share.

The last chapter of *Crime at Christmas* provides what Kitchin calls a "Short Catechism," a quasi–Socratic dialogue or vigorous Q-and-A between Malcolm Warren and the Reader, on the principles that, as Warren sees it, have governed the story now nearly ended. Early in this disquisition Kitchin has Warren make an extended statement about the nature and purpose of detective fiction: "A detective story is always something of an *étude de moeurs*—a study of normal people in abnormal circumstances. By normal people, I mean people whose lives come fairly close to our own, people whose psychology we can follow and sympathize with."[18]

This sounds straightforward enough until Warren/Kitchin only a couple of sentences later start discussing exactly why the signs and effects of extreme and fatal violence are indispensable for the particular kind of "study of manners and modes of living" that the detective novel should be: "You want the revolver shot, the bloodstained knife, the mutilated corpse—but largely because they bring out the prettiness of the chintz in the drawing-room and the softness of the grass on the Vicarage lawn."[19]

Warren goes on to try to clarify:

> ... I would say that the excuse for a detective story is two-fold. First, it presents a problem to be solved and shares, in a humble way, the charm of the acrostic and the crossword puzzle. But secondly—and this, to my mind, is its real justification—it provides one with a narrow but intensive view of ordinary life, the steady flow of which is felt more keenly through the very violence of its interruption.[20]

The Reader replies, "Most people would say that the softness of the Vicarage lawn is only noteworthy because there's a body lying on it. You say the body is only noteworthy because it is lying on a soft lawn." Warren demurs, "Not quite. Though I don't know," and then ventures the proposition, "After all, soft lawns are more real and permanent than dead bodies. At least I hope they are."[21] But are they? I suspect that whatever the question is for Warren, for Kitchin the question of which is "more real and permanent," a soft lawn or a dead body, is not a simple matter of yes or no, or one is and one is not.

Midway through the last of the Malcolm Warrens, *The Cornish Fox*, Warren has another experience of "serenity" and "ecstasy" in the perfectly ordinary-seeming circumstance of having a drink by himself while standing in a garden late one afternoon waiting for his host and hostess to come downstairs from dressing for the evening. The day has grown relatively warm, but a mist is rapidly forming and filling the sky: "It was a beautiful scene," Warren recalls, "and its charm increased as the mist gained in density and the lights became more varied and more subtle." He falls into a reverie remembering his intense aesthetic and emotional response of the previous day to hearing a skilled amateur singer perform Henri Duparc's song "*Extase*" ("Ecstasy") and he muses on the lyric's opening line, "On a pale lily, my heart sleeps in a slumber sweet as death." The line is repeated at the end of the song, but the "pale lily" has there become the "pale breast" of a human addressee. The imagined intersection of heart, breast, and death here is a bit eerily reminiscent of the way Warren had ecstatically immersed himself in the water in *Death of His Uncle*, imagined clothing his naked body in the grasses and mud of the pond, and brushed with his bare foot the rock holding down a corpse. But Warren's "serene" musings soon become contaminated with a "feeling of shame" at what he experiences as the disjunction between "the fairy-like view draped round me like a garment I was not worthy to wear" and "the hard crudity" of the life he finds himself living during his temporary abode in Cornwall, comprised of "anonymous letters, ... money, [fraudulent securities], dog-racing, the black-market, the drug-trade, and perhaps worse to come."[22]

As he confronts himself, asking, "Where was I going? What was happening to my soul?," he recalls a brief passage from Virgil's *Georgics*, "a line and a half spoken by Proteus, the sleepy god of the seashore to the hotheaded Aristaeus": "*Nam quis te, juvenum confidentissime, nostras / Jussit adire domos, quidve hic petis?*," which Kitchin translates in a footnote as, "Now who told you, most self-assured of men, to come and visit our houses, and what do you want here?" Warren immediately translates Proteus' aggressive query into a similarly aggressive questioning of his own motivations and desires: "Why had I come to Cornwall, spying round people's houses, and what did I really want there? And once more, the whole problem of the Cornish Fox had me in its toils."[23]

But, as we have seen, "the whole problem of the Cornish Fox" is not really a whole, it is but one (albeit the last) episode in the series of stories in which a man named Malcolm Warren experiences the agonies as well as the ecstasies of the intense pleasures and the grotesque contacts (physical and otherwise) that he has with human bodies living and dead, the race-track, "the black-market, the drug-trade," smoldering hatreds, out-and-out bloody murder—but also the kind of more or less secret serenity and bliss that Kitchin may have intermittently enjoyed with Clive Preen (and perhaps other men) in the course of what may have appeared to others to be "humdrum" relationships.[24] Malcolm Warren appears to enjoy such blisses and agonies almost entirely by himself, in ecstatic solitude, in the world of Kitchin's detective series. As readers, we can only speculate, as I have endeavored to do in some of these pages, about what Warren may or may not have gotten up to "between cases."

Research Note: I find the world in which Kitchin "clad" his character Malcolm Warren so richly coherent that I have devoted this brief consideration of Kitchin's detective fiction entirely to it, but I want to note here that Kitchin's 1938 ostensibly non-detective novel *Birthday Party* is also a "murder mystery" of sorts, with a plot that suspends itself between two fatal "accidents" (or "suicides") that take place at a country estate undergoing the radical change that was continuing to effect such places (and their owners and occupants) "between the wars." The question of the relation of *Birthday Party* to the Malcolm Warren mysteries is an interesting one. Researchers interested in gay histories and literary histories of the twentieth-century UK may also want to consider some of the work of man of letters William Plomer that verges on detective fiction, such as *The Case Is Altered* (1932, published by the Hogarth Press, as Kitchin's *Death of His Aunt* and *Crime at Christmas* had been). Better known to mystery readers (and much more numerous) are the detective novels published by prolific author Rupert Croft-Cooke, who was convicted of and imprisoned for "acts of indecency" with two sailors in 1955, and, under the pseudonym "Leo Bruce," published two extensive detective series, eight "Sergeant Beef" mysteries (1936–52) followed by a whopping twenty-three "Carolus Deene" mysteries (1955–74).

Note to Publishers: The greatest aid to the better understanding of Kitchin's work would be the making available to readers of *The Cornish Fox*, the fourth of the four Malcolm Warren mysteries, perennially listed on Amazon.com as "Currently Unavailable" and available at used-book websites in small numbers and only for rare-book prices. The first two Malcolm Warrens, *Death of My Aunt* and *Crime at Christmas*, are currently in print from "Faber Finds"/Faber & Faber paperbacks, but the third, *Death of His Uncle*, can at present be had only as a used book. Kitchin's quasi-murder-mystery novel *Birthday Party* is currently available from Valancourt Books, as are several of his other novels (see endnotes for further information about Valancourt's recent reprintings of Kitchin's fiction).

Notes

1. C. H. B. Kitchin, *Death of His Uncle* (1939; repr., New York: Harper & Row, 1984), 1.

2. But see the "Research Note" at the end of the essay above, regarding the evident murder mystery qualities of one of Kitchin's "non-crime" novels, *Birthday Party* (1938).

3. Nigel Nicholson and Joanna Trautmann, eds., *The Letters of Virginia Woolf*, Vol. 5 (New York: Harcourt Brace, 1979), 339–40.

4. C. H. B. Kitchin, *Crime at Christmas* (1934; repr., London: Faber and Faber, 2009), 15.

5. The story is told (among other places) in James E. Miller, Jr., *T.S. Eliot: The Making of an American Poet* (University Park: Pennsylvania State University Press, 2005), 385–86. Kitchin's friend and literary executor Francis King retells the story, which he says Kitchin told him. See Francis King, "Introduction" to C. H. B. Kitchin, *The Book of Life* (Richmond: Valancourt Books, 2009), vii.

6. LGBTQ Studies scholar David Robinson provides a stimulating meditation on the kaleidoscopic range of meanings that homosexuality bore in Kitchin's world and on the wide range of responses to same-sex desires and behaviors that a group of characters in a novel of Kitchin's evince (a "non-crime" novel that was published just a couple of years after Kitchin's first Malcolm Warren mystery appeared). See David Robinson, "Introduction" to C. H. B. Kitchin, *The Sensitive One* (Richmond: Valancourt Books, 2014).

7. **Spoiler Alert:** That is not to say that there is no observable "homo" action at all in the Warren series: in the resolution of the mystery in the closing chapters of *The Cornish Fox*, a strongly romantic, erotic lesbian attraction on the part of one of the female characters for another becomes clearly legible although it is not explicitly called "lesbian." Nevertheless, the apparently largely unrequited passion of an older woman for a younger remains a factor driving the plot invisibly forward until the murder is solved, when the younger woman tells Warren of the emotional history that the two women have shared, enabling him to put the pieces of the plot together into a harmonious whole.

8. C. H. B. Kitchin, *Death of My Aunt* (1929; repr., Harper & Row, 1984), 121; Kitchin, *Christmas*, 191.

9. Kitchin, *Uncle*, 105.

10. Kitchin, *Aunt*, 136–37.

11. Kitchin, *The Cornish Fox: A Detective Story* (London: Secker & Warburg, 1949), 27, 85.

12. Kitchin, *Christmas*, 162.

13. Kitchin, *Uncle*, 229.

14. *Ibid.*; Kitchin, *Fox*, 294.

15. Kitchin, *Uncle*, 97.

16. L. P. Hartley, Foreword to C. H. B. Kitchin, *A Short Walk in Williams Park* (1971; repr., Richmond: Valancourt, 2014).

17. Kitchin, *Uncle*, 185–86.

18. Kitchin, *Christmas*, 272.

19. *Ibid.*

20. *Ibid.*

21. *Ibid.*, 273.

22. Kitchin, *Fox*, 154.

23. *Ibid.*, 255.

24. I intend my use of the term "humdrum" (in scare-quotes) here and in the title of this piece as a tip of the cap to Curtis Evans' recasting of the implications of the term in his book, *Masters of the "Humdrum" Mystery: Cecil John Charles Street, Freeman Wills Croft, Alfred Walter Stewart, and the British Detective Novel, 1920–1961* (Jefferson, NC: McFarland, 2012). The implications of a revisionary aesthetic of the allegedly "humdrum" seem both ripe and rich for several modernist genres, and Evans has performed a considerable service to literary and cultural historians and theorists by showing some of the differences that such a reassessment can make in the flourishing field of modernist Mystery Studies. Similarly, a revisitation of (again) the allegedly "humdrum"—in and out of relation to such other aesthetic categories as the ordinary, the everyday, the abject, the sublime, the beautiful, the grotesque, the inexpressible, the unbearable, and the terrifying—may be of interest to some practitioners of feminist and queer literary and cultural studies.

BIBLIOGRAPHY

Hartley, L. P. Foreword to C. H. B. Kitchin, *A Short Walk in Williams Park*. 1971. Reprint, Richmond, VA: Valancourt, 2014.
King, Francis. "Introduction" to C. H. B. Kitchin, *The Book of Life*. 1960. Reprint, Richmond: Valancourt Books, 2009.
Kitchin, C. H. B. *Birthday Party*. 1938. Reprint, Richmond: Valancourt, 2014.
_____. *The Cornish Fox: A Detective Story*. London: Secker & Warburg, 1949.
_____. *Crime at Christmas*. 1934. Reprint, London: Faber and Faber, 2009.
_____. *Death of His Uncle*. 1939. Reprint, New York: Harper & Row, 1984.
_____. *Death of My Aunt*. 1929. Reprint, New York: Harper & Row, 1984.
Miller, James E., Jr. *T. S. Eliot: The Making of an American Poet*. University Park: Pennsylvania State University Press, 2005.
Nicholson, Nigel, and Joanne Trautmann, eds. *The Letters of Virginia Woolf*, Vol. 5. New York: Harcourt Brace, 1979.
Robinson, David. "Introduction" to C. H. B. Kitchin, *The Sensitive One*. Richmond: Valancourt Books, 2014.

"Two young men who write as one"
Richard Wilson Webb, Hugh Callingham Wheeler, Male Couples and The Grindle Nightmare

Curtis Evans

"By this time most readers know that Patrick Quentin and Q. Patrick are one and the same man—or rather, two young men who write as one. Between them they boast a few scattered BA's and MA's; their hobbies include everything but tropical fish, and their travels have taken in most of the world."—About the Author, Patrick Quentin, *Puzzle for Puppets* (Simon & Schuster, 1944)

Discerning critics and connoisseurs of vintage American crime fiction have long hailed expatriate Englishmen Richard Wilson Webb (1901–1966) and Hugh Callingham Wheeler (1912–1987), in their various pseudonymous incarnations of Patrick Quentin, Q. Patrick and Jonathan Stagge, as two of the most significant twentieth-century masters of the mystery form. Yet most accounts have failed to acknowledge a salient biographical fact about the two authors: that for nearly twenty years they not only crafted crime fiction together but spent much of their lives together. The mystery world has long acknowledged vintage crime writing couples of different sexes like Frances and Richard Lockridge, William and Audrey Kelley Roos, Darwin and Hildegarde Teilhet, John and Emery Bonett and G. D. H. and Margaret Cole, whose unions were publicized and sanctioned by both law and custom. Only very recently, however, have commentators on crime fiction evinced any real interest in Webb and Wheeler as a same-sex writing couple in a pre–Stonewall, pre-*Obergefell* era and of the queer subtext in much of their mystery fiction. In this essay I scrutinize the joint lives and careers of the two authors as well as the novel *The Grindle Nightmare* (1935), the first Q. Patrick mystery composed after Wheeler met Webb and joined him in the United States and one that—not coincidentally, I argue—gives great prominence to coupled male characters.[1]

The instigator of the deadly duo of Webb and Wheeler, Richard "Rickie" Webb, was born at Burnham-on-Sea, Somerset, the youngest of six children (four daughters and two sons) of Frederick Charles Webb and Grace Elizabeth Lucas, headmaster and mistress of a local girls' school. Rickie received his English education at Rutland's Oakham School, where he served as captain of the cricket team, and Clare College, Cambridge, from which he received a BA in 1923. After his graduation, Rickie, a diminutive, dark-haired globetrotter and dabbler in a diversity of fields, left England for Weimar Germany, at this time in the midst of its sexually frenetic cultural throes. He briefly attended the University of Berlin before departing for South Africa, where for a short time he conducted classes in Greek; then, at the fizzing height of the Roaring Twenties, he was placed in Paris as a British news agency correspondent. In 1926 the protean and venturesome young man again shifted career lanes, departing Paris for Philadelphia, where he became research manager for a pharmaceutical company, Smith, Kline and French Laboratories (SKF). This road proved quite a gainful one for Rickie financially, as in the mid–1930s he became instrumental in the manufacture, production and marketing of SKF's hugely successful amphetamine-based Benzedrine Sulfate inhaler. Quick to perceive the "exciting possibilities for Benzedrine Sulfate" (as an authority on the drug has noted), Rickie, his eye ever on the main chance, wrote a colleague in 1936: "If we haven't got a bearcat by the tail, then I'm a Dutchman."[2]

In his early years in Philadelphia, Rickie Webb resided downtown with two other individuals, Robert Elson Turner (1901–1979) and Frances Ritter Bartholomew (1873–1939), at rented lodgings in a row house at 2105 Locust Street (part of the city's modern "gayborhood" today). Likely for Rickie one of the main attractions of the city of brotherly love at this time was the tall, handsome, blue-eyed and bespectacled Bob Turner, scion of a prominent lawyer in Seattle, Washington. As a student Turner had attended classes at Hamilton College in Clinton, New York, where he majored in chemistry and French and joined the Alpha Delta Phi fraternity. According to the droll caption beside his college yearbook photo, "Toto," as Bob had been nicknamed by his ADPhi brothers, once had shown promise of becoming "the college aesthete," but behind "his coy smile and innocent looks" lurked "a world of guile and deviltry." This hidden "guile and deviltry" redounded on Toto spectacularly in his senior year, when he was expelled from Hamilton College for bootlegging and indicted by a federal grand jury. That his mother was president of the Seattle chapter of the Women's Christian Temperance Union added a layer of irony to the debacle.³

Embarrassed but not long sullied by his brush with bootlegging scandal, Bob Turner soon was back hitting the books, if not necessarily the bottles, this time at home in Seattle at the University of Washington, where presumably he was kept under greater parental supervision. After his graduation from UW, his parents unleashed him to study in Paris at the Sorbonne, where in 1926 he received a DUP (*Docteur de l'Université de Paris*). Presumably after having encountered Rickie in the City of Light, Turner later that year settled, like Rickie, in Philadelphia. There Turner initially taught courses at the University of Pennsylvania, before in 1930 obtaining a position at Bryn Mawr as an associate professor of French Language and Literature. Drawing on his undergraduate background in chemistry, he also joined Rickie in supervising lab research on Benzedrine for SKF. After leaving their Locust Street digs in the early Thirties, he remained Rickie's lifelong friend, serving not only as one of the two witnesses at Rickie's 1943 wedding (for more on the author's short-lived marriage, see below) but as one of the two executors and administrators of Rickie's estate after the author's death in 1966.⁴

Also lodging at the Locust Street residence with Rickie Webb and Bob Turner was Frances Ritter Bartholomew, head of the Eighth Ward Settlement House at 922 Locust Street. A generation older than her male co-lodgers, Frances Bartholomew was a progressive social liberal from a wealthy "Main Line" family who had long labored dutifully on behalf of the city's underprivileged African American population. A 1907 newspaper article described her as a "sweet-faced Quakeress ... unconscious of color differences in estimating the value of men...." Louis Martin, an African American who had been raised at the Eighth Ward Settlement House after the death of his mother in 1899, when he was but ten years old, warmly recalled "Ma Thol," as Frances Bartholomew was termed by the settlement house children, as a kindly, genteel lady who had "scandalous ideas" for her time, insisting on taking "her orphan charges to operas," "teaching them to waltz and two-step" and, most importantly, incessantly imploring them to get "*all* the education you can get."⁵

Possibly through the solicitous ministrations of "Ma Thol," Rickie Webb in 1930 found his first collaborator in crime fiction in Martha Mott Kelley (1906–1998), a Radcliffe graduate descended from famed Quaker abolitionist and feminist Lucretia Mott and a niece of prominent progressive social reformer Florence Kelley. "Patsy," as Martha Mott Kelley was nicknamed, had already demonstrated literary leanings, since her graduation from Radcliffe having published book reviews in *The Nation* and a short story in *Scribner's Magazine*. Together Rickie and Patsy devised the Q. Patrick pseudonym for their mystery novels by combining "Pat" and "Rick" to make "Patrick" and then adding the letter "Q" because, the pair later teasingly explained, they considered "Q" unquestionably the "most intriguing letter in the alphabet" (One suspects that Rickie, at least, with the letter "Q" may have had the word "queer" in mind.) In this first incarnation Q. Patrick produced *Cottage Sinister* (1931) and *Murder at the Women's City Club* (1932; published in the UK under the title *Death in the Dovecote*), both of which were well-received by reviewers. Frances Bartholomew may have been Rick and Patsy's model for Miss Riddle, the social worker character in the latter novel.[6]

After Patsy Kelley married and abandoned collaborative fiction writing with Rickie, he produced a successful solo detective novel, *Murder at Cambridge* (1933), which drew nostalgically yet quite murderously on his college days in England, before finding a promising new writing partner in another female Philadelphian, Mary Louise White (1902–1984). Together Rickie and "Mary Lou," as she was known to her friends, published, later in the same year, *S. S. Murder* (1933), a shipboard mystery that received good notices in the press. Descended from an old Quaker family, White had graduated from Bryn Mawr, done graduate work at Harvard and Yale and, like Rickie and his friend Bob Turner, spent time in Paris in the Twenties.[7] This second Q. Patrick incarnation was even shorter-lived than the first, however, for the same year that *S. S. Murder* appeared, Rickie met someone who proved his perfect partner: a prodigiously talented and strikingly handsome blue-eyed, young Englishman named Hugh Callingham Wheeler.

Born in London, the son of a Board of Trade Examiner, Hugh Wheeler attended Claysmore School and the University of London, where he was awarded a BA degree in English with honors in 1932. Before he ever crossed Rickie's path, Hugh already had demonstrated a marked streak of independent-mindedness. At Claysmore Hugh clashed repeatedly with his headmaster, Alex Devine, who wrote Hugh's father agitated letters complaining that his young charge was falling prey to bad company, including a "foolish and precocious" American boy and an "utterly immoral" novel by Aldous Huxley. "I am anxious about him," warned Devine, adding forebodingly that Hugh had "queer ideas" and was "particularly liable to outside influences that are dangerous." Especially vexing to Devine was Hugh's expressed disinclination to seek a scholarship to Oxford or Cambridge, since, Devine argued, the hallowed Oxbridge path "would lead naturally to the First Class of the Civil Service and do for the boy much more than anything else could."[8]

After his graduation from the University of London in 1932, Hugh met the visiting Rickie Webb, who soon was doing his best for the boy, as he saw it—though no doubt Hugh's old headmaster would have deemed the situation most perturbing indeed. In the company of his new mentor, the twenty-one-year-old Hugh on August 2, 1933, embarked aboard the *Norddeutscher Lloyd* on Rickie's return to Philadelphia, doubtlessly with visions of a lucrative American literary career dancing like Rockettes in his head. In a letter Hugh wrote to his mother on board the ship as it sailed into New York harbor (with characteristic irony he likened the Statue of Liberty to Lady Macbeth), Hugh avowed, "I still get along very well with Rickie," adding hopefully: "Long may it continue."[9]

By October of that year, Hugh was writing his brother that he and Webb were working together on a "quite pretentious novel." ("The best parts all are Rickie's," he added modestly.) The next two Q. Patrick novels, *The Grindle Nightmare* (1935) and *Death Goes to School* (1936), probably were written primarily by Rickie, though the first book often has been co-credited to Mary Louise White and the second to Hugh. The back cover of the *Grindle* dust jacket repeatedly signifies that Q. Patrick is a single individual, stating that "Q. Patrick is not his name, America not his birthplace, writing not his vocation.... A Jekyll and Hyde is Q. Patrick—by day an important Eastern executive—by night a recorder of macabre crime!" This declaration notwithstanding, however, it seems likely that Hugh had some influence on the composition of *The Grindle Nightmare*. In a late October letter to Hugh's parents, Rickie confided that he had suggested that he and Hugh—whom he was nursing through a bad bout with the grippe ("The poor fellow ... has been in bed about 10 days with temp. varying between 103 and 100 ... you can rely on my seeing he gets the best medical attention....")—work together writing "a mystery story of which I've already worked out the plot." This likely was *The Grindle Nightmare*, the most singular and impressive novel in the Q. Patrick oeuvre up to this point (see below).[10]

Whatever the exact origin of *The Grindle Nightmare*, from 1936 onward not only did Rickie and Hugh, thoughts of "literature" laid aside for now, together intermittently continue the Q. Patrick series of detective novels, they also introduced two additional mystery series, produced under a pair of new pseudonyms, Jonathan Stagge and Patrick Quentin, the latter pen name obviously a variation on Q. Patrick. Rickie devised the ingenious plots, upon which Hugh, a natural writer, expansively elaborated. Both men then honed the final drafts as Hugh typed.[11]

Inveterate travelers as well as writers, the couple throughout the Thirties frequently left Philadelphia to roam Bermuda, the Caribbean and Latin America together, not altogether incidentally providing settings for several of their crime novels. Passenger lists invariably place their two names adjacent to each other, with Hugh designated as a writer and Rickie as a business executive. Absent a period when Hugh, who followed Rickie's earlier example and became a naturalized citizen in 1940, did service during the Second World War in the U.S. Army Medical Corps, the two men from 1939 to 1952 divided their time between New York City and the Berkshires in western Massachusetts, long a favored rural retreat for members of the transatlantic social and cultural elite.¹²

In 1939–40 Rickie and Hugh resided in Tyringham, Massachusetts at the expansive Hickory Farm estate, which Rickie had rented from Lord and Lady Salter of London. The couple joined the local social whirl, attending, for example a luncheon party hosted by the Princess Stefano del Guidice Caracciolo di Luperano (the former Miss Dorothy Adrian of Poughkeepsie, New York), which included among the guests "Boy" Foster, son of multi-millionaire Giraud Foster, owner of the magnificent Gilded Age Berkshires mansion Bellefontaine, and stage actress Francesca Bruning and her theater critic husband, John Beaufort. Another time Rickie delivered a talk on mystery fiction to the Rotary Club at the nearby town of Great Barrington. Quite liking life in the Berkshires, Rickie in 1944 purchased Twin Hills Farm, located in Monterey, another village in the area. Here he and Hugh would reside until 1952.¹³

Admittedly there is to be considered the mysterious affair of Rickie's civil marriage, on May 21, 1943, to Frances Winwar (Francesca Vinciguerra, 1900–1985), a prolific Italian-born author known for her historical novels and biographies of myriad literary luminaries, including gay writers Oscar Wilde and Walt Whitman. The previous year Winwar had divorced her second husband of seventeen years, Bernard Grebanier, a distinguished Brooklyn College English professor who led a covert gay life. From these circumstances one can but conclude that the queer male was far from a closed book to Winwar. Scholar Mauro Boncompagni has speculated that Rickie, now past forty, may have hoped that a lavender marriage might hush whispers about his homosexuality, but alternatively or additionally the union might have been spurred by a notion that his local draft board would be less inclined to call up to active service a respectably wedded man. In any event, Rickie's marriage with Winwar ended officially in divorce five years later, without any evidence which I have seen that the husband and wife ever actually lived with each other.¹⁴

At their house at Twin Hills Farm Rickie and Hugh together after the war achieved the climax of their creative union, publishing seven Patrick Quentin novels, their most innovative and interesting group of mysteries, as well as three Jonathan Stagges and one Q. Patrick. Years later Hugh confided that although he frequently visited New York City, "Monterey is the only place where I can really write." By the publication of the tension-wracked Patrick Quentin novel *Black Widow* (1952), however, Rickie was fifty-one years old and in prematurely declining health. Informal photos taken of him with Hugh in Italy four years after the end of the Second World War show him paunchy and balding and appearing decidedly older than the glamorous and still boyish-looking Hugh, who remained on the right side of forty (though in one intimate breakfast table shot with Hugh, Rickie is stylishly attired in snazzy polka dot pajamas). After contributing to *Black Widow* and

Danger Next Door (1952), the final Q. Patrick tale, Rickie retired from the creative collaboration he had commenced sixteen years earlier with Hugh, his own powers having waned, it seems, as Hugh's had waxed. Rickie moved to France, leaving his protégé and longtime companion the farm in the Berkshires and the Patrick Quentin name, and passed away in Paris fourteen years later at the age of sixty-five. Hugh kept Twin Hills Farm as his main residence until his death at the age of seventy-five in 1987.[15]

Between 1954 and 1965 Hugh published additional Patrick Quentin novels, but after 1960 he became increasingly involved with writing for stage and film, enjoying distinguished success and gaining admittance to the golden social circles of prominent figures in the entertainment world. With two 1961 stage plays, *Big Fish, Little Fish* and *Look, We've Come Through*, Hugh is credited with being the playwright who made the greatest effort at this time to lighten Broadway's stifling environment regarding depictions of homosexuality; while as a group Hugh's film scripts—*Something for Everyone* (1970), *Cabaret* (1972), *Travels with My Aunt* (1972), *A Little Night Music* (1978) and *Nijinsky* (1980)—explore a collection of remarkably diverse sexualities. He achieved his greatest plaudits, however, with the libretti of the musicals *A Little Night Music* (1973), *Candide* (1974) and *Sweeney Todd: The Demon Barber of Fleet Street* (1979), for each of which he won Tony Awards.[16]

Histories of stage and film often acknowledge Hugh as a gay writer, but they never connect him in anything more than a cursory way with his prior life as an author of crime fiction with Rickie Webb, while most crime fiction histories have failed to allow that Hugh had anything beyond a working relationship with Rickie, or that their writing might have any queer subtext. In a piece in *Mysteries Unlocked: Essays in Honor of Douglas G. Greene*, a 2014 book I edited, Mauro Boncompagni and I addressed these subjects, which were also alluded to in a 2016 collection of Patrick Quentin short fiction published by Crippen & Landru, to which I contributed an introduction and Joanna Gondris, Hugh Wheeler's great-niece, an informative and fascinating afterword. Below in this essay, I provide a preliminary consideration of queer subtext in the crime fiction of Rickie Webb and Hugh Wheeler by looking at the 1935 Q. Patrick novel *The Grindle Nightmare*, the first mystery that Rickie Webb published after Hugh Wheeler came to the United States to live and write with him, and the work with by far the highest quotient of queer-themed material of any of the Q. Patrick novels up to that time.

Suggestive subtext is found in earlier Q. Patrick novels, particularly *Murder at Cambridge*, written by Rickie solo, yet something queer about *The Grindle Nightmare* is immediately indicated on the author biography found on the back panel of the dust jacket of the American edition (previously referenced above).[17] Under a drawing of a question mark and the back of the head and shoulders of a fedora'd man, is the teasing declaration, "Q. Patrick is an enigma! Q. Patrick is a riddle! Q. Patrick is a mystery!" One might ask oneself, *with just what secret is Q. Patrick teasing us*? When we are informed that Q. Patrick is a Jekyll and Hyde ("by day an important Eastern executive—by night a recorder of macabre crime!"), it conjures images of illicit activities performed in the shadows.

Grindle's back panel blurb also signifies, even allowing for inevitable hype, especial ambition for this particular novel. "This story will place him, once and for all" the publisher, New York's short-lived Hartney Press, trumpets, "among that group of storytelling princes who stand, proudly sequestered, at the pinnacle of the craft." What was it about *The Grindle Nightmare* that made it such an exceptional book? The critical blurb from *Punch* included on the dust jacket's front flap gets to the heart of the matter: "In this tale of terror in a 'green New England valley' Mr. Patrick set out to make a study of a perverted mind, and without a reserve he has succeeded in his terrible intention." A chorus of other reviewers in both the U.S. and the UK chimed in with this evaluation, William C. Weber in the *Saturday Review*, for example, awarding the novel the "Malignancy Medal for 1935" and concluding that "more nasty people and unpleasant events you'll never find between two covers." In short, *The Grindle Nightmare* constituted a remarkable early attempt, within the detective fiction genre, to explore the subject of aberrant criminal psychology.[18]

Set in the scattered New England valley community of Grindle, some twenty miles distant from Rhodes, home of Rhodes University Hospital, *The Grindle Nightmare* tells the story of a series of criminal horrors—animal mutilations and human torture slayings (the first victim is a young child)—that impact the people in the valley, members of the upper crust and their servitors alike. Through the rather dispassionate narration of the novel's main character Q. Patrick intellectualizes the terrible events as a problem to be solved rather than wallowing in terror and gore in the manner of so many modern crime tales, yet *The Grindle Nightmare* nevertheless is most unusual for its time, when writers of classic detective fiction tended to shy from portraying gruesome acts of violence or deeply damaged mental states. Many orthodox writers and readers of detective fiction in this era saw fictional murder strictly as a puzzle that should test the mind, not trouble the heart or turn the stomach; and they believed that a mad murderer violated the "rules of the game," as codified by such authorities as S. S. Van Dine and Ronald Knox.[19]

In its setting *The Grindle Nightmare* rather resembles the dysfunctional suburbs of the celebrated mid-century American crime writer Patricia Highsmith, displaying a gallery of unlikable middle and upper-class characters, any one of whom, the reader might well conclude, might be capable of nasty doings, including maneater Roberta Tailford-Jones and her cuckolded "emasculate" husband, Edgar, who was grievously wounded in the Great War. Q.

Patrick's writing is viperish when describing Roberta, "the most magnificent woman in our community," through the poisoned prose of the narrator of the novel, Dr. Douglas Swanson, a researcher and instructor at Rhodes University Hospital:

> To me she always suggests an insect, or rather, a series of insects. Her hair is burnished like the wing of a Japanese beetle. Her eyebrows point upward like heraldic grasshoppers. Her mouth is long and soft like a coral slug, while her frequently gesticulating hands are somehow reminiscent of a praying mantis. I might also mention that she does not like me any better than I like her.[20]

Living "in style as only bachelors can," Doug Swanson and his Rhodes colleague Dr. Antonio Conti, "one of the youngest and smartest professors of pathology in America," share the lease of a "charming little farm house" in Grindle. Not only is Toni surpassingly brilliant, Doug never tires of telling us, but he is an awesome physical specimen as well. When Doug first introduces readers to Toni on the second page of the novel, as the two are preparing for the cocktail party which they are hosting, Toni has only "just emerged magnificent from the shower." Later, after the party has commenced, Doug notes that Toni is "six foot four of splendid physique," in contrast with himself, whom Roberta Tailford-Jones has derided in the past as "that microscopic runt." Yet later Doug again takes time admiringly to observe Toni (through Roberta's lascivious eyes, he tells us): "the muscular expanse of chest, the splendid teeth, the dark Italian hair." After the party has ended and the guests have left, we find Toni, still under Doug's close scrutiny, taking off "his shirt in the living room." Toni has, it seems, "an unconventional habit of dressing and undressing anywhere but in the right place."[21] This is all just in Chapter One.

Modern readers might be pardoned at this point for assuming that Doug and Toni are snugly ensconced gay partners or at least that Doug is carrying a brightly flaming torch for Toni. Not so, however. We learn that Doug has what he sadly believes is an unrequited passion for the "gorgeously eupeptic" Valerie Middleton, a lovely young woman he naturally assumes is pursuing Toni, for what woman with intact senses would not be dazzled by the Italian-American's magnificence? Still, Doug notes that the desirable Valerie "has a cool, clear laugh like a boy's" and he later compares a handsome, stricken young man to a painting of the martyred, arrow-pierced Saint Sebastian, famously a gay icon, that "I had once seen in some gallery or other"; so Doug's desires perhaps are queerer than he realizes.[22]

What seems beyond doubt is the similarity, as couples, between Doug and Toni and what we know of Rickie Webb and Bob Turner. Like Doug and Toni at fictional Rhodes University Hospital, both Rickie and Bob were involved with institutional research, their work, as we know, taking place at Philadelphia, for Smith, Kline and French Laboratories. Doug and Toni enjoy a comfortable bachelor existence in Grindle, their housekeeping and cooking provided for them by Lucinda, their "efficient colored factotum" ("Our tidy house and well-ordered meals were the envy of the entire married community," boasts Doug), while Rickie and Bob had lived together for several years at their place on Locust Street, chaperoned, in a manner of speaking, by that "sweet-faced Quakeress," Frances Bartholomew. Finally, while Rickie Webb was very far from a "nonentity," as the self-effacing Doug terms himself at one point, at 5'6" Rickie did stand rather in the shade of the strapping Bob Turner, who measured just shy of six feet. (Like Rickie, Hugh had a slighter build than Bob; his height was 5'8" and his weight about 140 pounds.)[23]

Spoiler Alert: While Doug and Toni are the relatively sympathetic male sleuthing couple of the novel, there is balancing them another, altogether repellent, male couple: young medical students Gerald Allstone and Peter Foote, the fiendish Hydes to Doug and Toni's detecting Jekylls. The authors of the terrible crimes in Grindle, Gerald and Peter also are drawn from real life individuals, young men who numbered among the most notorious murderers in the United States from the between-the-wars period known as the Golden Age of detective fiction: Nathan "Babe" Leopold (1904–1971) and Richard "Dickie" Loeb (1905–1936), the slayers of young Bobby Franks.

The trial of this pair of precocious teenage college graduates, privileged sons of wealthy Chicago parents, for the thrill killing of a randomly selected boy riveted the nation in 1924, when Rickie Webb was at the University of Berlin and Bob Turner at the University of Washington. (Hugh Wheeler at the time was merely twelve years old, two years younger than the murder victim.) Of especial interest to gay men in the Twenties and afterward were the public hints and whispers that Leopold and Loeb were lovers. A decade later, Rickie, likely encouraged by Hugh, his youthful but sophisticated new living companion, decided to invoke the enduringly fascinating, if deeply disturbing, Leopold-Loeb case within the pages of *The Grindle Nightmare*, anticipating Meyer Levin's novel *Compulsion* by over two decades.[24]

Resemblance between the real life murderers Babe Leopold and Dickie Loeb and *Grindle*'s fictional slayers, Gerald Allstone and Peter Foote, is not total, though it is considerable. While Leopold and Loeb both came from wealthy Jewish families in Chicago and precociously had graduated from college before turning twenty, there were differences between the two young men. Leopold was extremely intelligent, yet socially awkward, while Loeb, though bright as well, was a poorer student and also athletic, handsome and popular. A crime fiction addict and fantasist, Loeb dreamed of becoming a master criminal and committing the perfect crime. With the lure of sex Loeb gradually drew Leopold, who was utterly besotted with him, into the world of his fantasies—though sex with Dickie was insufficiently frequent for Babe's satisfaction.

The joint pathological state that was generated by the coupling of these two youths has been termed a *folie á deux*, a condition where madness is communicated between two individuals, the stronger of the two transmitting to the weaker his own dangerous delusions. In *The Grindle Nightmare* Toni Conti posits *folie á deux* as the cause of the rash of terrors plaguing the valley when he pronounces that Peter Foote mentally infected Gerald Allstone, grandson of local tycoon Seymour Allstone. Doug Swanson first describes Peter and Gerald in Chapter One, upon their arrival—together naturally—at Doug and Toni's cocktail party, in a revealing description to anyone recalling Leopold and Loeb:

> As they entered they presented a violent contrast. Gerald was slight and meek....
> Although he did not wear spectacles, his eyes had a trick of peering myopically at random objects which had no significance in themselves. He was awkward in company.
> Peter Foote, on the other hand, was rather handsome in an easy, graceful way. Being the son and heir of very rich parents somewhere in Illinois, friends and self-assurance came easily to him ... from his travels he had acquired that well-groomed sophistication which blossoms so often and so unexpectedly upon the emancipated Middle Westerner. I had always found him most responsive as a student and Toni had said that he was the most brilliant and hardworking member of his pathology classes at Rhodes.[25]

Not all the details are the same, to be sure. (Had they been Q. Patrick and his publisher might have opened themselves up to lawsuits, as Meyer Levin did with *Compulsion*.) In life it was Leopold who was an arrogantly brilliant, though socially maladroit, student, Loeb who was a diffident scholar in college; but the overall similarity is telling. Q. Patrick even mentions spectacles (Leopold carelessly dropped his at the site where he and Loeb disposed of Franks' body, the spectacles becoming the clue—what in detective fiction the author Carolyn Wells called a "gravity clue"—that led to their undoing) and he coyly notes that Peter is the son of "very rich parents somewhere in Illinois."

Leopold and Loeb are briefly mentioned by name in *The Grindle Nightmare*, when Doug scoffs concerning Toni's theory of *folie á deux*: "It is my own belief that [*folie á deux*] was invented by alienists of small scruples in order to save wealthy murderers from the death penalty. No one had ever heard of it until the Loeb-Leopold case, and no one would have heard of it then, if a bunch of millionaires hadn't been involved."[26]

While it is never explicitly stated in *Grindle* that Peter and Gerald are lovers, like Leopold and Loeb, such a relationship seems implicit in Q. Patrick's portrayal of the pair. At Doug and Toni's cocktail party Roberta indulges in a spot of spiteful innuendo after the duo leave the party: "'Very odd,' spat Roberta, even before the door closed behind the two boys. 'Very odd how those two boys are always about together. Never seen them with a girl or anything.'" Doug dismisses this as random bitchery, "the kind of equivocal remark that Roberta made about any man, married or single, who was not actively engaged in having an affair with her"; yet modern readers surely will see things differently, just as some contemporary readers likely did.[27] **End Spoiler.**

With references to homosexuality, adultery, impotence, sadism and madness, *The Grindle Nightmare* is a classic detective novel ahead of its time within the genre for its treatment of mature subject matter; and it marked a significant advance in this regard over the previous Q. Patrick novels, written by Rickie Webb either solo or in collaboration with Martha Mott Kelley or Mary Louise White. To be sure, the extent of the influence young Hugh Wheeler, recently arrived in the United States from his native England, had on this fascinating crime tale is not certain. What is beyond question, however, is that queer subtext amply exists not only in *The Grindle Nightmare* but also in the increasingly sophisticated mysteries which Rickie and Hugh produced during the years of their creative partnership, when two men wrote as one.

NOTES

1. Douglas G. Greene's circumspect introduction to the publisher IPL's 1989 reissue of the Patrick Quentin novel *Puzzle for Players* notes only, concerning the personal relationship between the two men, that a "chance meeting with Webb gave Wheeler the opportunity to realize his ambition of being a writer." For more recent accounts of the personal relationship between Rickie Webb and Hugh Wheeler, see Mauro Boncompagni, "Patrick Quentin/Q. Patrick/Jonathan Stagge: A Phantasmagoria of Crime Writers," in Curtis Evans, ed., *Mysteries Unlocked: Essays in Honor of Douglas G. Greene* (Jefferson, NC: McFarland, 2014); Curtis Evans, "Puzzles for Posterity," Introduction to *The Puzzles of Peter Duluth* (Norfolk: Crippen & Landru, 2016); and Joanna Gondris, Afterword to *The Puzzles of Peter Duluth*. On the queer subtext in G. D. H. Cole's crime writing, see my essay on Cole in this volume as well as my chapter on the Cole in my book *The Spectrum of English Murder: The Detective Fiction of Henry Lancelot Aubrey-Fletcher and G. D. H. and Margaret Cole* (Greenville, OH: Coachwhip, 2015).

2. Biographical details for Rickie Webb can be found in Boncompagni, "Phantasmagoria" and Evans, "Posterity." On Rickie's college cricket playing see "Richard Webb," *Cricket Archive*, http://cricketarchive.com/Archive/Players/1030/1030137/1030137.html. On Rickie, SKF and Benzedrine, see Nicholas Rasmussen, *On Speed: The Many Lives of Amphetamine* (New York: New York University, 2008), 22–32. Rickie's Twenties residence in Paris and Berlin would have introduced him to the thriving queer communities in these cities. A Cambridge contemporary of Rickie's, gay novelist Christopher Isherwood (1904–1986), wrote of life in Weimar Berlin in works that inspired the 1966 stage and 1972 film versions of *Cabaret*, for the latter of which Hugh Wheeler, a friend of Isherwood's since the Fifties, would co-write the screenplay. On Weimar Berlin and gay English expatriates see Robert Beachy, *Gay Berlin: Birthplace of a Modern Identity* (New York: Knopf, 2014), chapter seven.

3. 1930 US Federal Census, Philadelphia, Pennsylvania, Roll 2096, Page 30A; "Robert Elson Turner (1901–1979)," www.Ancestry.com, at http://person.ancestry.com/tree/70062582/person/34206862518/story; Maurice Isserman, "Roaring Twenties: Cars, Parties and Wild Weekends, *Alumni Review Online* (Spring 2011), at

https://www.hamilton.edu/magazine/spring11/departments/the-hill-in-history. At American colleges in the 1920s, "aesthete" and "aesthetic" often served as euphemisms for homosexuality. See Nicholas L. Syrett, *The Company He Keeps: A History of White College Fraternities* (Chapel Hill: University of North Caroline Press, 2009), 203–207. On college bootlegging, a "commonplace in 1920s fraternities," see Syrett, *Company*, 202.

    4. *Bryn Mawr College Calendar, 1930–1931*, 17, at https://archive.org/stream/bryn mawrcalendar2324bryn/brynmawrcalendar2324bryn_djvu.txt. In 1940 Turner published the promotional pamphlet *Benzedrine Sulfate Protocol*. According to a communication to me from a Turner family member on Ancestry.com, Turner's "last partner" was a man named Phil.

    5. *A. M. E. Church Review* 24 (July 1907), 70; William Brinkley, "Degrees by the Dozen on $40 a Week," *Life* 39 (19 September 1955), 188–190, 192, 196, 200, 202, 204.

    6. On Martha Mott Kelley, see Boncompagni, "Phantasmagoria." The word queer was part of urban gay male argot at this time. See George Chauncey, *Gay New York: Gender, Urban Culture, and the Making of the Gay Male World 1890–1940* (New York: Basic Books, 1994), 14.

    7. Ann Waldron, *Eudora Welty: A Writer's Life* (New York: Anchor Books, 1998), 116. In 1935 Mary Lou White wed Edward C. Aswell, an editor closely associated with the works of Thomas Wolfe. Mary Louise Aswell, as she was now known professionally, later became the influential fiction editor at *Harper's Bazaar*, where she fostered the careers of such luminaries as Eudora Welty, Truman Capote and Carson McCullers. After two divorces Mary Lou moved to New Mexico, where she maintained a long-term relationship with the artist Agnes Sims, and authored a single solo suspense novel, *Far to Go* (1957).

    8. See Joanna Gondris, Afterword to *The Puzzles of Peter Duluth*.

    9. *Ibid*. On gay mentoring relationships in this period see Chauncey, *Gay New York*, 277–278.

    10. Gondris, Afterword; R. Wilson Webb to Mr. Wheeler, 26 October 1933 (letter in possession of Joanna Gondris). In an email from 29 November 2015, Mauro Boncompagni has pointed out to me that in the About the Author blurb on Mary Lou Aswell's novel *Far to Go*, Aswell states only that she collaborated on one Q. Patrick novel, *S. S. Murder*, making no mention of *The Grindle Nightmare*, which, like *Death Goes to School*, is copyrighted to Rickie Webb alone.

    11. A copy of *S. S. Murder* inscribed in May 1936, not long after the publication of *Death Goes to School*, to mystery writer Darwin L. Teilhet "with best wishes Q. Patrick" is signed beneath this inscription R. Wilson Webb and H. C. Wheeler, indicating that Hugh had been absorbed into the "Q. Patrick" partnership, even to the extent of having his name included on a book he had not been involved with writing. See *S. S. Murder* sales advertisement from the bookseller Bibliomania, at http://www.bibliomania.ws/shop/bibliomania/90405. Hugh did finally make a stab at a more pretentious novel with *The Crippled Muse*, which in a sign of increasing independence from Rickie he published under his own name in 1952. The *Saturday Review* praised *Muse* as an entertainment but complained that any deeper meaning at which the author might have been aiming "is all but crowded out by its plot." *Saturday Review*, 26 April 1952, 33.

    12. Bernard A. Drew, *Literary Luminaries from the Berkshires: From Herman Melville to Patricia Highsmith* (Charleston: The History Press, 2015), 72. On Rickie and Hugh's international travels see the passenger lists collected on Ancestry.com. On Hugh's naturalization see *Petitions for Naturalization from the U.S. District Court*

for the Southern District of New York, 1897–1944, Series *M1972,* Roll *1431,* National Archives and Records Administration, Washington, D.C.

13. Drew, *Luminaries,* 72; "Princess Caracciolo Berkshire Hostess," *New York Times,* 19 July 1940, 22. *Berkshire Eagle,* 3 October 1949, 15 June 1950, 28; 1940 U.S. Federal Census, Tyringham, Berkshire County, Massachusetts, Roll *T6271570,* Page 3A. The 1949 *Eagle* article on Rickie and Hugh refers to Twin Hills Farm as "their present place." Rickie and Hugh's household also included an additional individual, John R. Grubbs, their black cook and driver. Born in Addyston, Ohio, in 1916, Johnny Grubbs served as a cook in the U.S. Army during the Second World War, where he met Hugh, and returned with him to Twin Hills Farm in 1944. Grubbs would stay on there after Rickie departed, caring for Hugh when he was terminally ill, and after Hugh's death was the beneficiary of a trust that Hugh created. Grubbs remained at the house until his death in 2006. *Berkshire Eagle,* 26 February 2006; Joanna Gondris to Curtis Evans, 21 January 2016 (email). The editor of the Christopher Isherwood diaries terms Grubbs Wheeler's "black lover." See Christopher Isherwood, *Diaries,* Volume I: 1939–1960, ed. Katherine Bucknell (London: Methuen, 1996), 1011.

14. "Frances Winwar Wed to Richard W. Webb," *New York Times,* 22 May 1943; Alan M. Wald, *Exiles from a Future Time: The Forging of the Mid-Twentieth-Century Literary Left* (Chapel Hill: University of North Carolina Press, 2002), 164–165; Alan M. Wald, *American Night: The Literary Left in the Era of the Cold War* (Chapel Hill: University of North Carolina Press, 2012), 282; Gay poet and artist Harold Norse recalled that Grebanier, while still married to Winwar, propositioned him at New York's Everard (aka "Everhard") Baths. Harold Norse, *Memoirs of a Bastard Angel* (New York: Thunder's Mouth, 1989), 137–138. Homosexuality was grounds for exclusion from service in the U.S. armed forces in the Second World War, but social stigma attached to anyone so excluded. Allan Berube, *Coming Out Under Fire: The History of Gay Men and Women in World War II* (1990; repr., Chapel Hill: University of North Carolina Press, 1990), 20–21.

15. Drew, *Luminaries,* 72. In his essay in *Mysteries Unlocked,* Mauro Boncompagni speculates that Rickie's declining health might have been related to heavy Benzedrine use. Drewey Wayne Gunn writes that "townsfolk" contend Hugh died of "complications from AIDS." See Gunn, *Gay American Novels, 1870–1970: A Reader's Guide* (Jefferson, NC: McFarland, 2016), 58.

16. Alan Sinfield, *Out on the Stage: Lesbian and Gay Theatre in the Twentieth Century* (New Haven: Yale University Press, 1999), 218–219. Concerning Wheeler's extensive social connections in the entertainment world, which actually preceded the Sixties, see the letters to Hugh from Sir John Gielgud (1904–2000) that Richard Mangan collected in *Sir John Gielgud: A Life in Letters* (New York: Arcade, 2004). Gielgud evidently stayed at Twins Hills Farm in 1948 ("Thank you both for a heavenly and relaxing time," he wrote Hugh from New York, "and I was so happy to have the chance of knowing you, and all our gossip and witchery just couldn't have been more delicious….") and he maintained a correspondence with Hugh for the rest of Hugh's life (from 1957: "Did I ever thank you for the Judy Garland record? Anyway, you were sweet to send it"). Noting the recent success of Anthony Shaffer's mystery play *Sleuth* ("Tony is now a millionaire"), Gielgud in 1971 implored Hugh, "you simply must dramatise a Patrick Quentin, as we have all begged you to for so long" (pp. 119, 370). Gielgud's direction of *Big Fish, Little Fish* netted the distinguished thespian a Tony award. Correspondence from this later phase of Hugh's life is collected at the Howard Gottlieb Archival Research Center at Boston University.

17. For example, although the collegiate narrator of *Murder at Cambridge,* falls

in love at first sight, he assures us, with a lovely female student, he takes time to describe the easiness on the eyes of a male student, a tall, blue-eyed, "fair-haired youth in gorgeous sky-blue pajamas," before cynically concluding of such Cambridge men: "They are decorative but dumb; lovely but limited." Q. Patrick, *Murder at Cambridge* (New York: Farrar & Rinehart, 1933), 6–7.

18. *Saturday Review*, 10 August 1935, 14.

19. For a discussion of the aesthetics of Golden Age detective fiction see chapter One of my book *Masters of the Humdrum Mystery: Cecil John Charles Street, Freeman Wills Crofts, Alfred Walter Stewart and the British Detective Novel, 1920–1961* (Jefferson, NC: McFarland, 2012).

20. Q. Patrick, *The Grindle Nightmare* (New York: Hartney, 1935), 9, 22. Concerning the condition of Edgar Tailford-Jones, Doug amplifies: "Everybody in the valley knew that an unfortunately placed piece of shrapnel during the World War had left Edgar in the same predicament as Lady Chatterley's husband and the hero of *The Sun Also Rises*." Patrick, *Grindle*, 26.

21. Patrick, *Grindle*, 8, 9, 24, 27, 29.

22. *Ibid.*, 19.

23. *Ibid.*, 10, 27, 113. Doug and Toni's Grindle setup, managed so well by their "colored factotum" Lucinda, also seems similar to that of Rickie and his "friend"—as Hugh was designated in the 1940 census— when they lived in Tyringham in 1939–40, accompanied by a middle-aged half-French housekeeper, Marie Moore. Moore's truck driver husband had recently died in a horrific mishap resembling something out of Webb and Wheeler's crime tales. After gas fumes entered his cab during a New York haul he was making, he lost control of his truck, which ran off the road, hit a ledge, overturned and burst into flames, incinerating the driver, who was pinned inside the cab. 1940 U.S. Federal Census, Tyringham, Berkshire, Massachusetts, Roll T6271570, Page 3A; *Springfield Daily Republican*, 4 January 1939, 1.

24. Modern gay interest in the Leopold-Loeb case can be seen in the 1992 film *Swoon* and the 2003 stage musical *Thrill Me*. On the sexual relationship between Leopold and Loeb see especially Paul B. Franklin, "Jew Boys, Queer Boys: Rhetorics of Antisemitism and Homophobia in the Trial of Nathan 'Babe' Leopold Jr. and Richard 'Dickie' Loeb," in Daniel Boyarin, Daniel Itzkovitz and Ann Pellegrini, eds., *Queer Theory and the Jewish Question* (New York: Columbia University Press, 2003), 121–148. Franklin notes that while press and courtroom references to Leopold and Loeb's homosexual relationship "often were whispered or shrouded in innuendo," people were perfectly aware of what was being suggested: "What went unsaid in the course of the investigation and prosecution of Leopold and Loeb did so precisely because it went without saying" (p. 121). For example, when newspapers during the trial printed the text of Leopold's notorious "cocksuckers" letter to Loeb, the offending word was duly censored (see the *New York Times*, 2 June 1924), but the sexual nature of the relationship between the two teenagers that the letter implied remained sufficiently clear. For general accounts of the Leopold-Loeb affair, see Hal Higdon, *Leopold and Loeb: The Crime of the Century* (1975; paperback ed., Urbana: University of Illinois Press, 1999) (originally published under the title *The Crime of the Century: The Leopold and Loeb Case*) and Simon Baatz, *For the Thrill of It: Leopold, Loeb and the Murder That Shocked Chicago* (New York: HarperCollins, 2008). The first fictional work which clearly drew on the Leopold-Loeb affair is believed to have been Patrick Hamilton's 1929 British stage play *Rope*, which was filmed in 1948 by Alfred Hitchcock. Meyer Levin's novel *Compulsion*, which adhered closely to the facts of the Leopold-Loeb case, followed in 1956, inspiring stage and film adaptations as well as a lawsuit

from a still-jailed Nathan Leopold (Loeb had been murdered in prison in 1936), who claimed all this was a violation of his privacy and an attempt by others to enrich themselves at his expense.

25. Patrick, *Grindle*, 20.
26. *Ibid.*, 256–257. Until the murder of Loeb in 1936, the case generally was known not as the Leopold-Loeb case but the Loeb-Leopold case.
27. *Ibid.*, 27.

Works Cited

Books and Articles

Baatz, Simon. *For the Thrill of It: Leopold, Loeb and the Murder That Shocked Chicago.* New York: HarperCollins, 2008.
Beachy, Robert. *Gay Berlin: Birthplace of a Modern Identity.* New York: Knopf, 2014.
Berube, Allan. *Coming Out Under Fire: The History of Gay Men and Women in World War II.* 1990. 2d ed., Chapel Hill: University of North Carolina Press, 2010.
Boncompagni, Mauro. "Patrick Quentin/Q. Patrick/Jonathan Stagge: A Phantasmagoria of Crime Writers." In *Mysteries Unlocked: Essays in Honor of Douglas G. Greene,* ed. Curtis Evans. Jefferson, NC: McFarland, 2014.
Brinkley, William. "Degrees by the Dozen on $40 a Week." *Life* 39 (19 September 1955): 188–190, 192, 196, 200, 202, 204.
Chauncey, George. *Gay New York: Gender, Urban Culture, and the Making of the Gay Male World 1890–1940.* New York: Basic Books, 1994.
Drew, Bernard A. *Literary Luminaries from the Berkshires: From Herman Melville to Patricia Highsmith.* Charleston: History Press, 2015.
Evans, Curtis. *Masters of the Humdrum Mystery: Cecil John Charles Street, Freeman Wills Crofts, Alfred Walter Stewart and the British Detective Novel, 1920–1961.* Jefferson, NC: McFarland, 2012.
_____. "Puzzles for Posterity." Introduction to *The Puzzles of Peter Duluth.* Norfolk: Crippen & Landru, 2016.
_____. *The Spectrum of English Murder: The Crime Fiction of Henry Lancelot Aubrey-Fletcher and G. D. H. and Margaret Cole.* Greenville, OH: Coachwhip, 2015.
Franklin, Paul B. "Jew Boys, Queer Boys: Rhetorics of Antisemitism and Homophobia in the Trial of Nathan 'Babe' Leopold Jr., and Richard 'Dickie' Loeb." In Daniel Boyarin, Daniel Itzkovitz and Ann Pellegrini, eds., *Queer Theory and the Jewish Question.* New York: Columbia University Press, 2003.
Gondris, Joanna. Afterword to *The Puzzles of Peter Duluth.* Norfolk: Crippen & Landru, 2016.
Greene, Douglas G. Introduction to Patrick Quentin, Puzzle for Players. New York: International Polygonics, 1989.
Gunn, Drewey Wayne. *Gay American Novels, 1870-1970: A Reader's Guide.* Jefferson, NC: McFarland, 2016.
Higdon, Hal. *Leopold and Loeb: The Crime of the Century.* 1975 (as *The Crime of the Century: The Leopold and Loeb Case*). 2d ed. Urbana: University of Illinois Press, 1999.
Isherwood, Christopher. *Diaries,* Volume I: 1939–1960, ed. Katherine Bucknell. London: Methuen, 1996.
Isserman, Maurice. "Roaring Twenties: Cars, Parties and Wild Weekends." *Alumni Review Online* (Spring 2011). At https://www.hamilton.edu/magazine/spring11/departments/the-hill-in-history.

Mangan, Richard, ed. *Sir John Gielgud: A Life in Letters*. New York: Arcade, 2004.
Norse, Harold. *Memoirs of a Bastard Angel*. New York: Thunder's Mouth, 1989.
Patrick, Q. *The Grindle Nightmare*. New York: Hartney, 1935.
_____. *Murder at Cambridge*. New York: Farrar & Rinehart, 1933.
Rasmussen, Nicholas. *On Speed: The Many Lives of Amphetamine*. New York: New York University, 2008.
Sinfield, Alan. *Out on the Stage: Lesbian and Gay Theatre in the Twentieth Century*. New Haven: Yale University Press, 1999.
Syrett, Nicholas L. *The Company He Keeps: A History of White College Fraternities*. Chapel Hill: University of North Caroline Press, 2009.
Wald, Alan M. *American Night: The Literary Left in the Era of the Cold War*. Chapel Hill: University of North Carolina Press, 2012.
_____. *Exiles from a Future Time: The Forging of the Mid-Twentieth-Century Literary Left*. Chapel Hill: University of North Carolina Press, 2002.
Waldron, Ann. *Eudora Welty: A Writer's Life*. New York: Anchor Books, 1998.

Correspondence, Genealogical and Government Records, Newspapers, Periodicals

A. M. E. Church Review 24 (July 1907): 70.
Berkshire Eagle, 3 October 1949, 15 June 1950.
Bryn Mawr College Calendar, 1930–1931 at https://archive.org/stream/brynmawrcalendar2324bryn/brynmawrcalendar2324bryn_djvu.txt.
Gondris, Joanna, to Curtis Evans, 21 January 2016 (email).
New York Times, 19 July 1940, 22 May 1943.
1940 U.S. Federal Census. Tyringham, Berkshire County, Massachusetts. Roll *T627 1570*, Page 3A.
1930 U.S. Federal Census. Philadelphia, Pennsylvania. Roll 2096, Page 30A.
Petitions for Naturalization from the U.S. District Court for the Southern District of New York, 1897–1944. Series *M1972*, Roll *1431*. National Archives and Records Administration. Washington, D.C.
"Robert Elson Turner (1901–1979)." Ancestry.com. At http://person.ancestry.com/tree/70062582/person/34206862518/story.
Saturday Review, 10 August 1935.
Springfield Daily Republican, 4 January 1939.
Webb, R. Wilson, to Mr. Wheeler, 26 October 1933 (letter in possession of Joanna Gondris).

Queering the Investigation
Explanation and Understanding in Todd Downing's Detective Fiction

CHARLES J. RZEPKA

Until quite recently, almost nothing had been written on Todd Downing, a popular author of classical detective fiction—or "whodunnits"—during the last half of the genre's so-called Golden Age. This lack of interest is surprising in light of his output: nine novels for two major publishers between 1933 and 1941 and a well-received history of Mexico, *The Mexican Earth*, in 1940. Aside from capsule biographies in literary and historical encyclopedias, a single essay by Wolfgang Hochbruck published in 1993 stood for some three decades after the author's death in 1974 as the solitary contribution to scholarship on Downing's life and writings. Since then, two major works on the author have appeared in print: James Cox's *The Red Land to the South*, which devotes more than seventy pages to a close analysis of Native American themes in Downing's oeuvre, and Curtis Evans' *Clues and Corpses: The Detective Fiction and Mystery Criticism of Todd Downing*, which contains an extensive and detailed critical biography, as well as reprints of Downing's reviews of detective fiction and his only lecture on the genre. In short, Downing is just beginning to emerge as an object of major interest to scholars. He has yet, however, to be fully recognized as a queer writer. By that I mean not just a writer who was gay, but also a writer who queered the conventions of his chosen genre.

Born in 1902 in Atoka, Oklahoma, to Sam Downing, who was one-quarter Choctaw, and Maud Miller Downing, originally of Albia, Iowa, George Todd Downing (his family soon dropped the "George") grew up in a conservative, middle-class Republican and Presbyterian household with his younger sister by two years, Ruth. His father was a major player in Choctaw tribal affairs and Todd soon became closely attuned to his family's Native American heritage. But he was also drawn to the great literary and artistic traditions of the West. Highly intelligent and somewhat bookish, Downing earned his bachelor's and master's degrees at the University of Oklahoma, writing his thesis on Florencio Sanchez, a Uruguayan playwright. There he taught Spanish from 1925 to 1935, reviewing Spanish and French books for the university's scholarly journal, *Books Abroad*, while earning tuition money by leading American tours of Mexico, a country he soon grew to love. This love, powerfully augmented by his Native American sympathies, is reflected in the Mexican settings of his detective novels, in which pre–Columbian and *mestizo* (mixed-race) cultures, folkways, and pagan religious practices are often highlighted. Downing's second publisher, Doubleday, even cited the author's part-Choctaw descent in promoting the authenticity of his indigenous themes.

Scholars of Native American Studies like James Cox have celebrated Downing's obvious appreciation of and respect for America's native peoples and cultures. These attitudes suffuse *The Mexican Earth*, which tells the history of Mexico from a *mestizo* perspective, and eventually prompted the writing of *Chahta Anompa: An Introduction to the Choctaw Language*, along with a lecture, "Cultural Traits of the Choctaws," and a drama about the Oklahoma settlement, *Journey's End*, the latter privately printed. However, Downing's love of detective stories, a middle-class genre of popular fiction written at the time almost exclusively by and for white people, was just as pronounced. He even wrote a regular review column on the subject, "Clues and Corpses," for Oklahoma City's *The Daily Oklahoman* from 1930 to 1937. Oddly enough, despite the call for a pan-Amerindian "anticolonial resistance" that Cox has discerned in Downing's fiction, his two detective protagonists, U.S. Customs agent Hugh Rennert in the first seven books and Sheriff Peter Bounty in the last two, are white "colonials," that is, Euro-Americans with no trace of indigenous blood.[1] Rennert in particular is unmistakably a projected ego ideal of Downing himself, and Rennert's strongest and most passionate relationships, whether long-standing or casual, are with white males of northern European descent.

Curtis Evans has made an impressive, if necessarily circumstantial, case for Downing's gay sexuality, noting his life-long bachelorhood, his numerous and close male friends, and most tellingly, the many books by and about homosexuals and homosexuality that were discovered in his library after his death. These include a 1951 sociological study by Donald Webster Cory, *The Homosexual in America: A Subjective Approach*. Like the three other gay-themed books Downing acquired during this period of his life—*The City and the Pillar* by Gore Vidal, *The Divided Path* by Nial Kent, and *Quatrefoil*, by James Barr—*The Homosexual in America* was written by a gay man "with the conscious intention of portraying homosexuals in a sympathetic light," notes Evans, who adds that Downing's obtaining these four books "suggests he had something more than an academic interest in the subject of homosexuality."[2]

To the evidence of his library, we can add the following two facts about Downing's life—and death. His sister, Ruth Shields Downing, who left Atoka for New York City in 1932 and returned only to attend her parents' funerals, lived in a long-term lesbian relationship during her residence there, according to her adopted son Nenad Downing, and as we know from recent studies of its heritability, same-sex preference tends to run in families. There is also the suggestive but inconclusive evidence of Downing's death certificate. Evans cites the wrong organ but the correct immediate cause of death when he reports that Downing died of a heart attack. The embolism that killed him was pulmonary, not cardiac, but more importantly for our purposes, it was an unintended consequence of surgery to relieve what must have seemed a benign, if painful and embarrassing, condition: a "peri-anal abscess." Among other major risk factors for this condition is "regular anal sex."[3]

In trying to determine from all this circumstantial evidence whether or not Todd Downing was homosexual, we are obliged to keep in mind the fact that if he was, he preferred to remain in the closet his entire life. Do we have the right to "out" him, then, to claim him as a pioneering gay detective writer for the purpose of including him in a volume of critical essays on the subject, or as a recruit for canonical gay pride generally? Scholars of Native American literature need have no such qualms: Downing was proud of his Choctaw blood. If he had a sexual preference, however, he kept it well hidden.

Except, I would contend, in his writing. It is one thing to "out" a homosexual author for no other reason than to add him to a gay honor roll. It is quite another to try making sense of features in his work that resist explanation until we view them from a gay perspective. There is a strong case to be made for Downing as a writer who queered the genre of detective fiction in trying to come to terms with his own same-sex desires. Like his racial self-understanding, however, Downing's sexual identity is by no means a simple matter, and even if we could go back to the time when he was writing his detective novels and ask him if he was gay, his most likely response (supposing he could bring himself to be entirely frank) would be, "I don't know yet, but I'm trying hard to find out."

Whatever his degree of sexual self-understanding, the Todd Downing of the 1930s does fit into a recognizable, interwar male type of homosociality: "the bachelor." The Depression era bachelor was already a species headed for extinction, according to Howard P. Chudacoff, who considers 1880–1930 the "peak years of bachelor subculture in America." However, the type persisted up to the Second World War as economic hard times tended to delay marriage and thus prolong single male adulthood. By the 1920s unmarried adult males had become less of a boarding house phenomenon and were more likely to be integrated into "their own nuclear or extended family household," much like Todd Downing, who lived with his parents for a good part of his working life as a writer. The bachelor may or may not have had an active sexual life (with men and/or women), but in any case he strongly preferred the company of males to that of females, "establish[ing] intense and affectionate ties to male friends."[4] Hugh Rennert tends to be more sentimental and reserved than passionate and overt about such attachments. Deeply sensuous himself and responsive to the sensuousness of other men, he finds himself repeatedly drawn to beautiful males (especially if they are younger than he), with whom he will sometimes carry on an oblique flirtation. However, Rennert is at best only friendly with women, beautiful or otherwise.

To go beyond the "bachelor" designation and try to decide, once and for all, the question of Downing's sexuality at the time he was writing his detective novels would be to subscribe to a homo/hetero binary that, at least since the publication of Eve Kosofsky Sedgwick's *The Epistemology of the Closet* in 1990, has been called into question as an arbitrary, incoherent construct ill-suited for organizing the enormous variety of human sexual preferences. In fact, notes Sedgwick, it was precisely the dominance of this discursive binary from the *fin de siecle* onwards, with its axiomatic injunctions concerning what could and could not be said about one's sexuality, that stretched the "performative aspects of texts" to include gendered "sites of definitional creation, violence, and rupture in relation to particular readers, particular institutional circumstances"—by which I take her to mean particular genres of writing and their ideal readerships. For Todd Downing, Golden Age detective fiction, with its narrow range of targeted audience expectations and "rules"—written or unwritten—governing what could and could not be said about events unfolding at any given point in the narrative, offered precisely such a performative arena for the "relations of the closet." In that arena, as Sedgwick puts it, silence itself becomes "a speech act" that "accrues particularity by fits and starts, in relation to the discourse that surrounds and differentially constitutes it"—in Downing's case, the discourse of investigation.[5]

* * *

Regardless of Todd Downing's sexual orientation, whether conscious or unconscious, active or repressed, there is little doubt that his detective novels show more interest in male-to-male relationships—and male bodies in various states of undress—than in women generally or as objects of male desire specifically. Without even conducting a detailed survey, any close student of Downing's work can see that its beefcake quotient is well in excess of what we would expect, given his choice of genre. Where in the writings of Agatha Christie, Dorothy L. Sayers, Willard Huntington Wright, Anthony Berkeley,

John Dickson Carr or Rex Stout would we come across a description like this of a well-tanned, muscular, Nordic-featured man in "snugly fitting black trunks," standing on a floating dock and preparing to dive: "Angerman turned his back and stepped to the edge of the float, where he stood, a flaming bronze and black colossus straddling seashore and houses and palms." The point of view is that of detective Hugh Rennert, also in swimming trunks, sitting "tailor-fashion" and observing the shore through Angerman's muscular legs. "Slightly winded from the swim," he feels "a pleasing lassitude creep over his limbs" as the "salt water dry[ies]" on his "bare shoulders and arms."[6]

Two half-naked men on a swimming raft floating in the Gulf of Mexico might be unremarkable if there were some plausible reason for their being out there at all. But none is ever offered: Angerman simply insists, when the detective arrives to question a witness at the health spa where the Nordic superman works, that the two of them go swimming—despite Rennert's not having brought his swim suit. Not to worry, says Angerman: "He eyed Rennert's body and gave his size accurately." Retrieving a suit from the office, where they keep such things for visitors, Angerman takes Rennert to "the adjoining bedroom" where they continue their conversation while stripping and putting on their swimwear.[7]

Nearly every description of the male anatomy in Todd Downing's first seven books is visualized through the gaze of his chief protagonist Hugh Rennert, and those that are not often serve an identical, titillating purpose. As the image of Angerman the bronze colossus indicates, the detective is every bit as good at "eyeing" male bodies as Angerman himself. He generally likes them tall, well built, and with "full red lips," like Dr. Lipscomb in Downing's first book, *Murder on Tour*: "A handsome man, judged by any standards, masculine or feminine. Tall, well-built and dressed in a perfectly fitting light gray suit. [...] His mustache was a thin dark line above full red lips." Another character is later observed "running the tip of a red tongue over his full, red lips" and still another is "tall, with a well-proportioned, athletic figure" and possesses "a curious Byronic attractiveness," a phrase apparently invoking Lord Byron's celebrated male beauty, including his full, pouting lips. In *Vultures in the Sky*, one of Rennert's fellow train passengers is a "tall fellow, probably in his middle thirties, with a well-proportioned, athletic figure," while the "strikingly handsome face" of an older man displays "a curious mingling of asceticism and virility in its finely cut features": "The full lips"—"delicately chiseled"—"lent a note of sensuality." The men whom Rennert observes most closely while solving his cases seem to have been hired by the casting director for a 1930s swashbuckler—or a Regency romance. Eyeing the body of one young man he meets in Downing's fourth book, *Murder on the Tropic*, Rennert observes "a solid statuesque effect of strength unconscious of itself [...] outlined in all its impressive muscularity by the wind that tore at his clothing."[8]

No other sleuth in classical detective fiction gives the male body—face and figure—as much scrutiny as Hugh Rennert, and none of Downing's female characters come close to competing for his attention. Madame Fournier, the hotel keeper in Rennert's second adventure, *The Cat Screams*, seems to be saying as much when, as the detective begins to examine her guest register, she tells him, "The men [...] are more interesting, as always."[9] Downing's women, however, if not as interesting as his men, are allowed to be more openly *interested* in male beauty, sexually, than his male characters, and the author will sometimes get more erotic torque and traction in his prose by representing the male anatomy through the eyes of a female character, her gender providing safe cover for the author's queer voyeurism. Here is Downing describing how Janell Lincoln, the young ingenue of *The Last Trumpet*, sees Carlos Campos, the matador at her first bullfight:

> The Spanish say that the heart of a bullfight crowd is a woman's heart, captivated by colour and pomp and more than all else by blatant maleness. Campos must have known this, for he moved his legs so that the sunlight played upon his thighs and loins and revealed the rippling of the muscles under the tight trousers. The amphitheatre grew still again, filled with the orgiastic tremor of heavy breathing and hot, tense bodies perspiring under the sun.[10]

Employing a similarly re-sexed point of view, Downing follows the thoughts of entomologist Bertha Fahr in *Murder on the Tropic* as she recalls favorite passages from the bodice-rippers of her "gawky, timid" adolescence: "Terence Holderness dragged himself out of reach of the angry waves and lay upon the sand, his bronzed muscular chest rising and falling under a tattered shirt." This kind of fevered prose is, despite Downing's parodic intentions, not too dissimilar from the author's description of Campos in the ring or, for that matter, from other passages he apparently means us to take seriously in *Murder on the Tropic* itself. Thus, after stripping off the shirt of a young gunshot victim and dressing the wound, Rennert returns to the man's room later to find him still shirtless, "his muscular arms and shoulders ... dark bronze in the light."[11]

* * *

Like flashlight beams sweeping and interlocking in the dark, men's interest in other men, and Rennert's particularly, can make Downing's plots cast queer shadows. These shadows are longest in over-determined scenes of male encounter or conversation that would appear to be unmistakable tableaux of homosexual flirting if Downing had not provided a safely non-libidinous motivational context. The anodyne explanation might be apparent but finally inadequate—Angerman and Rennert do exchange relevant information on that swimming raft, but why there and not in the office?—or it can be delayed, thereby heightening the homoerotic effect. In some cases, the characters' motivations remain permanently inscrutable and, thus, even more intensely suggestive. What is particularly interesting about many of these scenes is how Downing can enlist the most important feature of the classical detective plot, namely, its suspension of full explanations until the story's final analepsis, to enhance any particular scene's immediate queerness.

Here are examples of all three types of queered explanation—inadequate, delayed, and none—spread over three different books. They require a bit of synopsis and ample quotation in order to convey their full effect, so I ask the reader's indulgence.

The Inadequate Explanation, or "Say! What is this anyway?"

In *Night over Mexico*, Downing's seventh book, Hugh Rennert is headed to Mexico City on business when a storm washes out the Pan-American Highway and strands him at a remote hunting lodge. He finds a recently murdered man outside and the closed circle of suspects typical of whodunnits inside, isolated from the rest of the world by the storm. They are soon joined by another stranded traveler, Dr. Gulliver Damson, a pudgy, balding, fussy, self-styled expert on Mexico who is gathering material for his new guidebook. Damson is delighted to make the acquaintance of Rennert, whose reputation as a detective familiar with life south of the border now precedes him wherever he goes. In fact, Damson cannot wait to get Rennert all to himself, and proposes that they share adjoining rooms in the hacienda. Rennert is dismayed. By this point in the series he is retired from the Customs Service and official detective work, and sees Damson as nothing more than a pest. Besides, he has just taken a room next to that of George Woodmansee, whose "slate-blue eyes met Rennert's in penetrating scrutiny" when the two were introduced, and whose "straw colour[ed]," "smoothly brushed hair emphasize[s] the bronze of his skin." Not surprisingly, Woodmansee's face is "strikingly handsome." Their two rooms even share a bathroom, a feature that Woodmansee pointedly remarks when he tells Rennert, "Keep that room if you can. If there has to be any changing about, we'll move together." Damson has other ideas: "You and I are bunking together to-night," he says to his new friend in the presence of Woodmansee.

> "You're mistaken," Woodmansee put in evenly. "*I'm* sharing Mr. Rennert's room with him...." He stood at ease, his well-shaped feet snugly clad in dark silk socks with magenta clocks.
>
> Damson glanced at him inimically and rested his rump against the wall. "I don't know who you are, but you're being very forward. Rennert and I have already made our arrangements."
>
> "Think so?" Woodmansee smiled. "Ask him."

At this point a fourth character named Kerwick poses the question Downing's readers must be asking themselves: "Say! What is this anyway?" To which Rennert replies, "I'm not quite sure myself." Turning to Damson "with scant politeness," however, Rennert sets him straight: "Mr. Woodmansee is right, Doctor. He and I have agreed to share quarters."[12]

Woodmansee, his "well-shaped feet" sporting those stylish "magenta clocks," will obviously win this rivalry for the hand of Rennert, with whom he will exchange an affectionate farewell (accompanied by reciprocal but rejected offers of long-term cohabitation) once the dust has settled. However, that will not happen before Damson (not a medical doctor, it turns out) corners the detective in his room and begins bathing a cactus wound in his foot "without much regard for the location of the wound" (what "location" *is* he regarding?). Just then, Woodmansee knocks at the door and Damson "admonishe[s]" Rennert "in a whisper: 'Don't answer it!'" When Rennert ignores him, Damson "snort[s]" in disgust, "Maybe someone else will listen to your fussing about a sore foot," and moves to a nearby chair as though interrupted in an attempt at seduction. When Woodmansee enters, he "grin[s] impudently at Damson, and greet[s] Rennert with a cheery 'Hello, room-mate! *We* have company, I see'" (italics in original). Later on Rennert, a chain smoker, assures Woodmansee that he's just stringing Damson along because the gullible Gulliver has cigarettes. "Go to it," replies Woodmansee. "And buy me some if you can. Then we'll send him out on his bald head and have the place to ourselves."[13] Alone at last!

Despite all the high-strung cattiness and cutting, Downing has provided Damson with an erotically innocuous excuse for his intense interest in Rennert (he wants information about Mexico), and will eventually provide an equally plausible cover-story for Woodmansee's possessiveness: Woodmansee is a secret agent on a mission to obtain radium for an unnamed foreign power, and he assumes that Rennert, the famous detective, stands a good chance of finding it in the course of his murder investigation. Neither excuse, however, can quite account for the emotional radioactivity emanating from this scene of two grown men jealously competing to become Rennert's roommate, and we are left with the feeling, if not the fact, that Rennert has become the *idée fixe* of two rival male suitors.

The Delayed Explanation, or Meet Me at the Pillar in the Square

While the apparent reason for Damson's desire to be with Rennert is, on its face, inadequate to explain the petulant intensity of the doctor's attachment, the reason for Woodmansee's attraction is not apparent at all until later in the story, which makes it in fact a version of the delayed explanation. A more suggestive and extended example appears in *The Last Trumpet*, in two scenes between Jarl Angerman, the "bronze and black colossus," and Darwin Wyllys, the brother-in-law of Angerman's employer at the Toniutah health spa, Dr. Torday. The first of these encounters appears early in the book when Wyllys first comes into Rennert's view as a nameless figure with "a delicately featured face, handsome and at the same time weak," hovering about the public square in Matamoros and trying to avoid Angerman's gaze:

> He was moving, with quick steps, in Rennert's direction, keeping inside the rows of pillars and taking care to place each group of idlers between himself and the street. Now and then he stopped—and watched.... The man was watching Jarl Angerman.... The fugitive (that's how R. thought of him) remained for a long time behind a pillar at the edge of this expanse.... There was a shifting, hunted look in [his eyes] which gave Rennert a start.[14]

Eventually, Angerman spots him: "The pale-faced man stood as if paralysed, and his eyes met Angerman's across the quivering heat waves which rose from the strip of asphalt":

> Angerman did not speak or make any gesture at all, but kept his eyes fixed, rather sadly, on the other's face. The latter went deathly pale, his lips trembled spasmodically and, as if under the compulsion of some unspoken command, he moved toward the huge white-clad figure.... Then Angerman lifted an arm ponderously, and laid it about the frail unsteady shoulders. He kept them in this embrace as he drew the man gently towards the automobiles.[15]

By withholding an explanation of this silent encounter, in classical whodunnit fashion, Downing challenges the reader to come up with hypothetical interpretations of what looks like a shameful recognition scene between a furtive male hanging about a public square and another male whose gaze he is trying to avoid, but who embraces him nonetheless upon discovery and apparently takes him home. Lacking any other context of understanding, we must at least entertain the obvious suggestion that this "fugitive" is cruising the square for a hook-up while trying to elude the eye of his male lover, who, upon catching him in the act, decides, "rather sadly," to forgive rather than rail at him. The scene's homoerotic aura has been burnished by a prose snapshot of Angerman's sculpted, "colossal" male beauty just half a dozen pages earlier, amplified in the same heat waves that here distort the two men's intersecting gazes: "his body was given colossal proportions by the heat waves which went up from the asphalt" and "his Nordic features, bronzed by the sun, had ... an impassive sculptured appearance."[16]

Later on, in the chapter where Rennert goes for a swim with Angerman on his visit to Toniutah, Darwin Wyllys refuses to sign the witness affidavit Rennert has brought, forcing Angerman to have a private talk with Wyllys in his cottage while Rennert waits outside in the hot sun: "Yet he had to repress a shiver. It was the recoil of his whole healthy being from what he knew was going on inside. Or what he thought was going on." Well, what *is* going on in there that would make a "healthy being" "shiver" with revulsion, and that cannot, apparently, be described in words? Is the "colossus" exerting sexual pressure—seductive or violent—on the slighter, smaller man? When Angerman emerges, he says that Wyllys will sign when they get back from their swim. "Why not do it now?" asks Rennert.

> "We must let him rest. He does not feel well now."
> Their eyes met.
> Rennert flicked away his cigarette. "I understand," he said thoughtfully.
> "I knew"—Angerman's voice was level—"that you would understand."[17]

As it turns out, Wyllys is a heroin addict. He was looking for a fix in Matamoros when Angerman caught sight of him. Angerman is merely a close friend trying to save Wyllys from himself. This information is strategically withheld from the reader until near the end of the book, but until it is revealed, the queer tonalities emanating from Angerman's relationship with Wyllys continue to reverberate.

No Explanation, or the Understanding

While the "understanding" between Angerman and Rennert regarding the former's relationship to Wyllys is eventually clarified, the same cannot be said for other silent flashes of intense male rapport scattered throughout Downing's fiction. These ambiguous moments of recognition seem to accumulate as we approach *The Last Trumpet* and become even more pronounced once Downing turns his attention to a new, more blatantly attractive detective protagonist, Sheriff Peter Bounty, whose name, in light of Downing's increasing fascination with onomastic puns ("Angerman," "Jester," "Hand," "Lack," "Reaper"), evinces an implicit promise of abundant phallic potency. We are first introduced to Bounty halfway through *The Last Trumpet*, when he asks if Rennert will help him out, as a deputy, in solving a series of murders involving some of Rennert's personal acquaintances. Bounty is an "imperturbable, mildly sensuous man of slight but wiry build," with "something feline about the indolent movements of his body" and a "virile, finely featured face and sleek flaxen hair," much like Woodmansee's in *Night Over Mexico*. Bounty's sensuous, cat-like behavior is underlined four pages later: "His chair gyrated slowly toward the sunlight which was pouring in the window behind him. He spread out his legs and stretched them, as if getting voluptuous pleasure out of the warmth on his thighs and loins. A sleek and graceful leopard sunning himself upon a rock."

Rennert's "liking for the sheriff had been instantaneous," and he thinks Bounty is "simpatico"—which would imply that Bounty's liking for him is equally spontaneous.[18] In short, they seem to have a crush on each other.

This love at first sight persists throughout the subsequent investigation until, upon leaving Bounty's office one day, Rennert asks the sheriff out for what amounts to their first date, a dinner at the Jester Hotel: "We can talk this business over," he says, referring to the case. "Or, if you prefer, we can forget it. I'd like to have you in either event. You're a bachelor, too, aren't you?" Bounty, an aw-shucks kind of guy who's used to "eating at a cheap lunch counter," hems and haws as he pictures the "swanky" decor of the hotel dining room. "Don't be a damn fool," says Rennert. "The two men studied and understood each other. Bounty's smile was slow and warm and satisfied." What exactly do the two men understand? That table manners do not matter, or that they do not matter when bachelors get lonely for the company of other bachelors? With what, exactly, is Bounty "satisfied," and what does Rennert mean by saying he wants to "have" Bounty, even if they do not discuss the case? Because the house at his citrus farm is unfinished, Rennert is not "having" him over for a meal as a guest: the two will be sharing dinner in a public dining room. There, Rennert's desire to "have" Bounty will get triangulated though the gaze of women sitting at nearby tables, much as we have seen Downing's interest in male beauty get triangulated through the eyes of Janell Lincoln and Bertha Fahr: "More than one pair of feminine eyes lingered on the polished and handsome occupant of the chair opposite Rennert's—and returned. Rennert was amused and elated and perhaps envious."[19]

"Envious" can be understood in an uncomplicated heterosexual sense: a straight man might understandably envy Bounty for his attractiveness to women. But what's "amusing" about that, unless it strikes Rennert as an incongruous affirmation of his own vector of desire? And why should he feel "elated" over it, unless his delight arises from the sense of having captured the appreciative attention of a man whose unmistakably sensuous virility has been endorsed so publicly?

Rennert's and Bounty's dinner date is extended when Rennert invites Bounty to share a cigar on the moonlit terrace of his unfinished house while he explains the details of the case. "Their chairs were huge and soft and designed for lazy men" (261), writes Downing—men who are, clearly, *simpatico*. Gradually the talk drifts, like the "cigar smoke" that "dissolve[s] into moonlight," to matters of life and death, work and play, the "lazy" occupants of these huge, soft chairs as exquisitely attuned to each other as the occupants of a pair of bathtubs in a Cialis commercial. But the spell is broken when Rennert tries to return his deputy's badge. Bounty reacts as if he has just been handed back an engagement ring:

> Bounty gazed at it and his voice was low and quick.
> "Keep it, Hugh. I'll have a vacancy on the regular force the first of the year."
> "I can't, Peter. You know that. There's no need to go into my reasons, is there?"
> "No," Bounty said reluctantly as he put away the shield. "No, hell, no. I understand."[20]

And perhaps, finally, Downing's readers do as well—at least the bachelors among them: Rennert is drawn to Bounty, but not ready for a long-term relationship.

Is it possible that at least some of Downing's readers made more explicit connections, directly recognizing—without the help of an English professor from Boston University—the homoerotic longing that galvanizes these "understandings" between Hugh Rennert and his male crushes? Short of uncovering a survey by Doubleday of its customers' reactions to the Rennert and Bounty books, we'll never know. There is no evidence of such an awareness in the reviews and, given the public's prevailing condemnatory attitude toward homosexuality at the time, that omission would indicate, if not total ignorance, then at least a thorough denial of what was suspected. As far as we can tell, it was Downing's choice to stop writing detective fiction, not his publisher's. Perhaps he was beginning to fear that his attraction to handsome, virile, sensuous men was becoming too apparent to elude casual recognition. But that can only be a matter of speculation, and after all, does it really matter? Writing presupposes an ideal audience—a sympathetic "People" that doesn't necessarily coincide with a buying "Public," to use the language of the poet William Wordsworth.[21] In the assumed sympathy or earned agreement of that imagined readership the writer seeks validation of his or her vision of life. Insofar as we can put ourselves in the position of Downing's ideal, intended readership, we stand a chance of sharing that vision, whether or not anyone who purchased his books ever did. The creation of ambiguous scenes of mutual male attraction was apparently deeply satisfying to Todd Downing. That is all that really matters.

And yet, there remains the possibility that at least one portion of Downing's readership did hear his deeper message loud and clear, and even that Downing knew it: in short, that the code to decipher his most alluring male characters' secret understandings was in the possession of his gay readership. James Levin has noted that the history of the gay novel in American can be said to have begun in the 1930s, when the first books to feature recognizably homosexual protagonists made their appearance. At precisely the same moment, according to George Chauncey, a "powerful campaign to render gay men and lesbians invisible—to exclude them from the public sphere" was launched in New York City and soon spread nationwide in a backlash against Prohibition-era permissiveness that set the stage for America's postwar homophobia.[22] Thus, it is not far-fetched to assume that an identifiable gay readership capable of being targeted by gay writers had emerged by the time

Downing began his writing career and that, in light of the hostile crackdown against "pansies" and "fairies" that Chauncey has identified, it had begun to attune itself to themes, characters, scenes, and "understandings" meant only for queer readers. Nor is it far-fetched to assume that Downing had begun to target a gay readership in this way. Here is one piece of evidence to that effect.

Peter Bounty will not find complete happiness with the bachelor he seeks until the end of *The Lazy Lawrence Murders*, published in 1941—if by "complete" we mean emotionally satisfying and reciprocated without the looming prospect of a breakup. Any such outcome was permanently negated by the fact that this would be the last detective novel Downing ever wrote. It ends with Peter Bounty and his new friend, James Somerset, one of the original suspects in the book's eponymous case, enjoying a quiet sunset together on a park bench in the picturesque tourist town of Saltillo. An English professor whose point of view Downing—an adjunct professor himself—adopted in the book's opening chapter and here resumes, Somerset seems intended to take the place of the author's previous ego ideal and Bounty-admirer, Hugh Rennert. "[I]nhaling the heady perfume of [Mexico's] violet-blue blossoms" and feeling its "promised peace beginning to pervade him," the professor listens to the sheriff with rapt attention as he recounts the details of the case. Somerset believes this feeling of peace is partly due to having just finished writing an article on Christopher Marlowe, although "the presence of Peter Bounty beside him might have something to do with it," not to mention his companion's delicate floral adornment: "Bounty looked Dionysian with an indigo-blue petal from a 'smoke' tree lodged on his flaxen hair," later joined by "another indigo-blue petal [...] about to light on his chin."[23]

Downing's overt reference to the androgynous Greek god of intoxication and sexual release sets the tone for Somerset's interjected words and thoughts in the course of Bounty's analepsis, a standard narratological feature of classic detection. As the discussion turns to blood types, for instance, and Bounty observes that the two of them share the same one, Somerset murmurs, "So that's why you and I have so much in common," "lightheadedly feeling that by some magic this talk of blood was bringing out its color all around him. Skullcap flowers bordering that gravel path became a more vivid scarlet and gold." In the midst of this dizzying floral profusion, Downing once again alludes to Bounty's feline sensuousness:

> Leaning back on the bench, Bounty locked his hands behind his head. The sun seemed to be sucking all impurities from the air as it disappeared over the rim of the valley, and in that interval of crystal lucidity his features lost their jaded look for one which a stranger might have called dissolute but which Somerset knew to be expressive of purring contentment.

The lull of a later pause reveals "no sound ... save plaintive strains from a guitar, muted by distance, and the trill and chatter of magpies settling for the night in the trees of the Alameda." In the silence following Bounty's summary of the case, the mounting sense of romantic intimacy and yearning between the two men becomes almost palpable as they watch "darkness gather like creeping lava in the gorges" of extinct volcanoes on the horizon, an image alluding to hot, powerful forces deeply buried and long pent up, but suddenly beginning to flow.[24]

The lava cools and petrifies, however, when a raucous crowd of Texas tourists appears in the Alameda. "'The eyes of Texas are upon you,' Bounty quoted with a sigh, 'till Gabriel blows his horn.'"[25] The jig is up, the lovers discovered, consummation postponed.

"The Eyes of Texas" is the school spirit song of the University of Texas at Austin. Written in 1903 and set to the tune of "I've Been Working on the Railroad," it is familiar to fans of college football throughout the nation and to multitudes who have never witnessed a college football game. It is especially well known to residents of Texas and Oklahoma, whose football rivalry had been thriving for almost four decades when *The Lazy Lawrence Murders* was written. With its overt reference to being watched, the song has an obvious meaning in this highly charged homoerotic context: "Watch out! We're not alone." But it also illuminates an otherwise opaque moment in the earlier history of Bounty's secret understanding with Hugh Rennert, in *The Last Trumpet*. As Rennert leaves Bounty's office after arranging their dinner date at the Jester Hotel, he hears Bounty singing "the low strains of *The Eyes of Texas*."[26] Reading back into this moment from the rupture of intimacy that concludes Downing's final novel, the song's monitory message becomes unmistakable: Bounty is reminding Rennert that in the dining room of the Jester Hotel in Brownsville, Texas, the two men's behavior will be under public scrutiny. All the more reason for Rennert's amusement at Bounty's virile attractiveness to every female in the room.

In the context of its fictional performances, "The Eyes of Texas" possesses a clearly coded meaning for Rennert and Bounty. But could this understanding of the song have been formal and explicit among Downing's gay readers, in or out of Texas? In a blog posted on the website *I Blame the Patriarchy*, dated February 23, 2014, and entitled "Planet Earth: what a wacky place to be gay," the pseudonymous "Twisty Faster" describes anti-gay legislation in Texas in reaction to the 2003 Supreme Court decision in *Lawrence vs. Texas* striking down the state's anti-sodomy laws. Among other things, she is incensed at the legal mandate that "education programs intended for persons younger than 18 years of age must ... [s]tate that homosexual conduct is not an acceptable lifestyle and is a criminal offense under Section 21.06, Penal Code." "The eyes of Texas are upon you," she concludes.[27]

For historical purposes this evidence is, obviously, useless, but it does show that "The Eyes of Texas" has lent itself, on at least one recent occasion, to a gay discourse of surveillance, which means the idea of its having been thus appropriated in America's interwar period is not far-fetched. Whether or not this meaning had become codified in the gay communities of the southern plains states by 1941, when *The Lazy Lawrence Murders* was published, the phrase points to Downing's own awareness of the fact that being gay in the Lone Star State, or its Sooner neighbor to the north, could be bad for your health, if not your literal survival. Three years later he was living in Philadelphia, where he wrote to his parents on July 15, 1944:

> You doubtless think I've forgotten you. But such is *not* the case. I am simply living such a full—and *happy*—life that I never get a chance to write the long letter which I want to write you. Maybe tomorrow I shall.
> (Postcard in possession of the author. Emphasis in the original.)

Apparently, the eyes of Oklahoma had become too much for Todd Downing.

NOTES

1. James H. Cox, *The Red Land to the South: American Indian Writers and Indigenous Mexico* (Minneapolis: University of Minnesota Press, 2012), 10.

2. Curtis Evans, *Clues and Corpses: The Detective Fiction and Mystery Criticism of Todd Downing* (Greenville, OH: Coachwhip, 2013), 76.

3. Information about Ruth Downing was obtained from a taped interview with Nenad Downing by Lavonne Ruoff, then a professor of English and now a professor emerita at the University of Illinois, Chicago, April 5, 1993 (copy in possession of the author). Ruth Shields Downing's roommate was Dr. Mary Jane Sherfey, an early researcher on female orgasm and sexuality and author of *The Nature and Evolution of Female Sexuality* (New York: Random House, 1972). On the heritability of homosexuality, see W. R. Rice, "Homosexuality as a Consequence of Epigenetically Canalized Sexual Development," *The Quarterly Review of Biology* 87 (2012): 343–368. "Peri-anal Abscess" is listed as the "Secondary Cause" of death on the "Certificate of Death," signed January 17, 1974. A certified copy of the document is in the possession of the author. On the risk factors for anal abscess see Camella Wint, Matthew Solan, and Brian Wu, "Anal-Rectal Abscess," *Healthline*, October 20, 2015, at http://www.healthline.com/health/anorectal-abscess#Overview1.

4. Howard P. Chudacoff, *The Age of the Bachelor: Creating an American Subculture* (Princeton: Princeton University Press, 1999), 5, 98, 247.

5. Eve Kosovsky Sedgwick, *The Epistemology of the Closet* (Berkeley: University of California Press, 1990), 3. The late 1920s represented the apogee of the classical detective story's formulization according to generic "rules," mostly propagated tongue-in-cheek by Golden Age writers themselves. For details, see Charles J. Rzepka, *Detective Fiction* (Cambridge: Polity, 2005), 12–15.

6. Todd Downing, *The Last Trumpet* (London: Metheuen, 1938), 87, 90–91.

7. Ibid., 85.

8. Todd Downing, *Murder on Tour* (New York: Putnam's, 1933), 31–32, 62, 191, 229; Todd Downing, *Vultures in the Sky* (London: Methuen, 1936), 8, 15–16. Todd Downing, *Murder on the Tropic* (London: Methuen, 1936), 216–17.

9. Todd Downing, *The Cat Screams* (New York: Doubleday, Doran, 1934), 12.

10. Downing, *Trumpet*, 11.

11. Downing, *Tropic*, 146, 204.
12. Todd Downing. *Night over Mexico* (London: Methuen, 1937), 53, 87, 103.
13. *Ibid.*, 124, 125, 129.
14. Downing, *Trumpet*, 30–31.
15. *Ibid.*, 31.
16. *Ibid.*, 24.
17. *Ibid.*, 84–85.
18. *Ibid.*, 113, 114, 117.
19. *Ibid.*, 174, 256.
20. *Ibid.*, 261, 270–71.
21. William Wordsworth, *Poetical Works*, Vol. 4 (London: Moxon, 1870), 384.
22. James Levin, *The Gay Novel in America* (New York: Garland, 1991), 28; George Chauncey, *Gay New York: Gender, Culture, and the Making of the Gay Male World, 1890–1940* (New York: Basic Books, 1995), 331. Levin cites in particular Blair Niles' *Strange Brother* of 1931, published by H. Liveright, a major publisher of serious fiction and poetry, which offered "a panorama of gay life in New York" in a tone of "liberal tolerance."
23. Todd Downing, *The Lazy Lawrence Murders* (New York: Doubleday, Doran, 1941), 262, 263, 272.
24. *Ibid.*, 267, 271, 275, 278.
25. *Ibid.*, 278.
26. Downing, *Trumpet*, 175.
27. Twisty Faster (pseud.), "Planet Earth: What a Wacky Place to Be Gay," *I Blame the Patriarchy*, at http://blog.iblamethepatriarchy.com/2014/02/23/planet-earth-what-a-wacky-place-to-be-gay/.

BIBLIOGRAPHY

Chauncey, George. *Gay New York: Gender, Culture, and the Making of the Gay Male World, 1890–1940*. New York: Basic Books, 1995.
Chudacoff, Howard P. *The Age of the Bachelor: Creating an American Subculture*. Princeton: Princeton University Press, 1999.
Cox, James H. *The Red Land to the South: American Indian Writers and Indigenous Mexico*. Minneapolis: University of Minnesota Press, 2012.
Downing, Todd. *The Cat Screams*. New York: Doubleday, Doran 1934.
_____. *Chahta Anompa: An Introduction to the Choctaw Language*. Durant, OK: Choctaw Bilingual Education Program, Southeastern State College, 1971.
_____. "Cultural Traits of the Choctaws." Durant, OK: Choctaw Bilingual Education Program, McCurtain County Superintendents of Schools, and Southeastern State College, 1973.
_____. *Journey's End*. Privately printed. Copy in the possession of Margaret Maxey Homer, Atoka, OK. Given her by Todd Downing, 1970.
_____. *The Last Trumpet*. 1937. London: Metheuen, 1938.
_____. *The Lazy Lawrence Murders*. New York: Doubleday, Doran, 1941.
_____. *Murder on the Tropic*. 1935. London: Methuen, 1936.
_____. *Murder on Tour*. New York: Putnam's, 1933.
_____. *Night Over Mexico*. London: Methuen, 1937.
_____. *Vultures in the Sky*. 1935. London: Methuen, 1936.
Evans, Curtis. *Clues and Corpses: The Detective Fiction and Mystery Criticism of Todd Downing*. Greenville, OH: Coachwhip, 2013.
Faster, Twisty (pseud.). "Planet Earth: What a Wacky Place to Be Gay." *I Blame the*

Patriarchy, at http://blog.iblamethepatriarchy.com/2014/02/23/planet-earth-what-a-wacky-place-to-be-gay/.
Hochbruck, Wolfgang. "Mystery Novels to Choctaw Pageant: Todd Downing and Native American Literature(s)." In Arnold Krupat, ed., *New Voices in Native American Literary Criticism*. Washington, D.C.: Smithsonian Institution Press, 1993. pp. 205–21.
Levin, James. *The Gay Novel in America*. New York: Garland, 1991.
Rice, W. R. "Homosexuality as a Consequence of Epigenetically Canalized Sexual Development." *The Quarterly Review of Biology* 87 (2012): 343–368.
Rzepka, Charles J. *Detective Fiction*. Cambridge: Polity, 2005.
Sedgwick, Eve Kosofsky. *Epistemology of the Closet*. Berkeley: University of California Press, 1990.
Wint, Camella, Matthew Solan, and Brian Wu. "Anal-Rectal Abscess." *Healthline*. October 20, 2015, at http://www.healthline.com/health/anorectal-abscess#Overview1.
Wordsworth, William. *Poetical Works*. 6 volumes. London: Moxon, 1870. Volume 4.

"A bad, bad past"
Rufus King, Clifford Orr, College Drag and Detective Fiction

CURTIS EVANS

> If you've a bad, bad past
> It finds you out at last.
> —From "A Bad, Bad Past" (Clifford Orr)

Introduction

The performance of female roles in college theatricals by young men decked out in feminine drag was a common practice at all-male American Ivy League universities in the first three decades of the twentieth century, declining only when the public began associating cross-dressing with sexual inversion. During this era of a rising, irreverent youth culture fostered by the trebling of the number of students attending colleges and universities, Rufus King (1893–1966) and Clifford Orr (1899–1951), two gay male authors of Golden Age American detective fiction, were closely connected with college theatricals in this era, King in the years immediately preceding the First World War, Orr in the years immediately following the conflict.[1] As a member of the Yale Dramatic Association, the handsome and ebullient Rufus King had such a flair for the feminine that he was dubbed the "Queen of the Yale Dramat," while Clifford Orr, a sharp-featured young man with wavy red hair, as a member of the Dartmouth Players wrote books and lyrics for musicals that provided opportunities for his fellow players, including his roommate, to shine on stage as women. King went on to become one of the most popular American mystery writers of the Thirties and Forties, unabashedly revealing in his crime fiction—particularly his stunning tour de force *Murder by Lat-*

itude (1930)—considerable evidence of his "bad, bad past" on the college stage, while intimations of a grimmer kind of queerness are evident in *The Dartmouth Murders* (1929) and *The Wailing Rock Murders* (1932), Orr's two Golden Age detective novels.

Rufus King: Queen of the Yale Dramat

Future prominent American songwriter Cole Albert Porter, born on June 9, 1891, and future prominent American crime writer Rufus Frederick King, born on January 3, 1893, both only children of wealthy parents, in overlapping years attended Yale University during the early part of the twentieth century. The families of both men desired that their promising young scions become respectable lawyers, but their careers did not pan out that way. While students at Yale, both Porter and King took to musicals and became key members—indeed, in their respective senior years, presidents—of the Yale Dramatic Association, popularly known as the Yale Dramat. (King also was a member of the Elizabethan Club, dedicated to conversation, tea and literature, and, like Porter, of the Pundits, a group of ten "devoutly literary" students who met weekly for dinner and lectures at the home of famed English professor William Lyon Phelps.) When King first came to Yale, the slightly older Porter already was writing musical plays for the Dramat. "Rufe" King, as he was known, was adept among the same-sex membership at playing women's parts, and he became one of the Dramat's star attractions. Testifying to King's prominence within the group, another member, Arnold Whitridge (grandson of Matthew Arnold), once penned the following envious couplet: *"Little Rufe King couldn't teach me a thing/I'm the Queen of the Yale Dramat."*[2]

Probably the best-known Cole Porter play in which Rufe King starred was *And the Villain Still Pursued Her* (1912), a send-up of *Uncle Tom's Cabin* and similar nineteenth-century melodramas. Another Yale man, the future Oscar-nominated actor Edgar Montillian "Monty" Woolley, played the villain, while little Rufe King, age nineteen, took the heroine's part, singing the ditty "The Lovely Heroine." ("Oh gee! It's heaven to be the lovely heroine/All the men woo me/And try to undo me/But that's not my line.") Quite the diva, King had other major star turns in Porter's college musicals, performing additional camp numbers like, "Oh What a Lovely Princess" ("Years have I waited for someone adorable/So far my luck is deplorable") and "The Prep School Widow" ("I find that school boys offer more/than many a college sophomore"); yet he also distinguished himself in drag roles in non-musical plays, such as Leo Tolstoy's *The Fruits of Culture* (Tanya), Carlo Goldoni's *The Fan* (Candida), George Bernard Shaw's *The Devil's Disciple* (Mrs. Anderson) and Jack Randall Crawford's *Robin of Sherwood* (Maid Marian, of course). In a

1913 review of the Dramat's staging of *The Fruits of Culture*, the *New York Times* lauded King as "one of the best impersonators of feminine roles that Yale has ever had." King's photo in drag in the part of "scheming maidservant Tanya" headed the article.[3]

During his senior year in 1914, King, a native New Yorker, had planned to enroll in Columbia Law School, but abruptly he charted another, for more unusual, course. A young man who had always loved recreation on the water (during his freshman year he had served as coxswain of Yale's crew team), King upon graduation spent a couple of years at sea as a shipboard wireless operator, enjoying a "romantic life of rolling ships and strange ports," and afterward worked a year in a Paterson, New Jersey silk mill. Drafted into military service after the United States entered the Great War, King served overseas in Europe, rising to the rank of first lieutenant in the field artillery. After the conflict King for a time joined the maritime division of the New York police, but by the mid–1920s he had settled down to make a career for himself as a novelist. Within a few years the fledgling author hit the bigtime with the publication of the mysteries *Murder by the Clock* (1929) and *Murder by Latitude* (1930), becoming one of the most popular and critically-acclaimed American detective novelists of the Thirties and Forties.[4]

King's wealthy New York physician father, Thomas Armstrong King, had passed away prematurely in 1928, leaving his son a substantial inheritance, suitably managed by a responsible trustee. "Dr. King somehow knew that Rufus needed his money looked after," the trustee's daughter observed. Throughout the Thirties and Forties King resided at a Manhattan apartment, summering at the upstate New York King family home at Rouses Point, located on Lake Champlain, less than a mile south of the U.S.-Canadian border, and wintering in Florida, often in the company of his mother, Amelia Sarony Lambert King, with whom he had a very close relationship. The trustee's daughter recalls that Amelia King was Rufus' most trusted reader: "She was given the manuscript half-way through" and "[i]f she could guess who the murderer was, he re-wrote." Although the trustee personally "found Rufus rather alarming," both his wife and young daughter hit it off with the author in a big way. "I adored Rufus," the daughter recalls, "he was an enchanting person ... my mother and Rufus laughed gaily and understood each other. When asked, he presented her a copy of [*Museum Piece No. 13*, one of his mystery novels], inscribed. Knowing him, my mother said, 'Now Rufus, please write something I can show to my dignified friends.' Upon which he wrote, 'For Jane, to show her dignified friends. With love to her, and nuts to them.'"[5]

For years Rufus King was a fixture of the social scene round Rouses Point, keeping up his interest in the stage, for example, by performing in and directing such works as an adaptation of W. W. Jacobs' short story *The Monkey's Paw* and his own original crime drama, *Invitation to a Murder*, at the

Little Theatre at Plattsburgh, the county seat. After the death of his mother in 1950 and his publication of a final crime novel the next year, King left New York, moving to Broward County, Florida, where he resided until his death from a heart attack in 1966.[6] Although a place was reserved for him in the family vault back at Rouses Point, King was cremated and his ashes scattered across Danica Bay, Florida. With King's demise memory of him as a mystery writer soon faded. In the last few years, however, several bloggers, including myself, John Norris and Mike Grost, have lauded King's crime fiction on our blogs, and in 2015 his books, out-of-print for decades, were reissued by Wildside Press, giving some hope that the author may yet experience a well-deserved renaissance.

King's background was one not only of wealth and privilege, but of artistry. In addition to writing crime fiction and taking the occasional turn upon the stage, King as a young man had dabbled at drawing and painting, endeavors in which he had a rich family heritage. Although his father came of old and straight-pathed New England stock, King's beloved mother was a French Canadian Catholic by upbringing, a daughter of Theodore Sarony Lambert, a photographer (he patented "Lambertype") and nephew of Napoleon Sarony (1821–1896), successor to Matthew Brady as the most famous photographer in the United States. Sarony, whose host of celebrity subjects included Oscar Wilde, Mark Twain, Sarah Bernhardt, Lillian Russell, Nikola Tesla, William T. Sherman and pioneering bodybuilder Eugene Sandow, though eccentric had immense talent and a genius for self-promotion, especially in the theatrical world:

> His flair for odd costumes, along with his flowing beard and mustache, made him an object of great wonder and attention, especially among artists and bohemians of all stripes. He often delighted in strolling down Broadway in an astrakhan cap, a calfskin vest with the hairy side out, and trousers tucked into highly polished cavalry boots ... but it was not his odd appearance nor the real Egyptian mummy that stood guard by the door to his studio which made him society's favorite. Sarony was particularly good at shooting theater people ... during his career he produced forty thousand photographs of members of the dramatic profession alone.[7]

Perhaps not surprisingly given their great-uncle's renown among artistes and theater folk, both Amelia Sarony Lambert's brother Thomas and sister Nora went into the acting profession. (Nora also took up painting.) Nor is it surprising that stage lights attracted young Rufe.

The homosexuality of Cole Porter and Monty Woolley, King's colorful pals from his Yale Dramat days (Wooley remained a lifelong friend), has long been noted in books, yet King's sexuality, like his life in general, has received little attention. Although ignored in King's publicity material, which stressed the author's martial prowess and rugged masculinity, King's close affinity with the feminine, both in his drag performances and his personal relationships, suggests on his part a certain queerness, a quality which is also prevalent in his crime fiction.[8] For the purposes of this essay, I focus on one especially striking novel in this regard, the second of King's two breakthrough mysteries: *Murder by Latitude* (1930), a thrilling tale of a vicious murderer run amok on an ocean liner.

Murder by Latitude is one of a number of Rufus King crime novels with maritime settings, other notable examples being *Murder on a Yacht* (1932) and *The Lesser Antilles Case* (1934), all of which take advantage of King's deep familiarity with the life aquatic. In *Latitude* a ruthless murderer, having already struck once on land, boards the ocean liner *Eastern Bay*, bound from Bermuda to Halifax, Nova Scotia and thereupon kills again, the victim this time being Mr. Gans, the ship's wireless operator (a post, it will be recalled, which King had once held as a young man). This slaying prevents the *Eastern Bay* from receiving messages from the New York police, who now have a description of the murderer to send Lieutenant Valcour, King's series sleuth, already on board the ship in search of the culprit. Now Valcour is left groping in the dark, pursuing a murderer with a deadly agenda to fulfill.

In *Murder by Latitude* King fashioned an ingenious and suspenseful detective novel, peopling it with an exceptionally intriguing cast of characters, including both crew and passengers. Among the crew, there is Mr. Gans, only briefly glimpsed in the novel before his demise, and his devoted friend, young Swithers, who when questioned by Lt. Valcour has difficulty concealing the misery he feels over his loss:

> "...I was with him [Gans] in his shack up to two bells."
> "Talking?"
> "Talking."
> "About anything special?"
> "Just a lot of bull, sir."
> "How did he seem?"
> "Seem?"
> "Yes, was he natural—not nervous, or depressed, or ill or anything?"
> "Just natural, sir. We were" — young Swithers, because of a nasty thick feeling that was bothering his throat, found a momentary difficulty in pronouncing the words—"just talking. Same as usual."
> "And when you left him at nine o'clock he was quite all right?"
> "Yes." Monosyllables were easiest.[9]

Then there are the passengers, including certainly Mr. Dumarque, a dandyish, epigram-tossing aesthete, but most strikingly of all the wealthy, middle-aged, much-married Mrs. Poole, a man catcher who harpoons—Valcour's word—younger men as husbands with steady determination and the skill of long practice. Her latest handsome catch, Ted Poole, throughout the novel is objectified through the eyes of his admiring and acquisitive spouse. While the pair is lounging on deck chairs, Mrs. Poole turns to look at Ted and thinks, "It was a pity he had his clothes on...." In an erotic reverie she imagines a tropics filled with Teds, as she had first seen him: flat on his back on the hot pinkish sands of Bermuda's Coral Beach, very young and wiggling all though his smooth brown hardness, wiggling from sheer pleasure of the drenching, burning sun which was offsetting the chill sea breeze, strong fingers scooping up pink gold and pouring it in lazy rivulets on bronze, his head rising like a turtle's, and brown eyes staring at her from above sienna cheeks. "I've only got two days left to get burned in," he had said.[10]

Such explicit expression in a Golden Age detective novel of sexual desire for a male body is unusual, especially in this implicitly homoerotic form, with the female character likely serving as a conduit for the male author's own feelings. King also eroticizes a later scene in the novel in which Ted, clad only in his underwear, is murdered while shaving, shortly after having performed what he facetiously terms the "six famous poses of the Perfect Athlete." When Popular Library issued *Murder by Latitude* in a paperback edition in 1950, it depicted on the cover the scene in the novel where Mrs. Poole dissolves into hysterics over Ted's corpse, but with one significant alteration: it became a now much younger Mrs. Poole who is dishabille, not the slain Ted—the objectification of the female, not the male, being the name of the game with Fifties mass market paperbacks.

By the end of the novel, the resilient Mrs. Poole, having rebounded emotionally, already is on the hunt for Ted's replacement. She finds a highly plausible candidate for marriage in the form of a virile young coast guard: "She smiled lazily ... and wondered exactly how broad it was—that chocolate-colored neck which pillared above a spotlessly white sweat shirt."[11] Mrs. Poole truly calls to mind the youth-vamping Cole Porter character which Rufe King had played nearly two decades earlier: the prep school widow, who finds that "school boys offer more/than many a college sophomore."

Spoiler Alert: Yet even more remarkable than Mrs. Poole is the murderer himself: a "girlishly pretty" male passenger, who, we learn in a bizarre back story, was raised as a girl for four years (from the ages of five to nine), in order to conform with a young Mrs. Poole's capricious desire to have a daughter "to play with" rather than a son. "[T]here is no masquerade in this whole big world more tragic than one of sex," intones Mr. Dumarque when he learns the truth from Lt. Valcour.[12] Rufus King, a master-mistress of sexual masquerade, could not have been more in his element as a crime writer than he was when he wrote *Murder by Latitude*. **End Spoiler.**

Clifford Orr: An Air of Ruined Insouciance

Four years after Rufus King graduated from Yale in 1914, future mystery author Clifford Burrows Orr, a native of Portland, Maine born on November 19, 1899, matriculated at Dartmouth University, where, like King, he became enmeshed in the world of college musicals. However, "Kip" Orr, as he was known, did not perform in them, confining his talents to writing books and song lyrics. Orr's college drama group, the Dartmouth Players, relied, like the Yale Dramatic Society, on young men to take the women's parts. *Rise, Please!*, a mock marital melodrama with book and lyrics by Orr which premiered at the Dartmouth Players' Winter Carnival on February 10, 1921, tells the story of young Jerry and Jean, whose impending nuptials are abruptly menaced by the appearance of Gertie Purell, a lady of questionable repute with whom the unfortunate Jerry has had a certain prior familiarity. After lamenting, in Orr's song "A Bad, Bad Past," of the steep price to be paid for youthful indiscretions ("For every girl that you have known/If you have seen her once alone/She'll trail you/And nail you."), poor Jerry does away with himself at the end of Act One. Act Two opens with the descent of a flock of newspapermen, singing that they scent "Scandal": "Please tell us the facts, sir./We're sure you won't object./His life was wrecked and we suspect/Some scandal!"[13]

Stage laughter aside, in the Twenties real-life fear of sexual indiscretions and public scandal struck at the heart of the Dartmouth Players, including very close to Kip Orr, who always seemed to be there, at least on the periphery, when something queer happened. Three days before *Rise, Please!* was to premier, John Harvie Dew Zuckerman, one of Orr's closest Dartmouth friends (the two young men roomed together their senior year and lived together for a year after leaving college), had been called upon to step in and save the day when the young man originally cast to play Jerry's bride was taken ill with appendicitis. Happily for the Players, Harvie Zuckerman had experience with women's parts, having played the female lead in the 1919 Dartmouth Players prom show, *Oh, Doctor!* Less happily for Zuckerman personally, about a month after his two performances as Jean at the Winter Carnival, he visited the President of Dartmouth, Ernest Martin Hopkins, seeking Hopkins' help in dealing with certain disturbing feelings he reported having.

President Hopkins promptly steered the young man to Dr. Charles Bancroft, "the most prestigious psychiatrist" in the state, sending ahead of Zuckerman a letter delicately explaining the nature of the prospective patient's problem:

> I do not think that in his case abnormality has gone to any detrimental extent as yet ... but I do feel very strongly that he needs to be helped on reversing certain tendencies of his...
>
> Sometime I want to talk with some of your authorities on mental hygiene in regard to the general problem of whether playing girls' parts in the dramatic performances makes a man effeminate or whether being effeminate qualifies him for playing girls' parts. I am considered, among the dramatic group, as being unduly concerned on the question and if so I want to get over it.
>
> The fact is, however, that we have had a distinct tendency among a considerable number of the men who have played the so-called leads in girl characters to develop exotic and

unnatural instincts which are thoroughly out of keeping with what the College means to stand for.

In one case, three years ago, the boy wandered off from Hanover and safeguarded the College reputation to the extent that he committed suicide in New York rather than here, but the underlying fact was that his affection for one of his dramatic club associates was not only unappreciated but was rebuffed. We have had one other case in which I would a good deal rather the boy would have committed suicide.

With Zuckerman there is nothing of this seriousness at all and as a matter of fact it is somewhat on the basis of his own recognition of conditions that I am bespeaking your help...

We have been remarkably free from the deviations from normal and the sex aberrations which have been so serious a condition in many of the colleges of the country and we have taken every possible precaution to watch and guard against any outbreak of this. I hope that we may be spared what many of the others have had to experience...

During the previous year officials at Harvard University had formed a co-called "Secret Court" to root out those at the school who were suspected of what Hopkins had termed "exotic and unnatural instincts," with the result that seven students were expelled (one of whom shortly afterward committed suicide). Harvard tried to keep its sexual inquisition from becoming public knowledge, but it seems not unlikely that the Dartmouth president might have heard something about it.[14] In any event, despite Hopkins' fervently expressed hope that Dartmouth be spared the "sex aberrations which have been so serious a condition in many of the colleges of the country," the plague of aberrancy struck Dartmouth only a few years later, the locus of contagion once again being found amid the Dartmouth players.

Among other things Harvie Zuckerman was advised, during his consultation with Dr. Bancroft, Superintendent of the New Hampshire State Asylum and Secretary of the National Committee for Mental Hygiene, to desist from impersonating women, to play tennis regularly and to cultivate a scientific hobby, such as ornithology or botany. Whether Zuckerman took up tennis and birdwatching in a big way is unknown, but he did stop playing female parts in college plays. On campus he began meeting regularly with a minister and gradually faded from active participation in the Dartmouth Players. (Later in life he converted to Protestantism, became a minister himself, wed and fathered several children.) Kip Orr, on the other hand, kept writing plays for the group and even became the Players' president during his senior year. He later told President Hopkins that a year had elapsed before he learned of Zuckerman's personal crisis.

In 1923, a year after Orr has completed his Dartmouth coursework, star Dartmouth Players Ralph Garfield Jones and William McKay Patterson—Jones had played villainess Gertie Purell in *Rise, Please!* and Patterson had taken the role of the bride's sister—bought, along with several other individuals, a house located across the Connecticut River from the college, in the hamlet of Beaver Meadow, Vermont. There the group played host to other young men currently or formerly associated with the Dartmouth Players, including Kip Orr. By 1925 the house at Beaver Meadow had become a center of sinister speculation, with President Hopkins concluding from dark stories he had heard that "going to or visiting in the house at Beaver Meadow ... was prima facie evidence of undesirability." As Nicholas Syrett has more bluntly put it in his essay "The Boys at Beaver Meadow," in this house "an all-male group of Dartmouth students and recent graduates ... had parties, stayed up late, drank alcohol, and had sex. With each other." Dartmouth responded to the shocking situation by expelling one student visitor to the house, while Jones and Patterson, who had graduated the previous year, were requested to resign from their college fraternity, to which request they hastily complied. By the next year the Players were importing women to play female parts and by 1929, men in drag had been banished entirely from the stage at Dartmouth.[15]

After leaving the college in 1922, Orr, unscathed by the Beaver Meadow affair, spent three years working at the *Boston Evening Transcript*, then for another three years was successively employed as publicity manager for publisher Robert M. McBride and as manager of publisher Doubleday, Doran's Wall Street bookshop. Upon deciding in 1928 to try making his living as a freelance writer, Orr that summer penned most of his first novel, *The Dartmouth Murders*, while lazing on Ogunquit Beach, Maine, a locale which had become a haven for bohemians and artists. The novel was accepted by the American publisher Farrar & Rinehart and issued in 1929 to good reviews, encouraging Orr to compose another mystery, *The Wailing Rock Murders*, published in 1932 by Farrar & Rinehart to even better reviews than Orr's first novel. The rising crime writer was said to have a third mystery, *The Cornell Murders*, in preparation, but it never appeared; and, indeed, no more detective fiction was ever to come forth from Orr's hand, though a film version of *The Dartmouth Murders*, entitled *A Shot in the Dark*, was released by a poverty row studio in 1935. Orr became a features writer for the *New Yorker*, in the two decades between 1932 and his death in 1951 publishing over 400 columns, many of them for the popular "Talk of the Town" section. (At the *New Yorker* Orr also was tasked with answering letters to the editor, including those from the many people puzzled or outraged by the ending of Shirley Jackson's famous story "The Lottery," originally published in the magazine.)[16] Although Orr's crime writing and journalism largely was forgotten after his death, in recent years his name has resurfaced, on account of his connection with the Beaver Meadow affair, in studies of college homosexuality in the 1920s.

During his lifetime Kip Orr unquestionably traveled a far piece from his relatively simple turn-of-the-century origins in Portland Maine. Orr's father as a younger man had possessed writing ambitions, but he gave them up when he married, becoming an advertising agent for a mercantile establishment, while his paternal grandfather had been "one of the most upright ... sea captains on the Maine coast," with his wife "very faithful members of the Baptist church" and in his own right a "noble member of the Sons of Temperance." Kip Orr had once wryly contrasted himself with his sea captain grandfather, noting that "I am seasick at the sight of a canoe," and doubtlessly he had been involved in activities at Dartmouth at which the pious man would very much have looked askance.[17] Orr was in fact gay, as his college association with the Dartmouth Players and the boys at Beaver Meadow have suggested to analysts of the Beaver Meadow affair. Certainly the lyrics to Orr's song "A Bad, Bad Past," warbled by a young man who on stage has just wed another young man in drag (played, in the event, by Orr's roommate), suggest a winking acknowledgment of some queer skeletons in the closet (e.g., "There's nothing you can hide/That's so/I know/I've often tried.")

At the *New Yorker,* Orr had a reputation as a waspish, embittered homosexual and confirmed alcoholic. In his controversial memoir, *Here at the New Yorker,* Orr's work colleague Brendan Gill painted a poignant picture of Kip in the 1940s, no longer laughing at life:

> He had been a brilliant undergraduate at Dartmouth and had written a successful mystery novel about the college.... Alcoholic and homosexual, Kip took terrible chances with his life, and it became a wonder that he wasn't murdered; more than once he was rolled, beaten up, and left for dead in some dirty doorway in the Village, and yet he survived to die sadly in the small college town where, for a little while, he had known good fortune. When I first encountered him ... his reddish pompadour was going grey and his large light-green eyes had lids shocking in their rolled-back redness. He had an air about him of ruined insouciance, and this was heightened by the fact that he wore good-looking, old-fashioned tweeds and English brogans with the exceptionally thick, light-colored crepe soles that were in vogue in the twenties. Thanks to those soles, Kip was able to steal up behind one in the corridors and suddenly whisper some abrupt, catty remark, or offer the latest gossip about some fresh office disaster, and one was more startled by the fact of his presence at one's ear than by anything he said.... For lunch Orr would drink a series of sweet Manhattans, signaling so discreetly to the waitress for a second, third, and fourth that in my earliest acquaintance with him I supposed him always to be sipping daintily at his first.[18]

Gill vividly recalled Kip—who back in 1929 had composed customarily ironic lyrics to the popular song "I May Be Wrong (But I think You're Wonderful)" (sung by Doris Day in the 1950 Kirk Douglas film *Young Man with a Horn*)—at cocktail parties when the piano was played, standing "at one end of the piano, drink in hand, listening raptly. As the evening wore on, his eyes would grow more and more watery, and it was odd and touching to see him, as happy in those moments as he would ever be, apparently dissolved in tears." Orr died at a nursing home in Hanover, New Hampshire, home of Dartmouth

University, in 1951, about five weeks shy of his fifty-second birthday.[19] Something of Orr's evident unhappiness—his sense, perhaps, of perennially being an outside observer of life—comes through in his pair of detective novels, deadly serious affairs in which the sardonic gaiety of his song lyrics is entirely absent.

Orr dedicated both of his detective novels to Dartmouth friends, *The Dartmouth Murders* to tall, slender, blue-eyed Franklin McDuffee, Dartmouth '21, a Rhodes scholar, prize-winning poet and Dartmouth English professor best known today for having written lyrics to the popular college song "Dartmouth Undying," and *The Wailing Rock Murders* to Bill North ("who hates this sort of thing"), who had been one of the co-owners of the house in Beaver Meadow and later was employed as a teacher at a boys' school. Like Orr himself, both North and McDuffee never married. A year older than Orr, McDuffee at the age of 41 committed suicide at Dartmouth by inhaling automobile exhaust fumes in his garage. Friends avowed that for several weeks he had been suffering from "melancholia."[20]

The Dartmouth Murders, the book Kip Orr dedicated to Franklin McDuffee, ironically opens with a suicide on campus, though in this case the purported suicide actually proves murder. In the first chapter of the novel, Dartmouth student Byron Coates is discovered dead, hanging by his neck from the rope ladder fire escape suspended outside his locked dormitory bedroom (in real life North Massachusetts Hall, where Orr himself had resided). After Byron's death is established to have resulted not from hanging but rather a particularly nasty form of foul play, Kenneth Harris, the dead boy's roommate and best friend, and Ken's officious father, an attorney and occasional detective novelist, act as an investigative team in the affair, somewhat in the manner of Ellery Queen and his police inspector parent, who debuted the same year in *The Roman Hat Mystery*, though in *The Dartmouth Murders* these roles are reversed, with Ken Harris functioning as the novel's Watson figure and retrospective narrator.

Throughout *The Dartmouth Murders*, Ken Harris evinces little interest in Byron's sister, Jean (she carries the same name as the bride in *Rise, Please!*), who is visiting from Vassar for the weekend. Jean "was handed over to me as a companion," notes Ken neutrally. "I was neither pleased nor displeased. She was, I thought, a nice girl, quite good-looking in a dark, slim way, but a little strange." The author soon transfers Jean as a romantic interest to another young male character in the novel. Ken musters much more enthusiasm for the late Byron, his friendship with whom he describes in what seems something of a semi-autobiographical passage:

> We were good companions, careless friends, and happy enemies when anything small enough arose to fight about. His claim to undergraduate fame lay in his really excellent baritone voice. Mine lay in a facility with the piano and an ability, after a fashion, to write

dancy tunes for the annual music shows. He was more of an athlete than I and dabbled a bit as a sophomore in both track and swimming, and he was also more studious, though his grades almost always fell slightly short of mine. Mine was the quicker wit, his the greater doggedness. We took to each other's friends as easily as we did to each other's clothes.

Ken emotionally describes the scene when he is asked to formally identify his dead friend's body: "I leaned forward and looked.... Byron was beautiful.... The tears welled in my eyes and I was glad that Father turned at once and made for the door."[21]

Recalling the morning of the day of Byron's death, Ken imparts that his friend had implored him, "If I die, for heaven's sake don't ship my letters home to Mother without sorting them first"—a suggestive request when one considers that it was an incriminating letter discovered after the suicide of a Harvard student which kindled that school's anti-queer inquisition in 1920. Obsession and sexual secrets play a great role in *The Dartmouth Murders*, though they concern matters other than homosexuality. In passing we learn that Byron was a reader of the English sexologist Havelock Ellis, a pioneer in the study of same-sex attraction, but Byron's peculiar difficulty seems to have arisen not from homosexuality but rather from his mother-fixation. Ken's feelings for Byron certainly leave room for speculation, however.[22]

In form *The Dartmouth Murders* is a competently executed but conventional detective novel that in its day garnered attention (including an eventual film adaptation) for the novelty of its college setting; Orr's second and final detective novel, *The Wailing Rock Murders*, is an altogether more remarkable affair. "Too good a book may undo a writer as well as too bad a one," wrote English author and crime fiction reviewer Charles Williams in his notice of the novel, "and what Mr. Orr is going to do for his next climax I cannot think."[23] Set on the rocky Maine cliffs near Ogunquit Beach, where Orr had written his debut mystery, *The Wailing Rock Murders* bears considerable similarity to the "old dark house" thriller popularized at the time though books and such hit films as *The Bat* (1926), *The Cat and the Canary* (1927) and, of course, *The Old Dark House* (1932), as well as to the horror-infused detective fiction of John Dickson Carr, though at the time of the publication of Orr's second novel Carr had not yet hit his stride as a mystery writer. Acknowledged as the Golden Age master of the locked room mystery, Carr was an adept at atmospherics, producing such spine-chilling mystery classics as *The Three Coffins* (1935), *The Burning Court* (1937), *The Crooked Hinge* (1938) and *He Who Whispers* (1946). As a detective novel Orr's second mystery does not rise to the exalted level of these Carr classics, yet it offers mystery fans a superbly shuddery and suspenseful read. Much of the plot of the well-regarded 1946 noir film *So Dark the Night* appears to have been adapted from *The Wailing*

Rock Murders, though unfortunately without acknowledgment of Clifford Orr.

The events of *The Wailing Rock Murders* take place over one hagridden evening and morning on an isolated stretch of Maine coast, where are found a whistling rock whose sound foretells of death and two identical neighboring cliffside houses, Victorian monstrosities described with distaste by the narrator of the novel, Spaton Meech, who shares the rationalist disdain, so typical of Golden Age detective fiction, for the romantic excesses of mid- to late-nineteenth-century architecture. Nearly seventy-six years old, Meech is a sleuth of long and esteemed repute, but in *The Wailing Rock Murders* he is more a figure of pathos than an archetypal Great Detective, striding confidently and nonchalantly through fictional annals of brilliant crime detection. "I am no writer," Meech tells us plaintively at the opening of the novel. "But I have no Watson to write for me. I have never had a Watson, lonely freelance that I have been for so long." Nor does Meech have the handsome countenance and form of many a gentleman detective, as his nickname, "Spider," indicates:

> They call me "Spider," and I know why. It is because I am slightly deformed from a spinal twist I received in a fall from a rope-swing when I was only five, and because my arms are very long and hang to my knees, and because my head is large and seems to lie on my chest when I walk, and because (on account of my shape) I prefer to sit cross-legged on tables or on the floor rather than to rest my hump against the unyielding back of a chair....
> Naturally I am a bachelor....[24]

Meech explains that this, his latest, most personal and perhaps final investigation, arose after his ward, Garda Lawrence, invited him to a weekend house party at the country mansion of Creamer and Vera Farnol. On the very night of his arrival at the perilously rock-perched Farnol abode, Meech discovered Garda slain in her locked bedroom, her throat "most horribly, most hideously slit." Before his investigation into Garda's savage murder is over, two more people will be dead, with every promise of a third death soon to follow—a resolution that is a long way from the "restoration of order" which is said to characterize Golden Age mystery. Indeed, the lack of comfort afforded readers of *The Wailing Rock Murders* is the most striking aspect of the novel. Meech begins and ends the tale an isolated and sad figure, someone always seen as essentially an outsider and denied a "normal" existence, despite widespread public acclaim for his cleverness. One can sense parallels with the life of the author himself, a "lonely freelance" who never seems to have found contentment in his life, despite the great promise he showed from an early age. "Kip Orr, too, sought death," claimed Orr's *New Yorker* colleague Brendan Gill, just like Franklin McDuffee in real life and Byron Coates in fiction—and, it is implied in the dreadful last line of *The Wailing Rock Murders*, like Spaton Meech will do as well.[25]

186 Part One: Locked Doors

NOTES

1. "A Bad, Bad Past," Nicholas L. Syrett, *The Company He Keeps: A History of White College Fraternities* (Chapel Hill: University of North Carolina Press, 2009), 186, 203–07; Laura Horak, *Girls Will Be Boys: Cross-Dressed Women, Lesbians, and American Cinema* (New Brunswick: Rutgers University Press, 2016).

2. William McBrien, *Cole Porter: A Biography* (New York: Vintage, 1998), 42, 44; George Washington Patterson, IV, ed., *History of the Class of Nineteen Hundred and Fourteen Yale College*, Vol. I (New Haven: Yale University Press, 1913), 221.

3. Robert Kimball, ed., *The Complete Lyrics of Cole Porter* (1983; New York: Da Capo, 1992), 13–14, 31, 35; *New York Times*, 19 January 1913.

4. Information drawn from author blurbs on dust jackets and *New York, Abstracts of World War I Military Service, 1917–1919,* Ancestry.com.

5. (Rouses Point) *The North Countryman*, 19 April 1928, 1; 2 April 2013 comment by janec at John Norris, Review of *Murder by the Clock*, 16 January 2012, *Pretty Sinister Books*, at http://prettysinister.blogspot.com/2012/01/first-books-murder-by-clock-rufus-king.html.

6. (Plattsburgh) *Daily Republican*, 29 January 1932, 5; (Sable Forks) *The Record-Post*, 9 May 1935; (Rouses Point) *The North Countryman*, 24 February 1966, 4.

7. Thomas S. Lambert obituary, *Anthony's Photographic Bulletin* 19 (1888): 220; Sean Corcoran, "Napoleon Sarony: Celebrity Photographer," 28 April 2015, *MCNY Blog: New York Stories*, Museum of the City of New York, at http://blog.mcny.org/2015/04/28/napoleon-sarony-celebrity-photographer/; David L. Chapman, *Sandow the Magnificent: Eugen Sandow and the Beginnings of Bodybuilding* (Urbana: University of Illinois Press, 1994), 71–72.

8. So reads this blurb from one of King's dust jackets:

> Rufus King has poured into [his series detective] Lieutenant Valcour the result of all his varied experience in adventure and crime detection. Mr. King has been a cavalry man on the Mexican border, an officer in the artillery during the war, where he fought in the battle that swayed back and forth across the Meuse. He admits that he was cited for holding the front line in the Bois de Sachet with two French .75s. He has been a wireless man on freighters, tankers and fruit ships, cruising the seven seas. He has salvaged a ship off Pernambuco and hauled it into port. He has beachcombed along the waterfront of Buenos Aires, has served in the marine division of the New York police, and in general has lived the sort of life which could be expected from the creator of so exciting and glamorous a detective as Lieutenant Valcour.

9. Rufus King, *Murder by Latitude* (Garden City, NY: Doubleday, Doran, 1930), 54–55. Lt. Valcour and another character, the sardonic Mr. Dumarque, reference the classical friendship of Damon and Pythias at one point in the novel, albeit with a cynical twist:

> "There should be no such thing, Mr. Valcour, as friendship. It is nothing but an institution for the coupling of compatible bores with whom the rest of the world has grown fatigued."
> "I'm inclined to agree with you. When one thinks of Damon and Pythias—"
> "Let us not." Mr. Dumarque's eyes shot fleetingly toward heaven. "One dreads to think on what subjects they conversed after the first six months" [*Ibid.*, 50].

10. King, *Latitude*, 27, 28.
11. *Ibid.*, 148, 303.
12. *Ibid.*, 276, 285, 304.
13. The information in this and the next two pages, including the excerpts from

President Hopkins' letter, is drawn from Nicholas Preti, "Rise, Please! Theatre of the Dead," 15 March 2015, *Mouth*, at http://dmouth.com/writing/2015/3/15/rise-please-theatre-of-the-dead.

14. See William Wright, *Harvard's Secret Court: The Savage 1920 Purge of Campus Homosexuals* (New York: St. Martin's, 2005).

15. Nicholas L. Syrett, "The Boys of Beaver Meadow: A Homosexual Community at 1920s Dartmouth College," *American Studies* 48 (Summer 2007): 9, 12.

16. Clifford B. Orr Correspondence, Maine Writers Correspondence, Special Collections, Maine State Library, *Maine State Documents*, at http://digitalmaine.com/maine_writers_correspondence/413/; Howard M. Solomon, "Creating a 'Gay Mecca': Lesbians and Gay Men in Late-Twentieth-Century Gay Portland," in Joseph A. Conforti, ed., *Creating Portland: History and Place in Northern New England* (Hanover, NH: University Press of New England, 2005), 297; Ruth Franklin, "'The Lottery' Letters," 25 June 2013, *New Yorker*, at http://www.newyorker.com/books/page-turner/the-lottery-letters. Howard Solomon has characterized Ogunquit at this time as having been a "place to escape the sexual and gender strictures of middle-class America—if only for a few weeks in the summer" (p. 297). Such an escape would have proved welcome for Orr.

17. Charles Nelson Sinnett, *Sinnett Genealogy: Michael Sinnett of Harpswell, Maine, His Ancestry and Descendants* (Concord, NH: Rumford, 1910), 95; Orr Correspondence.

18. Brendan Gill, *Here at the New Yorker* (1975; repr., New York: Da Capo, 1997), 301–03.

19. Gill, *New Yorker*, 302; *New York Times*, 12 October 1951.

20. *Edwardsville Intelligencer*, 16 January 1940, 7. As a student at Oxford McDuffee had won the prestigious 1924 Newdigate Prize for best composition in verse by an undergraduate.

21. Clifford Orr, *The Dartmouth Murders* (New York: Farrar & Rinehart, 1929), 2–3, 4, 89.

22. Orr, *Dartmouth*, 1–2. The name Byron, of course is suggestive (the sexually adventurous Lord Byron), as is "By," Byron's nickname in the novel.

23. Jared C. Lobdell, ed., *The Detective Fiction Reviews of Charles Williams, 1930–1935* (Jefferson, NC: McFarland, 2003), 93.

24. Clifford Orr, *The Wailing Rock Murders* (New York: Farrar & Rinehart, 1932), 4, 6.

25. Orr, *Rock*, 24; Gill, *New Yorker*, 301.

BIBLIOGRAPHY

Books and Articles

Anthony's Photographic Bulletin 19 (1888): 220.
Chapman, David L. *Sandow the Magnificent: Eugen Sandow and the Beginnings of Bodybuilding*. Urbana: University of Illinois Press, 1994.
Corcoran, Sean. "Napoleon Sarony: Celebrity Photographer." 28 April 2015. *MCNY Blog: New York Stories*. Museum of the City of New York. At http://blog.mcny.org/2015/04/28/napoleon-sarony-celebrity-photographer/.
Franklin, Ruth. "'The Lottery' Letters." *New Yorker*, 25 June 2013. At http://www.newyorker.com/books/page-turner/the-lottery-letters.
Gill, Brendan. *Here at the New Yorker*. 1975. Reprint, New York: Da Capo, 1997.
Horak, Laura. *Girls Will Be Boys: Cross-Dressed Women, Lesbians, and American Cinema*. New Brunswick: Rutgers University Press 2016.

188 Part One: Locked Doors

Kimball, Robert, ed. *The Complete Lyrics of Cole Porter*. 1983. Reprint, New York: Da Capo, 1992.
King, Rufus. *Murder by Latitude*. Garden City, NY: Doubleday, Doran, 1930.
Lobdell, Jared C., ed. *The Detective Fiction Reviews of Charles Williams, 1930–1935*. Jefferson, NC: McFarland, 2003.
McBrien, William. *Cole Porter: A Biography*. New York: Vintage, 1998.
Orr, Clifford. *The Dartmouth Murders*. New York: Farrar & Rinehart, 1929.
_____. *The Wailing Rock Murders*. New York: Farrar & Rinehart, 1932.
Patterson, George Washington IV, ed. *History of the Class of Nineteen Hundred and Fourteen Yale College*. Volume I. New Haven: Yale University Press, 1913.
Preti, Nicholas. "Rise, Please! Theatre of the Dead" (15 March 2015). *Mouth*. At http://dmouth.com/writing/2015/3/15/rise-please-theatre-of-the-dead.
Sinnett, Charles Nelson. *Sinnett Genealogy: Michael Sinnett of Harpswell, Maine, His Ancestry and Descendants*. Concord, NH: Rumford, 1910.
Solomon, Howard M. "Creating a 'Gay Mecca': Lesbians and Gay Men in Late-Twentieth-Century Gay Portland." In Joseph A. Conforti, ed., *Creating Portland: History and Place in Northern New England*. Hanover, NH: University Press of New England, 2005.
Syrett, Nicholas L. "The Boys of Beaver Meadow: A Homosexual Community at 1920s Dartmouth College." *American Studies* 48 (Summer 2007): 9–18.
_____. *The Company He Keeps: A History of White College Fraternities*. Chapel Hill: University of North Carolina Press, 2009.
Wright, William. *Harvard's Secret Court: The Savage 1920 Purge of Campus Homosexuals*. New York: St. Martin's, 2005.

Blog Comment, Government Records, Newspapers, Special Collections

Clifford B. Orr Correspondence. Maine Writers Correspondence. Special Collections. Maine State Library. *Maine State Documents*, at http://digitalmaine.com/maine_writers_correspondence/413/
Comment by janec (2 April 2013) to John Norris, Review of *Murder by the Clock*. 16 January 2012. *Pretty Sinister Books*. At http://prettysinister.blogspot.com/2012/01/first-books-murder-by-clock-rufus-king.html.
Edwardsville Intelligencer, 16 January 1940, 7.
New York Times, 19 January 1913, 12 October 1951.
New York, Abstracts of World War I Military Service, 1917–1919. Ancestry.com.
Plattsburgh *Daily Republican*, 29 January 1932, 5.
(Rouses Point) *The North Countryman*, 19 April 1928, 24 February 1966.
(Sable Forks) *The Record-Post*, 9 May 1935.

Foppish, Effeminate, or "a little too handsome"
Coded Character Descriptions in the Novels of Mignon G. Eberhart

RICK CYPERT

For much of the twentieth century, Mignon Good Eberhart was one of the best-known female mystery writers in America. Born to a middle class family in Lincoln, Nebraska, Mignon Good ultimately dreamed of a different kind of life, one she would live and one she would write about: the former, in luxurious settings of penthouses and estates; the latter, an elegant world into which murder intrudes. And into both of these lives, these worlds, issues of sexuality would emerge. A heterosexual, Eberhart dealt with an absence of physical intimacy in one of her marriages; an abusive relationship in the other; and, during an inter-marriage interlude, an indecisiveness about a suitor's character. A writer with a wide range of acquaintances in arts and publishing, Eberhart was sophisticated in the ways of the world as well as capable of describing the types of individuals she encountered, both for her narrative goals and as a means of perpetuating idealized gender roles and heteronormative relationships in her novels.

Over a writing career that spanned sixty years, Eberhart wrote fifty-nine novels and numerous short stories, essays, and plays. Her life itself spanned the twentieth century: Eberhart was born in 1899 and died in 1996. After attending Nebraska Wesleyan University, a small liberal arts college in her hometown, Eberhart married a young engineer, just graduated from the University of Nebraska, and the two embarked upon a whirlwind life that took them around the globe, settling and resettling in such varied locales as the sand hills of Nebraska, suburban Chicago, the Alps Maritime in France, vacation resorts in Florida, wartime Washington, D.C., a military base in Nevada,

New York City, and suburban Connecticut. In each of these residences and throughout her travels, Eberhart took careful note of her surroundings as a means for creating the realistic and atmospheric settings for which she was known.

Likewise, her contacts in the publishing world introduced her to people—artists, writers, entertainers, the wealthy, and other *Vanity Fair* celebrities—who would inspire her as she created characters that populated the often opulent, sometimes homey, settings into which she placed them. Although generally happy in her marriage to Alan Eberhart, she suggests in her letters to longtime friend and *Chicago Tribune* literary critic Fanny Butcher that there was an absence of physical intimacy in the marriage. The cultural identity for women in Mignon Eberhart's generation demanded modesty, propriety, fulfillment in marriage (whether genuine or performed), and absolute discretion. Men were selective and women were highly discreet when discussing intimate matters with others, if at all. That Eberhart chose to break these various taboos in her letters to Fanny reveals both the severity of the problem and Mignon Eberhart's fragile emotional state. Although the correspondence suggests that her husband's challenge was related to physical problems rather than a question of sexual identity, the lack of physical intimacy, just like the abuse she suffered from her second husband and her anxiety with the character of her would-be suitor in a third relationship, all provide reasonable biographical evidence for why Eberhart might explore issues of masculinity in the development of many of the characters in her novels. To the biographical perspective, as stated previously, we can add the pervasive cultural norm throughout much of the twentieth century for rigid gender roles and heteronormative relationships.

Not surprisingly, given Eberhart's mass appeal and the century and genre in which she wrote, we do not find a positive portrayal of male homosexuality (unstated and unnamed), except, perhaps, in older, non-threatening, fatherly "dandy" figure characters she introduced in several of her novels. There is, no doubt, a distinct disconnect here between Eberhart's own life and her work. Clearly Eberhart must have known homosexuals in the New York and Chicago social worlds which she inhabited. And Eberhart surely encountered numerous others in the art and literary world whose secret or not-so-secret lives must have provided her with an informed, if not tolerant, perspective on the subject. If that is the case, then we must consider the male homosexual characters from her novels as variations on a theme. They represented for Eberhart, and allowed her to convey to readers, the notion that seemingly accessible, attractive, emotionally communicative men, although appealing to women, might not actually be the type of man that is right for a woman. Aside from her second husband, Hazen Perry, the other named romantic involvement in Eberhart's life is the mysterious figure with the ambiguous name of "Kim." Whether he was too emotionally accessible, too effusive, too present is impossible to know. But Eberhart's brief references to him in her letters to Fanny Butcher potentially suggest such a possibility.

Nor is it insignificant that early in her career Eberhart met Gertrude Stein and Alice B. Toklas during Stein's *Lectures in America* tour (1934–1935), arranged by Eberhart's Random House publisher, Bennett Cerf. Having read a few of Eberhart's novels, Stein later enthused about the young mystery writer's atmospheric writing in letters to Fanny Butcher: "I am just reading the other Mignon Eberhart book *The White Cockatoo* and it is xtraordinarily [sic] good writing and pleases me a lot." In a letter after her return to France, Stein comments: "I have just been reading Mignon Eberhart's last book all about how Chicago looks and it's a pleasure; we did like it; I can still see it out of the window." Stein, no doubt, referred to either *The Dark Garden* or *The House on the Roof* for descriptions of downtown Chicago such as the following: "The fog was growing heavier, and there was a hint of sleet on the windshield. Bits of automobiles loomed out of the fog here and there into confused, futuristic paths of light; automobiles with their radiators or their rear fenders mysteriously gone. It was a kind of Cheshire-cat effect gone modern and very noisy."[1] Such descriptions would stand out to a modernist like Stein, just as Eberhart must have found elements of Stein's personality extremely appealing: her independence; her unsettling sense of humor; her playfulness with language; her rhetorical dexterity in conversation and public speaking—all traits that Eberhart might hope to develop for her own public persona as an up-and-coming writer. And certainly, Eberhart would have understood Stein's ability to suggest, to intimate, to provide a reader with clues.

Early in the century, Stein's playful short story "Miss Furr and Miss Skeene" (1922) had provided plenty of clues for perceptive readers about the nature of certain kinds of relationships between women. Another friend of Eberhart's, the romance novelist Faith Baldwin, though married, divorced, and remarried to the same man, maintained a relationship with her children's nurse, Gonnie, who travelled with her and regularly accompanied her on social occasions with the Eberharts, as the correspondence between Eberhart and Baldwin attests. One must "read" the exchanges in such correspondence, nonetheless, with caution.

In 1920, Faith married Hugh H. Cuthrell, who would become president of Brooklyn Union Gas Company, and the couple had four children. In 1927, Faith gave birth to twins (Ann and Steven), and shortly thereafter, she and Hugh separated. At that point, Faith tells the story this way:

> I was fortunate, just at this juncture to have a friend who had been with me at the hospital when Ann and Steven were born. She was extremely capable and very kind. She became attached to us all. After Hugh and I separated, I continued to live in the Bay Ridge house with the children, and she came to live with us. I shall here call her Mademoiselle "X"

which is the name by which she has been known in many of my articles and also through many of my radio talks. Also she prefers to be anonymous. Mlle. X had her own and quite important job at the time—a species of welfare work—but she managed to run the house and look after the children which allowed me to write. I owe her a debt which I can never repay.[2]

Mlle. X was the likely inspiration for one of Baldwin's novels, *District Nurse*, concerning a welfare worker in a large city. The mysterious companion of Faith Baldwin was no mystery to Mignon Eberhart, who throughout her letters to Fanny Butcher, refers to Faith and Gonnie. At the time Mignon Eberhart and Faith Baldwin met, Gonnie had been part of the Baldwin household for at least five years. In 1935, Mignon Eberhart dedicated her novel *The House on the Roof* as follows: "To Faith and to Gonnie." Wisely, the second "to" maintained a kind of distance between the two women, not cluing in the public that Gonnie could be "Mademoiselle X." By 1936, the two women had decided to relocate to New Canaan, purchasing a country estate with a pool after extensive house hunting: "We looked at many houses, Mlle. X and I. She looked at more. I think she looked at 40."[3]

As Lillian Faderman suggests in *Odd Girls and Twilight Lovers*, from the late nineteenth century through the early 1920s, intense emotional, often romantic relationships were common between young women, certainly among those attending many of the women's colleges such as Vassar, Smith, Mount Holyoke, and Bryn Mawr. Likewise, documented life-long "devoted friendships" and "Boston marriages" were often common between female professors, college administrators, and other women in a variety of professions, including, notably, Jane Addams, founder of Hull House in Chicago, and her life companion, Mary Smith. Such women, as Faderman explains, "saw women as productive beings who could support themselves by professional labor, and as pathbreakers they found a way to make that labor possible, to permit women not only to contribute to society but to be self-supporting so that they might pursue whatever living arrangement they wished." While the clinical concept of lesbianism emerged in the nineteenth century, based on the theories of Freud, and was explored throughout Europe, it received little attention in America until near the end of the century. In fact, as Faderman reports, "[t]he *Index Catalogue of the Library of the Surgeon General's Office* lists only one article on lesbians between 1740 and 1895," while "between 1896 and 1916" one finds approximately 100 books and 566 articles.[4]

While Mignon Good and her older sister Lulu were both heterosexual, they grew up in a time when the popular media began to focus on the "love that dares not speak its name." In 1913 while Mignon Eberhart's sister Lulu was attending Nebraska Wesleyan University, *Harper's Bazaar* printed an article titled "Your Daughter: What Are Her Friendships?" signed "by a College Graduate," informing parents that while most college friendships were innocent, "a tenth of them (how that figure is arrived at is never made clear) were morally degenerate and caused guilt and unhappiness because they were 'not legitimate.'"[5] Such articles represented an attack on female romantic friendships of the nineteenth and early part of the twentieth century and the accompanying cultural anxiety which continued to grow may in part explain the success of the romance genre in the twentieth century and the absence of female characters of the same age who are friends in the novels of Mignon Eberhart. In fact, the protagonist and her contemporary(ies) are typically in competition for the affection of the male lead.

Thus, in spite of Mignon Eberhart's awareness of same-sex attraction in the wide social circles in which she traveled in the publishing and arts world of the east coast, in her writing she not only reflected the general practices of the time by not publicly addressing the topic, but took things one step further by utilizing descriptions of certain male characters that were code for homosexuality. Interestingly, comparable code descriptions for female characters to suggest lesbianism do not occur in her works. The prevalence of coded descriptions for certain male characters, in contrast, is difficult to ignore.

Beginning with Eustace Federie in *While the Patient Slept* (1930), Mignon Eberhart included a certain kind of man in thirty-six of her fifty-nine novels. While these men vary in their type, they all are just a bit too ... either handsome, foppish, effeminate, high-voiced, pretty, nelly or something that Eberhart chooses not to label. While some may be interested in women, they are always more interested in themselves. Others may have little interest in women. Yet others are too boyish acting. Some even disguise themselves or cross-dress (always with wicked intent). In all cases, something about these gents just does not quite add up to their being a "real man." Often, Eberhart does not extensively address this facet of their character. Very often, though not always, it explains their criminal behavior (thirteen of them are murderers). In other instances, it explains why they are not the right mate for the heroine, in spite of their gallant efforts. After all, they dance with ease (one suspects better than the female protagonist); walk with grace; converse and behave in charming ways; and dress impeccably. And, of course, they are startlingly handsome or pretty. For Eberhart, that is just plain wrong.

In the case of Dr. Kunce in *From This Dark Stairway*, it is long, womanish eyelashes. For Paul Duchane in *The Dark Garden*, it is his "...handsome profile. Too handsome, especially when lit and warmed by a devastating charm which Paul could turn on and off as readily as he might an electric light." So sure of himself, Paul, drawing upon his striking resemblance to his late father, costumes himself accordingly and performs as a spirit to sway an elderly woman's judgment. Of Andy Crittendon, would-be suitor to Rue in *The Glass Slipper*, she observes: "Handsome, regular, boyish; queer, thought Rue, how much better she liked Andy when she was away from him." It is the idea of a stunningly beautiful man that is appealing, not the reality. Similarly, in *Speak No Evil*, Elizabeth, upon reencountering former beau Dyke Sanders, observes: "He was exactly as she remembered him; gracefully easy in motion, his smile and his dark eyes quick and gay.... There was, always, a kind of boyish impetuousness about him, which made him seem younger than in fact he was." But do such men represent danger? In *The Chiffon Scarf*, Eden Shore finds it hard to believe, since "...the young, curly-haired steward with his girlish mouth and mildly pleasant manner certainly could have had no possible motive for brutally murdering Creda Blaine." Or consider the character Walsh Rantoul in *The Man Next Door*, "...a young, slender man, small really, with blond hair and impeccable tailoring ... whose face had small almost doll-like features—startlingly regular, with round shallow eyes, and a trace of something fragile and effeminate around his small mouth and chin." Neville, a dandy from the Revolutionary period featured in *Enemy in the House*, is "both charming and handsome ... slim and delicately made; his hair curled romantically and ... frosted with perfumed powder." And Boyd in *Witness at Large* is "startlingly handsome in a romantic Byronic way; yet somehow his high forehead was a trifle too narrow, his nose barely too fine, his lips just a bit too handsomely curved. He was always thin and somehow airy in his movements—wispy ... just the same as he had always been in his easy, affable, butterfly way."[6]

Not always, of course, are these men delicate. Sometimes they are foreign, mysterious, feral—like Andre Durant in *The White Dress*: "Andre swam well and easily the way he walked or danced, with an extraordinary, apparently effortless grace and ease ... rather like the instinctive, perfect coordination of an extraordinarily slender and graceful animal.... Rather like an animal again, he knew instinctively she was looking at him and thinking about him for he turned and looked at her quickly across the few feet of clear pale water between them." Of the handsome boxer named Bert Prowde in *Danger Money*, regular guy Greg Cameron comments: "He's youngish, mid-thirties, fantastically good-looking. I wouldn't trust him with a nickel. That's wrong. I don't have reason to think he's dishonest. I don't know him. He just struck me as one of those handsome, well-mannered, too well-dressed ineffectuals. He may be a very decent fellow. I'm certainly letting myself talk." There is, nonetheless, always a contrast between the real man and the other, as in *The Bayou Road* where heroine Marcy notices: "They were oddly alike and as oddly unlike. Gene was very slim, blond, dressed like a fop in a frilled, if wilted, shirt, tight fawn-colored trousers creased from riding, a long black coat which looked and undoubtedly was very hot. The major in his trim blue uniform lounged on the steps too, yet even lounging, there was an alertness about him, something tough and firm." The slightly effeminate man, nonetheless, is one to watch, as Marcia observes of her ex-husband in *Message from*

Hong Kong: "Dino settled down on an ottoman. I hadn't noticed until then that below that thick light beard he wore a wide black tie, flowing a little as if he were a Gay Nineties dandy, and a pink waistcoat. He looked curiously effeminate with that long wavy hair, and curiously evil." On occasion the contrast is between relatives as in the scheming brother and sister team of Alexia and Nicky Senour in *Wolf in Man's Clothing*, or cousins, Richard and Dolores Welbeck in *Casa Madrone*. The similar appearances of the former pair enable Alexia to cross-dress as her brother for secret purposes. In the case of the Welbeck cousins, "what was strikingly handsome in Richard, however, was different in Dolores. A man's good looks are never a woman's good looks."[7]

Perhaps the most dangerous—and evil—effeminate man in the Eberhart canon, however, is Francis Maly in the early novel *The House on the Roof*. Maly is the roommate of protagonist Deborah Cavert's love interest, Anthony Wyatt. Suspicious that Deborah and Anthony have made some kind of secret pact concerning the recent murder in their apartment house, Francis visits Deborah at her apartment to inquire if she knows what is wrong with Anthony:

> "He's not himself," he said, watching her. "He's worried about something. I thought you might know what's wrong. He—I'm terribly fond of Anthony, you know. I'd hate to let him get involved in something that would—" "Would what?" said Deborah steadily. "Oh..." Francis Maly's slender brown hands moved. "Oh, that would be bad for him," he said lightly.... "I do assure you that I'm not trying to pry into my friend's affairs. You see, Anthony and I have shared the same apartment for two years. We've learned to know each other pretty well, and I'm enough older than he to feel a kind of—I suppose you'd call it protective instinct. It's silly, of course, for certainly Anthony Wyatt of all people is fully capable of taking care of himself. My excuse is that I'm rather a lonely sort of person. And he—Well, as I said, I'm pretty fond of him. I thought he might have told you—" He paused and then added slowly and with a kind of reluctance that was in itself alarming to Deborah: "It's just last night and today that I've noticed it." The words lay between them in a small, too meaning silence while Deborah wondered what she could say. Evidently his suspicions had been aroused; as evidently there was more than a tinge of disapproval in his bearing. She was not sufficiently worldly to weigh and measure the possible effect of that disapproval.[8]

Francis joins Anthony and Deborah at dinner,

> demand[ing] café royale and burn[ing] the brandy and sugar himself for it, his brown hands steady and adroit above each cup and the tiny blue flames reflecting themselves in his intent eyes. And it was very good and cheered what had been a somewhat somber dinner, and later they danced, Deborah dancing first with Francis, who was light and graceful as a feather and barely touched her as they moved, and then with Anthony. Anthony wasn't as good a dancer as Francis; Deborah was oddly conscious of his arm around her body holding her rather tightly against him as the floor became crowded, of her fingers in his hand.[9]

Not surprisingly, in reviewing the potential murder suspects, Deborah lingers on Francis:

> Besides, thought Deborah with a touch of malice, he would be rather admirably cast as the villain of the piece; his pleasant, civilized suavity, his observant, handsome eyes, his somewhat spectacular beauty, his graceful detached air, were all almost irresistibly suspicious.... The antagonism she had felt in him and had attributed to his own suspicion of her and, in a small degree, to some faint jealousy of her own relation to Anthony which excluded Francis, and which he must have recognized, might be owing to something else entirely.[10]

Francis Maly represents the most overt homosexual character that Mignon Eberhart portrayed. In this sense, Francis Maly resembles the various female characters in Eberhart novels who attempt to thwart the protagonist from connecting with her true love.

Often, however, the effeminate men in Eberhart novels are harmless, older gentlemen dandies, emotional eunuchs at it were, in need of care from the females who surround them. Their greatest sin is living a bit hedonistically and their over-fondness for cocktails. Such is the case with Clarence Siskinson in *The Dark Garden*, whose surname, resembling "sissy" fits with the description of him in the book: "He was a slender man with a lithe, delicately rounded body and a grace and neatness of motion that would have done credit to a ballet dancer ... he was almost entirely sober although somewhat impatiently waiting a before-dinner cocktail...." In *R.S.V.P. Murder*, Uncle Sisley is "...tall and rather weedy, around sixty, with thin gray hair and a kind of dandyish air" who uses words like "cad" and "perfidious" when roused to indignation. In *The Bayou Road*, Monsieur Lemaire is the protagonist's foppish, but frayed, older cousin who has a talent for prevarication and of whom the protagonist observes that one "[m]ight as well try to pin down a frayed but elusive butterfly." In *Next of Kin*, Clarence Fotheringay, the step-father of protagonist Mady Smith, provides the comic relief as he attends auctions, buying expensive but bizarre art objects, squires a wealthy widow about town, and advises everyone involved in the murder investigation to "cherchez la femme." Lovable Clarence Fotheringay, whose surname is certainly telling, provides young Mady with emotional support, "[b]ut if money could ever be said truly to go through people's fingers, then Clarence's finely boned and finely manicured fingers had that talent.... He reappeared, his coat off and a frilly pink apron tied around him; he carried a casserole of sorts in both hands. How could she feel irritated and impatient with anybody done up in a frilly apron and taking a happy turn at household chores?"[11] How indeed?

Regardless of the way they play out their role—as murderer, murder victim, effete snob, ineffectual gigolo, or comic relief dandy—the effeminate men in Eberhart's novels provide a stark contrast to the type of man that Eberhart, and presumably her readers, found appealing: strong, masculine, virile, protective, and ruggedly handsome. By describing in detail these effeminate, emasculated as it were, men, and contrasting them with her "real men" characters, Eberhart could reassure herself that whatever the physical limitations in her own intimate relationships, she was at least not involved with one of those types. From her earliest novels, strong male characters with names like Jim (7) or Richard (5) who are engineers (3) or military officers (8)—like husband Alan—provide solid support to the female protagonists. On occasion they are distant, preoccupied, not forthcoming with their feelings or some other quality that prevents the heroines from understanding right away that these men have the "right stuff." So instead these women listen to siren calls of other men, also handsome, sometimes effeminate, sometimes not, who may or may not have the heroine's best interests at heart. By the end of the novel, however, the heroines have discovered the real man, best suited to them, leaving the other kind to be dealt their justice.

Note: An earlier version of this essay was published in Rick Cypert, *America's Agatha Christie: Mignon Good Eberhart, Her Life and Works* (Susquehanna University Press, 2005).

Notes

1. Gertrude Stein to Fanny Butcher, January 1935, Fanny Butcher Collection, The Newberry Library; Gertrude Stein to Fanny Butcher, 1935, Fanny Butcher Collection; Mignon Eberhart, *The Dark Garden* (Garden City: Doubleday, Doran, 1933), 9.

2. Faith Baldwin, Autobiography, Faith Baldwin Collection, Howard Gotlieb Archival Research Center, Boston University.

3. Ibid.

4. Lillian Faderman, *Odd Girls and Twilight Lovers: A History of Lesbian Life in Twentieth-Century America* (New York: Columbia University Press, 1991), 15, 26, 31, 49.

5. A College Graduate, "Your Daughter: What Are Her Friendships?" *Harper's Bazaar*, October 1913, quoted in Faderman, *Odd Girls*, 51.

6. Eberhart, *Garden*, 14; Mignon Eberhart, *The Glass Slipper* (1938; repr., Philadelphia: Blakiston, 1941), 187; Mignon Eberhart, *Speak No Evil* (New York: Random House, 1941), 37; Mignon Eberhart, *The Chiffon Scarf* (Garden City: Doubleday, Doran, 1939), 180; Mignon Eberhart, *The Man Next Door* (New York: Random House, 1943), 8–9; Mignon Eberhart, *Enemy in the House* (New York: Random House, 1962), 57; Mignon Eberhart, *Witness at Large* (New York: Random House, 1966), 41.

7. Mignon Eberhart, *The White Dress* (New York: Random House, 1946), 33; Mignon Eberhart, *Danger Money* (New York: Random House, 1974), 39; Mignon Eberhart, *The Bayou Road* (New York: Random House, 1979), 217; Mignon Eberhart, *Message from Hong Kong* (New York: Random House, 1969), 87; Mignon Eberhart, *Casa Madrone* (New York: Random House, 1980), 80.

8. Mignon Eberhart, *The House on the Roof* (Garden City: Doubleday, Doran, 1934), 105–106.

9. Eberhart, *Roof*, 108–109.

10. Ibid., 232–233.

11. Eberhart, *Garden*, 27; Mignon Eberhart, *R.S.V.P. Murder* (New York: Random House, 1965), 47, 66; Eberhart, *The Bayou Road*, 128; Mignon Eberhart, *Next of Kin* (New York: Random House, 1982), 33, 34.

Part One: Locked Doors

BIBLIOGRAPHY

Baldwin, Faith. "Autobiography." Faith Baldwin Collection. Howard Gotlieb Archival Research Center, Boston University.

Eberhart Mignon. *The Bayou Road*. New York: Random House, 1979.

———. *Casa Madrone*. New York: Random House, 1980.

———. *The Chiffon Scarf*. Garden City: Doubleday, Doran & Co., 1939.

———. *Danger Money*. New York: Random House, 1974.

———. *The Dark Garden*. Garden City: Doubleday, Doran & Co., 1933.

———. *Enemy in the House*. New York: Random House, 1962.

———. *From This Dark Stairway*. New York: Doubleday, Doran, 1931.

———. *The Glass Slipper*. 1938. Reprint, Philadelphia: Blakiston, 1941.

———. *The House on the Roof*. Garden City: Doubleday, Doran & Co., 1934.

———. *The Man Next Door*. New York: Random House, 1943.

———. *Message from Hong Kong*. New York: Random House, 1969.

———. *Next of Kin*. New York: Random House, 1982.

———. *R.S.V.P. Murder*. New York: Random House, 1965.

———. *Speak No Evil*. New York: Random House, 1941.

———. *The White Dress*. New York: Random House, 1946.

———. *Witness at Large*. New York, Random House, 1966.

Faderman, Lillian. *Odd Girls and Twilight Lovers: A History of Lesbian Life in Twentieth-Century America*. New York: Columbia University Press, 1991.

Stein, Gertrude to Fanny Butcher. 1935 Letters. Fanny Butcher Collection. The Newberry Library.

PART TWO
Skeleton Keys

"The finest triumvirate of perversion, horror and murder written this spring"
Frank Walford's Twisted Clay

JAMES DOIG

"She loved ... and killed ... both men and women."—Claude Kendall dust jacket blurb on *Twisted Clay* (1934)

Twisted Clay, an outré crime novel by Frank Walford (1882–1969), a journalist and conservationist from Katoomba in the Blue Mountains region of New South Wales, Australia, has the distinction of being one of the most bizarre thrillers published during the 1930s, which is saying something given the excruciating literary excesses from that decade committed by such writers as J. U. Nicolson, R. R. Ryan and Harry Stephen Keeler.[1] When *Twisted Clay* was published in Great Britain and the United States in 1934, horrorstruck reviewers compared the novel to the classic terror tales of Edgar Allan Poe, Sheridan Le Fanu and Bram Stoker. Making *Twisted Clay* even more remarkable for its time is that it is set entirely in Australia and was written by an Australian author. On account of its lurid plot, which details the awful crimes of a psychotic "lesbian" serial killer, the novel was banned in Australia for nearly three decades, not actually appearing in print there until 1960; yet, make no mistake, *Twisted Clay* is a seminal work of Australian crime fiction.

Twisted Clay was first published in the United Kingdom by T. Werner Laurie in January 1934 and by Claude Kendall in the United States later that same year. The memorable narrator and anti-heroine of the novel is Jean Deslines, a girl fourteen years old when the novel opens and precocious in every conceivable way. Jean's mother having died giving birth to her during a terrible storm, Jean lives with her loving father and tyrannical grandmother in a "bleak old house on the crest of the Blue Mountains." Jean delights in causing trouble and then innocently denying she has done anything wrong. Early in the book she describes how as a twelve-year-old she led on a clergyman, drawing his hand around her waist and kissing him, knowing that her grandmother was spying on them through a window. Jean also enjoys sharing a bed with the family's buxom maid, but it is only when her savvy, university-educated cousin, Myrtle, tells her to read psychology textbooks that Jean concludes she is a lesbian. At first she is appalled, regarding herself as "something unhealthy, a gross abnormality which should have been strangled at birth," and she tries to commit suicide by boiling herself alive in the laundry tub. The textbooks inform her that lesbianism is caused by a deficiency of female hormones, giving her the notion that she might release her suppressed femininity by consorting with the opposite sex. After getting pregnant by the local bank manager's son, Jean confesses all to her long-suffering father, has an abortion and dumps her perplexed boyfriend. Soon afterwards she has a dream that recurs throughout the novel: Dressed as a slave girl, Jean witnesses the stabbing murder by barbarians of a Roman centurion who, when examined by a doctor, turns out to be a beautiful woman.

Events take a turn for the worse for Jean when she eavesdrops on a conversation between her father and the doctor who performed the abortion. She learns they plan to take her to Europe to undergo experimental hormone treatment that they hope will "cure" her lesbianism and improve her personality. The only way Jean sees to avoid the treatment is to murder her father. One night she takes him to the local cemetery, where a grave has been freshly dug. She smashes his skull with a shovel and then buries him in the grave. Although the doctor suspects Jean of the crime, she convinces the local police that she is an innocent victim who is routinely beaten and abused by her grandmother and the doctor. Just as it seems that Jean has escaped all suspicion, she starts to experience intermittent bouts of insanity in which her father appears and implores her to perform specific tasks; her first task is to go to the graveyard, dig him up and stop up the hole in his head because his brains are slipping out! Jean accomplishes this grisly errand over a couple of nights. When local suspicion falls on her she manages to deflect it onto the doctor. Meanwhile, her cousin Myrtle appears on the scene again and becomes infatuated with Jean; the two attend a fancy dress ball, Jean dressed as a slave girl and Myrtle as a centurion, suggesting that Jean's dream was clairaudient. The doctor employs a detective to investigate the case and the sleuth sees through Jean's charade of innocence. When in another fit of insanity Jean disinters the corpse of her father he is on hand to apprehend her and she is placed in a mental asylum.

Jean escapes from the asylum and finds that easy money can be made as a Sydney prostitute. However, her hatred of men and her intermittent bouts of insanity compel her to become a "Jill-the-Ripper" serial killer who ruthlessly dispatches her clients. She is able to live in an apartment undiscovered until she murders Myrtle, with whom she had resumed a relationship, in the flat. Once again she takes on a new identity, this time as a beautician. She even seems to be "cured" when she is seduced by "scar-face" Harry Lees, a rough, masculine criminal and drug dealer. The two go into business together and the partnership prospers. Unfortunately for Jean the detective reappears and she is forced to kill him. When she tells Harry what she has done, he is horrified and deserts her. Disillusioned once and for all, Jean gases herself in the kitchen, leaving behind for posterity her dark diary of depravity.

So there you have it: classic 1930s pulp that mixes crime and horror in generous proportions. How did an Australian country journalist and conservationist come to write this "high-octane mix of sex, crime, and morbid sensationalism," as Nicole Moore calls it in her study of literary censorship in Australia, *The Censor's Library*?[2] It appears that the book leapt fully formed from the intellectual milieu of the Blue Mountains writers groups that Walford was involved with at the time.

Born in Balmain, a suburb of West Sydney, in 1882, Frank Walford attended Fort Street Boys High School, the oldest government school in Australia. After his graduation in 1898, Walford divided his time between clerical work in Sydney and, according to various semi-autobiographical accounts, adventurous and sometimes illegal activities in northern Australia.[3] In 1912 he married Madge Owen and the following year he began a long journalistic career, initially with the *Cumberland Times*. He was also an active member of the Labour Party and ran unsuccessfully for a State parliamentary seat in 1913 and 1916. When his own Parramatta-based newspaper, *Walford's Weekly*, folded in January 1919, Walford and his wife moved to Katoomba, where for many years they played active and important roles in the life of the town and in the development of the Blue Mountains as a tourist centre.

Continuing to work prolifically as a journalist, Walford in the early to mid–1920s made contact with a group of writers, bushwalkers and rock climbers who later formed the Blue Mountains Club. The writers included Dr. Eric Dark and his wife, the celebrated novelist Eleanor Dark, Osmar White and Eric Lowe. No doubt through Dr. Dark's efforts, this writers group obtained, read and discussed important works on psychology and sexuality by such authorities as Sigmund Freud, Carl Jung, Havelock Ellis and Cesare Lombroso; and it was from this intellectual ferment that *Twisted Clay* was born in the 1930s. Not surprisingly, the female protagonists in Eleanor Dark's *Prelude to Christopher* and Eric Lowe's *Salute to Freedom*—novels written around the same time as *Twisted Clay*—are unconventional, independent woman.

Suggesting the challenging nature of the subject matter of Walford's crime novel, correspondence in the author's personal archive indicates that between December 1932 and February 1933 *Twisted Clay* (the original title of which was *Twilight*), was rejected by the London publishers Hamish Hamilton, William Heinemann and Jonathan Cape. Finally the venturesome Thomas Werner Laurie accepted the book. His firm, T. Werner Laurie, was friendly to then-controversial works of fiction, having published, for example, Andre Tellier's 1931 gay novel *Twilight Men*. (Laurie's daughter, Joan Werner Laurie, was later the life-partner of lesbian writer Nancy Spain.) Walford signed a contract to publish *Twisted Clay*, as it was now called, with T. Warner Laurie on September 19, 1933.[4]

In late January and early February 1934 newspapers in the United Kingdom received review copies of *Twisted Clay* from T. Werner Laurie, and shortly afterwards notices began to appear.[5] In its own publicity for *Twisted Clay*, Werner Laurie described the novel as "the most amazingly clever study of progressive insanity ever written," and reviewers tended to echo this sentiment in their own appraisals, On February 1, 1934, for example, the *Yorkshire Herald* described *Twisted Clay* as "remarkable and deeply interesting" and stressed the serious intent of the author: "There is a great deal more in the book than actually appears in print, and on concluding the story one is led to consider the problems of the present day, with its perversion, sterilisation and mental defectives." On February 14, the reviewer for the *Aberdeen Press and Journal* called the novel "a remarkable account of progressive insanity," while *The Western Mail*, under the heading, "Unsavoury," focused on the book's horror elements: "It contains some horrible scenes equal to the worst in *Dracula*." Frank Walford, the *Western Mail* avowed, "is a master of the morbid."

Review copies of the novel, including cuttings of published reviews, were sent to Australian newspapers in March and April; and notices began appearing in late March, initially in Walford's local newspapers. There were positive reports in the *Katoomba Daily News* on March 27 and the *Blue Mountains Times* on March 30, the latter paper speculating that "possibly *Twisted Clay* is the most ambitious novel yet attempted in Australia." A glowing April 4 review in Australia's leading literary magazine, *The Bulletin*, pronounced *Twisted Clay* "a masterpiece in its ghastly line," comparing it favourably with the realistic thrillers of Wilkie Collins, Émile Zola, Sheridan Le Fanu and, of more recent vintage, Marie Belloc Lowndes' *The Lodger*. The same reviewer wrote a few months later, in an article called "The Australian Novel," that *Twisted Clay* was the best novel of horror he had read. An April 18 review for the national newspaper, *The Sydney Morning Herald*, was also positive: "*Twisted Clay*, by Frank Walford, is a remarkable and peculiarly horrible study of progressive insanity.... This study in abnormal psychology has been most cleverly worked out, so that its qualities cannot be ignored; but most people will prefer to avoid it." Under the heading "A Modern Dracula," the *Daily Telegraph* similarly lauded the literary quality of Walford's writing in *Twisted Clay*, like *The Bulletin* comparing the novel to the works of Sheridan Le Fanu and stressing the author's serious intent.

Other reviewers were less persuaded than *The Bulletin* critic that *Twisted Clay* was an essay in realism. In a piece for *All About Books*, a monthly literary review, Nettie Palmer wrote that Walford's novel was an ingenious piece of "fantastic horror" but not in the least realistic, while the *Sunday Sun* dismissed the book as neither convincing nor worthwhile and *The Western Mail* of Perth described it as "too far-fetched." The *Woman's Mirror*, anticipating the Book Censorship Board, declared *Twisted Clay* to be "a most unpleasant book which may interest psychologists, but will be nauseating to the average reader." In April 1934 the *Blue Mountains Times* reported that the Library Committee was debating whether or not to purchase the novel for the public library.

The controversial American publisher Claude Kendall (whose brutal 1937 murder remains unsolved), brought *Twisted Clay* to the United States in 1934 with an advertising blitz that saw the shocker reviewed in newspapers across the country.[6] Clearly *Twisted Clay* made something of a sensation in the United States, judging from newspaper reviews. Some reviewers, such as Kenneth C. Kaufman (editor of the literary page of the *Daily Oklahoman*, a professor in the University of Oklahoma foreign languages department and mentor of Oklahoma detective novelist Todd Downing), were appalled. Kaufman primly noted that the protagonist of *Twisted Clay* was "a young girl, a homosexual, who ... indulges in all sorts of sexual experiments, of which the less said the better ... it just happens that I am not interested in sexual abnormalities." Others, however, were fascinated. In his syndicated "A Book a Day" column, the future Pulitzer Prize–winning narrative historian Bruce Catton deemed *Twisted Clay* "a creepy tale about the collapse of a mind" that was certain "to make you shudder." Meanwhile, the *Lexington Leader* reviewed the novel under the not altogether subtle heading, "Frank Walford writes one of the most amazing books ever printed," the *Dayton Daily News* opened its notice with the declaration, "This work will probably be regarded as one of the most notable books of the year," and the *Durham Sunday Herald Sun* memorably pronounced the shocker "the finest triumvirate of perversion, horror and murder written this spring."

While most reviewers treated *Twisted Clay* as a crime thriller and a study of abnormal psychology, others took a broader view. The *Baltimore News and Post* compared the book favourably with Radclyffe Hall's pioneering lesbian novel, *The Well of Loneliness* (1928), and other critics also mentioned the lesbian theme, which had been developed in additional American and English novels in this period.[7] *This Week* of Pittsburgh, which selected *Twisted Clay* as the Book of the Week, dubbed it "a modern Dracula" and declared that "for excitement and horror, [it] transcends any of the works of Edgar Allan Poe." Similarly, the *New York Mirror* compared the novel to the works of Poe and Baudelaire. These reviews were quoted on the back panel of other Claude Kendall books to ballyhoo *Twisted Clay*. No doubt the popularity of pulp fiction in the United States at this time, with its ubiquitous combination of sex and crime, made *Twisted Clay* more acceptable in the American market.

Certainly the book appears to have sold well where it was published. According to a short article in *The Bulletin* that followed the banning of *Twisted Clay* in Australia, by February 1935 the shocker had gone into two editions in the United Kingdom and three in the United States.[8] The online Australian literature database, AUSTLIT, notes that Walford's first three novels, including *Twisted Clay*, sold 20,000 copies overseas.

While contemporary critics noted the serious psychological concerns of the novel—the review in *The Sydney Morning Herald* is titled "Abnormal Psychology" and reviewers tended to call it a "study" or "account" of "progressive insanity"—most perceived that Walford's intention was to write a sensational bestseller. As H. M. Green wrote in *A History of Australian Literature* (1961), "*Twisted Clay* is a gruesome study of progressive insanity, but the study is obviously subordinate to a desire to excite and horrify."[9]

To be sure, Walford gave his novel serious credentials by having Jean Deslines read works by "Havelock Ellis, Lombroso, Freud, Stekel, Jung, Brown, Bousfield and others." Havelock Ellis is a particular influence: "I read the night out, only desisting when the rosy shafts of dawn entered my bedroom window. Then I flung Ellis on the floor, and lay thinking. I had absorbed enough to know that I was a Lesbian." The book is steeped in the psychology of "sexual inversion" of the day, which also influenced Radclyffe Hall's much tamer tragedy of lesbian awakening, *The Well of Loneliness*.[10]

Walford also cleverly casts *Twisted Clay* as a Gothic novel. At least one reviewer saw the tale as stemming "directly from Matthew Gregory Lewis' *The Monk* and [Horace] Walpole's *The Castle of Otranto*."[11] Jean Deslines' birth takes place during a terrible storm, typical of Gothic fiction:

> It was a bitter night when I first drew breath in this bitter world. A westerly gale lashed the Blue Mountains, and snow was driving under the eaves and verandas. The house trembled in the blast; once a resounding crash told that a pine tree had been torn up by the roots, to smash to earth in a ruin of flowers and shrubs. The electrical service was disorganised, and I was ushered into the world by the fitful gleam of candles which flickered and guttered even in the shelter of the bedroom. On the hearth glowed a fire of coke, before which I was washed and wrapped.

Yet *Twisted Clay* is no pastiche, but rather a reinterpretation of the usual Gothic tropes and themes. The Deslines' "bleak old house" in the Blue Mountains is akin to the decaying castle or rambling mansion of Gothic fiction, but in *Twisted Clay* it is transposed to an Australian setting, a "modern" country where there is no tradition of medieval superstition or ignorance. Rather than supposed vampires, hauntings and ghosts, the reader is confronted with entirely modern concepts of psychology, insanity and hallucination. Indeed, the young maiden of the novel is not stranded in an ancestral castle and menaced by a sinister uncle or relative who is after her inheritance or worse—rather it is Jean Deslines who is the menace, a deadly threat to all the male characters in the novel.

The novel works because Walford's writing is confident and assured—we sympathize with Jean's plight in much the same way that we can understand the murderous motivations of Patricia Highsmith's Tom Ripley. This is a difficult task to pull off; yet, although when reading *Twisted Clay* we may laugh occasionally at dated surface psychology and sexism (such as the lesbian's transformation by the love of a "real man"), Jean speaks to us as a genuine female antihero pitted against the forces of the male-dominated establishment.

Given the subject matter of the book, it was probably inevitable in Australia that *Twisted Clay* would be brought to the attention of the Commonwealth Book Censorship Board. On June 6, 1935, the Comptroller-General of the Department of Trade and Customs wrote to Sir Robert Garran, Chairman of the Censorship Board, asking him to consider whether *Twisted Clay* should be considered a prohibited import under the *Customs Act*. A few weeks later, two Censorship Board members scribbled their judgments on a sheet of paper.[12] According to Chairman Garran, the book was "crude and repulsive. The so-called 'psychology' in it is a cheap fake. I would ban." J. F. Meurisse Haydon, Professor of French at the Canberra University College, wrote, "I can see no redeeming feature in this story of progressive insanity. It could, I am sure, prove very harmful to a highly impressionable nature. I would certainly ban." *Twisted Clay* was placed on the prohibited list on July 15, 1935, and was not released from it until September 19, 1959.

Another blow to the fortunes of *Twisted Clay* was the paper shortage that resulted from the onset of the Second World War. After the war Walford tried through his English agent to have *Twisted Clay* reprinted. Werner Laurie appears to have declined the request, perhaps because of the paper restrictions that still applied to British publishers, which reduced their interest in reprinting older works (the publisher did release the rights for Walford's novels, however). Walford's Paris publisher, Les Èditions du Chêne, was approached in 1946, but declined to reprint the book in English or a French translation due to a perceived reaction by the French reading public against English translations which had flooded the French market. The following year Walford sent a copy of *Twisted Clay* to the Australian pulp publisher, The Shakespeare Head, which specialised in mystery fiction, but it was not accepted, presumably because the novel was still banned in Australia.[13]

Walford's fortunes improved when *Twisted Clay* was taken off the banned list in 1959. When the novel came up for review at Walford's instigation in May 1958, the Commonwealth Literature Censorship Board recommended that it continue to be treated as a prohibited import. However, the Appeal Censor reversed this decision in September 1959 and the book was released. Walford approached Penguin Books in early 1960 about reprinting the book, but the publisher declined. Horwitz Publications, however, jumped at the chance, and published *Twisted Clay* in September 1960, though the letter from Horwitz's senior editor, Ann Oxenham, accepting the book advised Walford that "it may be necessary to tone down some of the more startling passages—but editing would be very slight indeed." It is not clear whether any of the proposed edits were actually made in the Horwitz edition. In any case, *Twisted Clay* finally reached an Australian audience, selling 13,427 copies for the period up to March 30, 1961; and Horwitz quickly reprinted the novel in January 1962. *Twisted Clay* was still doing well as late as 1968, when 3,171 copies of the book were sold.[14]

Twisted Clay may be a serious novel—an indictment of contemporary attitudes and mores, and a brilliant reinterpretation and inversion of the Gothic novel—but it is also a rollicking good read, a pulp tour-de-force that keeps us riveted to the last page. Horwitz knew it was on to a good thing when it reprinted the novel in 1960 with the cover blurb, "An explosive novel of strange passions," and the declaration on the back cover: "Just released from the banned list!" Although Frank Walford continued to write novels, he was never able to emulate the success of *Twisted Clay*; indeed, about ten of his novels were never published. Walford died on May 30, 1969, better known for his journalism and conservation work than as the author of an Australian crime fiction classic.

NOTES

1. John Urban Nicolson (1885–1944) published *Fingers of Fear* (1937), recently reprinted by Valancourt Books. "Insanity, murder, as bloody as they come," panted a contemporary reviewer of the novel. R. R. Ryan was a pseudonym of Evelyn Grosvenor Bradley (1882–1950), who mostly under the Ryan pen name wrote psychological horror thrillers, most of them published between 1936 and 1940 and several of which have been reprinted by Ramble House. Beginning in the 1920s the wildly prolific Harry Stephen Keeler (1890–1967) authored numerous mysteries, considered some of the most bizarre in the history of the genre. Many of his works have been reissued by Ramble House. Frank Walford's *Twisted Clay* was reprinted by Salt in 2014.

2. Moore, *The Censor's Library: Uncovering the Lost History of Australia's Banned Books* (Brisbane: University of Queensland Press, 2012), 142.

3. For much of what follows see Jim Smith, "The Life of Frank Walford," *Aboriginal Legends of the Blue Mountains* (by the author, 1992), 69–74. In northern Australia Walford claims to have worked at different times as a timber getter, mule packer, prospector, drover, hunter and pearler as well as to have engaged in various illegal activities such as drug and people smuggling. See his semi-autobiographical novel,

A Fools Odyssey (London: Werner Laurie, 1942) and the following autobiographical articles serialized in the *Australian Journal*: "The Devil Ray," May 1946; "Living Contraband," June 1946; "The Bush Telegraph," September 1947; "Repayment in Kind," September 1948; "A Dead Certainty," November 1948.

    4. Letters dated 19 December 1932 (Jonathon Cape), 30 January 1933 (William Heinemann), and 2 February 1933 (Hamish Hamilton). The letters and contract are in Frank Walford's personal archive.

    5. All extracts from reviews of *Twisted Clay* that follow are from review clippings in Frank Walford's personal archive, kindly provided by Jim Smith.

    6. According to the *Catalogue of Copyright Entries* (1935), copyright was registered in the United States on May 21, 1934. Copies of about fifty reviews in U.S. newspapers are extant in Frank Walford's personal archive. On Claude Kendall's career and unsolved murder (the culprit appears to have been a male hustler), see Curtis Evans, "Murder of the Publisher: Who Killed Claude Kendall?" *The Passing Tramp*, 12 May 2013, at http://thepassingtramp.blogspot.com/2013/05/murder-of-publisher-who-killed-claude.html, "The Controversies of Claude Kendall," *The Passing Tramp*, 15 May 2013, at http://thepassingtramp.blogspot.com/2013/05/the-controversies-of-claude-kendall.html, and his introduction to the reissued Coachwhip editions of Willoughby Sharp's Thirties detective novels *Murder in Bermuda* and *Murder of the Honest Broker*, originally published by Claude Kendall.

    7. Lillian Faderman has complained of the lesbian-themed novels of this period: "Almost invariably [the lesbian] is 'twisted.' While in most cases her perversity has turned her into a vampire, sometimes she is nothing more than a confused sickie. Generally the message is that such women need to be locked up or put away, either for society's good or their own." See Faderman, *Surpassing the Love of Men: Romantic Friendship and Love between Women from the Renaissance to the Present* (New York: William Morrow, 1981), 341.

    8. *The Bulletin*, 6 February 1935.

    9. H.M. Green, *A History of Australian Literature* (Sydney: Angus & Robertson, 1961), 1140.

    10. See Moore, *Censor's Library*, 134–143.

    11. *Sydney Morning Herald*, 26 November 1960.

    12. National Archives of Australia, CRS series A3023 (correspondence files of the Book Censorship Board), file 1935/36.

    13. Innes Rose to Frank Walford, 16 August 1946; Letter from Les Èditions du Chêne dated 20 November 1946; Letters from The Shakespeare Head dated 19 February 1947 and 27 January 1948. Frank Walford Archive.

    14. See Frank Walford Archive.

Works Cited

The Bulletin. 6 February 1935.

Evans, Curtis. "The Controversies of Claude Kendall" (15 May 2013). *The Passing Tramp*. At http://thepassingtramp.blogspot.com/2013/05/the-controversies-of-claudkendall.html.

———. "Death's Dilletante." Introduction to Willoughby Sharp, *Murder in Bermuda* and *Murder of the Honest Broker*. Greenville, OH: Coachwhip, 2013. Originally published by Claude Kendall in 1934 and 1935.

———. "Dying High: *Death Rides the Air Line* (1934), by William Sutherland" (29 May 2013). *The Passing Tramp*. At http://thepassingtramp.blogspot.com/2013/05/the-controversies-of-claude-kendall.html.

———. "Murder of the Publisher: Who Killed Claude Kendall?" (12 May 2013). *The Passing Tramp.* At http://thepassingtramp.blogspot.com/2013/05/murder-of-publisher-who-killed-claude.html.
Faderman, Lillian. *Surpassing the Love of Men: Romantic Friendship and Love between Women from the Renaissance to the Present.* New York: William Morrow, 1981.
Frank Walford Archive. Letters and newspaper clippings.
Green, H. M. *A History of Australian Literature.* Sydney: Angus & Robertson, 1961.
Moore, Nicole. *The Censor's Library: Uncovering the Lost History of Australia's Banned Books.* Brisbane: University of Queensland Press, 2012.
National Archives of Australia, CRS series A3023 (correspondence files of the Book Censorship Board). File 1935/36.
Smith, Jim. "The Life of Frank Walford." *Aboriginal Legends of the Blue Mountains.* By the author, 1992. pp. 69–74.
Sydney Morning Herald, 26 November 1960.
Walford, Frank. "The Bush Telegraph." *Australian Journal*, September 1947.
———. "A Dead Certainty." *Australian Journal*, November 1948.
———. "The Devil Ray." *Australian Journal*, May 1946.
———. *A Fools Odyssey.* London: Werner Laurie, 1942.
———. "Living Contraband." *Australian Journal*, June 1946.
———. "Repayment in Kind." *Australian Journal*, September 1948.
———. *Twisted Clay.* London: Werner Laurie, 1934.

Wayne Lonergan's Long Shadow
A Forties Murder and Its Literary Legacy

DREWEY WAYNE GUNN

The Wayne Lonergan murder case of 1943–44 elicited a slew of newspaper reports at the time and over the next seventy years became the subject of numerous essays and book chapters as well as two entire books, stimulating the imaginations of at least seven novelists. Born in 1918 in Toronto, Canada, Wayne Thomas Lonergan came to New York in 1939, his ultimate goal appearing to have been finding some rich man or woman who would support him and ease his entry into society. While working as one of the cadre of handsome young men hired to push visitors in wheeled chairs around the 1939 World's Fair, twenty-one-year-old Wayne met forty-two-year-old William O. Burton, globetrotting heir to the Max Bernheimer brewery fortune and an amateur artist. Soon Wayne was serving as Burton's kept boy and hobnobbing with the likes of Somerset Maugham and Lucius Beebe, but in October 1940 Burton died of heart disease, leaving his sizeable estate to his daughter, Patricia. Not one to miss an opportunity, Wayne married the lovely young heiress, over her mother's objections, in the summer of 1941. Patricia is quoted by Dominick Dunne as saying, "If he was good enough for my father, he's good enough for me."[1] After Patricia gave birth to a son, Wayne doted on the child, but Patricia was more interested in New York's social life, frequenting such nightspots as El Morocco and the Stork Club. As the couple drifted apart, each took lovers (perhaps on occasion, the same one). When the United States entered the Second World War, Wayne was classified as 4-F because of his claim that he was a homosexual, but he concealed his sexuality (whatever it actually was) in volunteering for the Royal Canadian Air Force. His service had the benefit that Patricia could not divorce him as long as he was in the military.

On Sunday, October 24, 1943, Patricia's nude body was discovered in the locked bedroom of her three-floor apartment in the posh Manhattan neighborhood of Beekman Hill. She had been bludgeoned with a candlestick and strangled. It quickly came out that Wayne had been in town on a weekend leave and he was soon arrested in Toronto. His alibi was that he had picked up an American soldier and spent the night having sex with him, only to be robbed by the man and have his RCAF uniform stolen. Wayne said he had received the deep gashes on his chin in a struggle with the soldier. The Toronto police believed him at first; Mel Heimer reports one officer as saying, "A guilty man, I imagine, would not have offered us an alibi so degrading as this one." But holes soon appeared in Wayne's story, and he was extradited to New York for further interrogation. Meanwhile, the New York press was going wild; the story vied with war news for coverage. For gay historian Charles Kaiser, the case was singularly important for eliciting "the earliest extended discussion of homosexuality in the history of New York newspapers"—this several years before the publication of the first eye-opening Kinsey report, *Sexual Behavior in the Human Male* (1948).[2]

Under intense police grilling Wayne confessed to the murder and to having destroyed his blood-stained uniform. That Sunday morning he had gone to his and Patricia's apartment to deliver a stuffed toy to his son and found his wife nude in bed, recovering from her night out with another man. According to Heimer, Patricia's threat that Wayne would never be allowed see his son again triggered the murderous attack.[3] Contemporary gossip had it that while he remained clothed, she had performed fellatio on him and savagely bitten his penis. (Dunne dismisses the latter story for lack of evidence anywhere in the record, but the allegation took on a life of its own.) Wayne was indicted for murder in the first degree. The first trial was declared a mistrial, but the second one, which took place March 20–31, 1944, ended with a verdict of murder in the second degree. The judge sentenced Wayne to thirty-five years to life in prison. He was paroled in 1965 and deported to Toronto, where, according to Dunne, he was taken in by a woman executive before he met well-known actress Barbara Hamilton, with whom he lived until his death from cancer in 1986. His passing made the January 3 obituary page of the *New York Times*.

Soon after Wayne's arrest the writer Wolcott Gibbs, who lived two doors from the Lonergans' apartment, published a long article in the *New Yorker* highly critical of the sensational language used in the press coverage of the investigation. He records how, early in the coverage, all the articles began with innuendos about both Burton ("a penchant for picking up impecunious young men and lending a helpful hand") and Lonergan ("Indications of an abnormal psychological nature") before finally coming "right out with the word 'homosexual.'" After that Lonergan changed from being "handsome" and "boyish-looking" to the "sex-twisted 25-year-old Café Society playboy with the crew hair-cut and the easy sneer."[4]

In 1948 Raymond Chandler listed the Lonergan murder as number nine of "10 Greatest Crimes of the Century," noting that the motive for the slaying was "Dubious. Possibly quarrel over his right to see son." Seven years later Gold Medal Books brought out Mel Heimer's *The Girl in Murder Flat* (1955), the tenth in its series of "Classic Murder Trials" and an account of the Lonergan affair. The title reflects the fact that this was the third sensational Beekman Hill murder of a young woman within eight years. The bulk of the book recounts the trial, using excerpts from the transcript; as a result it focuses on Lonergan's flamboyant defense attorney almost as much as it does on Lonergan. Here we get to hear Lonergan's own voice, including such an exchange as this: "Q. What particular acts of perversion did you commit with this man? A. There are only two. Both of them. Q. You did that before you were married? A. Yes. Q. Did you get much satisfaction out of living with your wife or any other woman? A. Well, a certain amount." The language the author himself uses is more restrained than one might expect in a period still suffering from the "lavender scare" created by Washington politicians: nothing beyond "sexual aberrations," "degrading," and the like.[5]

In 1972 a crime reporter, Hamilton Darby Perry, weighed in on the matter with his own account, *A Chair for Wayne Lonergan*, with sixteen pages of photographs. The basic thesis of Perry, who interviewed Lonergan, is that his guilt was not proven beyond a shadow of a doubt and that it is quite possible another person committed the murder. Many pages are taken up with alternate theories. But Perry does fill in much more detail about events prior to the murder and continues Longergan's life up to the time the book appeared. In his 1997 history of New York, *The Gay Metropolis, 1940–1996*, Charles Kaiser devoted six-and-a-half pages to the murder, plus a page of photographs. Interested in the importance of the case to a developing gay identity, he quotes an entire article from the *Journal-American*, noting the type of vocabulary common in the 1940s when discussing homosexuality: "vice," "damage," "social cancer," "monster," "unnatural," "moral leper," "pervert," "degenerate," "evil," "unscrupulous," "contemptuous of decent people," "sinister."[6] For a 2000 *Vanity Fair* article, "The Gigolo, the Heiress, and the Candlestick," Dominick Dunne went over the now familiar ground with his own personal touch and an insider's access to people who knew Lonergan but would never have acknowledged it at the time, including one woman who claimed to have also known him in the biblical sense. In a throwaway line he intriguingly compares Lonergan to Patricia Highsmith's Tom Ripley. (Dunne's lively article was collected in book form in 2001.) Richard Goldstein devoted less than two full pages to the murder in *Helluva Town*, his 2010 history of the city during World War II. The only new information he adds with his account is the story of what happened to the Lonergan apartment. Most recently, Harold Schechter briefly summarizes the case in an epilogue to his

2014 book, *The Mad Sculptor*, about the second of the three Beekman Hill slayings. (Chandler gave this murder the number three spot on his list.) Schechter is undoubtedly correct when he says that the murder that dominated the headlines so fiercely in 1943–44 is now almost forgotten.

Yet this murder also directly impacted, to a greater or lesser degree, the creative imagination of writers of fiction, most (maybe all) of whom were in New York at the time, at least three of them actually knowing Lonergan. Poet and novelist Kenneth Fearing (1902-1961) used the Lonergan slaying as the basis for the murder in his celebrated crime novel *The Big Clock*, published by Harcourt, Brace in 1946. Social historian Alan Wald asserts that Earl Janoth, the murderer, and Steve Hagen, his best friend, were modeled after magazine magnate Henry Luce and his "partner and rival," Briton Hadden; yet Fearing, inspired by the revelations about Lonergan, made the relationship between the two men homoerotic. After Earl and his mistress quarrel, Earl brings up her lesbian affairs. She retaliates by questioning his relationship with Steve: "Do you think I'm blind? Did I ever see you two together when you weren't camping?" Earl's reaction is to feel "sick and stunned, with something big and black gathering inside." When she continues lashing out at him ("Why, you poor, old carbon copy of that fairy gorilla"), Earl, without realizing what he is doing, strikes her on the head with a brandy decanter and kills her. Earl flees to Steve's apartment and confesses his crime, obliquely referring to her accusations against the two men, but "Steve was unmoved." Steve later muses, "I liked Earl more than I had ever liked any person on earth except my mother. I really liked him."[7] But nothing physical occurs between the two men and the subject does not come up again. The novel's plot revolves around the irony that Earl hires one of his employees to track down a man who can place Earl at the scene of the crime, not knowing that the employee is himself the man. Charles Laughton played Earl and George Macready played Steve in the 1948 film version. Will Patton played the Steve role (here called Scott Pritchard) in the 1987 remake, *No Way Out*. There was also a 1976 French film version, *Police Python 357*, which apparently eliminated the gay angle.

After Kenneth Fearing's *The Big Clock* there appeared the second novel of Theodora Keogh (1919–2008), *The Double Door*, which in the United States was published in hardcover in 1950 by a small, offbeat publishing house, Creative Age Press, and reprinted in paperback by Signet (1952) and Ballantine (1963). It is a *roman à clef* based on the ballet impresario George de Cuevas. (The indefatigable Dominick Dunne also wrote an essay about him, collected in *The Mansions of Limbo*, 1991.) But the shadow of the Burton–Lonergans triangle hovers in the background. Charles de Tudelos owns adjoining houses in New York, connected only by a double door that he alone is allowed to use. His latest kept boy, teenager Giovanni Puchini, trespasses through it and catches sight of Tudelos' teenaged daughter, Candy. The attraction between the two is instant and mutual, and she manipulates him into taking her virginity. When Charles discovers the fact, Giovanni's days with him are numbered. There is no slaying here; rather, Charles sets Giovanni up to be charged with sodomy and corruption of a minor and sentenced to prison. Other plots intertwine. Charles' personal priest, though asexual or latently homosexual, has his own strange designs on Candy. Even more sinister is a longtime friend of Charles who, if one believes in sorcery, kills Giovanni's mother. The author's amoral universe is strongly reminiscent of Patricia Highsmith's; not surprisingly Highsmith admired Keogh's novels, and the two became friends. Keogh sought to conceal the fact that she was President Theodore Roosevelt's granddaughter.

Between these two novels two other authors attempted to recreate the story, hewing more closely to the facts. James Baldwin's biographer David Leeming records that in 1948 the author began his attempt, which he called *Ignorant Armies*. According to Leeming, Baldwin was preoccupied at the time with the "whole question of sexual dishonesty." For a time the novel progressed well, but "the characters suddenly stopped speaking, and he lost his sense of the novel's form." Leeming goes on, "The problem was, apparently, that there were two novels in *Ignorant Armies*: the bones of *Giovanni's Room* and *Another Country*." Although Giovanni kills his former boss in a rage and is subsequently sentenced to the guillotine, there is nothing in either published novel to remind readers of Wayne Lonergan. The English-born, naturalized American Brion Gysin, who knew Lonergan as part of the New York nightclub scene, finished *I Am Out*, his fictionalized account of the murder, in 1949, but it has never been published. (It was offered to Olympia Press in 1960, but the publisher turned it down.) According to Gysin's biographer, John Geiger, the novel "emphasized Lonergan's Catholic upbringing, and had monsignors and bishops swishing in and out of the scenes."[8]

A Nearness of Evil, the only novel by songwriter Carley Mills (1897–1962), was published in hardcover by Coward-McCann in 1961 and reprinted in paperback by Pyramid the next year (*Twisted Passions, Strange Desires—The Shattering Novel of a Beautiful Young Blueblood and Her Sensualist Father*). Although admittedly free with facts—most notably, keeping the Burton figure alive—*Evil* more closely adheres to the main outlines of the Lonergan case. An ardent nightclubber (Tennessee Williams left him, unable to accept his lifestyle), Carley Mills undoubtedly knew Lonergan, at least by sight. The novel opens with its straight narrator, the lawyer Alfie Fisher, calling upon Bobby Randall to inform him that he is nearly out of money and to advise that he remarry his ex-wife as a beard; he has had too many scandals while abroad. Alfie's mission is a success, but signs that Bobby's daughter, Diane, is likewise wayward are worrisome. The second part of the drama begins at the 1939 World's Fair, where Bobby has taken Diane. There he meets Neal

Hartigan, one of the young men hired to wheel visitors from attraction to attraction. Bobby and Neal quickly become a pair. Diane is equally attracted to the handsome man, declaring pertly that "if he's good enough for Daddy he's good enough for me." They start going out, causing a society columnist to remark, "Hartigan is going steady with both Randalls." Father and daughter turn against each other. Bobby decides to evict Neal from his apartment, but, after letting himself in unannounced, he is shocked to find Neal and the gay Howland Jotham packing up his things: "*Neal* was walking out on *him*."[9]

The next blow is the announcement of Neal and Diane's marriage. Diane lets drop that wedlock has not caused Neal to give up his "Jothaming." Soon, like him, she is picking up willing gigolos, including a high number of "pansies." Shortly after their son is born, Neal departs for Canada to join the RCAF. Then on October 17, 1943, Diane's body is discovered in her apartment. Neal is arrested; as an alibi he claims to have spent the evening visiting "gay bars," picking up an American soldier in one of them. A female friend is requested to corroborate Neal's alibi: "When asked by a reporter of her opinion of Hartigan's story, she replied, giggling, 'I think it's a terrible fairy tale.'" No motive for the murder emerges. During all this, Alfie's natural reaction is to protect Bobby, who is being presented by the press as "the evil genius who had touched off the whole chain of events leading up to the murder." The transcript of Neal's trial takes up several chapters. Both Bobby and Jotham are called, and the gay angle is pushed hard. After Neal abruptly changes his plea to murder in the second degree, Bobby leaves town. He settles in Cuernavaca, but departs after one of his "guests" turns out to be "under eighteen" and a British general's son to boot.[10] Finally Bobby ends up in Tangier, where his houseboy cuts his throat.

The notorious Lonergan murder case made its way into post-Stonewall fiction as well, including Karl Flinders' pornographic *The Boy Avengers* (1971) and Gordon Merrick's posthumously published 1997 novel *The Good Life* (completed by Charles G. Hulse), but it is the influence of the case on pre-Stonewall crime fiction which concerns us here. There have been, of course, other modern cases involving gay murderers. Several of them—the Butcher of Hanover, Leopold–Loeb, the Rotenburg Cannibal—became the basis for nonfiction accounts, novels, and films, but the majority are more or less forgotten. Why did the Lonergan case (which is merely sordid, not horrific like the three cited above) become such a sensation and the source of so many books and articles? The social milieu, the unusual nature of the romantic triangle, Wayne's flexible sexuality and his striking appearance, all must contribute in part to the fascination; perhaps at the time it was the sheer novelty of the forbidden being splashed across newspaper pages. Now that most of the people who followed the case as it unfolded are dying away, one wonders whether the trio finally will be allowed to rest in peace. Perhaps not: A brief search of the internet reveals that rehashes of the case continue to appear in tabloids.

Notes

1. Dominick Dunne, "The Gigolo, the Heiress, and the Candlestick" (2000), reprinted in *Justice: Crimes, Trials, and Punishments* (New York: Crown, 2001), 277.
2. Mel Heimer, *The Girl in Murder Flat* (New York: Fawcett Gold Medal, 1955), 21; Charles Kaiser, *The Gay Metropolis, 1940-1996* (Boston: Houghton Mifflin, 1997), 19.
3. Heimer, *Flat*, 23.
4. Wolcott Gibbs, "Five Days Wonder," *New Yorker* (Nov. 1943): 89, 90, 91.
5. Raymond Chandler, "10 Greatest Crimes of the Century," *Cosmopolitan* (Oct. 1948): 53; Heimer, *Flat*, 20, 21, 83.
6. Kaiser, *Metropolis*, 24.
7. Kenneth Fearing, *The Big Clock* (1946), reprinted in *Crime Novels: American Noir of the 1930s and 40s* (New York: Library of America, 1997), 430-31, 435, 442.
8. David Leeming, *James Baldwin: A Bibliography* (New York: Knopf, 1994), 52-53; John Geiger, *Nothing Is True, Everything Is Permitted: The Life of Brion Gysin* (New York: Disinformation, 2005), 76-77.
9. Carley Mills, *A Nearness of Evil* (New York: Coward McCann, 1961), 115, 117, 126.
10. Mills, *Evil*, 137, 138, 164, 165, 245.

Works Cited

Chandler, Raymond. "10 Greatest Crimes of the Century." *Cosmopolitan* (Oct. 1948): 50-53.
Dunne, Dominick. "The Gigolo, the Heiress, and the Candlestick." 2000. Reprinted in *Justice: Crimes, Trials, and Punishments*. New York: Crown, 2001. pp. 272-94.
Fearing, Kenneth. *The Big Clock*. 1946. In *Crime Novels: American Noir of the 1930s and 40s*. New York: Library of America, 1997. pp. 379-515.
Flinders, Karl. *The Boy Avengers*. New York: Olympia (Other Traveller), 1971.
Geiger, John. *Nothing Is True, Everything Is Permitted: The Life of Brion Gysin*. New York: Disinformation, 2005.
Gibbs, Wolcott. "Five Days Wonder." *New Yorker* (6 Nov. 1943): 86-92.
Goldstein, Richard. *Helluva Town: The Story of New York City during World War II*. New York: Free Press, 2010.
Heimer, Mel. *The Girl in Murder Flat*. New York: Fawcett Gold Medal, 1955.
Kaiser, Charles. *The Gay Metropolis, 1940-1996*. Boston: Houghton Mifflin, 1997.
Keogh, Theodora. *The Double Door*. 1950. London: Peter Davies, 1952.
Leeming, David. *James Baldwin: A Bibliography*. New York: Knopf, 1994.
Merrick, Gordon, and Charles G. Hulse. *The Good Life*. Los Angeles: Alyson, 1997.
_____. *The Lord Won't Mind*. 1970. Los Angeles: Alyson, 1995.
Mills, Carley. *A Nearness of Evil*. New York: Coward McCann, 1961.
Perry, Hamilton Darby. *A Chair for Wayne Lonergan*. New York: Macmillan, 1972.
Schechter, Harold. *The Mad Sculptor: The Maniac, the Model, and the Murder That Shook the Nation*. London: Head of Zeus, 2014.
Wald, Alan M. *American Night: The Literary Left in the Era of the Cold War*. Chapel Hill: University of North Carolina Press, 2012.

"Claude was doing all right"
Homosexuality, Hard-Boiled Crime Fiction and the Evolution of Ross Macdonald

Tom Nolan

Ross Macdonald (1915–1983), born and raised as Kenneth Millar, was abandoned at age four by his father; raised in Kitchener, Ontario, by an emotionally and financially unstable mother, and shunted into the care of other relatives in various Canadian provinces for months and years at a time. An inquisitive, observant, and vulnerable child, Kenneth was exposed in his youth and adolescence to many types of sexual behavior: homosexual, heterosexual, consensual, incompatible, married and adulterous, voyeuristic, amateur and professional.

At the age of seven, while living with an uncle and aunt in Wiarton, Ontario, he initiated frequent sexual play with a mentally retarded teenaged maid. At eight, male cousins on a farm introduced him, in whatever variations older and younger boys might devise, to "homo-sex," an activity which both excited and shamed him.

His first heterosexual intercourse seems to have come at thirteen, in Winnipeg, Manitoba, with a young woman working in a "beauty parlor"—bordello run by his father's sister. Here too he got drunk for the first time. At his Winnipeg boarding-school, and later while living in Medicine Hat, Alberta, he had sexual encounters with other male students; and fights, with still others.

There were sporadic sex episodes with males in his adolescence and an affair with a German girl during a trip to Europe in 1936, before Millar's marriage, in 1938, at age twenty-two, to the future author Margaret (Sturm) Millar. By then, Kenneth, after intense self-study of psychological and philosophical texts (from Freud to Kierkegaard), had suppressed his homosexual impulse, along with other behaviors (stealing, fighting) he deemed inimical to a civilized moral existence. Yet he wrestled in mind and spirit with homosexuality throughout his life, and his changing attitudes towards it were reflected in his fiction.

* * *

Margaret Millar had already written (with her husband's hands-on editorial assistance) four mystery novels by 1943, when Ken Millar, now studying and teaching at the University of Michigan, began penning his own first thriller, *The Dark Tunnel*, alone at night in his office in Angell Hall.

An espionage thriller set mostly on a Michigan university campus (with a flashback to Germany a few years earlier), *The Dark Tunnel* (published in 1944) presents scenes of then-shocking depravity: a passionate kiss between a young Nazi officer and (the reader later learns) a blonde man in "pansy drag"; an attempted assassination in a hospital by a male killer cross-disguised as a female nurse. In another sequence, a hotel's seasoned house-detective warns the book's protagonist (a young professor not unlike Ken Millar) about a female he's interested in:

"[T]ake it from me that that dame's poison with a red label and you keep clear of her. She's got the skull and crossbones on her."
"What do you mean?"
"She's a dike, friend. I've seen a million of them and I know. She likes women better than men. Now go back to your party...."

Shocking stuff, in 1944—and for years to come. A 1950 paperback edition of *The Dark Tunnel* would bear the somewhat spoiler-making cover-banner: THE STORY OF A HOMOSEXUAL SPY.

In 1943, Kenneth Millar was consciously building on the hard-boiled tradition of Dashiell Hammett (a writer he discovered in his teens) and Raymond Chandler (a more recent enthusiasm). Both those masters sneered at homosexuals in their books and used them to exemplify moral decay.

Chandler's 1939 debut *The Big Sleep* gave readers lurid peeks inside an L.A. shadow-world: "The fag gave you [a key].... He was like Caesar, a husband to women and a wife to men. Think I can't figure people like him and you out?" or "...[H]e swung on me.... It was meant to be a hard one, but a pansy has no iron in his bones, whatever he looks like."

A decade earlier, in Hammett's *The Maltese Falcon*, Sam Spade's secretary announces a visitor with the comment: "This guy is queer." Enter Joel Cairo, the perfume-scented, theater-loving ornament-hunter: "a small-boned dark man of medium height," wearing a tight-fitting coat and snug trousers, yellow gloves, a red jewel on his green cravat, fawn spats and patent-leather shoes. He walks with "short, mincing, bobbing steps" and speaks in "a high-pitched, thin voice."

* * *

Ken Millar had sensed, after having helped his wife on her first books, that he himself could produce detective-fiction; but having previously considered writing for the theater, or crafting mainstream fiction in the mode, say, of D. H. Lawrence, he was uncertain this genre was a worthy form to contain his talent. His doubts were dispelled by the counsel of no less than W.H. Auden, the best-known and arguably the greatest English poet of his generation—and Millar's graduate-school instructor at Michigan in 1941.

Auden was an habitual reader of mysteries. Detective story reviews done for London newspapers had been his first printed work. He knew and praised one of Margaret Millar's books when he came to dinner at Ken and Margaret's rental house in Ann Arbor. There was nothing shameful about detective stories, Auden assured Ken Millar, who took heart from the poet's endorsement of a form flexible enough to accommodate such estimable writers as Poe, Hammett and Chandler. Auden gave Millar the boost he needed to write *The Dark Tunnel* in a mere thirty nights.

Millar was grateful for Auden's literary encouragement—but he declined the poet's invitation to introduce him into New York literary circles, for instance at the *New Republic*, where Auden thought Millar could and should contribute. For the handsome Ken Millar, with his violet-blue eyes, to debut in Manhattan as the homosexual Auden's protégé, as it were, did not seem like a good idea.

Millar's wife was also intent on keeping her husband physically apart from Auden and his ilk.

Donald Pearce, a friend of Ken's from their Canadian college days, and in the early '40s a fellow grad-student with Millar at Michigan, would recall Margaret describing Auden's visit to the Millars' house in disparaging terms:

> "Oh, I just *hated* his black teeth, and his self-importance," she said. "Moreover, his pant leg slid up his shin, and here was this bare stretch of absolutely hairless leg. It was terrible!" And she said, "Pearce, pull your pant leg up." I pulled my pant leg up. She said, "That's exactly what a man's leg should look like!" Well, a few years later I learned in a letter from [a mutual friend] that Margaret thought I was a latent homosexual in love with Ken, because I was so devoted to him in many ways.... But when she asked me to exhibit my leg and saw that it was adequately hairy, that relieved her of any problem that she had regarding me, and I was a *welcome* person after that. Can you imagine?

Once the Millars had distanced themselves from Auden in public, though, they found room for his fictionalized image in their books. Margaret cast the first rock-candies: in "Last Day in Lisbon," a 1943 novelette with the minor character of a police interpreter, Duarte (almost an anagram): "a thin, shriveled little man with a lazy, insolent smile. He looked like a street urchin, and it was a shock to hear his voice. It was pure Oxford ... '[U]nfortunate' ... [h]e pronounced ... 'unfawtunit'"; and her 1944 semi-comic mystery *Fire Will Freeze*, one of whose road-company cast is "a refugee English poet whose genius is to madness near allied."

Margaret (who was also wary of other women "snatching Ken away," according to friends) may have prompted Ken also to take a satiric jab at his would-be mentor. In any case, when Millar finally did sketch Auden into a novel, it was a far more ambitious portrait.

Auden was the seed-inspiration for Francis Marvell, an English poet and playwright (Auden had also written for the stage) in *The Drowning Pool* (1950), the second Lew Archer novel by Ross Macdonald, Millar's pseudonym after his first four books. Marvell is nurturing a professional-personal relationship with the husband of Archer's client. With his "coltish sideways steps" and his "Adam's apple bobbing like a soft egg caught in his throat," the poet-playwright is a pretentious and unappealing figure. "His legs were pale and hairless above the drooping socks. His pale blond gaze seemed lashless.... He was an aging Peter Pan, glib, bland and eccentric..." Marvell has none of Auden's genius or warmth.

These were not flattering portraits. The Millars must have expected that mystery-reader Auden—familiar with Margaret's work, and likely to take an interest in Ken's—would see and recognize these exaggerated versions of himself. Ken Millar would eventually express apparent remorse for his literary abuse of the man whose enthusiasm for detective fiction gave Ken permission, as it were, to put his energies into the genre. But in the early 1950s, he was intent on maintaining a stone wall between himself and the sort of behavior seen by mainstream society—and himself—as perverted and dangerous.

* * *

Millar's fearful concerns regarding homosexuality were as much social as personal, said his friend Don Pearce:

> He spoke of how the great encyclopedic syntheses of everything known in the world had formerly been shaped by man.... [N]ow [circa 1952] it is women who are beginning to produce the new synthesis.... One thing that worried him more than anything else along this line was the presence and emergence of the homosexual. I can remember his telling me that a new kind of anarchy would result from the increasingly dominant presence of homosexuality in institutes of higher learning....

And Millar was afraid that an element of homosexuality lurked within his own being. A recent experience he had had during a train trip, when his sleepy gaze seemed to transform the slumbering blanket-wrapped male passenger next to him into a desirable female, shook him to the core, Pearce recalled: "He said, 'I wonder if I'm not a covert homosexual,' words to that effect."

Despite his abhorrence and fear of homosexuality, Millar tried to understand and perhaps make some accommodation with it. He used his Archer novels to explore humane options. Near the end of *The Drowning Pool*, with his client's husband separated from his wife and suffering paranoid delusions,

Archer pays Marvell the courtesy of giving him some life-affirming advice: "If you care about this man, you'd better get him a damn good doctor."

Many if not all Ross Macdonald novels contain young-man characters who seem in subtle ways to be symbolic examples of how Lew Archer (or, more to the point, his creator) might have turned out had circumstances taken a different twist. One such fellow is young Lance (Torres) Leonard, the pretty-boy wise-guy in *The Barbarous* Coast (1956) who progresses, in a particularly Southern California manner, from crooked boxer to potential movie-star—and the boyfriend of mobster Carl Stern.

A beaten-up Archer eavesdrops on Leonard's fretful dialogue with a sarcastic and bitter old thug, as they await Stern's arrival: "Carlie ought to been here long ago. You think his plane crashed?" "Yeah, I think his plane crashed. Which makes you a goddam orphan."

When Stern telephones later, he asks for Leonard. "Go and talk to him," the older hood tells Lance. "Put him out of his misery."

As vain and brutish as Leonard otherwise is, Macdonald shows his (and Stern's) emotional vulnerability in a sympathetic light. And when the young man comes to a bad end (still the inevitable fate of homosexuals in genre fiction circa 1956), Archer murmurs a poignant (if sardonic) epitaph over his corpse.

* * *

Millar/Macdonald in the 1950s was trying to understand the origins and behavior of his homosexual characters, the same as he looked for social and psychological explanations behind the rest of his fictional people. The author and his detective were moving beyond a simplistic black-and-white world of good people versus bad people, into a more complicated, realistic and humane post–Chandler vision.

As the Canadian-raised author turned his penetrating gaze upon Southern California (where he and his wife and daughter moved after World War II), he noted—as part, perhaps, of the general disintegration of the culture—a sort of mingling of the sexes within certain individuals.

Here, for instance, is a criminal who sits guarding Archer in *The Barbarous Coast*: "He was naked to the waist. Black fur made tufted patterns on his torso. He had breasts like a female gorilla."

And here is a guest at a "sophisticated" rich-folks party in *The Drowning Pool*: "A fat man with a cropped gray head, in a tweed suit with padded shoulders ... turned out to be a woman when she moved her nyloned legs."

Macdonald's worldview changed dramatically though in 1956 when the Millars' daughter was involved in a fatal hit-run accident in Santa Barbara, and the family moved to Northern California to escape the scandal. Ken Millar there underwent psychoanalysis, forcing himself to turn his probing vision on himself and his own neuroses and failings. He traced the causes of his psychic unease to his problematic childhood; and the insights he gained allowed him to alter his personality, he thought, for the better, as he attempted to incorporate rather than squelch the feminine forces that had helped (through many female relatives) to shape him.

In free-associative notebooks from this time, Millar seems to express remorse for having "betrayed" his "brother" Auden, whom he would later describe in public as a sort of "secular saint."

Millar came to see homosexuality as something caused as much by environment as any other factor—by boys growing up without fathers (as had Millar, and many of Auden's English generation of post–World War I sons).

Ross Macdonald's (and Lew Archer's) attitude towards and understanding of homosexuals changed. More and more, Macdonald showed how warped parents warped children in efforts to get them to meet abnormal expectations and desires.

In *The Zebra-Striped Hearse* (1962), a gruff-acting, insecurely-masculine Mama's-boy of a father (seen by a younger female paramour as being like a "sweet old lady") raises his unfortunate daughter "as a boy," a "he-she," to the detriment of her own social and sexual adjustment.

In "Little Woman," a 1950s story-fragment included in *The Archer Files*, an iron-willed mother with a girlish manner fawns over her long-suffering teenaged son:

> "Isn't he tall? Imagine little me giving birth to a great big fellow like Henry."
> He looked down into her upturned smile with a kind of disgusted resignation.... [T]hey almost could have been father and daughter instead of mother and son.... The boy's eyes met mine. They were tragic with pain and understanding. I left the room.

In later Macdonald books, homosexuals are viewed with greater empathy than in his earlier work. They may seem lonely, sad and thwarted, yet they are presented as people rather than caricatures.

In *The Zebra-Striped Hearse*, Archer's sympathy with Claude Stacy, "a big middle-aged American" hotel-keeper in Mexico, is heightened when he borrows clothes from the man after getting his own soaked: "I ... pulled on his blue turtleneck sweater. It had a big monogrammed 'S' like a target over the heart, and it smelled of the kind of piney scent they foist off on men who want to smell masculine." When the two chat about some of the people in Archer's case, the detective identifies further with the gossipy Claude: "Stacy's eyes had a feeding look, as if he lived on these morsels and scraps of other people's lives. Perhaps I feared a similar fate for myself." After he's walked a mile in Stacy's sweater, Archer takes amicable leave of the innkeeper: "[H]e did ask me when I had the time to call a friend of his who managed a small hotel in Laguna Beach. I was to tell the man that Claude was doing all right, and there were no hard feelings."

* * *

Near the end of his career, Macdonald told interviewer Paul Nelson it was possible he might write or already had written of homosexual characters without indicating they were such. Depicting a homosexual as an "average" individual not defined by sexual orientation: that was coming a long way, for the author of *The Dark Tunnel* or even *The Drowning Pool*.

That was a long way, too, for a Canadian-Californian born in 1915 who'd spent much of his childhood reading on his own, who never fit in with kids not as bright as himself ("Well, he was never 'one of the boys,' I can tell you that," one of his Kitchener street-hockey pals who later taught high-school with him there said fifty years later) and who, even in middle-age, was vulnerable to the same sort of insult any American male may receive any day out of the blue.

Collin Wilcox, a fellow mystery-writer and Bay Area friend of Ken Millar's, recalled an incident from a Millar visit to San Francisco in the late 1960s, after *The Goodbye Look* had made Macdonald a nationally best-selling author:

> We'd been out to dinner with friends, and he was staying at the Cliff Hotel [in the Tenderloin district].... I asked him if he felt like a nightcap, and he said sure. There was this small bar across from the Cliff, it looked okay.... This was probably a weeknight.... We sat in a booth and had a round; he insisted on paying.... There were just a few guys at the bar, and I think Ken and I [were] the only guys at a table. The bartender did the whole thing, came around from behind the bar, put the drinks down.... We had a second round, we paid him for that. Then we decided we were going to go. The guy says, "Wait a minute, you owe me for the first round." I said, "No, he certainly paid." And this guy just went berserk! It was the god-damnedest thing I've ever seen. He was raving, and he said, "You guys, you *fags* come in here—." ... It took me entirely aback.... Christ, I remember there were two or three guys at the end of the bar, and I had some perception that they might—I don't know, try to corral us or some damn thing. I think I might have said, "You know, this guy's very famous!" Well—that just made it worse! Then I thought I'd make a joke; I said to Ken, "You think I should leave him a tip?" He said, "*I think not.*"

Once the two writers left unscathed, Millar's thoughts turned, as they so often did and had since childhood, to books. "[The bartender] had been a small, kind of crab-like guy," Wilcox said, "in a red vest with brass buttons; and he had a strange, deeply-lined face. Ken said, 'He reminds me of a character in Dickens.' Yeah."

Works Cited

Chandler, Raymond. *The Big Sleep*. New York: Knopf, 1939.
Hammett, Dashiell. *The Maltese Falcon*. New York: Knopf, 1929.
Macdonald, Ross. *The Barbarous Coast*. New York: Knopf, 1956.
_____. *The Dark Tunnel*. New York: Dodd, Mead, 1944.

_____. *The Drowning Pool.* New York: Knopf, 1950.

_____. "Little Woman." First published in Ross Macdonald, *The Archer Files: The Complete Short Stories of Lew Archer, Private Investigator, Including Newly Discovered Case Notes.* Norfolk: Crippen & Landru, 2007. Edited by Tom Nolan.

_____. *The Zebra-Striped Hearse.* New York: Knopf, 1962.

Millar, Margaret. *Fire Will Freeze.* New York: Random House, 1944.

_____. "Last Day in Lisbon." 1943. Reprinted in Margaret Millar, *The Couple Next Door: Collected Short Mysteries.* Edited by Tom Nolan. Norfolk: Crippen & Landru, 2010.

Nolan, Tom. *Ross Macdonald: A Biography.* New York: Scribner's, 1999.

"Elegant stuff ... of its sort"
Gore Vidal's Edgar Box Detective Novels

CURTIS EVANS

Introduction: Spillane in Mink

Although not enjoying nearly the level of fame as the hard-boiled American crime fiction of Dashiell Hammett, Raymond Chandler and Ross Macdonald (not to mention the classic English crime tales of Agatha Christie), the trio of mid-twentieth-century "Edgar Box" detective novels by late man of letters Gore Vidal (1925–2012)—*Death in the Fifth Position* (1952), *Death Before Bedtime* (1953) and *Death Likes It Hot* (1954)—has hardly been forgotten. For many years the novels were frequently reprinted, and in 2011 all three of them were brought back into circulation in the United States, after an absence of two decades, by Vintage Books' Black Lizard, the hardboiled/noir imprint that also publishes Hammett, Chandler and Macdonald. When in 2012 Gore Vidal died at the age of 86, his Edgar Box mysteries in this sense stood with the works of the titans of twentieth-century American crime fiction.

Gore Vidal himself matter-of-factly termed the Boxes mere potboilers, pseudonymous quickies written simply to earn income after the supposed critical blackballing he received on account of his publication, at the precocious age of twenty-three, of the controversial bestselling gay-themed novel *The City and the Pillar* (1948). Certainly the years between Vidal's raising of *Pillar* and the appearance of his first Box, *Death in the Fifth Position* (1952), must have been cruelly disappointing ones for the author concerning his lofty artistic and monetary aspirations, for the mainstream novels he published at that time, though not quite so universally ignored and/or panned by putatively homophobic reviewers as Vidal claimed in his later years, sold disappointingly. Desirous of making more money, especially after having purchased with his *Pillar* profits Edgewater, a white-columned antebellum country mansion located on the banks of New York's Hudson River that had once been owned by a branch of the Livingston family (a move that symbolized the young man's intended arrival as a literary seigneur), Vidal industriously began putting pots to boil, taking full advantage of the greater freedom afforded genre fiction authors after the Second World War to include risqué subject matter in their books.¹

In 1950 Vidal produced a steaming women's melodrama, written under the pseudonym Katherine Everard, the surname being the author's sly pun on the name of New York's Everard (aka "Everhard") Baths, a trysting place renowned among the city's gay population. Issued strictly for the rental market by Vidal's publisher Dutton under the title *A Star's Progress*, the novel was promptly "pulped," so to speak, the same year by paperback publisher Pyramid as *Cry Shame!*, with a sexy young woman on the front cover and a lurid plot description on the back:

> At 13 she danced in a New Orleans honky-tonk and learned things she was too young to know! At 14 she ran off with a man four times her age and lived as his wife—in name only! Her strange affair with a screen idol who was "ambisextrous" shocked all of Hollywood! Her flagrant amour with a crown prince exploded in a page-one scandal! Here, told with compassion and artistry, is the story of a young girl who grew up—too fast!

This determined bit of whoring, as Vidal decades later termed his dabbling in pulp fiction, proved lucrative, with *Cry Shame!* selling over 400,000 copies in paperback; and, thus encouraged, the young author decided to try his hand at a detective novel. Vidal later claimed that the idea for this venture actually sprang fully formed from the mind of Victor Weybright (1903–1978), publisher of the New American Library (NAL) and its imprint Signet, businesses which stood at the forefront of the American paperback revolution, brandishing books, by authors as diverse as Mickey Spillane and William Faulkner, designed to conquer the fiction market with brightly illustrated and boldly sexual covers. Here is Vidal's reconstruction, in his 1995 memoir *Palimpsest*, of the luncheon conversation with Weybright which supposedly led to the making of Edgar Box (Vidal claims he proposed the name "Edgar," in honor of Edgar Allan Poe—though Victor Weybright assumed "Edgar" referred to the once hugely popular between-the-wars English thriller writer Edgar Wallace):

> "I'm quite aware that whatever you publish these days will be ignored or attacked. But I have a hunch that if you were to write something—well, popular, under another name, we could sell it.... You know, I've had great success with this Mickey Spillane—fantastic success...."
>
> "For God's sake, Victor, I can't even read him much less write like him!"
>
> "Of course not. What I was thinking ... you will recall S. S. Van Dine? ... Elegant stuff, you know. Of its sort. Well, we have Spillane, the lowbrow mystery writer. What we need now is an elegant one, to balance Spillane."²

Vidal's characteristically self-serving reminiscence of a forty-four-year-old luncheon tête-a-tête must be taken with grains of salt, for contemporary NAL records indicate that in fact Vidal had already written the novel that was to be published as *Death in the Fifth Position* before he lunched with Victor Weybright. However, it is noteworthy that in Vidal's recollection S. S. Van Dine served as a model for his proposed mystery series. Van Dine, who had passed away a dozen years earlier (when Vidal was barely a teenager) and promptly faded into obscurity, was the creator of the fancy pants American gentleman amateur detective Philo Vance, once one of the most prominent sleuths in Golden Age detective fiction and the antithesis of the hard-boiled private investigators created by Hammett, Chandler and their many followers, including Mickey Spillane, who had gained ascendancy in American mystery fiction by the middle of the twentieth century. Victor Weybright himself contemporaneously compared Edgar Box with S. S. Van Dine, writing in 1952: "I predict we can build Edgar Box into a major S. S. Van Dine type of mystery writer."[3]

In addition to the "elegant" S. S. Van Dine, another classical influence on the Edgar Box mysteries was Agatha Christie. During a March 2011 *New York Times* interview Vidal spoke quite favorably about England's Queen of Crime: "I liked Christie because I thought she was a great naturalist—those are real villages she writes about—and it's fascinating. I used to like to read her not for the mysteries but ... for the characters."[4] Suggestively, the same year that Vidal produced his first Edgar Box mystery, he also published a mainstream novel, *The Judgment of Paris*, which includes as one of its minor characters a bestselling woman detective novelist, Fay Peabody, who bears more than a passing resemblance to Christie (although, in an amusing twist, the competitive Mrs. Peabody expresses only scorn for her rival in the fictional murder business.) It seems apparent that it was not Mike Hammer but Philo Vance and Hercule Poirot who hovered as investigative muses over the shoulders of Vidal as he sat in his imposing octagonal study at Edgewater, working on the novel that became *Death in the Fifth Position*.

Although as "Edgar Box" Gore Vidal eschewed the extreme violence of Spillane's Mike Hammer, he added lavish lashings of sex to spice up the stories, much to the delight of Victor Weybright, who in contemporary correspondence lauded the series, pronouncing the second Box novel, for example, "daring and sexy but not hard-boiled...."[5] Vidal's randy series sleuth, public relations man Peter Cutler Sargeant II, is far from the archetypal sexless aesthete of classic mystery fiction, being more interested in warm bodies than cold ones. As tales of detection, one must admit, the Boxes are left dead and deeply buried in the boundless graveyard of Dame Agatha's less inspired imitators—although, to be fair, the plots improved over the course of the series, as Vidal honed his puzzle craft. Ultimately the Box series is most interesting for its sexual element, which satisfyingly melds with Vidal's lightly biting satirical foreplay. "Spillane in mink," pithily if paradoxically observed the *Saturday Review*'s Sergeant Cuff of the silkily sophisticated and sexy third novel in the Box series, *Death Likes It Hot*; and the phrase duly stuck.

If the Edgar Box novels are not masterpieces of detective fiction, how do they stand as examples of queer fiction from the Fifties? Here we run up against the reluctance of Gore Vidal, most of whose early fame rested on having published a pioneering gay novel, *The City and the Pillar*, to be categorized as a gay writer, or even a gay man, even though in *Palimpsest* he freely admits to having had gay sex, and lots of it, over the course of his life. Vidal, who professed the belief that everyone was bisexual by nature, scorned those he deemed had errantly identified themselves as gay (or straight for that matter). He felt as well the need to be in control during sex, the one in the "male" role exercising power by, to employ Vidal's blunt language, doing the fucking, not getting fucked. This attitude concerning masculinity and sexuality allowed Vidal in the first of the Edgar Box novels, *Death in the Fifth Position*, to present queer characters in a transgressive fashion that nevertheless seemingly stopped short of the line demarcated by American culture in the Fifties, although in fact the author may have come to feel that he had pushed too far against the boundary, for in the last two Box mysteries he effectively retired queer characters from his stage. While Gore Vidal's Edgar Box detective novels in my view thus mark somewhat halting steps in the forward advance of queer crime fiction, for their wicked wit and overall panache the books deserve space on the shelves, actual or virtual, of devotees of sophisticated vintage mysteries.[6]

Staying on Top of It All: Death in the Fifth Position

The first Edgar Box detective novel, *Death in the Fifth Position*, belongs to a tiny mystery subgenre, the ballet detective novel. (Additional examples are the three detective novels published from 1937–1940 by Caryl Brahms and S. J. Simon and Lucy Cores' 1944 mystery, *Corpse de Ballet*.) Vidal was well-suited to make a contribution to this particular field. Having suffered damage to his left knee from hypothermia sustained while he served as a maritime warrant officer in Alaska during the Second World War, Vidal took ballet lessons as restorative therapy after the end of hostilities. During this time he became quite interested in ballet and ballet dancers, especially male ones. With dancer Harold Lang, dubbed "the Beast of the Ballet" for his sexual voraciousness, Vidal had an affair, discussed by him in *Palimpsest*, and he likely was sexually involved as well, although more casually, with dancer John

Kriza, best known for his performance of the title role in Aaron Copland's ballet *Billy the Kid*. Louis Giraud, easily the most memorable character in *Death in the Fifth Position*, appears to have been compositely drawn from Lang and Kriza.[7]

Death in the Fifth Position concerns a rash of demises afflicting the Grand St. Petersburg Ballet Company during its performance at the New York City Metropolitan Opera House. Vidal's amateur detective in this novel (and its two sequels) is the aforementioned PR man Peter Cutler Sargeant II, Pacific War veteran and Harvard graduate, who has taken a temporary job with the Company. Vidal himself neither saw fighting in the Second World War nor earned, likely to his later chagrin, a Harvard degree (rather than enter college he published his first novel when he was twenty); but in other ways the author resembles Peter Sargeant. Like Vidal, Peter does not suffer fools gladly and he expresses loathing for Fifties McCarthyite Redbaiters and those he scornfully deems naively complacent balladeers of democracy and the American way. Peter additionally resembles Vidal in being a consummate sexual swordsman, though his coital conquests are female and Vidal's were male.[8] Peter's couplings with the fetching ballerina Jane Garden are described at length by Vidal. Yet it is the queer subject matter in *Position* that was especially "hot" for the Fifties. The Company's star male dancer, Louis Giraud (who "started life as a longshoreman in Marseilles" and was rumored to have been discovered in a bordello by a certain wealthy gentleman who, knowing a good thing when he saw it, carried him off to Paris), hits on every attractive man who crosses his sight—and for most men resistance is futile.

While Peter is intent, in between diversions with Jane, on solving the murders, Louis is bent on nailing Peter. This situation is humorously treated by Vidal, doubtlessly in contrast with how Mickey Spillane would have handled it. (Likely Mike Hammer would have slain Louis on the final page in some spectacularly unpleasant fashion.) Yet despite taking a mirthful approach to Louis' lustful pursuits, Vidal makes it clear to his readers that Peter, unquestionably all man, is not about to allow some ballet swish to deflower him, however macho the ballet swish may be. As Victor Weybright put it in his outline of the ideal modern fictional detective (what he termed the New Sleuth): "He must be absolutely certain of his identification with the male role."[9]

Louis and Peter's first passage of arms, in which Louis, clad only in a towel, traps Peter in his dressing room and makes a determined grab for him, is described by the imperiled sleuth as follows:

> We played tag for a moment and then he grabbed me, holding me the way a boxer holds another boxer in a clinch and both of us trying not to make any noise, for different reasons. I wondered whether to knee him or not; the towel had fallen off. I decided against it for the good of the company. I would be fired if I did. On the other hand I was in danger

of being ravished.... I couldn't stand like this forever pressed against his front while he fumbled and groped with his one free hand, embarrassing me very much. He smelled like a horse. Controlling myself with great effort I said in a very even and dignified voice, "If you don't let go of me, I will break every one of your toes." And with that, fairly gently, I put one hard leather heel on top of his left foot. He jumped at that and, breathing hard, I slid out the door.

I was mad as hell for several minute but then, since no damage was done, I began to see the funny side....[10]

With the humor removed from the sexual equation, this encounter between Peter and Louis reads like a wartime assault that Vidal in *Palimpsest* recalled experiencing. In a Seattle bar the night before he shipped out to Alaska, Vidal, as this story goes, picked up a married merchant mariner and the two proceeded to a hotel, where things promptly went awry from Vidal's perspective: "Suddenly, he was on my back. I tried to push him off. He used an expert half nelson in order to shove partway in. I bucked like a horse from the pain, and threw us both off the bed. We rolled across the floor, slugging at each other. Then, exhausted, we separated. He cursed; dressed; left. That was my first and last experience of being nearly fucked." When years later, in 1953, Vidal had sex with Beat writer Jack Kerouac (according to *Palimpsest*), Vidal made certain that he was the top man, recalling the incident with the merchant mariner: "...I finally flipped [Jack] over on his stomach, not an easy job as he was much heavier than I as was the merchant mariner in Seattle, whom he—only now does it strike me—physically resembled. Was I getting my own back on Jack's back?" "I liked the way he smelled," adds Vidal. Did Jack, like Louis, smell like a horse?[11]

Sex in all its forms as a contest for physical dominance was something Vidal clearly could understand and he no doubt expected that his presumed primary readership would understand it too. To be sure, in *Death in the Fifth Position* Vidal was daring in portraying a subsidiary queer character as a macho man rather than a flaming fairy. "He had a deep voice and he wasn't at all like the other boys in the company who were inclined to be rather tender," grudgingly observes Peter. "Louis had shoulders like a boxer." Yet because the queer character was a subsidiary one hailing from the queer world of ballet and stoutly resisted by the resolutely heterosexual male series sleuth, straight readers could derive from Louis' passes at Peter a sense of titillation without feeling compromised by any real threat of actual physical consummation.[12]

Admittedly, when Peter lets slip to Jane about Louis' assault on his male virtue, Jane's response makes clear that the fortresses of many men have fallen to Louis' sustained sieges, even those that appeared impregnable:

"[Louis] pads, you know."
"He what?"
"You know ... like a falsie: well, they say he wears one too, when he's in tights."

"Oh, no, he doesn't," I said, remembering my little tussle with the ballet's glamour boy.
"You, too?" She sat bolt upright.
"Me too what?"
"He didn't ... go after you, too, did he?"
"Well as a matter of fact he did but I fought him off." And I told her the story of how I had saved my honor. She was very skeptical. "He's had every boy in the company ... even the ones who like girls.... I expect he's irresistible."[13]

To this Peter tersely pronounces, "I resisted." For Peter and Vidal alike, staying on top is the key to constructing masculinity. At one point Peter gives expression to a bit of the sexual philosophy which Vidal had derived from his own self-need, bolstered by sexual continuum data from the Kinsey Report on *Sexual Behavior in the Human Male* (issued the same year the author published *The City and the Pillar*): "[Louis] certainly acts like a man and there may be, who knows, not much difference between nailing a boy to the bed and treating a girl in like manner." A man having sex with a man remains a real man, in other words, as long as he acts the part of a man by staying on top.[14]

The climax of Peter's investigation, as well as his personal peril of ravishment, comes in Chapter Seven, when he manfully accepts an invitation from Louis—strictly in the line of duty, of course—to go on a night crawl of gay hotspots, from Hermione's, a drag bar in the Village, to an anonymous Turkish bathhouse in Harlem. "I thought I knew a great deal about our feathered friends, the shy, sensitive dancers and so on that I've met the last few years in New York, but that night with Louis was an eye-opener," confides Peter. "[I]t was like those last chapters in Proust when everybody starts turning into boy-lovers until there isn't a womanizer left." However, the reader need not worry overmuch for Peter. After getting an eyeful of the colorful queens at Hermione's, Peter undergoes yet more manhandling from Louis at the bathhouse; yet the butch sleuth remains virgo intacta, though at times it seems like a near thing:

"Where'd you get those muscles, baby?" he asked, in a low voice.
"Beating up dancers," I said evenly. But I wasn't too sure of myself. Louis looked like one of those Greek gods with his clothes off, all muscle and perfect proportions, including the bone head.[15]

Admittedly, the detection in *Death in the Fifth Position* (assuming any reader ever has been much concerned about it at this point) will never win any competitions. Inexcusably from the standpoint of the puzzle purist, Vidal indulges himself in what can only be called an information dump near the end of the novel. Peter thereupon intuits the solution, but he has no proof to offer, since the whole thing is utterly conjectural. So that he can somehow solve the case Vidal has devised, the neophyte mystery author allows his hero, in most unsatisfactory fashion, literally to stumble over the proof he needs.

Death in the Fifth Position seems generally to have received good reviews, though the detection sometimes was faulted and a prim *Kirkus* reviewer was hostile to the entire Box enterprise: "More sex than gore in this unsavory concoction of murder in the ballet. Between courses of murder and sudden death, the author serves up a variety of affairs ... spiced with some excursions into perversion. The search for the murderer ... is not vital enough to wade through the rest of the story. Skip it." Even Anthony Boucher, dean of American mystery fiction critics, sniffed that he would have found the novel "more agreeable" had Edgar Box not strained so hard "to outdo Mickey Spillane and Adam Knight in sexiness."[16] Although Vidal maintained his high quotient of sex with his next two Edgar Box mysteries, the author, perhaps sensitive to such criticism in light of earlier critiques of *The City and the Pillar*, all but exiled gay characters from the pages, allowing them existence only in passing mentions from the principal players.

Country House Corpses and Copious Coitus: Death Before Bedtime *(1953) and* Death Likes It Hot *(1954)*

> "One of the guests ... drowned this morning."
> "Oh, isn't that awful! And on a weekend too."[17]
> —*Death Likes It Hot*

Both *Death Before Bedtime* and *Death Likes It Hot* are sexed-up, mid-century American versions of the highly-stylized closed circle, English house party mysteries associated with the Golden Age of detective fiction (roughly 1920 to 1940), of which Agatha Christie remains the most celebrated practitioner. *Death Before Bedtime* takes place in the Washington, D.C., mansion of an unscrupulous, ultra-conservative Midwestern senator with presidential aspirations, *Death Likes It Hot* in the Hamptons "beach house" of a socially ambitious matron. In both cases Peter Sargeant is hired by the mansion owner to perform a publicity job and thus is conveniently on hand when murder inevitably strikes.

Just as he drew on his personal experience with ballet and the gay demimonde when writing *Death in the Fifth Position*, Vidal with *Death Before Bedtime* looked back to his own troubled family history. The author's maternal grandfather, Thomas Pryor Gore (1870–1949), a United States senator from Oklahoma, began his political career as a Populist Democrat but later became known for his fervent isolationism, a stance which greatly influenced his young grandson. Although Vidal admired Senator Gore, he despised the senator's daughter, the flighty, narcissistic and tippling Nina Gore Vidal. Nina divorced Vidal's father when the boy was only nine years old and later, through her second marriage to Hugh Auchincloss, gave Vidal a connection, after a fashion, with the Kennedy family, a relationship ironically much-valued by Nina's extremely status-conscious son, no matter how intense his animus against his mother.[18] Vidal incorporates some of this background material into *Bedtime* in rather an interesting way. Although Leander Rhodes, the villainous Midwestern senator who is murdered early in the novel by means of explosives planted in his study fireplace, does not bear likeness to T. P. Gore, Senator Rhodes' dissipated daughter Ellen seems to have been inspired by Nina, whom a few years earlier the author had portrayed quite negatively in his fourth novel, *The Season of Comfort* (1949). How shocked would critics put off by the "perversities" depicted in *Death in the Fifth Position* have been had they discerned that, by having Peter bed Ellen in *Death Before Bedtime*, the author was symbolically nailing his own mother?

Bedtime opens memorably with Ellen Rhodes and the always ready, willing and able Peter about to commence copulation on a D.C.-bound train:

"You know, I've never gone to bed with man on a train before," she said, taking off her blouse.
"Neither have I," I said, and I made sure that the door to the compartment was securely locked.
"What innocents we are," she sighed, then: "I wish I had a drink."[19]

As this passage suggests, the two great interests that Ellen exhibits throughout the novel are booze and beaux. "For several years she had been living in New York," dryly notes Peter of Ellen, "traveling with a very fast set of post-debutantes and pre-alcoholics." When Senator Rhodes is blown up in Washington, D. C. in his own study, his houseguests act as all houseguests should in a classic house party mystery, where essentially death is a game; they are remarkably blasé about it, Ellen the most of the bunch:

I was surprised at how calmly the guests took the sudden, extraordinary turn in their affairs ... especially Ellen, who was the coolest of the lot.
"Do fix me a Scotch," she said.... I sat beside Ellen on an uncomfortable love seat....
"This is awful," I said inadequately, conventionally.
"I should hope to hell it is," said Ellen, guzzling Scotch like a baby at its mother's breast.
"It's going to tie us all in knots for the next few months."[20]

As Peter investigates the murder, the mercurial Ellen quickly loses interest in him and begins pursuing another eligible young male, a virginal writer for an advanced leftist intellectual magazine that was doing an expose on Senator Rhodes when the politician was sent to his account. Peter and the not-so-blushing Ellen are typically frank in their discussion of this matter:

"By the way, have you gotten into the Langdon boy yet?"
"What an ugly question!" she beamed; then she shook her head. "I haven't had time. Last night would have been unseemly.... I mean after the murder. This afternoon I was interrupted."

"I think he's much too innocent for the likes of you."

"Stop it ... you don't know about these things. He's rather tense, I'll admit, but they're much the best fun ... the tense ones."

"What a bore *I* must have been."[21]

Not for nothing is the cover of the new Black Lizard edition of *Bedtime* illustrated by a woman's eyes gazing out of a brandy snifter. The uninhibited Ellen is something of a female version of Louis from *Death in the Fifth Position*. To be sure, Vidal takes aim at additional satirical targets as well. Block-headed reactionary Midwesterners come under fire, as well as Vidal's literary rival, Truman Capote; yet the outrageous antics of Ellen, like those of Louis, are what seem most memorable to me.

A pleasing plentitude of suspects is milling around on the night of Senator Rhodes' murder, including, in classic fashion, his butler and private secretary; and the solution to the mystery is artistically apposite and subtly clued. In *Death Before Bedtime* Vidal demonstrated that he was learning the puzzle game—and playing it. He went on to produce the best-constructed Box with his last mystery, *Death Likes It Hot* (1954), dubbed at the time "a first-rate comedy of manners" by Anthony Boucher.[22]

The novel starts off with discussion of the latest New York newspaper death sensation: "The death of Peaches Sandoe the midget at the hands, or rather feet, of a maddened elephant in the sideshow of the circus at Madison Square Garden was at first thought to be an accident, the sort of tragedy you're bound to run into from time to time if you run a circus with both elephants and midgets in it. A few days later, though, there was talk of foul play."[23]

Sadly Peter Sargeant has no time to get involved with this tantalizing circus case, for he had already scheduled a trip to the Hamptons on New York's Long Island. Mrs. Veering, a wealthy Hamptons matron, is determined to become the next big thing in hostessing and has hired the publicity man to help her map out a campaign to attain her ambition. Soon Peter is on the Long Island Cannon Ball Express, on the way to his client's country house party, where death inevitably strikes, in the form of an offshore drowning of one of the guests. Foul play comes to be suspected, leading Peter to speculate: "The odds are that the murderer was among us, quietly eating stewed tomatoes and lobster Newburg." After another murder follows the original slaying, an interesting plot line develops—the best of the three Boxes in my view. Vidal even condescends to describe the layout of the house, which actually matters (though he really should have provided a floor plan), and he favorably mentions Agatha Christie.[24]

Much of the reader's fun in *Death Likes It Hot* is derived, as in the two previous Box mysteries, from the sardonic narration of Peter Sargeant, who is reminiscent in this respect of a vastly less idealized version of Raymond Chandler's great hard-boiled sleuth, Philip Marlowe. (There is nothing knightly, even in a shop-soiled sense, about Peter.) It soon emerges that Peter's client is a pronounced dipsomaniac reminiscent of the Mrs. Murdock character in Chandler's classic mystery *The High Window* (1942). Peter's deadpan observations concerning Mrs. Veering—"*a combination of Hetty Green and lush*"— and her avid pursuit of liquid refreshment are mordantly amusing: "Mrs. Veering stirred her orange juice with her forefinger: I wondered what pale firewater it contained. Probably gin, the breakfast drink."[25]

Through Peter the author also mercilessly mocks Mary Western Lung, noted children's writer—her most beloved work is *Little Biddy Bit*—and hostess of the nationally syndicated program *Book-Chat*. Miss Lung is quite the coyly amorous type, putting the move on all the available men in the house, including the police sergeant sent to check on the first suspicious death. "[W]e talked mostly about books," she later admits regretfully of her interview with him. "He likes Mickey Spillane."[26] Vidal seems to have it in for genteel women novelists in general (Agatha Christie excepted), another "noted penwoman" target of his ire being "Francine Karpin Lock," obviously southern regional novelist Frances Parkinson Keyes. Of traditional Hamptons society Peters holds a similarly low opinion, witheringly explaining at one point that belonging to the "nice" set at the local Ladyrock Yacht Club requires deploring "the presence in the community of such un-nice elements as Jews, artists, fairies and celebrities, four groups which, given half a chance, will, they feel, sweep all that's nice right out to sea."[27]

This being an Edgar Box novel, there naturally is an ample amount of sex that takes place between Sargeant and his fling of the moment, rich girl Liz Bessemer, including, so that the oceanside Hamptons setting does not go to waste, sex on the beach. There is a recurrent joke about how the quite amorous and uninhibited couple keeps copulating in the most uncomfortable of locations. "You know, darling, there are such things as beds, old-fashioned as they may sound," Liz chides Peter at one point. Surprisingly, Peter admits to himself that he finds Liz more desirable after lovemaking than before, a markedly new development for him. Sounding very much like Gore Vidal, who after the end of his affair with Harold Lang largely confined his sexual relationships to ephemeral "trade," Peter reflects that "usually, after the first excitement of a new body, I find myself drifting away." He makes haste to declare that "there would be no serious moments [with Liz] if I could help it."[28]

In between carnal bouts with Liz Bessemer, Peter gets in some detecting, explaining: "Justice didn't concern me much. But the puzzle, the danger, the excitement of following a killer's trail was all I needed to get involved."[29] Peter collars his criminal quarry, restoring order to the Hamptons, and the novel ends enticingly with the promise that Peter may end up getting involved in that Peaches Sandoe circus midget murder case after all. Sadly, we would never see from the hand of Gore Vidal a fourth Edgar Box detective novel, entitled *Death Clowns Around*, preferably with the irrepressibly lustful Louis Giraud making a return engagement, this time as a horny Hastings to Peter's priapic Poirot.

"Where'd you get those little grey cells, baby?"

NOTES

1. For personal background on Gore Vidal I have drawn primarily on these sources: Gore Vidal, *Palimpsest: A Memoir* (1995; London: Penguin, 1996); Fred Kaplan, *Gore Vidal: A Biography* (Bloomsbury: London, 1999); Tim Teeman, *In Bed with Gore Vidal: Hustlers, Hollywood and the Private World of an American Master* (New York: Magnus Books, 2013); Jay Parini, *Empire of Self: A Life of Gore Vidal* (New York: Doubleday, 2015). Jay Parini has written of Tom Teeman's luridly-titled but substantively-sourced volume, "It's a tell-all book, probably accurate." Parini, *Empire of Self*, 403. On the American paperback revolution see Geoffrey O'Brien, *Hardboiled America: The Lurid Years of American Paperbacks* (New York: Van Nostrand Reinhold, 1981), Kenneth C. Davis, *Two-Bit Culture: The Paperbacking of America* (New York: Houghton Mifflin, 1984) and Paula Rabinowitz, *American Pulp: How Paperbacks Brought Modernism to Main Street* (Princeton: Princeton University Press, 2014). Screenwriter Arthur Laurents recalled that during a stay at Edgewater in the early 1950s, Gore Vidal had "[f]our main topics: Harold Lang, Truman Capote, money and sex." Arthur Laurents, *Original Story By: A Memoir of Broadway and Hollywood* (New York: Applause, 2000), 340. Harold Lang was a dancer with whom Vidal had recently broken up (see pp. 228–29). Truman Capote, who with his fiction had outpaced Vidal in the race for critical acclaim, became one of Vidal's lifelong bêtes noires. In a 1995 preface to a Random House reprint of *The City and the Pillar*, Vidal claimed that "no major American newspaper or magazine would review [*Pillar*] or any other book of mine for the next six years," but this claim, though frequently repeated by Vidal over the years of his life, does not withstand scrutiny. According to Parini the "real problem" with Vidal's books at this time "lay in the fact that Gore had written half a dozen novels in less than five years, and none—not even *The City and the Pillar*—was more than the work of a brilliant apprentice, a young novelist searching for his voice." Parini, *Empire of Self*, 86. Interestingly, Vidal himself takes this same measured view in a 1974 interview published in the *Paris Review*, wherein he allows "my first years as a writer were very difficult because I knew I wasn't doing what I should be doing, and I didn't know how to do what I ought to be doing." See Gore Vidal, "The Art of Fiction No. 50," *Paris Review* (Fall 1974), at http://www.theparisreview.org/interviews/3917/the-art-of-fiction-no-50-gore-vidal.

2. Thomas L. Bonn, *Heavy Traffic & High Culture: New American Library as Literary Gatekeeper in the Paperback Revolution* (Carbondale: Southern Illinois Univeristy Press, 1989), 91; Vidal, *Palimpsest*, 248. The "Box" in Edgar Box was adopted on the spot, according to Vidal, from the surname of a couple being honored at a publisher's party he and Weybright were attending, lately identified by Wayne Gunn as scriptwriters Muriel and Sydney Box. See Drewey Wayne Gunn, "Gore Vidal Writing as Edgar Box" (review), 28 February 2011, *LambaLiterary*, at http://www.lambdaliterary.org/reviews/02/28/gore-vidal-writing-as-edgar-box/. However, Gunn has reminded us that "Box" also calls to mind the Edgar Allan Poe mystery story "The Oblong Box" (1844).

3. Bonn, *Culture*, 91, 93.

4. Stephen Heyman, "Gore Vidal, P. I.," *T: The New York Times Style Magazine*, 10 March 2011, at http://tmagazine.blogs.nytimes.com/2011/03/10/gore-vidal-p-i/. The three 2010 introductions to Black Lizard's 2011 reissue of the Edgar Box trio, which are credited to Gore Vidal, also emphasize the influence of Agatha Christie on the Boxes. However, Jay Parini has admitted that Vidal, though he attempted to do so, did not in fact write the introductions. Rather, Parini put them together for Vidal, after having asked the ailing author "questions that would lead to appropriate introductory material." Parini, *Empire of Self*, 396.

5. Bonn, *Culture*, 93.

6. Although he does not scrutinize the Edgar Box mysteries in his *Homosexuality in the Works of Gore Vidal* (Munster: LIT Verlag, 2002), Jorg Behrendt provides a useful analysis of Vidal's view of sexuality and power. "Vidal and his characters," Behrendt notes, "do not want to enter close intimate relationships because they are afraid to lose their positions of autonomy and power" (p. 121). For a convenient collection of Vidal's thoughts on sex, see Gore Vidal, *Sexually Speaking: The Collected Sex Writings* (Berkeley: Cleis, 2001). See also Dennis Altman, *Gore Vidal's America* (Cambridge: Polity, 2005). Vidal's notorious antipathy to Truman Capote (see note 1) was not based simply on insecurity over Capote's literary success or on any of Capote's perceived character defects (some of which Vidal himself seems to have shared), but also on a visceral dislike of the southerner's "flaming" homosexuality, as Frank Kaplan suggests when he observes that to Vidal Capote seemed "excessively and self-promotingly effeminate, an extravagant queen eager to use his mannerisms to make sure people remembered him...." Kaplan, *Gore Vidal*, 210. In Vidal's view the effeminacy of Capote, and that of queens in general, projected weakness. "[T]he queen world frightens and depresses me...," he reflected in 1950. Kaplan, *Gore Vidal*, 336.

7. Presumably referring to Lang and Kriza, Vidal once boasted to Leonard Bernstein that he had slept with two of the three original male cast members of the ballet *Fancy Free* (1944), to which Bernstein, not to be outdone, replied that he had slept with all three. (Besides Lang and Kriza, the other original male cast member was Jerome Robbins.)

8. Of Harold Lang's promiscuity during their relationship, Vidal in *Palimpsest* quips: "This hardly bothered me, since I was almost as promiscuous as Harold." Vidal, *Palimpsest*, 131.

9. Bonn, *Culture*, 90. In the same 1956 letter Weybright bluntly termed Sherlock Holmes "passé," Philo Vance "over-exotic," Perry Mason "pedestrian," and Spillane's Mike Hammer a "dull-witted, slap-happy, over-compensated effeminate character." *Ibid.*

10. Gore Vidal (as Edgar Box), *Death in the Fifth Position* (1952; repr., New York: Vintage Crime/Black Lizard, 2011), 23–24.

11. Vidal, *Palimpsest*, 95, 233.

12. Vidal, *Position*, 23. Compare the unconsummated Louis-Peter tussle with the male rape episodes in *The City and the Pillar* and Vidal's bestselling sextravganza *Myra Breckinridge* (1968), "part of a major cultural assault on the assumed norms of gender and sexuality which swept the western world in the late 1960s and 1970s...." Altman, *Gore Vidal's America*, 132.

13. Vidal, *Position*, 34–35. Peter finds the tables turned with Jane when he comes to suspect her of having had her own same-sex fling with a dancer.

14. On sexual identity being determined by what gender role one plays rather than who one has sex with, see George Chauncey, *Gay New York: Gender, Urban Culture, and the Making of the Gay Male World 1890–1940* (New York: Basic Books, 1990).

Vidal hearkens back to an early twentieth-century sexual culture that "divided into 'queers' and 'men' on the basis of gender status," rather than categorizing individuals as "homosexuals" and "heterosexuals" (as in the late twentieth-century) "on the basis of sexual object choice." "Attraction between equally masculine types, according to Vidal's ideology, is impossible and thus his characters cannot evolve in that direction" (p. 122), notes Behrendt in *Homosexuality in the Works of Gore Vidal*. In this view "sex between men is nothing but a game of exerting power and being dominated..." (p. 142).

    15. Vidal, *Position*, 192, 203. **Spoiler Alert:** Peter's solution to the mystery provides support for Vidal's thesis that exhibiting emotional weakness in sexual relationships by falling in love leads to disaster. Peter discovers that the murderer turns out to be the ballet choreographer, Jed Wilbur, whose motivation was his mad love for Louis. "You should see the way he looks at him, like a spaniel or something," Jane explains to Peter, while at the bathhouse Louis goes into more detail: "I used to be a pussycat for some older guys, when I was real young, but I didn't like it much and besides it isn't dignified.... I tell him all this a thousand times but he doesn't listen. He's made up his mind I'm his big love and there's nothing I can do about it. You'd think somebody who'd been around dancers as long as he has wouldn't feel that way, like a little girl, but he's got a one-track mind." Sentiment, in short, kills. Vidal, *Position*, 17, 201.

    16. *Kirkus Reviews*, 2 July 1952, *New York Times Book Review*, 22 June 1952. Adam Knight (aka Lawrence Lariar) was another NAL hard-boiled author, a forgotten Spillane imitator who in the Fifties published eight detective novels chronicling the adventures of Steve Conacher, "the exciting detective who can't be shocked or stopped by the wiles of scheming women or the whine of screaming bullets." One can see Gore Vidal's lip curling already. See David Pekasky, "Steve Conacher," *The Thrilling Detective Website*, at http://www.thrillingdetective.com/eyes/conacher.html. By 1956 *Death in the Fifth Position* had sold 197,000 of 335,000 paperback copies printed, which Bonn notes (p. 93) "must have been seen as something of a disappointment," especially given the paperback sales of *Cry Shame! Death Before Bedtime* sold 164,000 of 207,000 paperback copies printed and *Death Likes It Hot* 196,000 of 220,000 printed. After receiving an early royalty statement from NAL on *Death in the Fifth Position*, Vidal, though he conceded that it was "not bad for a cocktail hour project," nevertheless complained: "BUT STILL VERY LITTLE MONEY" (p. 93, n. 2).

    17. Gore Vidal (as Edgar Box), *Death Likes It Hot* (1954, repr., New York: Vintage Crime/Black Lizard, 2011), 49.

    18. After divorcing Nina, Hugh Auchincloss married Jacqueline Bouvier's mother, making Vidal's former stepfather Jacqueline Bouvier's current stepfather.

    19. Gore Vidal (as Edgar Box), *Death Before Bedtime* (1953; repr., Vintage Crime/Black Lizard, 2011), 9. The irony in Peter's retort to Ellen must have particularly amused Vidal.

    20. Vidal, *Bedtime*, 11, 36.

    21. Ibid., 65–66.

    22. *New York Times Book Review*, 23 May 1954. **Spoiler Alert:** The murderer turns out to be no less than Ellen Rhodes, her motive having been to stop her father from interfering in her life. Just like Nina Gore, the high-spirited Ellen constituted quite a handful for her political parents. Peter exposes Ellen only after the unhinged murderess, believing that he has discovered the truth about her, attempts to kill him. At the end of the novel Ellen is committed to an insane asylum, where she is last seen barking like a dog. Well aware of Ellen's sexual voraciousness, Peter expresses pity

for the asylum's "younger doctors." Nina, it seems, has been nailed by the author yet again.
 23. Vidal, *Hot*, 7.
 24. *Ibid.*, 120.
 25. *Ibid.*, 66, 74. Hetty Green (1834–1916) was a New York millionaire notorious for her miserliness.
 26. *Ibid.*, 39.
 27. *Ibid.*, 53, 63, 106. In *Death Before Bedtime* Vidal ribbed American novelist Mary Roberts Rinehart (1876–1958), the high priestess of the foreboding "Had I But Known" (HIBK) school of mystery. The previous year she had published *The Swimming Pool*, her final mystery novel.
 28. *Ibid.*, 51, 91. In 1950, not long after his breakup with Harold Lang, Vidal at the Everard Baths met Howard Auster, with whom he would live for the next fifty-three years, until Auster's death in 2003. Vidal repeatedly insisted that the two men had only a briefly sexual relationship, making long-term cohabitation possible for him.
 29. Vidal, *Hot*, 51.

WORKS CITED

Altman, Dennis. *Gore Vidal's America*. Cambridge: Polity, 2005.
Behrendt, Jorg. *Homosexuality in the Works of Gore Vidal*. Munster: LIT Verlag, 2002.
Bonn, Thomas L. *Heavy Traffic & High Culture: New American Library as Literary Gatekeeper in the Paperback Revolution*. Carbondale: Southern Illinois University Press, 1989.
Chauncey, George. *Gay New York: Gender, Urban Culture, and the Making of the Gay Male World 1890–1940*. New York: Basic Books, 1990.
Heyman, Stephen. "Gore Vidal, P. I." *T: The New York Times Style Magazine*. 10 March 2011. At http://tmagazine.blogs.nytimes.com/2011/03/10/gore-vidal-p-i/.
Davis, Kenneth C. *Two-Bit Culture: The Paperbacking of America*. New York: Houghton Mifflin, 1984.
Gunn, Drewey Wayne. "Gore Vidal Writing as Edgar Box." 28 February 2011. *Lambda Literary*. At http://www.lambdaliterary.org/reviews/02/28/gore-vidal-writing-as-edgar-box/.
Kaplan, Fred. *Gore Vidal: A Biography*. 1999; Bloomsbury: London, 2000.
Kirkus Reviews, 2 July 1952.
Laurents, Arthur. *Original Story By: A Memoir of Broadway and Hollywood*. New York: Applause, 2000.
New York Times Book Review, 22 June 1952, 23 May 1954.
O'Brien, Geoffrey. *Hardboiled America: The Lurid Years of Americans Paperbacks*. New York: Van Nostrand Reinhold, 1981.
Parini, Jay. *Empire of Self: A Life of Gore Vidal*. New York: Doubleday, 2015.
Pekasky, David. "Steve Conacher." *The Thrilling Detective Website*. At http://www.thrillingdetective.com/eyes/conacher.html.
Rabinowitz, Paula. *American Pulp: How Paperbacks Brought Modernism to Main Street*. Princeton: Princeton University Press, 2014.
Teeman, Tim. *In Bed with Gore Vidal: Hustlers, Hollywood and the Private World of an American Master*. New York: Magnus, 2013.
Vidal, Gore. "The Art of Fiction No. 50." *Paris Review* (Fall 1974). Gerald Clarke interviewer. At http://www.theparisreview.org/interviews/3917/the-art-of-fiction-no-50-gore-vidal.

_____. *Palimpsest: A Memoir.* 1995; London: Penguin, 1996.
_____. *Sexually Speaking: The Collected Sex Writings.* Berkeley: Cleis, 2001.
_____ (as Edgar Box). *Death Before Bedtime.* 1953. Reprint, New York: Vintage Crime/Black Lizard, 2011.
_____ (as Edgar Box). *Death in the Fifth Position.* 1952. Reprint, New York: Vintage Crime/Black Lizard, 2011.
_____ (as Edgar Box). *Death Likes It Hot.* 1954. Reprint, New York: Vintage Crime/Black Lizard, 2011.
Weybright, Victor. *The Making of a Publisher: A Life in the 20th Century Book Revolution.* New York: Reynal, 1967.

"Adonis in person"
Same-Sex Intimacy and Male Eroticism in the Detective Novels of Beverley Nichols

J. F. NORRIS

If any writer should have created a compassionate portrait of gay men and lesbians in fiction that writer should have been British bon vivant and gardening enthusiast Beverley Nichols (1898–1983). Best known for a series of memoirs and a veritable library of books on the splendor of English gardens, Nichols also dabbled in detective fiction, publishing five mystery novels between 1954 and 1960. His retired private detective, Horatio Green, seems an older, wiser and more subdued version of the author himself. Both share an uninhibited passion for flowers and gardening. Mr. Green's mandatory Great Detective quirk is his acute sense of smell, which allows him literally to sniff out clues that help him solve the puzzling and devilishly plotted murders the author devised.[1] Additionally, his adventures often lead him into the music and theater milieus which Nichols knew so well, where one is certain of finding a gay man or two, not to mention a few lesbians.

Horatio Green debuted in *No Man's Street* (1954), Nichol's first detective novel. In its pages we find an interesting lesbian couple who seem different from the usual stereotypes of the era; yet it is difficult to reconcile the depictions of these two women as seen through the eyes of Mr. Green. How are we meant to interpret the unfortunate choice of analogies he uses? Is this the fictional character's opinion of lesbians, or is it also that of the author? Though the portrayal seems motivated by sympathy, it comes off as awkward and bigoted.

Music critic Edward Carstairs, the murder victim in *No Man's Street*, was cruel in person and cruel on the printed page, making a name for himself with two extremes—laudatory hyperbole for those he admired or scathingly trenchant pans for those he deemed failures. Veronica Carstairs is his outspoken, brusque and self-absorbed sister. Mr. Green is taken aback by her brutal honesty when she declares that he should consider her the primary suspect in her brother's stabbing death. Sweeping in and out of the murder scene in the second chapter, she practically dismisses both the police and Mr. Green, who has been called into the case as a consultant (as is usual, we learn, when the murder has a tinge of the outré).

Mr. Green visits Veronica at her home and there discovers that she is in a relationship with a much younger woman, Sheila Crane, who was once a rising pianist and composer but now suffers from a severely damaged reputation due to one of Carstairs' nasty reviews. Sheila has turned to the bottle for solace and Veronica finds herself increasingly angry at being helpless to save her partner from destroying her life. Throughout this sequence Nichols once again gives us the painfully honest side of Veronica and allows her moments of a poignant breakdown, yet her confession scene is tainted by Mr. Green's perceptions. He seems uncomfortable being with her. See if you notice a pattern in these passages:

> "Her shoulders shook with sobs that seemed to wrench the body, but she made no sound. It was like a man weeping."
>
> "...he put his hand on her shoulder. It was the sort of gesture he would have made with a man."
>
> "...there was nothing in the least feminine, thought Mr. Green, about [her] handshake; it made him wince; it was a grip that could break a man's fingers, there was an unnatural brutal strength about it...."

A study of each description of Veronica finds Mr. Green always comparing her to a man. Veronica herself says "I am not a normal woman" as a lead-in to her confession about her love life with Sheila. She even intimates that Mr. Green may be gay himself when he plays coy and interprets the sentence as a self-deprecating joke. "You know what I mean," she says impatiently, while staring at him accusingly. He ought to know the code for "not normal" in this context.

Mr. Green does in fact come off as rather sexless and maternal, as is the case with many older gay male characters of this era. In later books his queer vibe is very present. Why is he so afraid of Veronica? Why can he only see her as a woman who seems more like a man? This is a troubling manner in which to present a lesbian in a book written by a man who was so full of life and acceptance for all types of people and who by his own confession was quite sexually uninhibited. Nichols has a few tricks up his sleeve, however.

Sheila's role in the story is perhaps the saddest part. Nichols paints her as a morose, hopeless drunk, slurring her words as she refills her glass repeatedly with straight whiskey. Is it any wonder when she is later found dead with her head in a gas oven? What else happens to the self-pitying drunken gay man or woman in books of this era? They turn to the most melodramatic form of suicide possible, of course. Veronica is not even given a chance to redeem herself as a compassionate figure, for rather than trying to save her lover she just accepts that she is dead and calls for a doctor to dispose of the body. It is the doctor who does his best to save Sheila. She passes away in a rest home only a few hours later, but not before giving a full confession to the murder of Edward Carstairs. Is this the end of the novel? Not quite.

It turns out that the behavior of Veronica and Sheila was orchestrated by the author for the purposes of his mystery plot and was presented in such a fashion as to bamboozle us. In essence the two women were tools of a skilled detective fiction writer's greatest gift—that of misdirection. Each woman was convinced that the other had killed Edward Carstairs. Mr. Green tells the group assembled for his traditional lecture in the final chapters that the two women were so devoted to one another and so deeply in love that they were willing to sacrifice themselves by confessing to the crime. In the end, Nichols does indeed seem to understand the often profound attachment that makes gay relationships so different and difficult to comprehend for so many "normal" men and women. These two friends—they are only described as either "friend" or "companion"—actually behaved like a married husband and wife. Imagine!

The mystery itself, like all of Nichols' well-written and tightly-constructed detective fiction, is fashioned from the pattern of an Agatha Christie novel, despite Nichols' many allusions to the Sherlock Holmes canon. *No Man's Street* is cleverly plotted with a few clues for the reader, many secrets in the past lives of the characters (with most of them having interesting motives for the murder of Carstairs) and a couple of the traditional eleventh hour surprises. If only the two lesbian characters were described less clumsily the book would be something of a landmark in postwar detective fiction for its depiction of a lasting devoted same-sex relationship that can succeed in the face of such stereotyped social ills as alcoholism and depression. The emphasis on perceived mannishness, however, is troubling for modern audiences—or at least to this reader.

The Moonflower (1955) marks the second appearance as a detective of Horatio Green, still retired but once again called upon to investigate a murder case that is right up his allée. The entire book is about gardening and flowers, and the murder itself is committed in a greenhouse with one of the most baroque murder means in the history of the genre. Only a true gardening enthusiast would think of something so devilish and only Mr. Green manages to uncover the secret—though this is not all he uncovers in the novel. Mr. Green is fascinated with the handsome, rugged features and impressive physique of Wilburfoss, the gardener on the Faversham estate. Marveling at this fine specimen of male beauty, the detective says half aloud, "He might have sat for Praxiteles." Instantly we know that he has imagined what Wilburfoss looks like underneath his green baize apron and natty gardening uniform.

When the time comes for Mr. Green to explain the motive behind the crime, the sleuth says that he and Superintendent Waller were so intent on proving the murder was committed for money that they were blind to the real reason, love. Nor was it garden variety love, but rather "the highest form of love—the love of a man for his friend." Though not explicitly a gay male relationship, the depth of feeling expressed between the two men in question is something not often encountered in fiction. The closest similar plot motif one can expect to find in this period would be in a novel set during wartime dealing with military culture and that profound male camaraderie which comes closest to physical love between two men (without the sex).

In the third fictional outing of Mr. Green, *Death to Slow Music* (1956), the murder is tied to a kind of David and Jonathan relationship traceable back to the Korean War. Once again we enter the world of musicians; but also in the cast we find actors, theater producers, carnival workers and a hidden clue in the life of a movie stunt double. There are uncanny similarities in the novel to the detective fiction of Agatha Christie, who like Nichols had a fondness for writing mysteries with artistic settings. The murderer in *Death to Slow Music* is not unlike the villains found in *Lord Edgware Dies* (1933) or *Three Act Tragedy* (1934), both of which feature egomania in a stage personality. The entire conceit of the plot eerily coincides with that of *The Mirror Crack'd from Side to Side* (1962), a novel published six years after Beverly Nichols concocted this story of the gruesome revenge of an embittered entertainer.

Money, wealth, beauty and power are the motivating forces in Nichols' penultimate detective novel, *The Rich Die Hard* (1957). Andrew Lloyd has exceptional tastes in art, music and furnishings; his home is a veritable museum display. However, as much as he has an appreciation for all things beautiful, including people, his life is devoted to making money, not displaying his wealth. He confesses to the police "My god is money" and tells another person "You know I do nothing unless it involves money."

Lloyd also has an insatiable sexual appetite and indulges himself with a live-in mistress tolerated by his aloof wife Nancy, who is more interested in Andrew's intellect than his body. This strange *ménage a trois* allows Nichols once again to express his gay sensibility as he scoffs at traditional marriage and satirizes the conventional views of love and sexuality. The mistress, Margot Larue, is found dead in a locked room from an apparently self-inflicted gunshot wound. Margot, who wanted Andrew all to herself, had threatened suicide many times over the nature of the odd three-way living arrangement in the Lloyd house. Any diligent reader of detective fiction knows that a dead body in a locked room is going to have been the result of foul play—and so does Mr. Green. The love of beauty plays its most important role in this entry in Nichols' mystery series, proving one character's undoing and revealing the motive for Margot's murder.

Nichols develops the beauty motif by introducing two stunningly handsome men into his cast of characters. There is Palmer, the Lloyds' butler, who is drawn to Mr. Green's gentlemanly ways and so desires to be of service to him that he gives special instructions to the footman to leave Mr. Green's valeting to him. His service goes beyond the call of duty into the realm of creepy obsequiousness. Palmer squeezes out toothpaste onto Mr. Green's toothbrush and tucks a handkerchief artfully arranged as a fan into Mr. Green's smoking jacket. "It is a pleasure to work for a man if he isn't temperamental," the butler pronounces. Palmer's attachment to Mr. Green makes the detective extremely uncomfortable. That Palmer has "startling good looks" adds to his discomfort. Nichols implies (though he never outright states) that there is some sort of physical attraction between the two men. "For Mr. Green," Nichols writes, "[Palmer] had conceived a feeling verging on adoration."

When he was a lad and new to London, Palmer's good looks, coupled with his penchant for wandering outside at night "marveling at all he saw," often led to his being mistaken for a hustler on the prowl by certain elderly gentleman. In his late teen years he was arrested by an opportunistic policeman who saw that "the most popular way to promotion was through the detention of homosexuals, or those who might conceivably be construed as such." This incident instilled in Palmer an intense dislike for all policemen, which explains his preference for confiding in Mr. Green rather than Supt. Waller. Beverley Nichols himself was no stranger to the world of hustlers and rough trade. Although he was in a relationship with actor Cyril Butcher for over fifty years, the author maintained a separate apartment in London intended exclusively for his frequent one-night stands. He picked up young men, especially guardsmen, in the same neighborhoods fictionally visited by Palmer.[2]

Palmer willingly divulges secrets about Andrew Lloyd to Mr. Green, to which the sleuth is more than willing to listen. The butler delivers a lengthy monologue, describing the night Lloyd in a quietly seething fury ordered a bonfire to be built and all his schoolboy clothes, books and other belongings from his schooldays burnt. Afterwards Palmer grows quiet and apologizes for nattering on so indiscreetly. "I hope you continue … to natter," a beaming Mr. Green tells him. "It may prove of the greatest assistance."

The other suspect whom Mr. Green finds himself liking a bit too much is Lord Richard Marwood. A young man of twenty-four with fair hair, blue eyes and a powerful build, Lord Richard "looked as though he would be happiest in rugger clothes." When Mr. Green meets Lord Richard, the latter man is wearing greasy overalls and working on his sports car. They have an almost instant rapport when the young man asks Mr. Green to correct his grammar. "I should be inclined to prefer the man who said 'That is me' to the man who said 'That is I,'" says Mr. Green. "Me too," comes Lord Richards' response and "the eyes of the two men met in a mutual twinkle." They discuss cars, with Lord Richard using feminine pronouns to describe his vehicle and Mr. Green a bit reluctantly following suit. Mr. Green takes advantage of Lord Richard's friendly manner and opens the driver's seat to get a feel for what looks like a luxuriously comfortable ride. He finds a slip of paper, pockets it, and then looks at the gas gauge, noticing that it registers nearly empty. Two more clues discovered almost serendipitously, and all thanks to a bit of unexpected male bonding.

With *Murder by Request* (1960), the fifth and final book in the Horatio Green series, Nichols' recurring motifs and themes come full circle. We find situations and relationships similar to those in earlier books, but this time they are more deeply felt and sometimes done with campy humor. As in all the Mr. Green books there are intense male friendships and an Adonis character, perhaps the queerest character Nichols created, apart from the lesbian couple in *No Man's Street*.

The story takes place at a spa resort where Mr. Green and his client Sir Owen Kent are staying. Kent has received threatening letters which promise that he will die within a specific date range of eight days. Green is given a list of the guests and staff at the spa in order to prepare for a job he thinks he is unsuited for—the prevention of Sir Owen's murder.

The male beauty in *Murder by Request* comes in the form of Mr. Garth, the spa's massage therapist. He is described as "Adonis in person" and "absolutely dreamy." One woman gushes out her erotic fantasy: "And wouldn't you love to be half strangled by him?" He may be drop dead gorgeous, but when Mr. Green first lays eyes on Garth he notices something a bit off:

> As he approached, Mr. Green realized why Mr. Garth had so devastating effect upon the women. He was about thirty, swarthy, tall, and powerfully built, with very dark hair growing close down on his forehead. He was the type to make a fortune on television in a Western serial. Everything about him was aggressively male, with the exception of his lips which were loose and curved in too delicate a bow for such rugged features.

Why is it that writers of this era focus on the shape of lips—whether full and sensuous or "too delicate"—to signal a male character being less than male? The obsession with facial features being signifiers for personality traits is almost a requirement in popular fiction of the early to mid-twentieth century. These qualifiers tend to be code for tagging a male character as gay. Not only are Mr. Garth's lips a tip-off; Mr. Green detects something odd in Garth's handshake, which is "cool and powerful and yet in some way cloying." (This is quite a talent, being able to convey all this in a quick grip.)

Even the less sensitive Supt. Waller is rattled by Garth's breathtaking appearance and manner, declaring: "No man with a face like that can be entirely normal." Nichols calls Garth's good looks the *beaute du diable*. When Waller comes for a massage treatment, he knocks on the door and Garth replies from within, "*Entrez.*" Queried by Waller about his use of the word, the therapist explains that when he is happy he thinks of Paris and thus he could not help letting slip with *Entrez*.

All thoughts of Garth being light in his loafers are put out of Waller's head, however, when the masseur goes to work on his tense muscles. His strength and grip are not cloying when he gets down to business. Garth begins to work like an artist, "swiftly, gently but with immense reserves of strength." Waller feels Garth's body "pressing behind him." Then Garth advises Waller: "Relax. I know it isn't easy the first time." This suggestive passage follows: "It certainly wasn't, thought Waller. To surrender so completely to any man, particularly a man like Garth who.... But before he could formulate the thought there was another jerk and the crack came. And with it a sudden feeling of lightness and ease...." One cannot help but suspect that Nichols managed to sneak in a gay sex scene without having two men actually do the deed.

We get another sampling of Nichols' interest in a different kind of male bonding when Waller visits Button, another masseur. Smaller and shorter than Garth, Button is summed up as "a dog who has lost his master." A veritable shrine to Sir Owen Kent, Button's room seems to have been designed by the masseur as a pathetic retreat for his hero worship. Waller notices several photos of Sir Owen in gaudy frames and even a patchwork quilt made of Sir Owen's old neckties. Button has a scrapbook filled with press cuttings about the man leading up to his funeral, and he lovingly shows the photos to Waller, at one point lamenting: "That's not a very good one, sir, the one of the grave." When, earlier in the novel, Mr. Green comes across the corpse of Sir Owen, he finds Button cradling the dead man's head and crying out, "He's gone, sir. He's gone." Only now does the glare of hatred he gave the guests that night and his perceived role of an avenger take on full meaning.

Button's devotion to Sir Owen recalls many instances of male bonding on display in the Mr. Green series. There is the friendship between Julian and Nick in *Death to Slow Music*, Palmer's rapport with Mr. Green in *The Rich Die Hard* and the fraternity between Wilburfoss and Meadows in *The Moonflower*. One might even see a parallel in the relationship between Nichols and his faithful secretary Ted, the author's advisor and confidante throughout the writing of each of his detective novels. Ted, Nichols explains in his foreword to *Death to Slow Music*, was chosen for "two special merits—a meticulous regard for detail and an exceptionally sensitive and revealing face." We learn that when Ted's face darkens and Nichols tells him "you've put on your expression," the author knows that his proffered idea is no good or worse— "ridiculous"—and he retreats into his study to think of something else.

248   Part Two: Skeleton Keys

Pervading the Horatio Green mystery series are moments when vulnerable men are seen neither as weak nor powerless, but as fully human. The most powerful passages, those with the tenderest exchanges and the brightest humor, more often than not are saved for scenes that take place between two male characters. Nichols' men come to life when they abandon their masculine posturing and let their career facades drop. They seem capable of being their most expressive, their most honest and real selves when confiding in other men, who with luck prove true friends or commiserating soul mates in one respect or another.

Notes

1. With the exception of this preternaturally acute sense of smell, writes Bryan Connon in his biography of Nichols, "Mr. Green was an idealized portrait" of the author. "Mr. Green was a knowledgeable author and a lover of music and cats, had a sharp intellect without being an overt intellectual, a strong sense of humor, and was always even-tempered and mild-mannered, a perfect gentleman," notes Connon, before adding: "It was a self-portrait with which not all of his acquaintants would agree." Bryan Connon, *Beverley Nichols: A Life* (1991; repr., Portland, OR: Timber Press, 2000), 244.

2. Christopher Petkanas, "Fabulous Dead People | Beverley Nichols," *T Magazine*, New York Times, 12 Jan. 2011, http://tmagazine.blogs.nytimes.com/2011/01/12/fabulous-dead-people-beverley-nichols/?_r=0. Photographer and theater designer Cecil Beaton recalled listening with incredulity to Nichols' "accounts of male brothels and rough trade pick-ups, and 'where to go to pick up sailors, marines and guardsmen.'" Philip Hoare, *Noel Coward: A Biography* (1995; repr., Chicago: University of Chicago Press, 1998), 123.

Works Cited

The Detective Novels of Beverley Nichols

Death to Slow Music. London: Hutchinson, 1956.
The Moonflower. London: Hutchinson, 1955.
Murder by Request. London: Hutchinson, 1960.
No Man's Street. London: Hutchinson, 1954.
The Rich Die Hard. London: Hutchinson, 1957.

Additional Works Cited

Connon, Bryan. *Beverley Nichols: A Life.* 1991. Reprint, Portland, OR: Timber Press, 2000.
Hoare, Philip. *Noel Coward: A Biography* 1995. Reprint, Chicago: University of Chicago Press, 1998.
Petkanas, Christopher. "Fabulous Dead People | Beverley Nichols." 12 Jan. 2011. *T Magazine. New York Times.* At http://tmagazine.blogs.nytimes.com/2011/01/12/fabulous-dead-people-beverley-nichols/?_r=0.

More Than Fiction
Troublesome Themes in the Life and Writing of Nancy Spain

BRUCE SHAW

Nancy Brooker Spain was born in Newcastle-upon-Tyne on September 13, 1917, and met her untimely death in a light aircraft accident on March 21, 1964, while en route to attend the Grand National, together with Joan Werner Laurie, her partner of fourteen years, and several other individuals. She was forty-six years old, a time of life by which many people have established careers and relationships, often facing mid-life crises of some sort, but might expect another twenty years or more of productive work before retirement.

Spain's writing came to my attention while I was researching leading British crime humorists of the Golden Age. In *Jolly Good Detecting* (2014), I placed her as the fourth of the "Best of the Farceurs" after Margery Allingham, John Dickson Carr and Edmund Crispin. Her detective novels are satirical, puzzle-solving romps full of puns, characters with unusual names (following an old tradition Dickensian and earlier), camp portraits (of perhaps insider gay and lesbian origins), and melodrama. Her crime writing career took up little more than a decade, at which point she stops abruptly. Her last crime novel, an inchoate effort titled *The Kat Strikes*, was published in 1955. By then, evidently, her heart was no longer in it. According to Spain in her autobiographical volume *A Funny Thing Happened on the Way*, she wrote the "thriller" when living in the house she had built on the Greek island of Skiathos. Arguably, she was distracted at the time because the house proved an expensive white elephant that had to be sold at a loss, in the sale of which for an obscure reason she included the typewriter on which she had written the book.

The three autobiographies are more evenly spaced: the first, *Thank You, Nelson* in 1945, *Why I'm Not a Millionaire* eleven years later in 1956, and eight years later *A Funny Thing Happened on the Way* in 1964, the year that she died. A gap of approximately ten years or a little less seems reasonable for autobiographical updates. The two biographies in 1948 and 1953 respectively, on Mrs Beeton, writer of cookbook fame and Eleanor Tennant, are familial and hero-worshipping. Beeton is Nancy's grandmother's sister, and Eleanor Tennant a tennis player who coached Hollywood celebrities such as David Niven and Carole Lombard, the latter said to have supplied the nickname "Teach" to their coach, hence Spain's title *Teach Tennant*.

Contrary to a first impression, Nancy Spain's oeuvre does not cease with *The Kat Strikes*. Spain switched to children's books and annuals: *The Tiger Who Saved the Train*, *The Tiger Who Couldn't Eat Meat*, and *My Boy Mo*, all published in 1959, four years after Nancy stopped writing her crime series and seven years after the birth of her son Tom. Tom, then, was a three year old toddler about the time Nancy ended her crime writing. The annuals came out in 1962 and 1963.

Journalism was Nancy Spain's chief profession. She wrote her crime tales while she was with several print businesses: as *Daily Express* columnist and book critic; as contributor to the original *She* magazine founded by Joan Laurie; in *News of the World*; and on the radio programs *Women's Hour*, *My Word!* and *Juke Box Jury*. Elements of her personal and professional life creep regularly into her fiction. For example, in *Murder, Bless It* (1948) a minor character, Miss Novello, tells Natasha's daughter Pamela, that she "ran a camp paper in Chicago ... with a friend. Called *City Life*," an obvious allusion to *She* magazine.

Nancy Spain's liking for people, particularly celebrities, comes through in her fiction, where the emphasis is as much on character sketches as it is on the crime of murder. In a short dedication to the Bouverie House edition of *Poison in Play* (1945), as well as the standard disclaimer that the tale and its characters are fictional, Spain addresses "Dear Kay-Kay," writing that she and her dedicatee both like best murder stories of "the kind where the characters and background are more important than the crime itself." Kay Jones "had become Nancy's closest friend" when Nancy was in the Women's Royal Naval Service in 1943. As First Officer, Jones headed the recruitment and applications department of the WRNS, where she helped out Nancy on several occasions, for example giving her a lighter, more manageable work load in the office and delivering asthma remedies when Spain was laid up in the Hospital for Women in Vincent Square, and where Spain met briefly with Rating Werner Laurie, a woman she was destined to see more of seven years later.

In her public role as a journalist writing columns for newspapers, and the partying that went on in the background, Nancy Spain led a flamboyant lifestyle. She liked to mix with a coterie of writers and the wealthy who were often eccentric, many gay and lesbian (the latter with whom Nancy had numerous affairs), or bisexual (Nancy and Joan, it might be argued). She affected the wearing of trousers and other "mannish" attire, a practice dating from her schooldays and reappearing in characters in the novels. But she could switch in one day from jeans and shirt to a standard black cocktail dress. It depended on the occasion and the company.

* * *

There is a vexed side to Nancy Spain, an unfortunate trait of disorganization and lack of forethought, not only in some of her later writing but also in her face-to-face encounters with literati and others. She is reported in the Wikipedia as having "a scatty style of column-writing" that got her and her newspaper into trouble more than once, notably in two successful libel suits brought against the paper by Evelyn Waugh (whom she is said to have admired). There is her flawed novel *The Kat Strikes* and disorganization in the autobiographies, particularly *A Funny Thing Happened on the Way* in which the chronology is haphazard, to say the least, and difficult to reconstruct from context.

In her own words, Spain was "black-balled" from Britain's Detection Club after running afoul of one of its members, Christianna Brand, who used such epithets against her as "Little Nothing Sacred" and "Little Spoil-Sport." Whether Brand spoke in wit or malice is not clear. Nancy reports herself as "a frivolous person" in *Why I'm Not a Millionaire* and Brand's lambasting as a joke against herself for careless plotting in her stories and as a fault of character from childhood at Roedean School for Girls, but I think it hurt her too.

On the other hand, Nancy Spain had many friends, valued them highly and cared a great deal about what they thought of her. By her own admission, she was unsure of herself, agonized over her character faults real or imagined, and to a large extent endeavored to hide them behind an extrovert style that was probably not all play-acting. Spain projects these feelings into her characters. For instance, Natasha Nevkorina, the beautiful and socially poised extrovert, is described at one point in *Murder, Bless It* as: "(like everyone worth anything at all) ... subject to appalling fits of meaningless depression."

Nancy wore her heart on her sleeve, especially in the autobiographies, in her admiration for several women partners or would-be partners. She idolized Joan Werner Laurie, saying that Joan was the best thing that ever happened to her, and contrasts Joan's steady, organizational abilities against her own slapdash ways. In a panegyric on Joan Laurie in *Why I'm Not a Millionaire*, Spain writes:

> Until I met Jonnie [Nancy's pet name for Joan Laurie] I was a miserable sort of creature, a failure, hating everybody, living in a sort of ivory tower of work, refusing to allow Real Life in the shape of Family Life to intrude on me at all.... On the day that I began to make judgments with Jonnie's hot, beautifully controlled mind assisting me, the whole pattern of

my behaviour changed.... Jonnie and Nicky awakened my fondness for humanity, which had lain hidden for so long; hidden away under a sort of barrage of smart attempts at wit and brisk repartee and clever little detective books.

On the whole we tend to place our beloveds on a pedestal. Joan Laurie was not always what Nancy makes her out to be. What Nancy perceives as a "hot beautifully controlled mind" was a very different matter to others who worked under Laurie. "While people were drawn to Nancy, so warm and funny, Joan kept the world at bay," notes Rachel Cooke. "She was cool and steely and rather humourless. At work she could be terrifying: a stickler, and a martinet. When the internal telephone rang three times—the signal that Miss Laurie was on the line—her staff would shiver inwardly."

* * *

If we believe Nancy, she and Joan led an idyllic companionship, but it was a domestic arrangement that the critic Ralph Wood implies has a "darker side." Wood's evaluation of Nancy's eighth novel, *Not Wanted on Voyage* (1951), touches upon a mystery difficult to unravel. Ralph Wood writes:

> Nancy Spain's biographical notes say she had a son by Philip Youngman Carter, Margery Allingham's husband. The boy was brought up as the youngest son of Joan Werner Laurie, Spain's partner. A character in "Not Wanted on Voyage," an author, has a neurotic lover who cannot have her own children. So his wife has allowed their daughter to be brought up as the lover's child.

The evidence I relied upon when I wrote *Jolly Good Detecting* was incomplete, and I made errors. I stated, incorrectly as it turned out, that a number of critics note that Spain lived in an open lesbian relationship with Joan Laurie and between them they raised Tommy, the product of Laurie's six-year marriage with Paul Seyler. I went on to say, "The other son, Nicholas ('Nicky'), was evidently the child begotten between Nancy Spain and Philip Youngman Carter, Margery Allingham's straying husband." I could not have got it more wrong. It was the other way around. (Charitably, we might call it a typo.)

Writing about Dorothy L. Sayers in an earlier chapter of *Jolly Good Detecting*, I get it right:

> In Nancy Spain's case she bore Thomas Bartholomew Laurie Seyler out of wedlock in 1952 after what was likely a one-night stand with Margery Allingham's husband Philip Youngman Carter. Spain and her partner Joan Werner Laurie included Tom in their family together with Joan's male child Nick Laurie, passing Tom off as Joan's child.

Back to page 211 and I say that the Wikipedia entry on "Nancy Spain" states that Nancy's son was "publicly unacknowledged during her lifetime." Furthermore, on the same page I cite Margery Allingham's biographer, Julia Jones: "While she talks about Nicky, her affair with Carter appears to have been a well-kept secret, for Margery Allingham did not identify Spain as one of Carter's paramours, as far as her biographer Julia Jones says." I add: "Spain in her autobiography does not allude to this while she records meeting Margery and Philip on several occasions." Barry Pike describes Philip Youngman Carter as "a gregarious and convivial man, who disliked solitude and greatly enjoyed entertaining his friends and associates," to which I observe that Carter was attractive to women and that Margery, who suffered manic-depression (bipolar condition), was often difficult to live with.

Margery Allingham had her suspicions from the early 1930s and by 1951 discovered her husband *in flagrante* in his London flat with an unnamed woman. Jones tells us that Nancy Spain visited Allingham's D'Arcy House: "Margery couldn't help wondering whether what Nancy really wanted was a book review for her magazine or the promise of a story for Joan Werner Laurie's *She*." Nancy Spain records those visits to Margery Allingham as well. This led me to say cautiously that it looked unlikely but not impossible that Nancy Spain was the woman Margery Allingham found with Philip Youngman Carter in his flat. If so, I added, Margery evidently did not hold a grudge, for fifteen years later, Jones tells us, she grieved for the deaths of Spain and Laurie.

While *Jolly Good Detecting* was in press, Rachel Cooke published *Her Brilliant Career* (2013), a study of ten notable mid-twentieth-century British career women. The book contains a more accurate account of the relationships among Joan, Nancy and the two boys. "Nicky" is Nicholas Werner Laurie, the son of Joan Werner Laurie by a soldier of fortune named Paul Seyler. Thomas Bartholomew Laurie Seyler, who was brought up in the joint household as Nicholas' younger brother, was in fact Nancy Spain's son. There was a sixteen year age difference between the two boys: Tom Seyler was born to Nancy Spain on 27 August 1952, while Nicholas Laurie Seyler was born to Joan Laurie on 3 March 1936.

Joan Laurie and Nancy Spain carried out a deceptive, if not illegal, act by falsifying the birth certificate. As Cooke says:

It was Joan who registered the birth.... The boy's father was recorded as Paul Clifford Seyler, a cattle rancher of Buenos Aires—a double falsehood, given that the man in question had been dead for two years. The baby's mother was named as Anne Brooker Seyler, formerly Brooker—in other words, a fictitious character with elements of both women's names.

The subterfuge led to a complication after their deaths:

When two people with interchangeable wills die at the same time, the law decrees that whoever was the oldest at the moment of their deaths died first. Nancy, then, had died first. Her estate had therefore passed to Joan, with the result that it would now pass to Nick as Joan's eldest child. Tom would get nothing, nor had any provision been made for his guardianship. In the end.... Nick was prevailed upon to share, and two separate trust funds were established.

Because responsibility for Tom was uncertain in the family, no one was willing to take him on, and in the end he was placed with his school head teacher, a man given to fits of rage who was clearly an unsuitable foster father. Matters became even more complicated when several women who had been Nancy's lovers "came out of the woodwork," as Cooke puts it, claiming interests in the properties they and Nancy had co-owned, for "Nancy had a small portfolio of secret love nests."

Cooke says that Tom was not told his mother's identity until he was nineteen when one of the estate's trustees divulged the secret. Nick had known about this since just after the air crash, perhaps because he was older. Nick felt at first hurt that he had not been told by Joan and Nancy, and after the passing of many years became angry about it. Tom for his part was relieved to learn the truth because he loved Nancy more, and subsequently he began personal enquiries into the identity of his father. Eventually Nancy Spain's doctor Nelly Newman told him that the man he was searching for had been the husband of Margery Allingham. Julia Jones reports this as well, in an Afterword to the 2009 edition of *The Adventures of Margery Allingham*. Tom followed this up, read Allingham's profile in *Who's Who*, and found that Margery's husband was Pip Youngman Carter who died in 1969. Nelly confirmed this, whereupon Tom Seyler changed his surname to Carter.

Rachel Cooke cries, "Oh the layers of misery that are here," refers to Nancy Spain's usual effusive style on Allignham in *Why I'm Not a Millionaire*, and wonders whether this is cruel, brazen or only "the result of Nancy's willed absent-mindedness." Nancy maintained this subterfuge/absent-mindedness to the end, although she was not to know it, in *A Funny Thing Happened on the Way*, finished within days before the aircraft accident. In it, Tom is referred to by the nickname "Bodge" and as "Jonnie's younger son." Returning to Cooke: "As for Tom, his life was not easy. After university he had a series of breakdowns and spent the rest of his life struggling with mental illness. He died in 2012 [aged sixty] in the bathroom of the psychiatric wing of Yeovil District Hospital."

Julia Jones revisits this troublesome theme in her essay "Intuition's Reckless Compass," implying that one of the pitfalls in being a literary biographer is that new information comes to light after one's work has gone to press and publication, not to mention sometimes ethical questions. This cannot have been easy for Julia Jones because Tom Carter had become a valued personal friend, one thinks during Jones' research. Jones' article is contained in Curtis Evans' collection *Mysteries Unlocked*, published in 2012, apparently overlapping Cooke's *Her Brilliant Career* and my *Jolly Good Detecting* a year later. (Because of the close publication dates, Jones missed Cooke and I missed Jones!)

Jones notes that Margery Allingham's sister Joyce, who was Jones' chief informant, was unaware of Tom's identity and was "shocked, upset, uncertain how to react" when it came out through two leaks. Joyce was reassured by the literary executor of Youngman Carter's estate that all was well. The first leak was to a BBC researcher, Natalie Wheen, for a radio program in 1993. Evidently, Wheen could not account to Jones why she left out Pip Youngman Carter's name in the broadcast (the focus was on Spain's motherhood) but that she encountered "surprising levels of hostility" when she did the research. Did the hostility come from Tom Carter who (see above), "had a reputation as someone odd and possibly difficult?" Much later, the *Daily Telegraph* published a leaked preview from Rose Collis' *A Trouser-Wearing Character: The Life and Times of Nancy Spain* (1997).

There is a third factor in Julia Jones' analysis which we can add to those of ethical matters and the difficulties of being a biographer: the relationship between an author's fiction and their real-life experience. Jones was alerted to this when she found what appear to be links between characterization in Margery Allingham's novel *The China Governess* (1963) and Tom Carter's history. Jones wonders whether Margery Allingham really knew of her husband Pip's misbehavior with Nancy Spain and its result but preferred to fictionalize it in *The China Governess*.

* * *

All composition is in a sense autobiographical because it comes from a writer's mind, so when we notice the recurrence of the same themes, favorite words and phrases in a series of works we can be fairly safe in supposing that something is up. In Nancy Spain's case, dominant themes are the depiction of child characters in the crime stories together with complicated interpersonal relationships having to do with companionship and marriage, and underlying lesbian elements with more overt gay (male) elements. They appear satirized alongside many other social mores, different human types and national habits. Some human behavior is depicted in madcap fashion, as in the literally riotous fracas at the end of *Cinderella Goes to the Morgue* (1950). Spain's slapstick is one reason why I rank her along with John Dickson Carr and Edmund Crispin, who use the form too.

Spain is at her most acerbic in woman-to-woman encounters. In *Death Goes on Skis* (1949), a character of the mannish sort is Toddy, described as: "a tough, gentlemanly young woman in Glastonbury boots with a polished Eton crop." She becomes the object of another woman's venom through which the author's personal dilemma shines:

"Why can't you be like everybody *else*?" said Regan passionately. "And get married? And have children?"

"*Kiddies*...," said Toddy in a tone of withering disgust."

Much later in the novel we read what sounds very like Nancy's painful self-assessment: "Toddy, in spite of her bluff, masculine appearance, was not the forthright, open-hearted character she appeared to be. Hers was a warped, subtle, tortuous nature."

Nancy Spain's generalized dislike of young children appears in the autobiographies and crime novels especially, and I think verges upon outright hatred. One but more usually two or more children are described as little horrors, continually getting sick, injured or misbehaving. In *Murder, Bless It*, "little Niall and Mopsie Niall ... ran, shouting, like insane dwarfs, up and down the bus." Near the close of the novel one of the adults, a misanthrope named Polygon, kicks the male child hard. As far as I recall, this is the only physical violence visited upon a child in the novels by an adult. Violence among children, however, is rife. It recurs in an unlikely place, the short story Spain contributed to a collection of ghost stories edited by Lady Cynthia Asquith, "The Bewilderment of Snake McKoy" (1956):

> School sports in England are a desperate business. While the tiny tots are slaughtering one another in the three-legged race, the parents are expected to mullarky around with the teachers, always keeping a civil tongue in the head. So I found myself with Madam Head Teacher, telling me about Butch's lack of discipline.

Butch is a girl child. The passage is comparable to that found in *Poison for Teacher* in which is described an invented sport called Bally Netball.

Nancy Spain stopped writing the crime novels through which her greatest dislike of young children is expressed in 1955, the publication date of *The Kat Strikes* and also the year in which her son Tom reaches the age of three. I think that when faced with the role of motherhood Nancy found it not all bad. She confesses this in *Why I'm Not a Millionaire*, but we have to note that she continues with the deception that Tom is Joan's son and not her own:

> Thomas Bartholomew Laurie Seyler was probably the most important of all. For on my fondness for Tommy, the baby whom I have seen grow up to become a prospering boy now four years old, depends the remainder of the revolution in my heart that makes me fond of children, and therefore, being fond of children, fond of people, too.

One might think that the first three years of Tom's early childhood may have been a little trying considering Nancy's daily work routine. In *Why I'm Not a Millionaire* (232) she explains:

> I have got into the habit of getting up at five a.m. to work. This is surprisingly enjoyable, particularly in the summer.... I work until seven, when I am always so ragingly hungry that I go and get myself breakfast. This regime, carried out faithfully, morning after morning, produces the necessary tight string of continuity to finish a long piece of work like a book. So after breakfast I have a whole ordinary day left for broadcasting, journalism, answering the bloody telephone and meeting people. This is the way that I managed to finish two detective novels, two books for children (and I illustrated them myself, too, which I deeply enjoyed) a short novel, various magazine stories and this book. In the daytime I was writing my stuff for the *Daily Express*, SHE and working on various programmes for the B.B.C.

Where did the responsibilities of looking after an infant fit in with this demanding schedule? Perhaps Joan Laurie took up a lot of the slack, but she too would have been very busy, running the magazine. *Not Wanted on Voyage* (1951) and *Out Damned Tot* (1952) were written in those years so I think Nancy's mixed feelings about very young children still held sway. Yet Cooke observes (above) that Thomas found Nancy the more caring of his two mothers. The reason why Nancy made such a heart-hearted attempt on "Kat" and turned to writing books to amuse young children (1959, when Tom is seven) looks like a further step into motherhood, an important one considering that not all mothers write books for their progeny.

Nancy Spain's practice of disowning the child while doing everything else to give the growing person economic and quasi-family support might be explained by her commitment to journalism and the socializing that accompanied it, as well as by society's disapproval of single mothers in those years, or shame at having been compromised in her lesbian partnership with Joan Werner Laurie, not to mention her affairs with other women. All of this appears somehow enmeshed with a virtually pathological hatred of children that might have its roots in her own childhood experiences on the school grounds of Roedean. It found expression over again in her writing, and especially in the crime novels, and softened in the end, one might guess, as motherhood grew upon her.

WORKS CITED

Allingham, Margery. *The China Governess.* London: Heinemann, 1963.
Asquith, Lady Cynthia, ed. *The (2nd) Second Ghost Book (2).* London: Pan, 1961.
"Bourse (Paris Métro)." *Wikipedia, The Free Encyclopedia.*
"Cecil Beaton: The Randy Dandy of Photography & Fashion." *The Selvedge Yard: A Historical Record of Artistry, Anarchy, Alchemy & Authenticity.* At http://thes elvedgeyard.wordpress.com/2009/04/18/cecil-beaton-the-randy-dandy-of-photography-fashion/.
Classic Crime Fiction. "Nancy Spain Bibliography." At http://www.classiccrimefiction.com/nancy-spain.htm.
Collis, Rose. *Lesbian Portraits.* M. Q. Publishers, 1997.
_____. *A Trouser-Wearing Character: The Life and Times of Nancy Spain.* London: Cassell, 1997.
Contrasola. "LESBIAN PORTRAITS (14) Joan Werner Laurie and Nancy Spain—SHE Magazine." Blog, 28, 2010. [Extract from Rose Collis 1997.] At http://contrasola.blogspot.com/2010/10/lesbian-portrets-14-joan-werner-laurie.html?zx=9ceecfd d659fa095.
Cooke, Rachel. *Her Brilliant Career: Ten Extraordinary Women of the Fifties.* London: Virago, 2013.
Evans, Curt J. "Two by NANCY SPAIN." At http://mysteryfile.com/blog/?p=7630.
Fisher, L. R. Review of Poison for Teacher. Amazon.com. At http://www.amazon.co.uk/Poison-Teacher-Lesbian-Landmarks-Nancy/dp/1853817465/ref=sr_1_1?s= books&ie=UTF8&qid=1308017960&sr=1-1

Hennegan, Alison. "Introduction" (1993) to Nancy Spain, *Poison for Teacher*. London: Virago, 1949/1004. pp. ix–xvii.
Jones, Julia. *The Adventures of Margery Allingham*. Essex: Golden Duck, 1991/2009.
_____. "Intuition's Reckless Compass: Margery Allingham's *The China Governess* and the Problem of Literary Biography." In Curtis Evans, ed., *Mysteries Unlocked: Essays in Honor of Douglas G. Greene*. Jefferson, NC: McFarland, 2012. pp. 122–132.
Pike, Barry A. "Philip Youngman Carter." The Margery Allingham Society. ND/ c. 2009. At http://www.margeryallingham.org.uk/philip.htm
Shaw, Bruce. *Jolly Good Detecting: Humor in English Crime Fiction of the Golden Age*. Jefferson, NC: McFarland, 2014.
Spain, Nancy. "The Bewilderment of Snake McKoy." In Lady Cynthia Asquith, ed., *The Second Ghost Book*. London: Pan, 1961.
_____. *Cinderella Goes to the Morgue: An Entertainment*. 1950. Reprint, London: World, 1963.
_____. *Death Before Wicket*. London: Hutchinson, 1945.
_____. *Death Goes on Skis*. London: Hutchinson, 1949.
_____. *A Funny Thing Happened on the Way*. London: Hutchinson, May 1964.
_____. *The Kat Strikes*. London: Hutchinson, 1955.
_____. *Murder Bless It*. London: Hutchinson, 1948.
_____. *My Boy Mo*. London: Hutchinson, 1959.
_____. *Not Wanted on Voyage*. 1951. Reprint, Harmondsworth: Penguin, 1956.
_____. *Out Damned Tot*. London: Hutchinson, 1952.
_____. *Poison for Teacher*. 1949. Reprint, London: Virago, 2004.
_____. *Poison in Play*. London: Bouverie House (Hutchinson), 1945.
_____. *R in the Month*. London: Hutchinson, 1950.
_____. *The Saturday Book 15*. London: Hutchinson, 1955.
_____. *The Tiger Who Couldn't Eat Meat*. London: Max Parrish, 1959.
_____. *The Tiger Who Saved the Train*. London: Max Parrish, 1959.
_____. *Why I'm Not a Millionaire: An Autobiography*. London: Hutchison, 1957.
_____, ed. *The Beaver Annual*. London: Fairhaven, 1962.
_____, ed. *The Butlin Beaver Annual No. 2*. London: Fairhaven, 1963.
"Spain, Nancy–Murder, Bless It (1948)." http://gadetection.pbworks.com/w/page/7931556/Spain, Nancy.
Wood, Ralph. "Not Wanted on Voyage (1951)." At http://gadetection.pbworks.com/w/page/7931262/Not-Wanted-on-Voyage.

Man to Man
The Two-Men Theme in the Novels of Patricia Highsmith

NICK JONES

"The theme I have used over and over again in my novels is the relationship between two men," wrote Patricia Highsmith in her guidebook for budding writers, *Plotting and Writing Suspense Fiction* (1966, revised 1981), pointing to *Strangers on a Train* (her debut, 1950), *The Blunderer* (1954), *The Talented Mr. Ripley* (1955), *A Game for the Living* (1958), *The Two Faces of January* (1964) and (to an extent) *The Glass Cell* (1964) as examples of the "two-men theme." ("[S]even of my eleven novels," Highsmith put it at the time.) It was a theme she would return to thereafter as well, in *Those Who Walk Away* (1967) and four further Tom Ripley novels—*Ripley Under Ground* (1970), *Ripley's Game* (1974), *The Boy Who Followed Ripley* (1980) and *Ripley Under Water* (1991)—with elements of it appearing in *The Tremor of Forgery* (1969), *A Dog's Ransom* (1972) and others of her books.

Highsmith is typically unforthcoming in *Plotting and Writing Suspense Fiction* as to why the two-men theme is such a feature of her work, reasoning, "Themes cannot be sought after or strained for; they appear"; but the dynamics which inform that theme are also those that characterize much of her work and help to make that work so queasily compelling: the fluidity of identity, the nature of obsession and the tension between attraction and repulsion. All those are evident in her canon right from the start with *Strangers on a Train*, wherein Guy Haines is both disgusted and fascinated by Charles Anthony Bruno (whom, Highsmith later admitted on the November 11, 1976, edition of BBC2's *The Book Programme*, she based on "a very spoilt boy" she had met in Texas when she was seventeen—"really quite a psychopath"). When Bruno first raises the notion of swapping murders, Guy muses: "All he despised.... Bruno represented. All the things he would not want to be, Bruno was, or would become." And yet despite himself Guy likes Bruno—indeed, by the time he finally decides to kill Bruno's father, he's forced to admit that he's "like Bruno," that "Bruno was like himself"—and even: "He loved Bruno."

The obsessive male relationships that Highsmith delineates in her novels are frequently the catalysts for terrible acts—chiefly murder but also mutilation, deception, forgery and blackmail. Yet Highsmith is not especially judgmental about these acts or the men who perpetrate them. Morality is a malleable concept in the Highsmith universe. While Guy Haines and *The Blunderer*'s Walter Stackhouse meet sticky ends (in markedly different ways), *The Glass Cell*'s Philip Carter and *The Talented Mr. Ripley*'s Tom Ripley manage to evade "justice." Indeed, Highsmith's sympathies could be said to be more aligned with those of her protagonists who get away with it than those who get their collars felt (or worse).

Tom Ripley is the clearest example of this—a swindling murderer who not only gets off scot-free in his debut novel but proceeds to do so in four sequels too. Of all her male leads, Tom was the one Highsmith most identified with; later novels in the five-book Ripliad are littered with opinions and asides—Tom's frustration at the haphazard nature of the telephone service in France (where Highsmith lived for a time), his thoughts on the architectural deficiencies of the Pompidou center (which in *The Boy Who Followed Ripley* he compares to a blow-up doll), his politics (left-wing)—that are ostensibly Tom's but recognizably those of his creator, while Highsmith was even known to sign letters to friends "Tom." She said of *The Talented Mr. Ripley* in *Plotting and Writing Suspense Fiction*: "No book was easier for me to write, and I often had the feeling Ripley was writing it and I was merely typing."

The male relationship at the core of *The Talented Mr. Ripley* is that between Tom, who at the outset of the novel is a twenty-five-year-old purposeless New Yorker engaged in a half-hearted IRS scam, and Dickie Greenleaf, the idle, itinerant, wealthy former college associate of Tom's whose father tasks Tom with travelling to the Italian coastal town of Mongibello in order to try and convince Dickie to return home. As with *Strangers on a Train*, there is a form of love at the heart, or at least center, of this relationship. It is Dickie's spurning of Tom's love—epitomized by the scene in which Dickie catches Tom trying on his clothes—and his disgust at Tom's warped morality—characterized by Tom's fascination with Carlo, an Italian criminal who proposes a bizarre drug-smuggling-by-corpse scheme (a scheme Highsmith revealed in *Plotting and Writing Suspense Fiction* was originally to have formed the basis of the plot)—that drive Tom to kill Dickie. But Tom is in love with the *idea* of Dickie rather than with Dickie himself; he covets Dickie's comfortable lifestyle and ready access to European high culture—hence why he dresses up as Dickie and eventually assumes his identity—and idealizes him, choosing to ignore the vain, self-centered reality of who Dickie actually is, until the episode with Carlo finally forces him to confront the truth:

> He stared at Dickie's blue eyes that were still frowning, the sun-bleached eyebrows white and the eyes themselves shining and empty, nothing but little pieces of blue jelly with a black dot in them, meaningless, without relation to him. You were supposed to see the soul through the eyes, to see love through the eyes, the one place you could look at another human being and see what really went on inside, and in Dickie's eyes Tom saw nothing more now than he would have seen if he had looked at the hard, bloodless surface of a mirror. Tom felt a painful wrench in his breast, and he covered his face with his hands. It was as if Dickie had been suddenly snatched away from him. They were not friends. They didn't know each other. It struck Tom like a horrible truth, true for all time, true for the people he had known in the past and for those he would know in the future: each had stood and would stand before him, and he would know time and time again that he would never know them, and the worst was that there would always be illusion, for a time, that he did know them, and that he and they were completely in harmony and alike.

It is evident that it is not really love that causes Tom to fixate on Dickie but something darker: an absence in Tom's psychological make-up, a hole that he needs to fill, something missing in his persona. Herein resides the inexorable magnetic pull innate in all of the male relationships in Highsmith's novels. Romantic love—or what passes for it in the minds of Highsmith's protagonists—can only partly explain the transgressive and violent actions of Tom in *The Talented Mr. Ripley* or Guy and Bruno in *Strangers on a Train*; and there is little (romantic) love lost between Walter Stackhouse and Melchior Kimmel in *The Blunderer*, or Rydal Keener and Chester MacFarland in *The Two Faces of January*, or Ray Garrett and Edward Coleman in *Those Who Walk Away*. The men in these books are like separate halves of incomplete jigsaw puzzles, each missing vital constituent pieces, each representing something the other desires or needs, lacks or has lost.

For Walter Stackhouse, that desire is a similar one to Guy's in *Strangers on a Train*: the need to be rid of his wife, Clara, preferably by murderous means; and in the shape of Melchior Kimmel, who is suspected of murdering his own wife and yet remains at liberty, he finds a source of inspiration (although in the event Clara kills herself). For Rydal Keener, it is a desire for a little adventure and a baser desire for Chester McFarland's wife, Colette; but his interest in Chester is also informed by the fact that Chester reminds him of his domineering but now deceased father, another absence in his life. And for Ray Garrett, it is a raw, gaping wound that he cannot help but probe: the recent suicide of his wife, Peggy, as personified by his father-in-law, Coleman, whom Ray repeatedly seeks out and who in turn blames Ray for Peggy's death and intends to kill him.

In *Those Who Walk Away*, the dreadful gravity which anchors Highsmith's male relationships can be seen at its starkest. The dangerous fascination and accompanying animosity between Ray and Coleman is all-consuming and all-pervading, lasting the course of the book; there is no murder a la *The Talented Mr. Ripley* or *The Two Faces of January* to act as a pressure valve and turn the narrative in a new direction; the sole death, Peggy's, occurs before the novel opens. Instead we are presented with an extended game of cat and mouse in and around Venice, with Ray and Coleman continually prowling around the lagoon city on the hunt for one another, occasionally clashing violently but inconclusively, with a kind of cathartic fight at the climax which leaves as much unanswered as resolved.

What are we to make of the relationship between Ray and Coleman, or that between Rydal and Chester, or between Tom and Dickie, Stackhouse and Kimmel, Guy and Bruno and the rest—of this "two-men theme" that reoccurs so frequently in Highsmith's work? The temptation is to project onto the theme Highsmith's personal biography, to ascribe intentions and read into it things that might not necessarily be there. It is true, for instance, that Highsmith was known to idealize her female lovers in much the same way that Tom idealizes Dickie, and that she admired gay men and felt more comfortable with them than she did with gay women; and yet when Highsmith was so reticent about explaining her own work, it would be foolish to assign meaning to a theme that she herself steadfastly refused to illuminate. And in any case, it is not as though Highsmith felt she could only write about gay relationships obliquely—as if she were somehow afraid to tackle the subject head on: she did so directly, and arguably as autobiographically as she was ever to do so (albeit pseudonymously), in *The Price of Salt* (1952), her second novel (published under the alias Claire Morgan but eventually issued under her own name as *Carol* in 1990)—a novel that notably deals in similar themes of infatuation and obsession as her crime fiction and yet presents a relatively hopeful ending.

Perhaps a more fruitful line of enquiry may be found in Highsmith's literary influences. As her biographer Andrew Wilson points out, "...the themes and philosophical arguments that lie at the heart of her fiction reflect the bleak existentialist writings of Dostoevsky, Kierkegaard, Nietzsche, Kafka, Sartre and Camus, all of whom she read." She called Dostoevsky her "master," and was as fascinated by dualism—of which the two-men theme is a manifestation—as the author of *Crime and Punishment* was. According to Wilson, "She traced her fascination with duality and ambiguity back to her own childhood, acknowledging that the strands of love and hate which were woven through her character had their roots in her early relationship with her parents. Yet she knew that such dark, murky territory was a fertile breeding ground for her fiction." Another thematic influence was Proust, whose concept of, as Wilson puts it, "the illusory nature of love" can clearly be seen in Tom's idealizing of Dickie in *The Talented Mr. Ripley*.

"It often happens that a writer has a theme or a pattern that he uses over and over again in his novels," wrote Highsmith in *Plotting and Writing Suspense Fiction*. "He should be aware of this, not in a hampering way, but to exploit it well and to repeat it only deliberately." She maintained that themes "should be used to the fullest, because a writer will write better making use of what is, for some strange reason, innate." The two-men theme was one that Highsmith exploited repeatedly in her work, from some of her earliest published short stories ("Uncertain Treasure," published in the August 1943 issue of *Home & Food*, which centers on a cat-and-mouse pursuit around New York between a "cripple" and a bookkeeper over an unclaimed bag) to the last novel published in her lifetime (*Ripley Under Water*, which pits Tom Ripley against an equally twisted antagonist in the shape of his near-neighbor David Pritchard). Through it she was able to explore the things which interested and excited her: notions of identity and duality, of homosexuality and repression, of idealized love and unhinged hatred, of attraction and repulsion, of cruelty and madness, of forgery and dishonesty, of violence and abnormality, of morality and, rather more appositely, amorality. In different novels the two-men theme signifies some or sometimes all of these things; it is not in and of itself the destination, but rather the idiosyncratic vehicle via which Highsmith allows herself—and us—to tour her obsessions.

Highsmith was often winningly matter-of-fact when discussing her own work. "How can a writer answer the question of how does he write a book?" she queried in a piece for the H. R. F. Keating-edited *Whodunit? A Guide to Crime, Suspense & Spy Fiction* (1982), before adding: "A writer writes on enthusiasm, a rather embarrassing emotion to explain. Better just to write the book." As such, a few plausibly mundane and characteristically technical clues as to why she continually employed the device of two men becoming murderously infatuated with one another in her crime stories can be found in *Plotting and Writing Suspense Fiction*. Highsmith notes, "…I prefer the point of view of the main character, written in the third-person singular, and I might add masculine, as I have a feeling which I suppose is quite unfounded that women are not so active as men, and not so daring," before going on to state:

> I prefer two points of view in a novel, but I don't always have them … keeping a single point of view throughout a book, as I did in *The Talented Mr. Ripley*, increases the intensity of a story—and intensity can and should offset a possible monotony of a one-person viewpoint. Using two points of view—as I did in *Strangers on a Train*, of the two young men protagonists who are so different, and in *The Blunderer*, Walter and Kimmel, again vastly different people—can bring a very entertaining change of pace and mood. This is why I prefer the two-person point of view, if the story can possibly take it.

In the end, it is perhaps best left to a great admirer of Highsmith's to elucidate the elusive qualities of the two-men theme she so favored: Graham Greene, who in his foreword to the short story collection *Eleven* (1970; U.S.

title *The Snail-Watcher and Other Stories*) wrote of, in his words, "Miss Highsmith's dubious men":

> Actions are sudden and impromptu and the motives sometimes so inexplicable that we simply have to accept them on trust. I believe because it is impossible. Her characters are irrational, and they leap to life in their very lack of reason; suddenly we realize how unbelievably rational most fictional characters are as they lead their lives from A to Z, like commuters always taking the same train. The motives of these characters are never inexplicable because they are so drearily obvious. The characters are as flat as a mathematical symbol. We accepted them as real once, but when we look back at them from Miss Highsmith's side of the frontier, we realize that our world was not really as rational as all that.

WORKS CITED

Greene, Graham. Foreword to *Eleven*. London: William Heinemann, 1970.
Highsmith, Patricia. *The Blunderer*. London: Cresset Press, 1956.
_____. *Carol* (and Afterword to). 1952. Reprint, London: Bloomsbury, 1990.
_____. *Nothing That Meets the Eye: The Uncollected Stories of Patricia Highsmith*. London: Bloomsbury, 2005.
_____. "Not-Thinking with the Dishes." In H. R. F Keating, ed., *Whodunit? A Guide to Crime, Suspense & Spy Fiction*. London: Windward, 1982.
_____. *Plotting and Writing Suspense Fiction*. Bowling Green, OH: Poplar Press, 1983.
_____. *Strangers on a Train*. London: Cresset Press, 1950.
_____. *The Talented Mr. Ripley*. London: Cresset Press, 1957.
_____. *Those Who Walk Away*. London: William Heinemann, 1967.
_____. *The Two Faces of January*. London: William Heinemann, 1964.
Jones, Nick. "The Great Tom Ripley Reread, 1: The Talented Mr. Ripley." *Existential Ennui* (10 September 2012).
_____. "The Great Tom Ripley Reread, 4: The Boy Who Followed Ripley." *Existential Ennui* (7 March 2013).
_____. "Patricia Highsmith, Graham Greene and Eleven." *Existential Ennui* (23 June 2015).
_____. "Singular Points of View: Patricia Highsmith and A Dog's Ransom." *Existential Ennui* (18 June 2015).
_____. "Those Who Walk Away." *Existential Ennui* (20 June 2014).
Wilson, Andrew. *Beautiful Shadow: A Life of Patricia Highsmith*. London: Bloomsbury, 2003.

Kiss Kiss Bang Bang
Joseph Hansen's Known Homosexual

Josh Lanyon

"I did a couple of books that seemed to me to be better than okay. One of these was published in 1968 as *Known Homosexual*, and it was my first try at writing a mystery. It's in the book shops these days under the title *Pretty Boy Dead*. I still like it."—Joseph Hansen, *Bay Windows* interview, 1988

Six years before he penned *Fadeout* and changed the private detective sub-genre forever with the introduction of gay insurance investigator Dave Brandstetter, Joseph Hansen wrote a number of gay erotic quasi-literary works using the pseudonym James Colton (James Coulton in one instance). Though every one of these works had elements of a crime story, it was not until *Known Homosexual* in 1968 that Hansen took his shot at writing an actual mystery.

Or perhaps "who-dunnit" is the right term, for all three versions of this novel: *Known Homosexual*, *Stranger to Himself* and *Pretty Boy Dead*, are as much about character and identity as they are about figuring out who murdered beautiful but morally bankrupt Jesse Coy Randol.

Known Homosexual *(1968)*

The prologue begins like the opening reel of a neo-noir classic. A young black man, Steve Archer, awakens in an unfamiliar bed in an unfamiliar room. Another young man—a stranger to Steve—is sleeping soundly in a window seat overlooking a choked and overgrown garden. Steve doesn't remember the events of the last few hours. He knows only that he must get home to Coy, his lover: "He needed Coy Randol, needed him the way he needed air, food, water. He had to get home from wherever this was and tell him so, tell him that no matter what he'd done, Steve Archer couldn't live without him." In glorious if faded Technicolor we watch Steve leave the house, paying no attention to the address or the street as he winds his way down through the Hollywood Hills, "hibiscus bushes flaming with blossom crowding the sidewalks," arriving home to find the coroner's van leaving and the police waiting for him.

Coy is dead, murdered, after a loud and ugly fight the evening before. Steve is arrested and what follows is—again like a classic hard-boiled crime movie—a prolonged flashback of Steve's life leading to the moment of his arrest. In fact, ninety percent of the novel is told in retrospect.

The son of a well-to-do, upper middle-class family, nineteen-year-old Steve disappoints his strict, politically ambitious father when he impregnates Lacey, a white trash classmate. His father, disgusted by what he believes is yet another demonstration of Steve's animalistic sexual appetite and inability to stick to his own class and race, disowns him, and Steve, a budding playwright, must give up dreams of Stanford University to support his simple-minded and whorish bride.

Unsurprisingly, the marriage is not a success and Lacey eventually leaves him for their lesbian landlord. Steve gets another shot at success as a playwright, but his script is based too obviously on his own family, and his father threatens legal action. And so, at last having reached what he believes is rock bottom, Steve falls in with the charming and amoral Jesse Coy Randol, a religious student at Galilee College.

Steve Archer is Colton's only attempt at writing from the point of view of an African American. Though young black men often serve as romantic interests in Colton's work, and interracial romance is a frequent theme, *Known Homosexual* (in all its variants) is the only story where the lead character is not white. Nowadays there would likely be jibes about appropriation and authenticity, but in the 1960s this was groundbreaking stuff, a pioneering work into territory to which James Baldwin had laid claim.

All the more so because Colton makes no effort to whitewash Steve. As main characters go, Steve is not easy to like: arrogant, humorless and not exactly overflowing with empathy. He is often angry—and occasionally expresses that anger through physical abuse.

> Bernie said, "You're really a very corrupt person, aren't you, Steve? You're really empty." She fumbled a cigarette between her lips. The flame of the butane lighter trembled when she lit it, "Your generation makes me shudder."
>
> "Why?" Steve asked. "Because we look at what's there? We don't soften the focus? We don't add romantic violins to the soundtrack?"

Bernie is wrong. Despite his flaws, Steve is not corrupt. He is almost brutally honest. And he is not empty—though he also is not brimming with the milk of human kindness. It is easy to forget that he is a high school senior when the story begins, and that he does mature and evolve during the course of the novel. He learns from—and sometimes tries to fix—his mistakes. He has guts and integrity. Though born to affluence and privilege, he is not afraid of hard work.

Steve rejects his parents' most beloved sacred cows: wealth and respectability. He is closest to his god-fearing and down-to-earth grandmother, who regards the sacrifices and achievements of her offspring with skepticism similar to Steve's.

It helps to view *Known Homosexual* in historical—and sexual—context because Steve is very much a child of the Sixties, even if he is not noticeably politically aware. By 1968 the Age of Aquarius had dawned. The antiwar movement was in full swing and *Make Love Not War* was the battle cry of a generation. Free Love was not just a slogan on a t-shirt, it was a social movement. But the novel is written pre-Stonewall. In that sense, perhaps Steve's social attitudes *are* a political statement. He does not share the prejudices and hang-ups of his parents. He is unapologetically gay—which is not to say that he does not fear the very real consequences of arrest and disgrace.

It is impossible to consider this book without giving equal consideration to the extensive erotic content—nor would it make sense given that the sexual orientation of most of the characters is the only thing that separates them from the rest of the world. Colton—later Hansen—takes great pains and exerts great skill throughout the course of his career to make his point: *we are just like you.*

Known Homosexual was by far the most sexually explicit book Colton had written to date, and the extensive erotic content is both exuberant and evocative. Even the little throwaway lines are astonishing in their invention and lyricism:

> "Jimmy's mouth left his, and for half a second he saw Jimmy's cock standing, a naked angel, slipping back its gleaming hood."

And ...

> "They lay then, alongside, foot to head, cock to mouth, hands straying over each other's humid skins, and every muscle wire-tight, tried, tried for the prize, the shout of stars."

And ...

> "Coy cried out. His hands twitched like broken birds on Steve's shoulders. He kicked jerkily, rubbed his legs together, a cricket frantic to make a new kind of music."

This is by no means something as simple as porn. Barring its explicit sexual content, this was a novel that could have been published by any mainstream publisher of literary fiction. Brandon House was not a mainstream publisher, of course. In fact, they were a publisher of what we now call "vintage sleaze," but for a mainstream audience these erotic scenes would deliver a political wallop. In fact, by stressing their very normalcy Colton created something that could be viewed as downright subversive.

Unlike the haunted and harried gay characters—or caricatures—that had previously populated so much mystery fiction, Steve and Coy are handsome, healthy and mostly happy. The message for readers: there is no shame in sex between men—and no apology will be offered.

It is not being gay that gets Steve into such terrible trouble. It is loving Coy.

Coy Randol is another masterpiece of characterization. A blue-eyed, golden-haired boy with the face of an angel and a body made for sin. Coy is a liar, a cheat, a thief, a whore and a blackmailer ... but somehow Colton finesses this portrait of a male femme fatale so that we believe (even if we have trouble understanding why) Steve is crazy about him. Coy is funny and playful and free-spirited, he is loyal to Steve, whom he adores, and he too has nerve and strength of will. Coy even possesses a strange innocence. He is weirdly appealing, for all his flaws. But his flaws are myriad—and eventually prove fatal.

Religious hypocrisy is a frequent theme in Colton's—and later Hansen's—work, and Coy is the living incarnation of all that is wrong with organized religion. A former child preacher, this student of divinity is a consummate con artist. The catch is he has partially conned himself too. He plans eventually to become a rich television evangelist and live in a mansion like a former mentor, Brother Olin Swett.

There are a few passages ominous in their foreshadowing:

> Then Steve remembered and felt cold. The story had been in the papers—how Brother Olin Swett had died. The father of a fourteen-year-old boy had caught them in a motel room and shot the evangelist full of holes. Steve studied Coy.
> "It doesn't shake you," he wondered, "the idea of making a racket out of it?"
> "Religion?" Coy asked. "Oh, Steve, it won't be me. They made a racket out of it a long time ago."

When Coy's patron, Sister Myra Lusk, a successful radio evangelist, is forced to cut off Coy's financial support, he turns to hustling to supplement his income. Steve finds out, beats him to a pulp, then takes a second job pumping gas to get them out of debt. When he discovers Coy is attempting to blackmail one of their acquaintances, he finally ends their relationship. And while he is off getting drunk and blacking out, Coy is murdered. Is it any wonder the police immediately suspect Steve?

In the final eighth of the book Steve is alibied by Billy Rice, the "deer-eyed" young man he went home with the night Coy was murdered. Steve sets out to find Coy's killer. Frankly, his motive for doing so is a bit weak and he does not investigate so much as hurl accusations and then listen to all the potential suspects explain how they arrived in quick succession at his apartment only to find Coy already dead. The fact that every suspect has a believable (by fictional standards) motive for wanting Coy out of the way is a feat in itself.

By speedy process of elimination, Steve figures out that the only possible murderer is, in fact, Sister Myra Lusk, Coy's religious benefactress. In a final and admittedly melodramatic scene, Steve confronts Myra while she is on the air hosting her radio show, and she admits she slew Coy in a fit of righteous indignation after discovering that he was having carnal relations outside of wedlock—and with a "black beast of Sodom" to boot.

Steve's rushed investigation of suspects is the weakest section of the book. However, the structural flaw is inevitable given how much page time has been devoted to Steve's life and love affair with Coy. And, after all, the real focus of the book is Steve and his circuitous journey to manhood.

Stranger to Himself *(1977)*

Nine years later the freshly edited *Stranger to Himself* was published by Major Books under Joseph Hansen's own name. With the exception of a couple of short stories, it is the only Colton work he reclaimed.

The most obvious change was the removal of most of the explicit erotic content.

There are a number of possible reasons for this. The most obvious is that it is all but impossible to write about sex and be taken seriously as a mystery novelist, and by 1977 Hansen had carved out a name for himself as a highly respected writer of crime fiction in the tradition of Ross Macdonald or even Raymond Chandler.

The book does not suffer for the pruning. The sex scenes, though vibrant, were never emotional turning points and the dialog was always of the "oooh baby" variety. What remains is what is important. The glimpses of Steve and Coy's very ordinary and appealing domestic life:

> They carried the drinks into the living room where winter sunlight poured through the French windows. Coy put a Montovani record on the stereo. The couch had clean lines. It was upholstered in nubby, expensive beige. Coy sat at one end, legs tucked under him like a girl. Steve dropped down next to him. There was a low, plain rectangular coffee table, Danish teak. Steve stretched his legs across it, barefoot. He looked at Coy, eyebrows raised.
> "Okay?"
> "It's your table as much as mine," Coy smiled.

This is true intimacy, and one of a number of scenes far more revealing and romantic than any reference to "naked angels" or "shout of stars."

One of the things that struck me in reading *Stranger to Himself* was the delicate characterization of Billy Rice. Billy is the boy in the room where Steve wakes up at the start of the novel. And he is the boy Steve ends up with at novel's end. He has probably the least page time of any character in the novel, and yet he is key.

He is Steve's salvation. And unlike Steve and Coy, Billy is unable to "pass" as anything but gay: "On a cushioned seat under the window a boy lay asleep, one knee up, one arm flung out, a fragile-looking kid of nineteen or twenty, sunburned skin, sunstreaked brown hair, genitals neat in their shadowy notch."

Steve instinctively recognizes Billy as "a nice enough faggot," and the cops instantly label him a "flit with guts." Billy collects Bette Davis memorabilia, reads movie mags, and seems to live on his own in a crumbling Hollywood Hills mansion that has been sublet into apartments. But though we never get his backstory—or really any of his story—he is one of the most memorable characters in the novel. He demonstrates great courage, great generosity, and great kindness to Steve when Steve needs it most. In fact, Billy seems to represent a change in Steve's fortune—even if after their first meeting Steve dismisses Billy in favor of returning to Coy.

For all the tweaking Hansen does to various characters and dialog in *Stranger to Himself*, he does not change a single vowel of Billy's characterization.

Another point of interest is that Billy and Steve do not have sex. They are about to consummate their relationship at the novel's end. More, Billy has apparently been saving himself for Steve: "Billy set the tall green wet bottles on the dresser. He slid off his shorts. 'All I've minded was the wait.' He knelt on the bed. 'I wasn't cut out to be a nun.'"

Granted, this difference stands out more in *Known Homosexual* where Steve has sex with just about everyone *except* Billy, but from the first reference to what we later learn is a chivalrous distance and "genitals neat in their shadowy notch" it is obvious there is something special about this boy.

Most of the novel's other edits are stylistic. Nothing of substance changes. But neither do the abstracts of tone or mood or theme. Hansen seems to be merely fine-tuning his already carefully crafted prose. He adds a bit of exposition and reiterates a clue concerning Coy's religious medal, but essentially the alterations have to do with breaking up paragraphs, dramatic beats and little softenings of Steve's character.

"Forget it" becomes "'Forget it,' Steve said, appreciating the offer."

There also are a few dialog updates:

"Swinging" becomes "Far out."

"To get cozy with a Negro" becomes "To get cozy with a jig."

The final encounter with Jimmy Pike, the man whose seduction of both Steve and Lacey contributes to the collapse of their marriage, is slightly extended and Coy's funeral scene is expanded and embellished to great effect.

Some of the stylistic choices are questionable. The final line of the final chapter—"He slid steeply into darkness"—is removed and the chapter ends with Sister Myra gurgling, "Agh, agh…." One of the previous three "aghs" has been cut, a reminder of exactly how painstaking Hansen was over every single detail.

The next to last line of the novel also changes.

"I don't like people staring at me while I'm making out" becomes "I've taken a dislike to people staring at me while I'm making out."

The mass market cover of *Stranger to Himself* features two fully adult male disembodied heads, one white, one black, and a sexy looking girl with pigtails. The blurb reads: He was BLACK … He was HOMOSEXUAL … He was wanted for MURDER …

It sends a mixed message, to say the least.

The change in title is confusing as well. *Who* is the actual stranger to himself? Is it Steve or is it Coy? It is debatable whether either of them are really strangers to themselves. And is self-discovery the real point when the cover cites "Joseph Hansen author of *Troublemaker*"?

Pretty Boy Dead *(1984)*

Seven years later Gay Sunshine Press released the trade paperback novel *Pretty Boy Dead*, clarifying both genre, theme and audience. This time the cover features a black youth and a white—possibly napping but, given the title, likely dead—youth.

As far as text, the changes are all cosmetic tweaks, with Hansen reversing a few of his creative decisions in *Stranger to Himself*.

Steve's brusque "Forget it" is back.

The "He slid steeply into darkness" is back. And Myra gets her rule-of-three "aghs" again.

The somewhat artificial "I've taken a dislike to people staring at me" is retained, even though it is hard to picture anyone other than *Laura's* Waldo Lydecker spitting that one out *in flagrante delicto*.

What is intended by the closing lines remains a bit oblique. Men making love to men has proven a risky business, and it is probably no coincidence that a life-sized cutout photo of Bette Davis from *The Letter*—a movie about obsession, blackmail and murder—stands in the room. But the novel is not really about obsession or voyeurism. I am not certain that it even ultimately about identity, though I believe this was Hansen's original intent when he wrote *Known Homosexual*.

Given the minimal changes, it appears that Hansen was simply unhappy with how the novel had fared at Major Books and reclaimed his rights once they reverted in order to try one last time to get the book the audience he felt it deserved.

Unfortunately, the schism that makes *Pretty Boy Dead* such an interesting novel is what dilutes its power in the final analysis. Part murder mystery, part coming-of-age novel, part testament of gay life in the mid-to-late 1900s.... The book is all of these and yet it is not the best example of any of these—even by Colton. *Hang-Up* is a better mystery. *Lost on Twilight Road* is a better coming of age story. And any of the Brandstetter novels probably offer as incisive a portrait of gay life in the twentieth century.

The difficulty in pinning down what the novel is actually about is reflected in the disparate attempts at targeting an audience through title changes and different cover art.

But why *this* novel? Why did Hansen keep trying to find a new audience for this particular work? Is the answer something quite obvious: that Hansen believed *Known Homosexual* was the strongest of those early works and the most likely to click with his newfound audience?

Or was there something fundamentally and personally important about this novel? It is tempting to theorize that Steve Archer's journey possessed symbolic meaning or deep significance for its author, but that seems unlikely given that Hansen, the son of Midwestern farmers, would seem to have little or nothing in common with this particular protagonist.

But maybe that *is* the point. Was Colton reminding us that, like the characters in *Known Homosexual*, we are all too prone to base our understanding of any individual on one or two key facts—and are therefore never able see the complete picture?

Works Cited

Colton, James. *Hang-Up*. North Hollywood: Brandon House, 1969.
_____. *Known Homosexual*. North Hollywood: Brandon House, 1968.
_____. *Lost on Twilight Road*. Fresno: National Library, 1964.
Hansen, Joseph. *Pretty Boy Dead*. San Francisco: Gay Sunshine Press, 1984.
_____. *Stranger to Himself*. Canoga Park: Major Books, 1977.

I Am the Most!
Camping It Up in George Baxt's Pharoah Love Mystery Series

J. F. NORRIS

Pharoah Love. "That's a hell of a name for a detective, ain't it, man?" With those first words uttered by George Baxt's iconoclastic fictional detective, mysterydom would never be the same. For Pharoah Love has the distinction of representing the double whammy of two minority classes: he is black and he is unapologetically gay. Pharoah is a celebration of all that is hip and swinging. His speech is peppered with hipster Sixties slang, he calls everyone "cat" and he has no problem talking about sex. In fact in his first case, *A Queer Kind of Death* (1966), over the course of his unorthodox murder investigation Love stalks Seth Piro, lover of a young man who was electrocuted in his bathtub; meets him for a "date" in a gay bar; makes innuendoes about Seth's attractiveness; and encourages Seth's burgeoning friendship. Seth dreams about Pharaoh, and Pharoah fantasizes about Seth's naked body. As the men give into their desires and passions, they become locked in a relationship that disregards all police protocol.

A Queer Kind of Death was lauded for perhaps all the wrong reasons. Anthony Boucher in his oft-quoted June 12, 1966, *New York Times* book review said it was set in a "Manhattan subculture" populated with characters "wholly devoid of ethics or morality" and that "staid readers may well find it 'shocking.'" It may seem strange for him to have used such negative words to sing praises for Baxt's groundbreaking book, but Boucher was never known for being too freethinking about human sexuality. Rather he was more of a champion for ingenuity and originality in fiction writing, especially when he encountered a distinct crime fiction voice like Baxt's; he can be forgiven for being mildly condemning. To be sure, the characters in *A Queer Kind of Death* do behave unethically and at times immorally, but are they any different in their behavior from the characters in the work of Cornell Woolrich, Raymond Chandler or Gil Brewer? The only difference is that most of Baxt's characters are gay. How odd that straight fictional characters get away with betrayal, adultery, corruption, brutality, cruelty and a gamut of criminal activity, yet are rarely accused of being "wholly devoid of ethics or morality."

Were it to be reviewed today, Baxt's novel might be lauded with an array of newly positive traits for a story of this type: irreverent, bawdy, vulgar, sexually frank—all terms that sell fiction by the wheelbarrows full these days, and ironically all the kind of thing that addicts of noir and pulp crave. Tantalizing phrases like those Boucher used allowed skirting the matter of the book's overt sexuality, something which was necessary then to market it to a conservative reading audience, publishers not yet having perceived that there was a distinct and notable gay readership for this kind of mystery novel.

Boucher's problem is that he failed to be "in the know." The novel is imbued not with an absence of morality but a campy spirit and a wholly gay worldview where there are no real taboos. It never takes itself too seriously even when dealing with crimes as deadly serious as murder. *A Queer Kind of Death* may well be one of the earliest send-ups of a traditional detective novel, while also flirting with the concept of being the first gay noir. Despite Baxt's shameless camp humor and sardonic jokes there is a deadly serious edge to the story. Murder, betrayal and the revelation of dark secrets will be the undoing of the majority of the characters. In the final pages Pharoah and Seth will enter into an unthinkable pact that could only take place in a noir tale.

But what truly makes this novel a candidate for the label of gay noir is its unabashed eroticism of the male body. No *femme fatales* on display here, rather we have buff and uber-macho *homme fatales*. That Baxt never holds back in his discussion of gorgeous young hustlers who exploit their bodies and use men just as the traditional *femme fatales* use men is something that book reviewers of the 1960s would find uncomfortable for sure. Ben Bentley, the murder victim, is a handsome male model by way of male prostitution. He is repeatedly referred to as a whore and was known to use his body to win friends and influence people—mostly older, rich men. Open Ben's address book to the C section and you'll find a "familiar epithet" under which is a list of men's names followed by asterisk ratings. Under the F section, "headed by another familiar word" there are fifty-three names, some duplicates of the C list and many with red check marks next to them. In rummaging through his dead lover's belongings Seth also uncovers evidence of blackmail, a wad of bankbooks totaling over $60,000 in five different accounts and the beginnings of Ben's audacious autobiography titled *Available*. Then there's Adam Littlestorm, a Native American "caretaker" with the body of an Olympic athlete. Adam at one time compromised his dreams for a gold medal by becoming a masseur for wealthy businessmen and was not unwilling to perform a few extra favors or accept a few extra gifts. Pharoah riffs on this idea of trade—a gay slang word originally coined for men who sell their bodies. "Time to trade a lot of things. Protection traded for information. Pride traded for affection. Loneliness traded for love. Inferiority traded for domination. Will everybody be willing to swap?"

Prior to writing novels George Baxt made his living as a scriptwriter, first in television and then for motion pictures. Throughout his life he was involved in the entertainment industry in one manner or another. But his first love was always the movies. His knowledge of obscure cinema and forgotten supporting character actors was unrivaled by any so-called movie expert. Cinema historian Clive Hirschhorn, author of *The Warner Bros. Story* (1979), recalls Baxt inviting himself for a visit in order to discuss several mistakes he found in the book. He said that Baxt "was able to name players in some of the stills that nobody else had been able to do.... [H]e could practically name all of the girls who dance on the aeroplane wings in *Flying Down to Rio*."

That knowledge turns up in all of the Pharoah Love books. In *A Queer Kind of Death* a smarmy book publisher is described as having an "Adolphe Menjou mustache," while the epileptic millionaire Jameson Hurst melodramatically adopts "an attitude Norma Shearer would have recognized as her very own." Late in the book a male character imagines he is delivering an Oscar acceptance speech and makes a silly reference to *A Star is Born*: "I won the Oscar! Ladies and gentlemen! This is—Mrs. Norman Maine! I mean Gabriel Ward!" The characters not only are likened to old movie actors and actresses, they behave with the histrionic passions often found in those movies. Everyone seems to be hot tempered and vociferous and when not exploding in passionate outbursts they delight in repartee and wiseacre humor.

The camp nature of the book unfortunately often cascades into offensive territory. It is not a fine line Baxt is crossing here; there is no subtlety at all. There is no arguing that passé vaudeville shtick like an Austrian psychoanalyst who speaks in a cartoon phonetic dialect, the abundance of racial epithets (kike, Hebe, dinge, blackamoor), and frequent jokes playing on tired movieland stereotypes of Native Americans are not at all funny to a contemporary reader. But in a subculture "wholly devoid of ethics or morality" it might have been excused as outrageous humor to a 1960s audience. This kind of thing never ages well unless it is done to mock the characters who are speaking. It occurs so frequently in a *Queer Kind of Death*, with aspersions against Jews and blacks leading the parade of insults, that it cannot be viewed as satirical or campy. It is simply cringe inducing.

In *Swing Low, Sweet Harriet* (1967), the immediate sequel to *A Queer Kind of Death*, Pharoah and Seth continue their strange relationship built on emotional blackmail and Baxt's love of old movies explodes in glorious Technicolor. *Swing Low, Sweet Harriet* is a love letter to the big budget Busby Berkeley movie musicals. If *A Queer Kind of Death* gave us a taste of George Baxt's fondness for old movies, then this second novel delivers a smorgasbord of his cinematic obsessions. And while the majority of the characters in the first book were male and sex was ever present, in the sequel Baxt gives us a mostly female cast with an extremely different worldview that blends fantasy and reality. Gay sensibility is expressed through such motifs as escaping into a fantasy world, the worship of movie divas and the popular crime fiction motif of masquerade and disguise. *Swing Low, Sweet Harriet* is a murder mystery that probably has limited appeal to anyone not fully aware of all the in jokes and allusions to Hollywood and the faded glory of movie queens.

Not a single character in the book is meant to be taken seriously. So baroque and grotesque are the portraits of these former movie queens that it hard to call them characters at all. No one resembles anything remotely like a normal human being in *Swing Low, Sweet Harriet*. Sweet Harriet Dimple, apparently suffering from both a bipolar personality disorder and schizophrenia, has mood swings as frequent as an angry cab driver in gridlocked traffic and engages in conversations with herself using multiple voices, causing people to rush away from her (that is if they have not already fled in terror as she literally tap-dances down the sidewalks of midtown Manhattan). Madeleine Cartier is a Shirley Temple lookalike even though she is approaching her sixth decade. And the ridiculously named Flora and Fauna Fleur, a mother and daughter team, are every bit as cartoonish in their stereotypical relationship of overprotective stage mother and slavish child that gives a creepy new dimension to the concept of codependent parenting.

Baxt's love affair with aging movie stars, the bitchiness, the selfishness of every character in the book, the mockery of everything from Mama's boys to pretty boys is all taken from the trunk of old school gay gags. Reading a Baxt novel is like watching an early John Waters movie or going to a drag club and listening to a has-been crossdressing comic doing insult jokes. This second entry in the Pharoah Love series is sort of a homage to Grand Guignol style movies about murderous matrons and half-crazed spinsters like *Whatever Happened to Baby Jane?*, *Hush…. Hush, Sweet Charlotte*, *Whatever Happened to Aunt Alice?*, and *Die! Die! My Darling!*, where some veteran actress played a lunatic killer diva trapped in a past of tortured memories and tragic death. The novel is filled with in jokes about those movies as well as movie mania and movie trivia.

The premise of the novel is a murder mystery but the puzzle is merely a flimsy framework on which to stage the zany antics of the cartoon cast. The movie actresses were all involved in the long gone days of big budget glossy movie musicals produced and directed by Barclay Mills. Mills was mysteriously murdered back in 1932 and now Seth, who is ghost writing Ms. Cartier's memoirs, and the true crime writing duo of brothers Peter and Robert Moulin are all interested in digging up that past. But someone is desperate to keep what happened at that nearly forgotten pool party a secret. There is no real detection at all, just a lot of slowly revealed secrets, some of which are easily guessed based on the names of the characters alone. It is not a coincidence that Mills and Moulin are used as surnames. Most of Baxt's mysteries revolve around puns and wordplay and he is fond of hidden relationships and alternate identities, which crop up repeatedly in all three books.

The last book in the trilogy is an all-out farce and probably the funniest of the three books to a modern audience. While *Topsy and Evil* (1968) is also plagued with an unfunny use of comic dialects—the Boston Brahmin accent is lampooned in one woman's speech pattern while another speaks in drawn out final consonants ("Igorrr sayyyy nothinggggg")—this blemish is easy to overlook when encountering a dizzying abundance of literary allusions and movie references brilliantly used for comic effect. The sheer number is nothing short of madcap genius. Try these on for size:

- The murder victim is named Guru Raskalnikov and was bludgeoned with a blunt instrument (just as Dostoevsky's famous anti-hero did in the pawnbroker).
- Raskalnikov's dying last word is a barely audible whisper of "Rosebud!"
- Jo Alcott has three sisters named Meg, Beth and Amy.
- A true crime expose of the bathtub electrocution death in the first book is called *In Cold Water*.
- An obsequious valet is named Igor Isogul (spell that name backwards). His physical description matches exactly that of a character from the films *Son of Frankenstein* and *Ghost of Frankenstein*, even to the point of his having survived an execution by hanging that leaves him with a crooked neck.
- "The second Mrs. DeWinter just had her first encounter with Mrs. Danvers" is typical of the numerous movie characters and plots referenced.

So as not to leave out the eggheads and intellectuals, Baxt drops allusions to the writing of Bernard Malamud and Sheridan Le Fanu and adds some 1960s current events talk with catty snipes directed at Kurt Kiesinger and Lee Harvey Oswald's mother. Like a gossipy queen dishing the dirt at a theater party Baxt spares no malice. But even the most knowledgeable reader may be drawn to an internet search engine to look up some of Baxt's more obscure references when reading the books in the Pharoah Love series. Who these days remembers that Kurt Kiesinger was tied to Nazi Germany? Who remembers Kiesinger at all?

Topsy and Evil is a pulpy over-the-top revenge fantasy telling the story of Archimedes Zoltan, a master criminal businessman bent on taking control of the country's financial resources and dominating the world, and Topsy Alcott, his avaricious partner in crime with ulterior motives. The two of them attempt to cover up the death of Raskalnikov, Zoltan's one time advisor and Topsy's former lover. Complicating matters are yet another true crime investigation by the Moulin brothers; Madeleine Cartier's impending marriage to Zoltan; a performance artist named Ocelot who is about to make her debut at Tara, Topsy's chic night club; a planned prison escape for Flora and Fauna Fleur, who were incarcerated at the end of book two; and the mysterious disappearance of Pharoah Love himself.

"Where is Pharoah Love?" the characters keep asking themselves. Satan Stagg, Love's protégé and another handsome black policeman, is curious whether the black detective has vanished due to the Moulin's book *In Cold Water*, which implicates Love in a cover-up while also accusing him of murder. Multiple plot threads converge in one literally blazing finale, in which the villains get what is coming to them, Love's disappearance is explained and family secrets are exploded in a most farcical manner.

Adhering to the late Sixties motto "Let it all hang out!" Baxt gave himself free rein in this final volume. The Pharoah Love trilogy ends in a riotous explosion of wild mirth, pulp magazine melodrama, multiple mysteries and movie mania run amok. Baxt's humor flourishes in this new uncensored mode. His mysteries are not filled with the screwball antics of Alice Tilton's Leonidas Witherall and company or the cocktail-soaked drunk humor found in Craig Rice's novels. No longer is the author merely writing gags and resorting to low comedy and farce. The puns result not in groans but smiles and laughs, vulgar comments give way to risqué and naughty innuendo:

- *Topsy and Evil* is both a pun and an allusion to characters in *Uncle Tom's Cabin*.
- "Nisei come, Nisei go," says a Japanese-American prisoner about her talent for jail escapes.
- "How I loved to hear your shaggy-doge stories," says Topsy about someone who spent time in Venice.
- A plastic surgery service called Goldberg Rejuvenation Clinic is known for its "Goldberg variations."
- Ida's Place dares to capitalize on the Sixties gay bar trend of employing half-clad staff. A female character says of these new "bottomless" waiters: "What's with the way these waiters are undressed? They carry so little with such pride."

Although the novel tends to follow the formula of a 1940s thriller in its multiple viewpoints and slow revelation of the true motivations of its many villainous characters, Baxt still holds a final ace up his sleeve for the closing pages. Baxt has not forgotten his Manhattan subculture and the last surprise is not only intended to shock but to subvert the traditions of the old-fashioned crime novel as only a gay writer could do. The reason for Pharoah Love's disappearance and the hints dropped throughout the story in the scenes with the sexy Ocelot are what makes the book something of a tour de force. It may be the first time in crime fiction—dramatic or comic—in which a murderer attempts to elude the police by means of a complete identity transformation. Masquerade, disguise and role reversal is a prominent plot device in Golden Age detective fiction, a staple in any crime writer's bag of tricks. Women bind their breasts and glue on mustaches and beards to become men; men wear dresses, wigs and elaborate makeup to mimic a women's appearance. They do this all in order to bamboozle the police and escape detection, but never to shed for good their gender or sexual identity. Baxt takes this idea of masquerade to a most extreme and permanent level. How many fictional killers have been willing to give up their identity and undergo a full sex change operation simply to escape a prison sentence?

Works Cited

Baxt, George. *A Queer Kind of Love.* New York: Simon & Schuster, 1966.
_____. *Swing Low, Sweet Harriet.* New York: Simon & Schuster, 1967.
_____. *Topsy and Evil.* New York: Simon & Schuster, 1968.
Hirschhorn, Clive. *The Warner Bros. Story.* New York: Crown, 1979.
Vallance, Tom. "George Baxt, Author of 'Outrageous' Mystery Novels." *The Independent.* July 9, 2003.

About the Contributors

J.C. **Bernthal** is a private researcher for the crime writer Sophie Hannah. He holds a Ph.D. from the University of Exeter and is the editor of *The Ageless Agatha Christie* (McFarland, 2016) and the author of *Queering Agatha Christie* (Palgrave Macmillan, 2016).

Brittain **Bright** teaches crime fiction, film studies, and writing. She earned a Ph.D. at Goldsmiths, University of London; her dissertation was on the role of place in interwar detective fiction. Her research focuses on the work of Gladys Mitchell.

John **Curran** is the author of the award-winning *Agatha Christie's Secret Notebooks* (HarperCollins, 2009) and *Agatha Christie's Murder in the Making* (HarperCollins, 2011). He earned a Ph.D. at Trinity College Dublin; his dissertation was on "The Golden Age of Detective Fiction." His most recent book is *Tom Adams Uncovered: The Art of Agatha Christie and Beyond* (HarperCollins, 2015).

Rick **Cypert** is a professor of English at Nebraska Wesleyan University where he teaches courses in linguistics, rhetorical theory, pedagogy and writing. He is the author of biographies of Mignon Eberhart and Charlotte Armstrong as well as co-editor of collections of short stories by these two authors.

James **Doig** works at the National Archives of Australia in Canberra. He has a Ph.D. from Swansea University, Wales. He has edited several anthologies and collections of vintage Australian supernatural tales, including *Australia Ghost Stories* (Wordsworth, 2010), *Ghost Stories and Mysteries by Ernest Favenc* (Borgo Press, 2012), and *The Devil and the Marsh and Other Stories* (Ash Tree Press, 2004).

Curtis **Evans** received a Ph.D. in history in 1998. He is the author of *Masters of the "Humdrum" Mystery* (McFarland, 2012) and *Clues and Corpses: The Detective Fiction and Mystery Criticism of Todd Downing* (Coachwhip, 2013) and the editor of *Mysteries Unlocked: Essays in Honor of Douglas G. Greene* (McFarland, 2014). He blogs as *The Passing Tramp*.

Drewey Wayne **Gunn** is a professor emeritus at Texas A&M University–Kingsville. He is the author of *The Gay Male Sleuth in Print and Film* (Scarecrow, 2005). McFarland has published his most recent books: *Gay Novels of Britain, Ireland, and the Commonwealth, 1881–1981* (2014) and *Gay American Novels, 1870–1970* (2016).

About the Contributors

Nick **Jones** is the editor of numerous illustrated books, including *The Art of Neil Gaiman* (Harper Design, 2014), *The Art of Movie Storyboards* (Ilex, 2013) and *500 Essential Cult Books* (Sterling, 2010). He was a music journalist at *Mixmag* and now writes for *Marvel Fact Files, The Walking Dead: The Official Magazine* and his own blog, *Existential Ennui*.

Josh **Lanyon** is the pen name of American writer D.L. Browne, an Eppie Award winner, a four-time Lambda Literary Award finalist for Gay Mystery, and the first recipient of the Goodreads Favorite Male/Male Author Lifetime Achievement award.

Michael **Moon** has published books on embodiment in Walt Whitman's poetry, "outsider artist" Henry Darger, and the impact of proto-gay childhood on literature, art and film in the work of figures from Henry James to Andy Warhol. His latest book *Arabian Nights* (Arsenal Pulp Press, 2016) is on Pasolini's film. He has taught at Duke, Johns Hopkins, and Emory University.

Tom **Nolan** is the author of *Ross Macdonald: A Biography* (Scribner, 1999), editor of *The Archer Files* (Vintage/Black Lizard, 2015) and co-editor (with Suzanne Marrs) of *Meanwhile There Are Letters: The Correspondence of Eudora Welty and Ross Macdonald* (Arcade, 2015).

J. F. **Norris** writes about crime, supernatural and adventure fiction from the late 19th to the mid–20th century. His essays have appeared in *CADS (Crimes and Detective Stories); (Give Me That) Old-Time Detection*; and the anthology *Beat Girls, Love Tribes, and Real Cool Cats* (Verse Chorus Press, 2016). He has contributed to many websites including *Thrilling Detective, Mystery*File*, and his blog *Pretty Sinister Books*.

Moira **Redmond** is a journalist with a long-held interest in Golden Age detection. After a career working with the BBC and other radio outlets, the online magazine *Slate* and writing a book about etiquette, she now blogs as *Clothes in Books* and writes about books for *The Guardian*.

Charles J. **Rzepka** is a professor of English at Boston University. He is the author of numerous articles and books including *Detective Fiction: A Cultural History* (Polity, 2005) and *Being Cool: The Work of Elmore Leonard* (Johns Hopkins, 2013). He also co-edited *A Companion to Crime Fiction* (Blackwell, 2010) with Lee Horsley.

Bruce **Shaw** studied social anthropology at the University of Western Australia. He earned a Ph.D. in English at the Flinders University in South Australia. He is the author of two books of literary criticism: *The Animal Fable in Science Fiction and Fantasy* (McFarland, 2010) and *Jolly Good Detecting* (McFarland, 2014) as well as the coauthor of several books of Aboriginal Australian life histories.

Noah **Stewart** has spent most of his life dealing with mysteries (buying them, selling them, and most of all reading them), and in recognition received an award from the Matthew Baillie Begbie chapter of Crime Writers of Canada for "services to detective fiction." He is one of the founding members of the third-oldest AIDS-based service organization in the world, AIDS Vancouver.

Lucy **Sussex** has published widely, having edited five anthologies, and written five short story collections, including the award-winning neo-Victorian novel, *The Scarlet Rider* (Ticonderoga Publications, reprinted 2015). Her *Blockbuster: Fergus Hume and the Mystery of a Hansom Cab* (Text, 2015) won the Victorian Community History Award.

Index

Achilles 28
Across the Footlights (novel) 22
Adams, Samuel Hopkins 4, 33–39
Addams, Jane 192
The Adventures of Margery Allingham 254
aesthetes 21, 58, 124n22, 126, 135, 140, 151n3, 177, 227
"Afternoon at the Seaside" (play) 57
Agatha Christie: Curtain Up 57
Agatha Christie's Marple (television series) 59, 64
Agatha Christie's Poirot (television series) 62, 64
Aird, Catherine 108
Albert, Prince Consort 19
Alleyn, Roderick 44
Allingham, Joyce 254–255
Allingham, Margery 9, 11, 93, 249, 252, 253, 254, 255
Altman, Dennis 70, 71
And the Villain Still Pursued Her (play) 174
And Then There Were None (novel) 72
Another Country (novel) 214
Antinous 27, 28
Apollo Belvedere 27
The Archer Files (short fiction collection) 222
Arnold, Matthew 174
Arvin, Newton 14n8
Ashbrook, Harriet 33
Ashley, April 101
Asquith, Lady Cynthia 256
Asquith, H.H. 126
Aswell, Edward C. 151n7
Aswell, Mary Louise *see* White, Mary Louise
At Bertram's Hotel (novel) 123n3
Atlas, Charles 7
Atoka 156, 158
Auchincloss, Hugh 233, 236n18
Auden, W.H. 219, 220, 222
Austen, Jane 120

Auster, Howard 239n28
Average Jones 34

bachelors 20, 30, 42, 71, 147, 148, 157, 158, 159, 166, 167, 168, 185
"A Bad, Bad Past" (song) 173, 179, 182
Baldwin, Faith 191–192
Baldwin, James 214
Bancroft, Dr. Charles 179, 180
The Barbarous Coast (novel) 221
Barr, James 157
Barrett, Wilson 25
Bartholomew, Frances Ritter 140, 141, 142, 147
Bartlett, Adelaide 122
Bartlett, Edwin 122
The Bat (film) 184
Bates, Norman 33
Battle, Superintendent 63
Baudelaire, Charles 205
Baxt, George 1, 10, 273–278
The Bayou Road (novel) 194, 196
Beaton, Cecil 248n2
Beaufort, John 144
Beck, Philip 22, 25, 29
Beebe, Lucius 210
Beef, Sergeant 136
Beekman Hill 212, 213, 214
The Beetle (novel) 33
Beeton, Mrs. Isabella Mary 250
Behrendt, Jorg 237n6, 238n14
Bellefontaine 144
The Benson Murder Case (novel) 42
Bentley, Philip 26
benzedrine 140, 141, 151n4, 152n15
Beresford, Tommy 74, 75
Beresford, Tuppence 74, 75
Berkeley, Anthony 42, 159
Berkeley, Busby 276
Berkshires 143–144, 145
Berlin 140, 148, 150n2
Berlin, Isaiah 122

285

286   Index

Bernhardt, Sarah 176
Bernheimer, Max 210
Bernstein, Leonard 237*n*7
Bernthal, J.C. 5
Betjeman, John 124*n*22
"The Bewilderment of Snake McKoy" (short story) 256
The Big Clock (novel) 213
Big Fish, Little Fish (play) 145, 151*n*16
The Big Sleep (novel) 218
Billy the Kid (ballet) 229
Birthday Party (novel) 136, 137*n*2
bisexuality 8, 124, 226, 228, 251
"The Black Legend" (blog essay) 11, 15*n*13
Black Lizard 225, 237*n*4
Black Mask (magazine) 44
Black Widow (novel) 144
Blathwayt, Raymond 26
Blazey, Winifred 5
Bletchley Park 67, 68, 73, 75
Bloch, Michael 123*n*1, 124*n*22
Bloch, Robert 33
Bloody Murder 122*n*1
Bloomsbury 126, 127
The Blunderer (novel) 259, 260, 261, 263
The Body in the Library (novel) 64
Bohemians 29, 127, 176, 181
Bollars, Antoine 25, 30
Boncompagni, Mauro 144, 145, 151*n*10, 151*n*15
Bond, James 124*n*22
Bonett, Emery 139
Bonett, John 139
Bonn, Thomas L. 238*n*16
Boston marriages 192
Boucher, Anthony 10, 44, 45, 232, 273
Boulton, Ernest 23
Bounty, Sheriff Peter 157, 165–169
Bouvier, Jacqueline 238*n*18
Box, Edgar *see* Vidal, Gore
Box, Muriel and Sydney 236*n*2
The Boy Avengers (novel) 215
The Boy Who Followed Ripley (novel) 259, 260
"The Boys at Beaver Meadow" (essay) 181
Braddon, Mary 18
Bradley, Mrs. Beatrice Adela Lestrange 5, 78–91, 95
Brady, Matthew 176
Brahms, Caryl 227
Brand, Christianna 42, 251
Brando, Marlon 7
Brandstetter, Dave 2, 10, 13*n*1, 265
Brazen Tongue (novel) 91
Breaking the Code 69
Brewer, Gil 274
Brickell, Chris 22
Bright, Brittain 5
Bristow, Joseph 28
Bronski, Michael 7, 13

Brontë, Emily 108
Brood of the Witch Queen (novel) 37
Brooklyn College 144
The Brooklyn Murders (novel) 115
Bruce, Leo 7, 136
Bruning, Francesca 144
Bryn Mawr 141, 143, 192
The Burning Court (novel) 34, 184
Burton, William O. 210
Butcher, Cyril 245
Butcher, Fanny 190, 191
Byron, Lord 160

Cabaret (play/film) 145, 150*n*2
Cain, James M. 11
Cambridge University 140, 142
camp 7, 9, 10, 23, 175, 246, 249, 274, 275
Camus, Albert 262
Candide 145
Canguilhem, George 72
Capote, Truman 14*n*8, 151*n*7, 234, 236*n*1, 237*n*6
The Captive (play) 39*n*1
Cards on the Table (novel) 61–62, 64
A Caribbean Mystery (novel) 52–53
Carol (novel) 9, 262
Carr, John Dickson 6, 34, 160, 184, 249, 255
Carter, Philip Youngman ("Pip") 9, 252, 253, 254
Carter, Tom *see* Laurie, Thomas
Casa Madrone (novel) 195
The Case Is Altered (novel) 136
The Castle of Otranto (novel) 205
The Cat and the Canary (film) 184
The Cat Screams (novel) 161
Catton, Bruce 204
Cecil, Mr. 42
Cerf, Bennett 191
A Chair for Wayne Lonergan 212
Chandler, Raymond 8, 11, 212, 213, 218, 219, 225, 227, 234, 235, 269, 274
Chatterley, Lady 153*n*20
Chauncey, George 3, 4, 14*n*6, 39*n*1, 167–168
chemical castration 69
Chicago 148, 189, 199, 191
The Chiffon Scarf (novel) 194
The China Governess (novel) 255
Chitterwick, Ambrose 42
Choctaws 156, 157, 158
Christie, Agatha 4, 5, 6, 7, 11, 33, 50, 52–65, 67–76, 94, 98, 99, 123*n*3, 159, 225, 227, 232, 234, 235, 237*n*4, 244
Chudacoff, Howard P. 158
Cialis 166
Cinderella Goes to the Morgue (novel) 255
The City and the Pillar (novel) 157, 225, 228, 231, 232, 236*n*1, 237*n*12
Claysmore School 142
Clift, Montgomery 7
Climpson, Miss 47, 48

the closet 3, 12, 62, 68–69, 158–159
Closet Queens 123*n*1
Clues and Corpses 6, 156
code 3, 4, 21, 25, 26, 27, 28, 30, 40, 46, 49, 53, 67, 68, 69, 73, 98, 101, 167, 169, 193, 242, 246
Cold War 7, 14*n*8
Cole, G.D.H. 5, 6, 114–122, 122–123*n*1, 124*n*22, 150*n*1
Cole, Humphrey 122
Cole, Margaret 6, 114, 120–122, 122–123*n*1
college musicals/theatricals 6, 173–181
Collins, Wilkie 18, 203
Collis, Rose 255
Colton, James *see* Hansen, Joseph
Come Away, Death (novel) 83
Compulsion (novel/play) 148, 149, 153*n*24
Conan Doyle, Arthur 4, 18, 79
Connon, Bryan 248*n*1
Cooke, Rachel 252, 253, 254, 257
Copeland, Jack 69
Copland, Aaron 229
Cores, Lucy 227
The Cornell Murders (novel) 181
The Cornish Fox (novel) 125, 130, 131, 133, 135, 136, 137*n*7
Corpse de Ballet (novel) 227
Cory, Donald Webster 157
Cottage Sinister (novel) 142
Cox, James 156
"cozy" crime fiction 1, 11
Crawford, Jack Randall 174
Crime and Punishment (novel) 262
Crime at Christmas (novel) 125, 126, 130, 131, 134, 136
Crime Queens 2, 4, 5, 9, 11, 44
The Crippled Muse (novel) 151*n*11
Crispin, Edmund 249, 255
Croft-Cooke, Rupert 7, 136
Crofts, Freeman Wills 114
The Crooked Hinge (novel) 184
Cry Shame! (novel) 226, 238*n*16
Cuff, Sergeant 228
Curran, John 4
Cypert, Rick 7

Dalgliesh, Adam 95
Damon and Pythias 186*n*8
Dane, Clemence 47, 51*n*1
Danger Money (novel) 194
Danger Next Door (novel) 145
Dannay, Frederic 13*n*1
Dark, Eleanor 202
Dark, Eric 202
The Dark Garden (novel) 191, 193, 196
The Dark Tunnel (novel) 218, 219, 223
The Dartmouth Murders (novel) 174, 181, 183–184
Dartmouth Players 173, 179–182
"Dartmouth Undying" (song) 183

Dartmouth University 6, 179–181, 183
The Daughter of Time (novel) 95, 100
A Daughter's a Daughter (novel) 59–60
David, Bette 271
Daviot, Gordon 94
Day, Doris 182
Dean, James 7
Death and the Maiden (novel) 85
Death Before Bedtime (novel) 225, 232–234, 238*n*16, 236*n*22, 239*n*27
Death Goes on Skis (novel) 255
Death Goes to School (novel) 143, 151*n*10, 151*n*11
Death in Ecstasy (novel) 5, 44
Death in the Fifth Position (novel) 9, 225, 227, 228–232, 234, 238*n*15, 238*n*16
Death Likes It Hot (novel) 225, 228, 232, 234–235, 238*n*16
The Death of a Millionaire (novel) 6, 114–122, 123*n*3
Death of His Uncle (novel) 125, 129, 131, 133, 134, 135, 136
Death of My Aunt (novel) 125, 126, 127, 128, 129, 136
Death on the Nile (novel) 64, 72
"Death Sits in the Dentist's Chair" (short story) 12
Death to Slow Music (novel) 244, 247
de Cuevas, George 213
Deene, Carolus 136
de Lauretis, Teresa 88
Depression 158
de Sade, Marquis 69
Detection Club 47, 94, 122*n*1, 251
The Devil's Disciple (play) 174
The Devil's Elbow (novel) 81, 87–90
Devine, Alex 142
Dickens, Charles 223, 249
Die! Die! My Darling (film) 276
Dietrich, Marlene 45
Dionysus 168
District Nurse (novel) 191
The Divided Path (novel) 157
A Dog's Ransom (novel) 259
Doig, James 8
Dolman, Glen 26, 29
Dostoevsky, Fyodor 262, 277
"The Double Clue" (short story) 53, 60
The Double Door (novel) 213–214
Douglas, Lord Alfred 24, 43
Douglas, Kirk 182
Downing, Ruth 156, 158, 170*n*3
Downing, Sam 156
Downing, Todd 6, 156–170
Dracula 204, 205
drag 3, 6, 22, 23, 25, 173, 174, 175, 176, 181, 182, 218, 231, 276
"dropping hairpins" 4, 41
The Drowning Pool (novel) 220–221, 223
Dunedin 19, 20

288   Index

Dunne, Dominick 210, 211, 213
Duparc, Henri 135
Dyson, the Rev. George 122

Eberhart, Alan 190, 197
Eberhart, Mignon 7, 189–197
Edgewater 226
Edwards, Martin 94, 122–123n1, 124n22
effeminacy 21, 22, 37, 40, 41, 42, 43, 45, 60, 61, 69, 179, 193, 194, 195, 196, 197, 237n6, 237n9
Eighth Ward Settlement House 141
Elephants Can Remember (novel) 72
Eleven (short story collection) 263
Eliot, T.S. 127
Elizabeth II, Queen 69
Elizabethan Club 174
Ellis, Havelock 184, 202, 205
El Morocco 210
Emmerson, Owen 70, 71
End of an Ancient Mariner (novel) 122
Enemy in the House (novel) 194
enigma codes 68
Eustis, Helen 33
Evans, Curtis 5, 6, 7, 138n24, 156, 157, 158, 176, 254
Everard, Katherine 226
Everard Baths 152n14, 226, 239n28
An Experiment in Love (novel) 106
"Extase"(song) 135
"The Eyes of Texas" (song) 169–170

Fabian, Warner (pseudonym of Samuel Hopkins Adams) 39n1
Fadeout (novel) 2, 13n2, 265
Faderman, Lillian 51n1, 192, 208n7
The Fan (play) 174
Fancy Free (ballet) 237n7
Far to Go (novel) 151n7, 151n10
Faulkner, William 226
Fearing, Kenneth 213
femininity 5, 22, 37, 85, 86, 87, 88, 89, 94, 96, 99, 111, 201, 242
feminism 45, 85, 90
Fingers of Fear (novel) 207n1
Fire-Tongue (novel) 37
Fire Will Freeze (novel) 219
First World War 69, 146, 153n20, 173, 222
First You Dream, Then You Die 11
Five Little Pigs (novel) 64
Flaming Youth 39n1
Fleming, Ann 124n22
Fleming, Ian 124n22
Flinders, Karl 215
The Flying Death (novel) 34
Flying Down to Rio (film) 275
folie a deux 149
Foot, Michael 121
Foster, "Boy" 144
Foster, Giraud 144

The Franchise Affair (novel) 95
Franks, Bobbie 148
Freud, Sigmund 28, 30, 78, 79, 80, 81, 82, 83, 83, 84, 89, 90, 192, 202, 205, 217
From This Dark Stairway (novel) 193
The Fruits of Culture (play) 174, 175
A Funny Thing Happened on the Way 249, 250, 251, 254

Gaboriau, Emile 18, 19
Gaitskill, Hugh 121, 122, 124n22
A Game for the Living (novel) 29
Gant, Robert 22, 23, 30
Garber, Marjorie 98
Garland, Judy 152n16
Garland, Rodney 7
Garran, Sir Robert 206
Gaudy Night (novel) 108
The Gay Detective (novel) 7
The Gay Metropolis 212
Gay New York 3
gay sleuths *see* Brandstetter, Dave; Grant, Inspector Alan; Green, Horatio; Kent, Professor Chester; Love, Pharoah; Marple, Miss Jane; Poirot, Hercule; Rennert, Hugh; Vance, Philo; Warren, Malcolm
Geiger, John 214
gender identity 4, 5, 22, 33–39, 39n1, 79, 89, 93, 98–103, 237–238n14, 279
The Gentleman Who Vanished (novel) 22
Ghost of Frankenstein (film) 277
Gibbs, Wolcott 211
Gielgud, Sir John 152n16
"The Gigolo, the Heiress and the Candlestick" (essay) 212
Gilbert and Sullivan 21, 22
Gill, Brendan 182, 185
Gill, Gillian 73
Giovanni's Room (novel) 214
The Girl in Murder Flat 212
The Glass Cell (novel) 259, 260
The Glass Slipper (novel) 193
Glyn, Elinor 48
Goldberg, Jonathan 73
Golden Age detective fiction 4, 6, 9, 11, 40, 41, 43, 45, 46, 50, 79, 89, 93, 107, 108, 114, 120, 148, 153n19, 156, 159, 170n5, 173, 174, 178, 184, 185, 227, 232, 249, 279
"The Golden Age of Gay Fiction" (essay) 10
The Golden Age of Murder (book) 94, 122n1
Goldoni, Carlo 174
Goldstein, Richard 212
Gondris, Joanna 145
The Good Life (novel) 215
The Goodbye Look (novel) 223
Goodis, David 11
Goodwin, Archie 85
Gore, Thomas Pryor 232, 233
Grand Guignol 276
Grant, Inspector Alan 95–103

Grebanier, Bernard 144, 152*n*14
Green, Hetty 235, 239*n*25
Green, H.M. 205
Green, Horatio 241–248
Green, Julius 57
The Green Carnation 43
Greene, Douglas G. 150*n*1
Greene, Graham 263
"Greenshaw's Folly" (short story) 58
Greenwich Village 1, 231
Greenwood, Kerry 24
The Grindle Nightmare (novel) 6, 140, 143, 145–150, 151*n*10
Grost, Mike 106–107, 176
The Group (novel) 106
Growing Up into Revolution 114, 123*n*1
Grubbs, John ("Johnny") R. 152*n*13
Gunn, Drewey Wayne 8, 13, 236*n*2
gunsels 4, 43–45
Gysin, Brion 214

Haarmann, Fritz ("Butcher of Hanover") 215
"Had I But Known" mystery fiction 239*n*27
Hadden, Briton 213
Hadrian 28
Haggard, H. Rider 79
Hall, Radclyffe 127, 204, 205
Halley, Janet 71
Hallowe'en Party (novel) 59–60, 69, 99
Hamilton, Barbara 211
Hamilton, Patrick 153*n*24
Hamilton College 140
Hammer, Mike 227, 229, 237*n*9
Hammett, Dashiell 8, 11, 44, 218, 219, 225, 227
Hamptons 232, 234, 235
Hang-Up (novel) 10, 272
Hansen, Joseph 1, 10, 13, 13*n*1, 265–272
happy couples 4, 49, 50
hard-boiled crime fiction 2, 8, 11, 44, 125, 218, 225, 227, 234, 238*n*16, 266
Harker, Jamie 12, 13
Hartley, L.P. 133
Hartney Press 146
Harvard University (secret court) 180
Harward, Nancy 22, 30
Hastings, Arthur 60, 61, 70
Hawthorne, Julian 34
Haydon, Jeffrey Frederick Meurisse 206
He Who Whispers (novel) 184
The Heart in Exile (novel) 7
Heimer, Mel 211, 212
Helluva Town 212
Henderson, Jennifer Morag 93
Her Brilliant Career 253, 254
Here at the New Yorker 182
heteronormativity 6, 48, 51, 60, 71, 189, 190
Hichens, Robert 43
Hickory Farm 144
Hickson, Joan 70

The High Window (novel) 235
Highsmith, Patricia 9, 10, 11, 12, 206, 212, 214, 259–264
Hirschhorn, Clive 275
Hitchcock, Alfred 153*n*24
Hochbruck, Wolfgang 156
Hogarth Press 125, 126, 136
Holmes, Sherlock 237*n*9
Homophile Movement 7
The Homosexual in America 157
Hopkins, Ernest Martin 179–180, 181
The Horizontal Man (novel) 33
Horton, Edward Everett 41
The House on the Roof (novel) 191, 192, 195–196
Hudson, Rock 7
Hull House 192
Hulse, Charles G. 215
"Humdrum" detective fiction writers 114, 123*n*2, 138*n*24
Hume, Fergus 1, 4, 18–30
Hume, James 19
Hume, Mary 19
Hush…Hush Sweet Charlotte (film) 276
Huxley, Aldous 142

I Am Out (novel) 214
"I May Be Wrong (But I Think You're Wonderful") (song) 182
Ignorant Armies (novel) 214
"Intuition's Reckless Compass" (essay) 254
inversion 22, 38, 39*n*1, 89, 106, 111, 173, 205, 207
Invitation to Murder (play) 175
Isherwood, Christopoher 150*n*2
The Island of Fantasy (novel) 26, 27, 28, 30

Jackson, Shirley 181
Jacobs, W.W. 175
James, P.D. 95
Japp, Inspector 61, 62
Jekyll and Hyde 146, 148
Jennings, Richard 127
Jolly Good Detecting 249, 252, 253, 254
Jones, Julia 253, 254, 255
Jones, Kay 250
Jones, Ralph Garfield 181
Joss: A Reversion (novel) 33
The Judgment of Paris (novel) 227
Jung, Carl 202, 205

Kafka, Franz 262
Kaiser, Charles 211, 212
Kaplan, Frank 237*n*6
The Kat Strikes (novel) 249, 251, 256
Kaufman, Kenneth C. 204
Keating, H.R.F. 263
Keeler, Harry Stephen 200, 207*n*1
Kelley, Florence 141
Kelley, Martha Mott ("Patsy") 141, 142, 150

290   Index

Kendall, Clause 204, 205, 208n6
Kenney, Rowland 122
Kent, Nial 157
Kent, Professor Chester 34, 35, 37, 38
Keogh, Theodora 213, 214
Kerouac, Jack 230
Keyes, Frances Parkinson 235
Kierkegaard, Soren 217, 262
Kiesinger, Kurt 277
King, Amelia Sarony Lambert 175
King, Francis 137n5
King, Rufus 6, 173–178, 186n8
King, Thomas Armstrong 175
Kinsey Reports 3, 211, 231
Kitchin, C.H.B. 5, 125–136
Knight, Adam 232, 238n16
Known Homosexual (novel) 1, 10, 265–272
Knox, Dilwyn ("Dilly") 67, 68
Knox, Ronald 146
Kriza, John 228, 237n7

Labouchere amendment 19, 20, 30
Lambert, Nora 176
Lambert, Theodore Sarony 176
Lambert, Thomas Sarony 176
Lang, Harold 227–228, 236n1, 237n7, 237n8
Lanyon, Josh 10
"Last Day in Lisbon" (short story) 219
The Last Trumpet (novel) 161, 164–165, 169
Laughton, Charles 213
Laurels Are Poison (novel) 81, 85
Laurents, Arthur 236n1
Laurie, Joan ("Jonny") Ann Wener 9, 203, 249–257
Laurie, Nicholas 9, 252–254
Laurie, Thomas 9, 250, 252–257
Laurie, Thomas Werner 203
lavender color as gay code 42–43, 63
lavender marriage 40, 144
"lavender scare" 7, 14n8, 212
Lawrence, D.H. 219
Lawrence, Gordon 23, 25, 30
Lawrence v. Texas 169
The Lazy Lawrence Murders (novel) 168–170
Leaves of Grass 26
Leeming, David 214
Le Fanu, Sheridan 200, 203, 204, 277
Leopold, Nathan 148–149, 153–154n24, 154n25, 215
lesbian pulp fiction 7, 8
The Lesser Antilles Case (novel) 177
The Letter (short story/film) 271
Levin, James 167, 171n22
Levin, Meyer 148, 149, 153n24
Lewis, Matthew Gregory 205
Liberace 7
The Life of G.D.H. Cole (book) 114
Linton, Eliza Lynn 21
A Little Night Music (play/film) 145
Little Richard 7

"Little Woman" (short story fragment) 222
Lockridge, Frances 139
Lockridge, Richard 139
Loeb, Richard 148–149, 153–154n24, 154n25, 215
Lombard, Carole 250
Lombroso, Caesare 80, 202, 205
Lonergan, Patricia Burton 8, 210–217
Lonergan, Wayne Thomas 8, 210–217
Look, We've Come Through (play) 145
Lord Edgware Dies (novel) 60–61, 244
Lost on Twilight Road (novel) 272
"The Lottery" (short story) 181
Love, Pharoah 10, 273–279
Lowe, Eric 202
Lowndes, Marie Belloc 203
Luce, Henry 213

Macbeth, Lady 143
Macdonald, Ross 8, 217–223, 225, 269
Macready, George 213
The Mad Sculptor 213
Madame Midas (novel) 22, 25
The Making of Americans 72
Malamud, Bernard 277
The Maltese Falcon (novel) 44, 218
The Man from the River (novel) 122
"man-haters" 4, 45–46
The Man in the Queue (novel) 95, 97
The Man Next Door (novel) 194
Mangan, Richard 152n16
Mansfield, Jayne 7
The Mansions of Limbo 213
Mantel, Hilary 106
Marlowe, Christopher 168
Marlowe, Philip 125, 234
Marple, Miss Jane 50, 52, 53, 55, 57, 58, 59, 64, 69, 70, 71
Marsh, Ngaio 5, 11, 44, 93
Marsh, Richard 33
Martin, Christina R. 94
masculinity 7, 9, 43, 79, 82, 97, 98, 176, 190, 228, 231
mashers 21, 25
Mason, Perry 237n9
Masters of the "Humdrum" Mystery (book) 138n24, 153n19
Mattachine Society 13n1
Maugham, Somerset 210
McCarthy, Mary 106
McCarthyism 229, 234
McCullers, Carson 151n7
McDermid, Val 93, 96, 103
McDuffee, Franklin 183, 185
McEwen, Geraldine 70
McKenzie, Julia 70
Meaker, Marijane 14n8
Meiwes, Armin ("Rotenberg Cannibal") 215
Melbourne 19, 20, 22, 23, 25
Melville, John Joseph 29, 30

Menjou, Adolphe 275
Menzies, Laura 85–87
The Mermaids Singing (novel) 103
Merrick, Gordon 215
Message from Hong Kong (novel) 194
The Mexican Earth 156, 157
Mexico 156, 157, 162, 168
Millar, Kenneth *see* Macdonald, Ross
Millar, Margaret 217–221
Miller, Maud 156
Mills, Carley 214
The Mirror Crack'd from Side to Side (novel) 58–59, 244
"Miss Furr and Miss Skeene" (short story) 191
Miss Pym Disposes (novel) 5, 105–112
The Missing Aunt (novel) 124n22
Mitchell, Gladys 4, 5, 33, 78–91, 93, 108
Mitchison, Dick (Baron Mitchison) 122
Mitchison, Naomi 122
The Monk (novel) 205
Monroe, Marilyn 7
Moon, Michael 3, 5, 6
The Moonflower (novel) 243–244, 247
Moore, Aimee 30
Moore, Nicole 202
Morgan, Claire *see* Highsmith, Patricia
Morocco (film) 45
El Morocco 210
Morrell, Lady Ottoline 126
Mott, Lucretia 141
The Mousetrap (play) 55–56, 73
The Moving Finger (novel) 53–54, 69
Mrs. McGinty's Dead (novel) 55
Murder at Cambridge (novel) 142, 152–153n17
The Murder at Crome House (novel) 121
Murder at the Munition Works (novel) 121
Murder at the Women's City Club (novel) 142
Murder, Bless It (novel) 250, 251, 256
Murder by Latitude (novel) 6, 173, 175, 177–178
Murder by Request (novel) 246–247
Murder by the Clock (novel) 175
A Murder Is Announced (novel) 50, 54–55, 69
Murder Is Easy (novel) 62–64
The Murder of Roger Ackroyd (novel) 72, 79
Murder on a Yacht (novel) 177
Murder on the Orient Express (novel) 72
Murder on the Tropic (novel) 160, 161
Murder on Tour (novel) 160
Murphy, Agnes 20, 30
My Bo Mo (children's book) 250
Myra Breckinridge (novel) 237n12
Mysteries Unlocked 145, 152n15, 254
The Mysterious Affair at Styles (novel) 74
The Mysterious Mr. Quin (short story collection) 69
The Mystery (novel) 33

Mystery Fiction: Theory and Technique 1, 2
Mystery*File 12
The Mystery of a Hansom Cab (novel) 1, 18, 19, 22, 24, 25, 29
The Mystery of the Butcher's Shop (novel) 82

N or M? (novel) 67, 73–76
The Nation (journal) 141
National Committee for Mental Hygiene 180
Nemesis (novel) 57–58, 64, 69
Nevins, Francis M. 11, 12
New American Library 226, 238n14
New Hampshire State Asylum 180
New Republic 219
New York City 141, 143, 144, 158, 167, 171n22, 190
New York Sun (newspaper) 33
New Yorker 181
New Zealand 19, 20, 21
News of the World 101
Next of Kin (novel) 196
Nichols, Beverley 9, 241–248
Nicolson, John Urban 200, 207n1
Nietzsche, Friedrich 262
Night Over Mexico (novel) 162–163, 165
Nijinsky (film) 145
Niles, Blair 171n22
Nine Times Nine (novel) 44
Niven David 250
No Man's Street (novel) 241–243, 246
No Way Out (film) 213
Noir/neo-noir 1, 8, 11, 185, 225, 262, 274
Nolan, Tom 8
norms 5, 9, 71–73, 100, 102, 237n12
Norris, J.F. 4, 10, 15n13, 176
Norse, Harold 152n14
Not Wanted on Voyage (novel) 252, 257
Nyria (novel) 21, 30

Oakham School 142
Obergefell v. Hodges 139
"The Oblong Box" (short story) 236n2
Odd Girls and Twilight Lovers 192
Ogunquit Beach 181, 187n16
Oh, Doctor! (play) 179
Oklahoma 6, 156, 157, 169, 170, 204, 232
The Old Dark House (film) 184
One Woman's Wisdom (novel) 20
Orr, Clifford 6, 173, 174, 178–186
Oswald, Lee Harvey 277
Out Damned Tot (novel) 257
Oxenham, Ann 207
Oxford University 142

Packer, Vin 14n8
Palimpsest (memoir) 226, 228, 230, 237n8
Palmer, Nettie 204
Pangborn, Franklin 41
"pansy craze" 3, 13–14n6
paperbacks and the paperback revolution 3,

292 Index

7, 13n1, 18, 236n1, 24, 136, 178, 213, 214, 218, 226, 236n1, 238n16, 271
Parini, Jay 236n1, 237n4
Paris 140, 141, 150n2
Park, Frederick 23
Patterson, William McKay 181
Patton, Will 213
Passenger to Frankfurt (novel) 72
The Passing Tramp (blog) 15n13
The Patient (play) 57
Patrick, Q. 6, 139–150, 151n10, 151n11; *see also* Kelley, Martha Mott; Webb, Richard Wilson; Wheeler, Hugh Callingham; White, Mary Louise
Pearce, Donald 219, 220
peri-anal abscess 169, 170n3
Perry, Hamilton Darby 212
Perry, Hazen 190
Phelps, William Lyon 174
Philadelphia 140–143, 147, 170
physique magazines 7, 14n8
The Picadilly Murder (novel) 42
Pike, B.A. 86, 253
Plato 21, 27
Plotting and Writing Suspense Fiction (book) 259, 260, 263
Poe, Edgar Allan 22, 200, 205, 219, 226, 236n2
Poirot, Hercule 59, 60, 61, 62, 64, 69, 70, 95, 227, 236
Poison for Teacher 256
Poison in Play (novel) 250
The Poisoned Chocolates Case (novel) 42
Popular Library 178
Porter, Cole 2, 174, 176; and Yale Dramat songs ("Oh What a Lovely Princess," "The Lovely Heroine," "The Prep School Widow") 174, 178
Porter, Dorothy 70
Postern of Fate 72
Praed, Rosa 21, 30
Prelude to Christopher (novel) 202
Presbyterianism 21
Pretty Boy Dead (novel) 265, 271–272; *see also* Known Homosexual
The Price of Salt (novel) *see* Carol
Printer's Error (novel) 81
prissies/sissies 4, 41–43
Propper, Milton M. 12, 15n13
prostitutes and rent-boys 21, 23, 24, 202, 274
Proust, Marcel 262
Psycho (novel) 33
pulp fiction 1, 7, 8, 10, 12, 14n6, 44, 202, 205, 206, 207, 226, 274, 278; *see also* lesbian pulp fiction
The Pundits 174
Pym, Miss Lucy 107–112

Quatermain, Allan 79
Quatrefoil (novel) 157
Queen, Ellery 6, 13n1, 34, 98, 183
queens 237n6
A Queer Kind of Death (novel) 1, 10, 273–276
"The Queer Story of Adam Lind" (short story) 18, 19
Quentin, Patrick 6, 139, 143, 144, 145, 152n16; *see also* Webb, Richard Wilson; Wheeler, Hugh Callingham

Radcliffe 141
Rand, Lou 7
"The Rats" (play) 57
The Red Land to the South 156
Redmond, Moira 5
Regiment of Women (novel) 47, 51n1
The Religious Body (novel) 108
Rennert, Hugh 157–169
Rice, Craig 278
The Rich Die Hard (novel) 244–246, 247
Rinehart, Mary Roberts 239n27
Ripley, Tom 206, 212, 260
Ripley Under Ground (novel) 259
Ripley Under Water (novel) 259, 263
Ripley's Game (novel) 259
Rise, Please! (play) 179
The Rising of the Moon (novel) 82–85
Ritchie, Kenneth (3rd Baron Ritchie of Dundee) 126, 127
Robbins, Jerome 237n7
Robin of Sherwood (play) 174
Robinson, David 137n6
Rodean School 251, 257
Rodell, Marie F. 1, 2–3, 4, 8, 10, 13n2
Rohmer, Sax 37
The Roman Hat Mystery (novel) 183
Roos, Audrey Kelley 139
Roos, William 139
Roosevelt, Theodore 214
Rope (play) 153n24
Royal Canadian Air Force 210, 211
R.S.V.P. Murder (novel) 196
Rule of Three (play collection) 57
rules of detective fiction 2, 146, 170n5
Russell, Lillian 176
Ryan, R.R. 200, 207n1
Rzepka, Charles 6

Saint Sebastian 147
Salter, Lady 144
Salter, Lord 144
Saltillo 168
The Saltmarsh Murders (novel) 80
Salute to Freedom (novel) 202
same-sex attraction and homosociality 10, 20, 22, 28, 48, 57, 97, 98, 103, 109–112, 119–122, 128, 134, 137n7, 140, 158, 163, 167, 184, 193, 210, 215, 217, 220, 238n14, 245, 259, 262, 263
same-sex couples, companions and lovers 4, 6, 9, 14n8, 20, 21, 22, 27–30, 44, 45, 47–50,

52, 55, 59, 60, 64, 69, 80, 87–90, 101, 112, 127, 128, 131, 133, 134, 136, 139, 140, 142–145, 147–149, 150n1, 151n4, 151n7, 151n9, 151n11, 152n13, 153n24, 157–159, 164–169, 183–184, 191–192, 202, 203, 210, 213, 235, 237n8, 238n15, 239n28, 241–247, 249, 251–255, 257, 259–262, 265, 268, 270, 273, 274, 275
Sanchez, Florencia 157
Sandow, Eugene 176
Sargeant, Peter Cutler 227
Sarony, Napoleon 176
Sartre, Jean-Paul 262
Sayers, Dorothy L. 2, 11, 33, 46, 47, 49, 50, 51n1, 87, 108, 159, 252
"Scandal" (song) 179
Schechter, Harold 212, 213
Schenkar, Joan 12
Scribner's Magazine 141
The Season of Comfort (novel) 233
Seattle 140, 141
Second World War 2, 3, 7, 54, 73, 101, 115, 143, 152n13, 152n14, 206, 210, 212, 226, 228, 229
The Secret of Lonesome Cove (novel) 4, 33–39
Sedgwick, Eve Kosofsky 28, 159
self-hatred 11–12
sensation novel 18, 33
sexual identity 238n14
Seyler, Paul 252, 253
Shaffer, Anthony 152n16
Shaw, George Bernard 174
Shaw, Captain Joseph 44
She (magazine) 250, 253, 256
Shearer, Norma 275
Sherfey, Dr. Mary Jane 170n3
Sherman, William T. 176
A Shilling for Candles (novel) 95, 97
shilling shockers 18–19; *see also* paperbacks
A Short Walk in Williams Park (novel) 133
A Shot in the Dark (film) 181
Simon, S.J. 227
Sims, Agnes 151n7
The Singing Sands (novel) 95, 97
Sir John Gielgud: A Life in Letters 152n16
The Slave (play) 25
Sleuth (play) 152n16
Slide, Anthony 5
Smith, Kline and French Laboratories 140, 147
The Snail-Watcher and Other Stories (short story collection) 264
So Dark the Night (film) 185
Something for Everyone (film) 145
Son of Frankenstein (film) 277
Sorbonne 141
South Africa 140
Spade, Sam 125
Spain, Nancy 9, 203, 249–257

Speak No Evil (novel) 194
Speedy Death (novel) 79–80
Spillane, Mickey 8, 9, 226, 227, 229, 232, 235, 237n9, 238n14
spinsters 71, 81, 276
Spotted Hemlock (novel) 108
S.S. Murder (novel) 142, 151n10, 151n11
Stagge, Jonathan 6, 139, 143, 144; *see also* Webb, Richard Wilson; Wheeler, Hugh Callingham
A Star Is Born (film) 275
A Star's Progress (novel) *see Cry Shame!*
Statue of Liberty 143
Stefano del Guidice Caracciolo di Luperano, Princess 144
Stein, Gertrude 72, 191
Stekel, Wilhelm 205
stereotypes and clichés 4, 5, 11, 26, 33, 40–51, 51n1, 54–65, 71, 85, 95, 241, 275
Stewart, Noah 4
Stoker, Bram 200
Stonewall 1–3, 7, 11, 12, 13, 13n1, 139, 215, 267
Stork Club 210
Stout, Rex 160
Strachey, Lytton 126
Strange Brother (novel) 171n22
Stranger to Himself (novel) 265, 269–271; *see also Known Homosexual*
Strangers on a Train (novel) 10, 259, 260, 261, 263
Strong Poison (novel) 1946
Stryker, Susan 13
Studies of the Greek Poets 28
A Study in Scarlet (novel) 18
The Sun Also Rises (novel) 153n20
Sussex, Lucy 4
"Swan Song" (short story) 64
Sweeney Todd: The Demon Barber of Fleet Street (play) 145
The Swimming Pool (novel) 239n27
Swing Low, Sweet Harriet (novel) 10, 275–277
Swinging Sixties 4, 7, 8, 10, 52, 237n12, 267, 273, 278
Swoon (film) 153n24
Sydney 23–25, 202
Symonds, John Addington 21, 26, 20
Symons, Julian 122n1
Symposium (treatise) 27
Syrett, Nicholas 181

Table Talk (magazine) 20
Taken at the Flood (novel) 64
The Talented Mr. Ripley (novel) 10, 259–263
Teach Tennant 250
Teeman, Tom 236n1
Teilhet, Darwin 139, 151n11
Teilhet, Hildegarde 139
Tellier, Andre 203
Tennant, Eleanor 250
Terry, Ellen 29

294 Index

Tesla, Nikola 176
Texas 169–170, 259
Tey, Josephine 4, 5, 10, 93–103, 106–112
Thank You, Nelson 249
Thatcher, Margaret 70, 71
Theosophy 21, 30
Third Girl (novel) 52
Thomson, Sir Basil 116–117, 123*n*11
Thompson, Jim 8, 11
Those Who Walk Away (novel) 259, 261, 262
Three Act Tragedy (novel) 244
Three Blind Mice (radio play/short story) 55; see also *The Mousetrap*
The Three Coffins (novel) 184
The Three Musketeers (novel) 86, 90
Thrill Me (play) 153*n*24
The Tiger Who Couldn't Eat Meat (children's book) 250
The Tiger Who Saved the Train (children's book) 250
Tilton, Alice 278
To Love and Be Wise (novel) 5, 95–103
Toklas, Alice B. 191
Tolman, Deborah L. 83
Tolstoy, Leo 174
Tom Brown's School Days (novel) 21
Toper's End (novel) 124*n*22
Topsy and Evil (novel) 10, 277–279
Tour de Force (novel) 42
Tourneur, Nigel 29
Transcendent Detective 34
transmigration of souls 21, 22, 36, 38
transvestism 23, 98, 100, 101–102
Travels with My Aunt (film) 145
A Tremor of Forgery (novel) 259
A Trouser-Wearing Character (book) 255
Turing, Alan 68, 69
Turner, Robert Elson 140, 141, 147, 148, 151*n*4
Twain, Mark 176
Twelve Horses and the Hangman's Noose (novel) 86
Twilight Men (novel) 203
Twin Hills Farm 144, 145, 152*n*13
Twisted Clay (novel) 8, 200–207
The Two Faces of January (novel) 259, 261

Ulrichs, Karl Heinrich 39*n*1
Uncle Tom's Cabin (novel) 174, 278
Unforbidden Fruit (novel) 39*n*1
University of London 142
University of Texas 169
Unnatural Death (novel) 46–49, 87
Uranian 26, 27

Valcour, Lieutenant 177, 178, 186*n*9
vampires ("predatory" lesbians) 4, 46–49, 51*n*1
Vance, Philo 42, 43, 227
Van Dine, S.S. 42–43, 146, 159, 226, 227, 237*n*9

Vane, Harriet 46, 108
Vanzetti, Bartolomeo 123*n*4
Vassar 106, 192
Venus Urania 27, 29, 30
Victoria, Queen 19
Vidal, Gore 8, 9, 157, 225–239
Vidal, Nina Gore 232, 233
Viztelly (publisher) 18
Vultures in the Sky (novel) 160

The Wailing Rock Murders (novel) 174, 181, 183, 184–186
Wald, Alan 213
Walford, Frank 8, 200–207, 207*n*3
Wallace, Edgar 226
Wallace-Crabbe, Chris 27
Walpole, Horace 205
Walton, Samantha 79
The Warner Bros. Story 275
Warren, Malcolm 125–136
Watson, Dr. John 80, 85, 183, 185
Waugh, Evelyn 251
"ways of evasion" 21
Webb, Richard Wilson 6, 139–153; see also Patrick, Q.; Quentin, Patrick; Stagge, Jonathan; Wheeler, Hugh Callingham
Weber, William C. 146
The Weeping Willow Murders (novel) 13*n*4
Weimar Germany 140
The Well of Loneliness (novel) 127, 204, 205
Wells, Carolyn 34, 149
Welty, Eudora 151*n*7
West, Raymond 53
Westmacott, Mary 59
Weybright, Victor 226, 227, 229, 236*n*2, 237*n*9
Whatever Happened to Aunt Alice? (film) 276
Whatever Happened to Baby Jane? (film) 276
Wheeler, Hugh Callingham 6, 139–153; see also Patrick, Q.; Quentin, Patrick; Stagge, Jonathan; Webb, Richard Wilson
Wheen, Natalie 245
When I Lived in Bohemia 18
While the Patient Slept (novel) 193
White, Mary Louise ("Mary Lou") 142, 150, 151*n*10
White, Osmar 202
White, Stewart Edward 34
The White Cockatoo (novel) 191
The White Dress (novel) 194
Whitemore, Hugh 69
Whitman, Walt 26, 144
Whitridge, Arnold 174
Whodunit? A Guide to Crime, Suspense & Spy Fiction 263
Why I'm Not a Millionaire 249, 251, 254, 256
Wiegman, Robyn 71, 72
Wilcox, Collin 223
Wilde, Oscar 20, 21, 24, 29, 30, 43, 144, 176

Williams, Charles 184
Wilson, Andrew 262
Wilson, Elizabeth A. 71, 72
Wilson, Superintendent Henry 115–117, 122, 124*n*22
Wimsey, Lord Peter 46, 47, 48, 49, 95, 108
Winwar, Frances (Francesca Vinciguerra) 144, 152*n*14
Witherall, Leonidas 278
Witness at Large (novel) 194
Wodehouse, P.G. 80
Wolf in Man's Clothing (novel) 195
Wolfe, Thomas 151*n*7
Women's Royal Naval Service (WRNS) 250
Wood, Ralph 252
Wooley, Monty 174, 176
Woolf, Leonard 125

Woolf, Virginia 125, 126
Woolrich, Cornell 11, 12, 274
Wright, Willard Huntington *see* Van Dine, S.S.
Wuthering Heights (novel) 111

The X Factor (television program) 101

Yale Dramatic Association ("Yale Dramat") 173–176
Yale University 6, 173–174
Young, Ian 7, 13
Young Man with a Horn (film) 182
The Zebra-Striped Hearse (novel) 222–223

Zola, Emile 203
Zuckerman, John Harvie Dew 179

www.ingramcontent.com/pod-product-compliance
Lightning Source LLC
Chambersburg PA
CBHW051210300426
44116CB00006B/512